Resettling Displaced People

Resettling Displaced People

Policy and practice in India

Editor

Hari Mohan Mathur

Routledge
Taylor & Francis Group
LONDON NEW YORK NEW DELHI
Council for Social Development
New Delhi

First published in India 2011
by Routledge
912 Tolstoy House, 15–17 Tolstoy Marg, Connaught Place,
New Delhi 110 001

Simultaneously published in the UK
by Routledge
2 Park Square, Milton Park, Abingdon, Oxfordshire OX14 4RN

First issued in paperback 2015

Routledge is an imprint of the Taylor & Francis Group, an informa business

Typeset by
Star Compugraphics Private Limited
D-156, Second Floor,
Sector 7, Noida 201 301

British Library Cataloguing-in-Publication Data
A catalogue record of this book is available from the British Library

ISBN 13: 978-1-138-66270-4 (pbk)
ISBN 13: 978-0-415-58621-4 (hbk)

Contents

Part V: An alternative view

List of Abbreviations

ADB	Asian Development Bank
AfDB	African Development Bank
ANE	Autordade Nacional de Estradas
BC	Borough Committee
CBA	Cost–Benefit Analysis
CBO	Community-based Organisation
CCL	Central Coalfields Limited
CD	Community Development
CD/R&RO	Community Development/Resettement and Rehabilitation Oficr
CIL	Coal India Limited
CMTPA	Chief Municipal Town Planner and Architect's Department
CPI (M)	Communist Party of India (Marxists)
CPR	Common Property Resource
CSESMP	Coal Sector Environmental and Social Mitigation Project
CSRP	Coal Sector Rehabilitation Project
CSS	Center for Social Studies
CSR	Corporate Social Responsibility
CUIP	Community Infrastructure Upgrading Project
CV	Compensation Variation
CVM	Contingent Valuation Method
CWC	Central Water Commission
DACS	District Compensation Advisory Committee
DFID	Department for International Development
DP	Displaced Person
DPR	Department de Pistes Rurales
EIA	Environmental Impact Assessment
EIR	Extractive Industries Review
EPAP	Entitled Project Affected Person
EPW	Economic and Political Weekly
ESMP	Environmental and Social Mitigation Project
EV	Equivalent Variation
FDI	Foreign Direct Investment

FPIC	Free Prior Informed Consent
FSF	Four-Stage Framework
GDP	Gross Domestic Product
GEF	Global Environment Facility
GoO	Government of Orissa
GoT	Government of Tanzania
GPS	Global Positioning System
HAL	Hindustan Aeronautics Limited
IAS	Indian Administrative Service
IDA	International Development Association
IDC	Industrial Development Corporation
IDCO	Orissa Industrial Infrastructure Development Corporation
INTACH	Indian National Trust for Art and Cultural Heritage
IPDP	Indigenous Peoples Development Plan
IPR	Industrial Policy Resolution
IRDP	Integrated Rural Development Plan
IRRM	Impoverishment Risk and Reconstruction Model
ISED	Institute for Social and Economic Change
JRY	Jawahar Rozgar Yojna
KMC	Kolkata Municipal Corporation
LAA	Land Acquisition Act
LAMATA	Lagos Metropolitan Transport Authority
LF	Left Front
MCL	Mahanadi Coalfields Limited
MD	Managing Director
MMSD	Mining, Minerals and Sustainable Development
MNC	Multinational Corporation
MOU	Memorandum of Understanding
MP	Madhya Pradesh
MW	Megawatt
NAC	National Advisory Council
NALCO	National Aluminum Company
NBA	Narmada Bachao Andolan
NCA	Narmada Control Authority
NCL	Northern Coalfields Limited
NDA	National Democratic Alliance
NGO	Non-governmental Organisation
NRRP	National Rehabilitation and Resettlement Policy

NWDT	Narmada Water Disputes Tribunal
OCP	Open Cast Project
OD	Operational Directives
OECD	Organisation for Economic Cooperation and Development
OIC	Officer in Command
OMC	Orissa Mining Corporation
OMS	Operational Manual Statement
ONGC	Oil and Natural Gas Commission
OP/BP	Operational Policy/Bank Procedure
OSATIP	Orissa Scheduled Areas Transfer of Immovable Property
PA	Protected Area
PAP	Project-affected Person
PCB	Pollution Control Board
PESA	Panchayats (Extension of Scheduled Areas) Act
POSCO	Pohang Iron and Steel Companay
RAP	Resettlement Action Plan
R&R	Resettlement and Rehabilitation
ROW	Right of Way
RPDAC	Rehabilitation-cum-Periphery Development Advisory Committee
SC	Supreme Court
SCAS	State Compensation Advisory Committee
SC/ST	Scheduled Caste/Scheduled Tribe
SD	Sustainable Development
SECL	South Eastern Coalfields Limited
SEZ	Special Economic Zone
SHG	Self-Help Group
SIA	Social Impact Assessment
SIL	Sterlite Inustries Limited
SLCRR	State Level Council on Resettlement & Rehabilitation
SP	Superintendent of Police
SSP	Sardar Sarovar Project
TBVSS	Tehri Bandh Virodhi Sangharsh Samiti
TC	Trinamool Congress
THDC	Tehri Hydro Development Corporation
TISCO	Tata Iron and Steel Company
TISS	Tata Institute of Social Sciences

TSP	Tribal Sub Plan
UK	United Kingdom
UN	United Nations
UN CESCR	United Nations Committee on Economic, Social and Cultural Rights
UNDP	United Nations Development Programme
UNEP	United Nations Environment Programme
UNIDO	United Nations Industrial Develoment Organisation
USA	United States of America
USSR	Union of Soviet Socialist Republics
VAL	Vedanta Alumina Limited
WBIDC	West Bengal Industrial Development Corporation
WBPCB	West Bengal Pollution Control Board
WC	Ward Committee
WCD	World Commission on Dams
WCL	Western Coalfields Limited
WTA	Willingness to Accept
WTP	Willingness to Pay
WWF	World Wildlife Fund

Foreword

The process of development is currently uprooting millions of poor from their homes, livelihoods, and ways of life across the country. Given the growing pressures to acquire large tracts of land, now increasingly for projects in the private sector, displacement on an even more massive scale is likely to continue bedeviling development in the foreseeable future. Still, resettlement and the risks of impoverishment associated with population displacement, remain largely a neglected issue.

There is a tendency not to take resettlement problems seriously until they take on crisis proportions. Projects often remain focused on evicting people in the way, not on resettling them. The condition of relocated people shows no improvement even years after their shifting to the new place. When resettlement is not done well, projects which ought to be seen as beneficial become a focal point for discontent and protests. Much ongoing opposition to development stems from the past poor resettlement performance which has been pathetic, and which has often left most affected people in poverty of the worst kind.

The struggle that the affected people are currently waging against their displacement has political repercussions, which cannot be easily overlooked. This struggle has assumed violent proportions and is posing a grave threat to internal security. It is these developments that have finally brought resettlement policy issues on the development agenda. The government of India issued its first national resettlement and rehabilitation policy in 2004. This policy was soon followed by another policy with some minor changes, which has been in force since 2007. In addition, there is now a move to go beyond policy and have a law on the subject. Simultaneously, the archaic land acquisition law is also being amended — the result of years of struggle by affected groups.

Although the adoption of a national policy on resettlement is an important step forward, compliance with its provisions should not be taken for granted. The people interested in projects are often in a hurry to get on with the job, and if they can, they would not hesitate to relax or even disregard policy requirements and implementation procedures. As experience has shown, many inadequacies in resettlement arise from failure to implement the existing guidelines.

The fact is that the policy is unlikely to produce any tangible benefits without a properly conceived resettlement strategy and a fully equipped resettlement agency. Studies have shown that the poorly equipped resettlement agencies routinely fail, and only add to the misery of the people displaced. Yet, many projects still operate without a regular resettlement unit to deal with the complex problems of resettlement. A major challenge is to equip both public and private sector development agencies with knowledge, skills and attitudes they need to manage resettlement issues that arise in development work.

To all those working to ensure a better future for the displaced people, I recommend this volume as a useful source of reference and as a valuable guide to understanding the many complex issues surrounding the policy and practice of resettlement in India today.

Muchkund Dubey
President, Council for Social Development, New Delhi
May 2010

Acknowledgements

First, I wish to thank all my co-authors, whose known expertise and interest in issues of resettlement policy and practice have contributed enormously to the effort that has gone into the production of this publication.

Professor Muchkund Dubey, President, CSD, first suggested the idea for this volume, and then provided the necessary support and guidance for its fruition at every step. He has also written a Foreword for this volume. My very special thanks to Professor Dubey.

Some articles included in this volume were first published in a special resettlement issue of *Social Change* (36[1], March 2006), the quarterly journal of the Council for Social Development (CSD). Michael Cernea, Walter Fernandes, M. P. Roy and I were among the contributors to this special issue. With the exception of Roy's article, all the others appear in this volume in a revised and updated form. The paper by Felix Padel and Samarendra Das also first appeared in *Social Change* in a later issue (38[4], December 2008), but they have rewritten it for this publication. I am thankful to CSD for granting permission to reprint these articles from their journal.

I would also like to take this opportunity to thank N. J. Kurian and Sakarama Somayaji for the assistance they provided to this project in its initial stages.

Finally, thanks are due to the anonymous reviewer for his comments, which proved helpful in updating the script. The team at Routledge provided much assistance in facilitating the publication of this volume, and this I must acknowledge most gratefully.

Hari Mohan Mathur

Introduction and overview

Hari Mohan Mathur

Some 60 million people have been displaced in India in the years since Independence, and, as a result, mostly reduced to a state of permanent poverty. Still the resettlement of people displaced by development projects has, until recently, remained largely a neglected issue. Even today, the problem gets attention only when a crisis situation erupts, demanding immediate attention. The interest the government has shown in resettlement issues in the past few years is a mere response to the growing protests by farmers against acquisition of their land, and is widely seen as a political move aimed at containing this antagonism. The hurriedly revised national resettlement policy, issued in 2007, which is no great improvement on the earlier 2004 version, primarily arose in the context of strong opposition to the creation of special economic zones (SEZs). The government is not going to abandon or even go slow on its development agenda just because the projects involve displacement. It regards this agenda as critical to achieving the goal of poverty reduction and inclusive growth.

In recent years, the government's economic policies have undergone a significant change. These allow the private sector a major role in the development process, which, until recently, was exclusively a public sector affair. The new policies proactively seek investment from domestic as well as multinational corporations by creating an investment-friendly environment. The spectacular economic growth witnessed in recent years is indeed the outcome of these policy changes. Encouraged by this success, the planners are determined to proceed further on this path with even greater vigour. In order to touch greater heights in economic growth, policies are being further liberalised and laws amended overnight under the growing impacts of globalisation, liberalisation and privatisation. In addition, the government is assiduously wooing new investments in practically all sectors of development, ranging from manufacturing cars to retailing toiletries (Sinha 2009). Investments are indeed flowing in, as never before. Any large investment, especially foreign direct investment (FDI) coming to India, is now seen as the success of the economic reform agenda. It also immediately becomes the big headline news.

However, in the excitement over the inflow of large investments, nobody seems to be taking time to reflect on the likely social impact of these developments. As a consequence, even some basic questions tend to escape the attention of policymakers, investors and the others concerned. How much land will these development projects gobble up? Where will the land come from? How many people will lose land? Can land requirement not be reduced, and people saved from the avoidable pangs of displacement? What needs to be done to rebuild the lives of people who will be affected? Will compensation alone be enough for their adequate resettlement? Are right policies and mechanisms in place to address resettlement problems that come with such large investments? Insufficient attention paid to such basic issues of resettlement policy and practice is the reason why displaced people often end up impoverished, in a condition worse than before (Mathur 1998 and 1999; Cernea 2000; Downing 2002; Oliver-Smith 2009).

Businesses require large tracts of land. They need land not only in tribal and rural areas, but in urban areas as well. To be viable, SEZs in particular need to be connected to ports, airports, roads, power stations, that too in one contiguous area. Hence, the land generally preferred has to be close to densely populated urban centres (Tripathi 2007). The land in tribal areas, rich in natural resources, continues to be the preferred option for those looking for investment in mining and related industrial projects (CSE 2008). Overall, the investor-friendly development climate has created demand for land on a scale which is becoming hard to meet (Mathur 2009).

The insatiable appetite of private industry — now SEZs in particular — for land is definitely not good news for farmers. They know that this is going to trigger displacement on an unprecedented scale, hurting them much more than dams and other development projects ever did in the past. (Padel and Das 2008) Fearing displacement from their land and livelihood, farmers are now up in arms against new projects. And with NGO support, and in some cases with political support as well, they are fiercely opposing the establishment of new development projects because they expect them to do nothing but ruin their lives, as in the past (Asher 2007; Sahu 2007)

Farmers are increasingly beginning to perceive the government as being on the side of large corporations, assisting them in making huge profits at their expense, and completely ignoring people's basic livelihood concerns (Shiva and Jafri 1998; Padel and Das 2010).This belief is further confirmed by the fact that those demanding better resettlement from large corporations have often been met with brutal repression, as in the recent incidents of police firing which killed dozens of protestors in Kalinga Nagar, Singur, Nandigram and elsewhere (Kalshian 2007). The government has also lost trust of the people. Its track record fails to give people any reason to hope for adequate assistance in resettlement after they are forced off their lands. The claims of providing fair resettlement have been found to be hollow in most cases.

In the face of protests, which in some cases are turning aggressive, there is a danger that the process of development may get slowed down, if not halted completely. Investors are currently finding it hard to get their projects off the ground. They face an almost impossible task in getting land for industry. Doing business has never been an easy task in India because of its complex regulatory regime and other constraining factors, but now the land acquisition problem has further worsened the situation. Huge investments are now on hold because of farmers' agitations that have spread all over the country like wildfire (Saran 2008).

The difficulties in getting land, even the tracts promised by the government, are forcing companies to scale down or even completely abandon their projects in mid-stream. The recent shift of Tata's small car Nano factory from Singur in West Bengal to a new site in Gujarat is one example. The Korean steel giant POSCO has long been threatening to move its large investment from Orissa out of India. Other companies are hesitating to come forward with new investment proposals.

Many who were hoping to get jobs with upcoming projects now see the opportunities slipping away before their own eyes and are getting frustrated at the turn of events. For millions of people, development indeed offers a chance to escape from the poverty trap. Generally, the benefits from projects far outweigh the project costs, and that is the reason why they are undertaken. By creating new opportunities, well-planned projects can indeed improve living conditions for all. However, the downside of development is that some who carry the costs are often left to languish in irreversible poverty at the losing end of the process. This happens mostly due to the callous manner in which the resettlement task is generally approached. Generally, the good intentions of policy fail to get translated into good practice.

Nowhere has resettlement worked satisfactorily, but that is no reason to assume that it will not work, ever, anywhere. There is a growing view that the impoverishment of a displaced population should not be considered inevitable and is preventable. As grim as prospects may seem, opportunities do exist to improve lives even in displacement situations. This, however, requires people-oriented resettlement policy, imaginative planning, an effective implementation apparatus, supported by financial resources and high-level commitment (Scudder 2005). Projects do generate many benefits, and these can be shared with the affected people, as has indeed been done successfully at several places (Van Wicklin III 1999).

Many useful lessons have been learned from recent resettlement experiences, and as result, a lot more is known today on what reforming resettlement involves (Cernea and Mathur 2008). The first and foremost need is to adopt policies that minimise displacement and properly compensate and resettle the displaced people. Simply having a good resettlement policy is not enough though. A policy by itself cannot ensure adequate resettlement; it needs to be applied. For a policy to live up to its promise, projects also need to have the capacity for effective planning and implementation of resettlement.

A new awareness in dealing with resettlement issues is now growing and it is not restricted to government agencies. Corporations which previously viewed resettlement issues as peripheral to their operations now recognise that they also have social responsibilities towards their stakeholders, especially towards those who give up their land, without which no development can ever take place. Many factors have influenced this shift in perspective on resettlement from being a burden to a business opportunity. First, enlightened corporations understand that if they do not provide adequate resettlement, people will fight back and even force them to roll back their projects. Second, business reputation means a lot, especially to large corporations, and they do not want their name to be mired in controversies that are better avoided. Third, corporations are now under the close watch of NGOs and human rights activists for their actions, which leaves them no option but to do resettlement well. It is becoming difficult to get away without compensating and resettling the affected people properly.

In addition, the displaced people are also now a better organised group, in a position strong enough to demand resettlement that improves their lives and does not impoverish them. Their voices today are being heard in both national and international forums with the attention that they deserve. They are not opposed to development, as is often mistakenly believed. On the contrary, they too want to be a part of India's growth story; but for too long, displaced people have only been victims of development. The challenge now is how to do resettlement that also makes them beneficiaries of development. No development can ever be sustainable if a sizeable group of people sees in it nothing but the inevitability of displacement and impoverishment as the only future for itself.

Organisation of the book

This volume looks at emerging issues in resettlement policy and practice, the wide gap between what they promise and what is delivered, approaches to reconstructing livelihoods, and the growing threats of massive displacement arising from the rapid privatisation of development processes under the pressures of globalisation. In addition, it questions the existing theoretical resettlement models, and emphasises the need to rethink.

The contributors to this volume represent a wide background: government, PSUs research institutions, universities, civil society, NGOs and international development agencies. They are all experts, well known in their professions, including some who have played a significant role in shaping resettlement policies and in implementing resettlement projects at the grassroots level around the world. Also, there are a couple of young researchers with strong contributions.

The 15 papers in the volume are divided into five parts: The Governance Challenge, Emerging Issues in Resettlement Policies, Compensation and the Resettlement Process, Privatising Development, and An Alternative View.

Part I: The governance challenge

At the outset, Mathur introduces a broad discussion on resettlement issues surrounding development projects. The chapter is intended to serve as a background to the theme of this volume. Involuntary resettlement, he emphasises, is an inherently impoverishing process; it hurts a large number of people and is often unavoidable in the development process. Those displaced by projects confront a variety of impoverishment risks, mostly ending up worse off than before, an outcome just the opposite of what development aims for. Yet, this is not a problem that is going to go away in the foreseeable future, given the current emphasis on rapid economic growth and the consequent pressures of acquiring land, now increasingly for private industry as well. Experience suggests that though things have often gone wrong in resettlement, impoverishing millions in the process, the problem is not unmanageable altogether. Much can, in fact, be done to soften the adverse impact of displacement and even improve the living standards of displaced people. A better understanding of the issues involved is, however, required if resettlement is to be addressed in a way that projects generate benefits but harm none. Against this background, Mathur looks closely at selected issues of resettlement policy, planning and management that critically affect the resettlement outcomes, using examples from a variety of projects in India as well as in other countries.

Part II: Emerging issues in resettlement policy

The contributors to Part II address significant recent policy responses to resettlement issues. The first chapter is focussed on a much debated resettlement policy issue in India. The next two chapters deal with the issues concerning the World Bank policy on involuntary resettlement, issues that have a wider significance. The wide gap that exists between policy and practice is highlighted in the final chapter.

The debate on what should be an acceptable national resettlement policy to address the problems of people displaced by dams and various other development projects has gone on for over two decades, but Iyer contends that a satisfactory outcome does not seem to be in sight as yet. In 2004, the government of India after much dithering did come up with a national policy, but that failed to live up to expectations. Civil society groups felt completely let down, and denounced it as primarily designed to serve needs of the big business at the cost of the poor who would lose their land and livelihood. They had hoped that the policy would reflect their contributions, which they had informally made to the policy development process, but that clearly did not happen. Later, the same year, a new government took over, and the civil society group saw in this change a chance to have the damage undone. They did quickly succeed in persuading the government to replace the existing policy with a new one, and the National Advisory Council (NAC) started consulting with those involved in these issues, especially the civil society groups, on the basis of which it also prepared a draft policy. This draft was submitted to the government, which was expected to formalise the policy taking into consideration the draft and other relevant factors. In 2007, the government did issue a new policy, but to the puzzlement of the civil society, this was not on the lines of the NAC draft, to which some of them had even contributed formally as members of the council.

The criticism against the new policy grew. In response, the government came forth with two draft legislations. One Bill was meant to give legislative backing to the policy, as there was a feeling that without it the policy would not work. The other Bill was intended to amend the Land Acquisition Act, which had long been under attack for being the source of most displacement and resettlement problems. Iyer takes a close look at the new policy and legal initiatives in his critical essay, pointing out that while these documents and the civil society groups seem to be espousing the same policy principles, in the same language too, that is definitely not the case. His analysis of the two Bills, section by section, gives him no reason to cheer and he concludes that the battle has not been won yet. While it is good that the government is thinking in terms of a law on resettlement, and also amending the outdated Land Acquisition Act, much work still remains to be done to sort out weaknesses and questionable features of these Bills in consultation with NGOs, and not only with those who are part of the government.

Cernea draws attention to an important recent change in involuntary resettlement policy, which seems to have remained largely unknown. This pertains to a new element in the definition of displacement introduced by the World Bank in 2004 in its updated policy which was issued in 2002. The World Bank resettlement policy now defines the 'restriction of access' of indigenous and other people in parks and protected areas as 'involuntary displacement', even when physical displacement and relocation are not involved. The new policy broadens the definition of 'displacement' and goes beyond physical (geographical) relocation to also include occupational and economic dislocation, not necessarily accompanied by physical relocation of the local users. This is for the first time in the history of World Bank policy that 'loss of access' is being explicitly recognised as a form of displacement. Other major development agencies, such as the Asian Development Bank, the Inter-American Bank and the African Development Bank, responded positively to the broader definition of restriction of access as displacement, and have incorporated this change in their own resettlement policies. This policy change has direct relevance for tribal populations living in remote areas, whose condition worsens further due to the biodiversity conservation projects. As a result of the policy change, these people, when denied access to parks and protected areas, will now be entitled to reconstruction assistance on the lines of what was available so far to other physically relocated displaced people.

Can a general resettlement policy meet the varying requirements of resettlement projects in all sectors? Appleby brings up in his paper this important policy issue in involuntary resettlement. The World Bank's policy on involuntary resettlement, first issued in 1980, originated primarily from experience with high dams that were then causing great misery to a large number of people over vast areas. Although the policy is mainly based on those early experiences with high dams, it is now applicable uniformly to any project that acquires land. Projects as diverse as mining, industry, power generation, urban development, nature conservation, gas pipeline, transport, airports and ports are all governed by this single, all-embracing policy. Development practitioners in areas other than dam projects often argue that many provisions of this policy are not relevant to their particular situations, implying that the extra work involved in adhering to the policy is wasteful and avoidable. The contention, especially of transport engineers, is that their projects with minor impacts are not quite comparable with dam projects that involve extensive dislocation. While there is some force in this argument, transport projects — specifically road projects — often have severe impacts, which, if not redressed, can leave behind a trail of impoverishment among roadside communities. Despite such criticism, the fact remains that, operationally, the resettlement policy is not as rigid as it first seems. For example, the 2002 revision of the Bank policy developed a new instrument that takes care of such specific cases — the Abbreviated Resettlement Plan. In Appleby's view, the key question is not whether the policy applies, but how it should be tailored to the sector's context, and the capacity to effectively implement and monitor the resettlement operations. To better understand this complex policy issue, the author examines the development of the World Bank's involuntary resettlement policy with a focus on its relevance and application in the transport sector, roads in particular. Finally, he also looks at what the next necessary steps may be to ensure that the policy works.

Padel and Das find rather alarming the disjunction between policy and practice that lies at the heart of the displacement trauma. According to resettlement policies, including those of the World Bank and the governments in India, the living standards of project-affected people are supposed to go up, not down, but this hardly ever happens. This discrepancy is the result of a failure to analyse and incorporate displaced people's perspective while designing projects that cause resettlement. This, in turn, fuels strong resistance. From the viewpoint of corporations and governments supporting their projects, the protestors are holding up investments worth millions of rupees. From the viewpoint of protestors threatened with displacement, the corporations and governments are treating them with gross injustice. They seem to neither understand nor care about their lives that are being torn apart in pursuit of profit. This, in essence, is the reality gap: a gulf of understanding, or rather the lack of it, between those imposing and those suffering displacement. The authors voice their deep concern especially for the tribal people and their forced displacement, and the harassment of human rights activists championing their cause. Specifically, the displaced people demand the following: stringent attempts to avoid displacement, no further displacement until those previously displaced are first properly resettled and their standard of living improved, respect for their right to free, and informed consent prior to approval of any project affecting their land and resources. They want the process of consulting them to be real, not in the form of present public hearings where people's voices are routinely silenced by coercive means. In conclusion, Padel and Das emphasise the need to put only those officials in charge of resettlement who are properly trained, and have an attitude of serving the people.

Part III: Compensation and the resettlement process

The third part includes five chapters, focussed on approaches to and practices in rebuilding the lives affected by development projects, arguably the most challenging issue in resettlement. The compensation criterion is re-examined in the first chapter, in the light of new theoretical developments. The next two chapters are concerned with resettlement options: the hugely acceptable 'land for land' option and the 'self-employment in lieu of land loss' for which there are virtually no takers. The ongoing process of displacement and resettlement in a controversial dam project in the Himalayas is vividly described in the fourth chapter. The role of local political factors in decisions concerning eviction and rehabilitation of low-income urban residents is brought into sharp focus in this part's last chapter.

Garikipati addresses the critical compensation issue in resettlement, which, in recent years, has sparked a new interest, especially among economists who had all along tended to skirt this vexed problem, leaving anthropologists and other related social scientists to grapple with it. This interest seems largely to be in response to the growing criticism from resettlement researchers against economists for not giving adequate attention to this problem, which is much needed. Economists who have now devoted some attention to this subject have come to the conclusion that the compensation principle is indeed deeply flawed. This criticism of the compensation principle confirms the long-held view of resettlement researchers that compensation by itself is not enough to ensure adequate resettlement, and that compensation inadequacies are at the root of impoverishment, which is often the fate of the displaced people. Garikipati looks afresh at the compensation criterion in the light of the theoretical discourse that has emerged from economists' criticism of the compensation principle. Her argument is that although the criterion implies the use of 'willingness to accept' (as against 'willingness to pay') in evaluating project-costs, yet this was excluded from the cost-benefit analysis till recently. She then demonstrates through a case study of the Sardar Sarovar Project (SSP) the usefulness of the criterion in eliciting willingness of those displaced to accept compensation. The displaced people were consulted for their preferences from among four hypothetical compensation packages. The resettlement policy implications of the findings resulting from this consultative exercise are enormous. The author limits her comments on three provisions of the resettlement policy:

- Commons: This provision was envisaged to minimise disruption of livelihood due to relocation, but this intention could not be translated into reality mainly due to the unavailability of suitable land. The findings suggest that as an alternative, cash transfers or price subsidies too could have been well accepted.
- Community resettlement: This was expected to rebuild the community away from the original place, as those displaced mostly belonged to close-knit social groups. The findings suggest that this is not an arrangement necessarily acceptable to all, certainly not to those who suffered social exclusion and have had opportunities to interact with other outside communities (via markets, for example). Such people or groups would prefer to accept cash and move out, leaving their communities behind. This provision will, however, be more acceptable among groups that practice labour-sharing.
- Universal provision of land: The assumption was that land-based compensation would be preferred by all displaced people. The finding, however, shows that one-third respondents had already accepted cash compensation, contradicting the very assumption of this policy provision.

Garikipati is of the view that the cash alternative is potentially superior to land-based compensation as with cash in hand, theoretically, the displaced have a wider set of choices. There is, however, a danger in giving cash to those unfamiliar with the market economy. The results from this study also suggest that the displaced people will be served better by a tailor-made resettlement scheme which takes into account their preferences, rather than by the one that only offers a standard compensation package to all.

In the second chapter in this part, Dhagamwar looks at the land option issue in resettlement. Whether pro- or anti-dam, those involved in the Narmada debates were unanimous from the beginning that the

Land Acquisition Act was unjust to the displaced people. But, no one was quite clear what one should demand in return for lost land and livelihood. The affected people were mostly tribal people, and alternate land and forest were what they craved for, not something unreasonable given their circumstances. Therefore, the demand then raised was for land alone. However, conditions have changed vastly since. Displacement now is not caused by dams so much as by the projects of other kinds, such as industrial, mining, power generation, highways and airports, to name a few. Projects are not displacing tribal people alone; they are increasingly affecting non-tribal people as well. Like many other present projects, the SEZ in Nandigram was not going to displace tribal people. But the demand for land continues to come up even today, no less loudly than before. If the national resettlement policy issued in 2007 is any indication, the government also seems to concede it in principle, even when it is well known that meeting such a demand would be nearly impossible. In the 1980s, the Sardar Sarovar Project tried to provide land to the people affected, but it simply could not. Dhagamwar is quite emphatic that it is not that such experiences are ignored; the fact is that no one seems even aware of them. The government simply acts according to old ideas. Again, the government in Orissa does not even consider it necessary to properly scrutinise proposals for land requirement of private industry, fearing that any restrictions in this regard would drive away projects to other states. Other than land, tribal people have very few options for survival. But that is surely not the case with non-tribal people. They are more mobile and adaptable. In fact, people from villages are pouring into cities every day. The harsh truth is that landholdings are too small to sustain even small families. However much land may be given to the affected people, it will always prove inadequate for the growing family. They will need non-land-based skills and education. The time to take this route to resettlement was in the 1950s, when the first projects were launched. Dhagamwar concludes that much time has since been lost, but it is never too late to start on the right path. However, harping on 'land for land' as the only way to reconstruct lost livelihoods must now stop.

Continuing the discussion on resettlement options, Roy focusses on the self-employment option, which failed to win over people who had lost their livelihoods due to a coal mining project. While approving the Coal Sector Rehabilitation Project of Coal India Limited

(CIL), the World Bank simultaneously approved the Coal Sector Environmental and Social Mitigation Project (CSESMP). The objective was to ensure adequate resettlement to the people adversely affected by coal mining. For long, the CIL was able to provide jobs in lieu of land as a resettlement option, and people found the arrangement quite workable. But the job option is no longer feasible as mechanised opencast mining has greatly reduced the demand for labour. This has necessitated a major policy change. The CIL now assists those who lose land with self-employment schemes. As Roy shows, people have not responded positively to this option as they do not feel convinced that they can depend on these schemes to make a living on a sustainable basis. Although this project (1996–2002) still remains to be fully evaluated, indications are that the outcome of this particular income restoration strategy has remained well below the initial expectations.

The Tehri dam, located at the confluence of Bhagirathi and Bhilganga rivers in the state of Uttarakhand, is the subject of Bisht's chapter. This dam has long been mired in a fierce controversy. With the closure of the last of the three tunnels on 29 October 2005, the inundation began swiftly. For the media, this was big news, but not for the project area people. Although reliable data on the affected population does not exist, the dam is estimated to have displaced 85,600 persons, including a significant number from Tehri. As people are still being displaced, the number may well go up, crossing the mark of one hundred thousand. This resettlement on a massive scale is the subject of research which Bisht recently carried out, using the methodological tools of ethnography. His findings provide a fresh perspective on the impact of displacement on the rural population, and the daily problems which they face during the ongoing resettlement process. The dam caused displacement in two phases. It first occurred in the early 1970s and was triggered by land acquired from 13 villages for project works, a staff colony and to build New Tehri town. The submergence of villages in the reservoir area necessitated displacement for the second time. This displacement was on a much larger scale, involving a total of 109 villages. People had begun feeling the pangs of this displacement much before the actual displacement began, right from the day the decision to build the dam was announced. All development activities came to a halt, as any expenditure on them was seen as completely wasteful. The whole place looked like a picture of total neglect. Nothing reassuring happened during all these years to remove a sense of uncertainty from their minds. Those who were economically better off took an early decision to move elsewhere, but most others, not so fortunate and largely dependent on resettlement assistance, had to stay back. It was the long time that the process took that hurt them the most. Bisht also dwells at length on several other aspects of the resettlement process, including the policy shortcomings, inadequate civic facilities at resettlement sites, gender biases, livelihood challenges, hostile attitude of the local host population, and so on.

Most resettlement literature is focussed on projects that relocate people in remote rural and tribal areas, especially dams. In presenting a study of forced eviction and rehabilitation in Kolkata, Medha Chandra shifts the scene from the usual dam-centric research to the realm of urban resettlement studies, adding significantly to an area of growing concern in resettlement. Eviction and rehabilitation issues have often been at the root of many social and political conflicts, but have received far less attention than dam-induced displacement and resettlement issues, at least until recently. In Indian cities, low-income residents living without legal tenure in informal settlements, as well as high-income group encroachers of residential and commercial areas, happen to be frequent targets of evictions. The past few decades have seen massive evictions in almost all large cities, fuelled mostly by middle-class concerns about decline in the environmental quality, something informal urban settlers are routinely blamed for. Most studies of urban evictions tend to focus on legal aspects of squatting on municipal lands, canal banks, strips of land along railway tracks and other public properties, and the relocation and rehabilitation of encroachers. This, however, is not the subject of the present study. Chandra looks at urban evictions from a different perspective, not from the viewpoints of town planning or municipal laws. She looks at the social and political factors that determine who is to be evicted and who is to get compensation in the event of eviction. Often, the law may not be relevant to the making of these decisions, and may even be quietly sidestepped. It is micro-politics that colours the decision of a municipality to evict a certain group from urban land. Conflicts between urban municipalities, informal urban settlers and higher-income residents are quite frequent. Using case studies of B. P. Nagar and K. Gardens, two adjacent wards in south Kolkata, this paper focuses on the politics surrounding evictions and rehabilitation of low-income urban residents. It examines how the environmental conflict over access and control over urban water bodies resulted in eviction from one informal settlement, but not from the other informal settlement. It is interesting to note that of the two informal settlements, one that lacked legal status remained untouched by evictions, despite strong protests by residents of the surrounding area. While residents of the other informal settlement, who did have land deeds, got evicted. How and why did such seemingly illogical events take place? This is precisely the question that is under the scanner in this paper replete with deeply insightful field data.

Part IV: Privatising development

Discussion in the fourth part centres on issues that have emerged in the wake of a significant role that private capital has come to play in the development process under globalisation pressures. While privatisation is held up as a way to faster growth, it has, at the same time, created a huge demand of land for industry, especially for special economic zones (SEZs), and this is threatening the lives and livelihood of millions of smallholders all over India. The first chapter in this part dwells on some new developments that have brought displacement back as an issue for wide public discussion. The second chapter is focussed on land acquisition issues that the SEZs have brought to the fore, and the strong protests by the affected people against their displacement, which these issues have provoked. The failure of the West Bengal government to come up with a resettlement policy acceptable to people getting affected by acquisition of land for private industry is the subject of the third chapter. The final chapter is a case study of the disastrous impact of investor-friendly development policies on the tribal people in Orissa.

The displacement debate seems to go on and on, with its end nowhere in sight yet. Fernandes observes that the debate has in fact been further reinvigorated by a series of recent events which, in addition to the ongoing processes of globalisation, liberalisation and privatisation, include the refusal of the government to even discuss the report of the World Commission on Dams (WCD), the judgment of the Supreme Court on the Sardar Sarovar dam, the setting up of SEZs, and the promulgation of the National Rehabilitation Policy 2007. The message, loud and clear, that these developments convey is rather disappointing. It seems, presently, neither the government nor the judiciary is sensitive to the sufferings of the displaced people.

In such a situation, there is unlikely to be any end to the people's sufferings in the foreseeable future. The acquisition of land on an unprecedented scale is currently going on at breakneck speed, especially for private large corporations, impoverishing in the process a much larger number of people than ever before. Besides dams, much displacement is now also occurring from mining, industrial, transport and urban development, and other infrastructure projects. Estimates vary about the number of people displaced, but about 60 million displaced in the years since Independence in 1947 is the figure that most researchers find provisionally acceptable. A cause for serious concern is that those worst hit happen to be among the poorest — members of the scheduled castes/tribes (SC/ST) and other backward castes. Fernandes contends that the massive transfer of lands from the poor to the big businesses is directly linked to the processes of globalisation, liberalisation and privatisation. This is evident from the fact that laws are being routinely amended to facilitate privatisation of even those common property resources on which poor communities have subsisted since time immemorial. The anger among the displaced people who have lost their land and livelihood is growing, and often finds expression in the form of protests. Brutal repression usually follows when people mount such protests against their displacement, and in recent years, police firing has killed several protestors. Such a situation cannot be allowed to continue forever, and Fernandes' plea is to look for a solution that is fair to the displaced people and ensures that they are among the first beneficiaries of the development process, and do not end up as its victims.

In their paper, Asher and Atmavilas look at SEZs, which have been under attack ever since their establishment in 2005. The idea behind creating SEZs was to promote high economic growth and job creation opportunities, and a number of concessions were offered to those willing to set up industry in these enclaves. SEZs require large tracts of land, close to large cities with well developed infrastructure, such as ports, airports, roads, water and power. Farmers have been at the forefront of agitations against SEZs all over the country as these zones threaten to dislodge them from their land and livelihood for the sake of private industry, leaving them impoverished. The acquisition of land for mines, industry, dams, ports, roads, power plants and other development purposes has gone on in India for decades, but what has fuelled the current strong resistance to land takeover is the nature and extent of state involvement in handing the best agricultural land to extra-state enclaves governed by private interests. Asher and Atmavilas highlight in their paper some of the major issues related to land acquisition in this context. A widespread concern that has emerged is the adverse impact of SEZs on food cultivation and availability. The claims of SEZ proponents, that the new jobs created will go a long way in reducing the growing unemployment, remain unsubstantiated. These claims do not account for the livelihoods that will be lost in the process of creating SEZs, and are therefore quite unreliable. Moreover, new jobs will not necessarily go to those who will be losing land, as most farmers are ill-equipped to meet the demand for the kind of skills which the modern industry requires. Even so, the authors contend, the government seems determined to be acting more as a veritable broker of land, resources and power for corporations and realtors than as one protecting the rights of its poor citizens. In these circumstances, farmers and other affected groups have no option but to vent their anger through agitations, strikes, marches – weapons known to the weak. And this is beginning to yield results: the government of Goa was forced to cancel its SEZ plan. The resounding 'no' verdict of the first ever referendum on the issue of land acquisition in Raigarh is another example. Such examples of political transformation and democracy-in-action at the grassroots are indeed a hopeful trend and appear to be on the rise across the country, regardless of the SEZs or other attempts at land grab.

Issues surrounding the SEZs in West Bengal are discussed in Guha's chapter. According to him, although there was no concrete plan to create any SEZs till 2006, the government of West Bengal enacted the Act in 2003. This was two years ahead of the enactment of the SEZ Act by the government of India in 2005. It was in 2006 that the government of West Bengal first earmarked a large tract of land in Nandigram in East Medinipur district for a chemical industry project. There is no provision in the West Bengal SEZ Act to address resettlement issues that come with displacement. With no resettlement in sight, and faced with the prospect of losing their lands and livelihoods, the affected farmers then put up a strong resistance against their displacement. The agitation was promptly supported by certain political elements. This forced the government to backtrack on its SEZ plan meant to attract investment. For the time being, the government may not proceed with its SEZ plan, but the plan is not being abandoned altogether. If and when politically propitious circumstances emerge, the government may restart encouraging investments in SEZs to promote development. This, according to Guha, is the appropriate time when the government should be formulating a resettlement policy, which may be acceptable to the people losing land for development purposes, but nothing of the sort seems to be happening. This means that land for industry will continue to be acquired under the old colonial Land Acquisition Act of 1894, in which there is a provision for compensation but nothing on resettlement. Guha provides two cases of land acquisition for private industry in the wake of liberalisation to illustrate the changes that have taken place in the policies of the government — a government that claims to speak for small farmers and sharecroppers who form its support base, yet does nothing to ensure that they are compensated fairly and timely, and also get back land earlier acquired but now lying unused. Finally, the author gives a brief account of civil society movements in West Bengal, which gained prominence during recent protests against land acquisition for SEZs in Singur and Nandigram. His assessment is that the civil society is too weak to exert pressure on the government to enact a humane resettlement policy to address the problems of displacement caused by development projects.

The challenging issues that have emerged in the wake of growing importance of private capital in the development process under pressures of globalisation are the focus of this final paper in part four. In recent years, India's economic policies have undergone a dramatic transformation. Much emphasis now is on privatising development and attracting investment, especially foreign direct investment. Mathur examines the impact of such policies on the tribal people of Orissa, a resource-rich state, which is currently witnessing huge MNC-led investment in mining, steel and other development sectors. The rich natural resource endowment, and now the new investor-friendly policies, make Orissa an attractive investment destination. A number of large corporations indeed are lining up to invest in this state. As most natural wealth is concentrated in tribal areas, the growing demand for land is leading to displacement on a massive scale. For the tribal people, land is their only source of sustenance and, therefore, they are fiercely resisting its takeover. This, in turn, has led to clashes with the police, resulting in some protestors even losing their lives. Such events reinforce the belief among the displaced people that the government is interested only in helping private industry make profits at their expense, leaving them to languish in perpetual poverty. Mathur concludes that in this situation they see no end to their sufferings.

Part V: Conclusion — An alternative view

In the fifth and final part, the current theoretical resettlement models are questioned and instead a human rights-based approach is suggested in their place.

Perera questions the current resettlement models, finding them of limited value in understanding economic, social and cultural impacts of physical displacement that are caused by state-sponsored development interventions, and in finding ways to minimise these impacts. They focus more on how to assist people who have already been displaced than on the processes that cause physical displacement in the first place. Moreover, the models take for granted the difficulties and trauma the displaced communities and persons encounter as a result of physical displacement, by emphasising that subsequent development interventions will provide the displaced persons with 'development opportunities' to improve their income and livelihood. The author demonstrates that the rationale for 'development opportunity' stems from modernisation and development theories that emphasise that a wholesale change must take place in order to break the vicious circle of poverty, ignorance and low productivity. By justifying physical displacement as a 'development opportunity', the theoretical frameworks circumvent the need to focus on impoverishment and social disarticulation, inevitable in displacement situations. Hence, Perera makes a plea to discard the current resettlement and rehabilitation frameworks and instead focus more on human rights-based approaches to development, displacement, and resettlement.

References

Asher, Manshi. 2007. 'SEZs surge, but so do Protests'. *Civil Society*, August: 6.

Cernea, Michael M. 1995. 'Understanding and preventing impoverishment from displacement: Reflections on the state of knowledge'. Keynote address presented at the 'International Conference on Development-induced Displacement and Impoverishment', 3–7 January, University of Oxford.

Cernea, Michael M. and Hari Mohan Mathur (eds). 2008. *Can compensation prevent impoverishment? Reforming resettlement through investments and benefit-sharing*. New Delhi: Oxford University Press.

Centre for Science and Environment (CSE). 2008. 'Rich lands poor people: Is sustainable mining possible? State of India's environment: A citizens' report 6'. New Delhi: CSE.

Downing, Theodore E. 2002. *Avoiding new poverty: Mining-induced displacement and resettlement*. London: International Institute of Environment and Development.

Kalshian, Rakesh (ed.). 2007. *Caterpillar and the Mahua flower: Tremors in India's mining fields*. New Delhi: Panos South Asia.

Mathur, Hari Mohan. 1999. 'The impoverishing potential of development projects: Resettlement requires risk analysis'. *D+C Development and Cooperation*, 6: 24–26.

———. 2008. 'Managing the consequences of development-induced displacement', in Hari Mohan Mathur (ed.), *India social development report: Development and displacement*, pp. 179–95. New Delhi: Oxford University Press/Council for Social Development.

———. 2009. 'Investor-friendly development policies: Unsettling consequences for the tribal people of Orissa'. *The Asia and Pacific Journal of Anthropology*, 10(4): 318–28.

Mathur, Hari Mohan and David Marsden (eds). 1998. *Development projects and impoverishment risks: Resettling project-affected people in India*. New Delhi: Oxford University Press.

Oliver-Smith, Anthony (ed.). 2009. *Development and dispossession: The crisis of forced displacement and resettlement*. Santa Fe, NM: School of American Research.

Padel, Felix and Samarendra Das. 2008. 'Cultural genocide: The real impact of development induced displacement', in Hari Mohan Mathur (ed.), *India—social development report: Development and displacement*, pp. 103–15. New Delhi: Oxford University Press and Council for Social Development.

———. 2010. *Out of this earth: East india adivasis and the aluminium cartel*. New Delhi: Orient BlackSwan.

Sahu, Bighneswar. 2007. 'Defying the juggernaut', in Rakesh Kalshian (ed.), *Caterpillar and the Mahua flower: Tremors in India's mining fields*, pp. 178–91. New Delhi: Panos South Asia.

Saran, Rohit. 2008. 'From the editor'. *Business Today*, 17(19): 4.

Scudder, Thayer. 2005. *The future of large dams: Dealing with social, environmental, institutional and political costs*. London and Sterling, VA: Earthscan.

Shiva, Vandana and Afsar H. Jafri. 1998. 'Stronger than steel: An Indian people's movement against indiscriminate economic development'. *The Ecologist*, 28(6): 349–53.

Sinha, Prabhakar. 2009. 'Government eases FDI norms: Move to open up all sectors including retail, insurance'. *The Times of India*, 12 February, Jaipur, p. 1.

Tripathy, Salil. 2007. 'India must face its SEZ reality'. *Far Eastern Economic Review*, 170(4): 27–30.

van Wicklin III, Warren A. 1991. 'Sharing project benefits to improve resettlers' livelihoods', in Michael M. Cernea (ed.), *The economics of involuntary resettlement: Questions and challenges*, pp. 231–65. Washington DC: The World Bank.

Part I

The governance challenge

1

Making resettlement work: Policy, planning and management

Hari Mohan Mathur

The purpose of development is to promote economic growth, alleviate poverty and improve living standards for all, and the outcome is generally beneficial. Sometimes, the consequences can, however, be quite disruptive for the project area people. Projects may acquire their land, forcing them to relocate. The adverse social and economic impacts of such displacement are now well known. People lose their home, land and livelihood, and are often left to face on their own an uncertain future in unfamiliar, if not hostile, places. These are among the risks of impoverishment that frequently come with projects that involve involuntary resettlement (Cernea 1996, 2000; Mathur and Marsden 1998).

Worldwide experience has shown that most people who experience forced relocation are unable to regain their losses, ending up worse off than before (McDowell 1996; Downing 2002). In India, the track record of efforts undertaken to resettle displaced people remains quite dismal. Thus, as a result of development efforts that are intended to improve living conditions for people, millions have become worse off, a situation in direct opposition to what development stands for. Generally, the worst affected happen to be the poor. The fact is that the process of development is unintentionally adding to their numbers, and not reducing poverty.

Involuntary resettlement associated with development projects is, however, not a problem that will go away in the foreseeable future. With government aiming to achieve new highs in economic growth, and the private sector emerging as a major player in the development process under globalisation pressures, displacement in the years ahead is set to occur on a much larger scale than before. The growing impoverishment, in turn, is fuelling opposition to projects, which is increasingly turning aggressive, demanding even rollback of otherwise well-meant initiatives in some cases.

It is, however, becoming obvious that the lack of attention to resettlement issues not only harms the project area people, but has other serious implications as well. Project costs go up when discontented people mount protests that can completely upset implementation schedules, resulting in huge time and cost overruns. Providing adequate resettlement assistance to those displaced by development projects is, therefore, not only ethically correct, but also makes good economic sense. The cost of not doing adequate resettlement can often be much more than doing resettle-ment well.

Experience suggests that, though stubborn, resettlement problems are not insurmountable. A fuller understanding of the issues involved in managing resettlement is, however, essential if projects are to stay on track, harming none and yet generating benefits for all. This paper attempts to look closely at selected legal, policy, planning and management issues that critically affect resettlement outcomes.

Legal framework for land acquisition

Laws to specifically deal with resettlement issues generally do not exist. What exist are laws regulating the acquisition of privately owned land. Most of these laws were not enacted with the resettlement issues in view, as resettlement was not an issue when these laws were made. In India, the law on land acquisition was enacted in the nineteenth century, when maintenance of law and order, and not development, was the main focus of the colonial government. This archaic law, still operative, was not intended to address the problems that people now face due to acquisition of their land for dams, thermal power stations, mining operations, highways, airports, SEZs and other development projects.

In India, lands, buildings and other immovable properties are mostly acquired under the Land Acquisition Act of 1894 (as amended in 1984), which is presently under further amendment (Iyer, in this volume). This law, based on the doctrine of eminent domain, gives the state unilateral powers to take over privately owned land for a public purpose on payment of compensation. For a large number of people who have no formal title to land but otherwise depend on it, including landowners, subtenants, sharecroppers, landless labourers, encroachers and shifting cultivators, there is no compensation whatsoever. Experience indicates that the exercise of eminent domain operates wholly to the disadvantage of people whose land is acquired (Ramanathan 2008, 2009). No doubt persons who lose their land are entitled to compensation, but the amount is never enough to buy an equivalent piece of land. This happens because the compensation amount is determined on the basis of the land's market value, not its replacement value. No wonder people losing their land are seldom able to re-establish themselves, swelling instead the number of development-induced poor.

A major criticism of the Indian land acquisition law is that it does not define public purpose. This is left to the state agencies to determine on a case by case basis, but their decisions regarding land requirement for projects can often be arbitrary, leading to the acquisition of land far in excess of actual requirement, causing displacement that is better avoided. Appa and Patel (1996) cite several cases of unnecessary and unjustified acquisitions and displacement for a variety of projects in Gujarat.

The laws for land acquisition are not much different in other countries either. In Africa, as de Wet (1999) has shown, when it comes to taking over private land for development projects, the state is under no obligation to demonstrate public purpose. Legal frameworks exist to uphold the interests of the state, not those of the project-affected people. On the basis of his experiences with World Bank-assisted projects involving resettlement, Shihata (1993: 41–42) noted that

> in many countries the national legal framework of resettlement operations is incomplete.... Resettlement legal issues are treated as a subset of property and expropriation law. For various reasons, these national laws do not provide a fully adequate framework for development-oriented resettlement.... New legislation often must be introduced, or existing laws must be modified, in order to plan and carry out involuntary resettlement adequately.

Policy guidelines on resettlement

There were also no resettlement policies anywhere until the late 1980s. In the absence of policy, projects addressed resettlement issues as they arose in a purely ad hoc manner, through promulgation of instructions that were specific to the project causing displacement. Gradually, sector-specific policies applicable to all projects within that particular sector merged. There was no uniformity either in project-specific instructions or sector-specific policies, which varied from project to project and sector to sector. Often, the affected people received resettlement assistance that differed markedly from one project to the other in the same country.

In Latin American countries, as Mejia (1999: 166) pointed out:

> Lack of an official resettlement policy that defines institutional responsibilities, rights of those displaced, financing mechanisms, land acquisition, compensation, indemnification, and titling is one of the most common problems in resettlement planning. No Latin American or Caribbean country has a national policy for involuntary resettlement caused by development projects, nor are we aware of any comprehensive sectoral policy except for the one in the Colombian electricity sector.

A policy signifies government commitment to ensure adequate resettlement. It is the project-affected people who suffer the most in the absence of such a commitment. They do not know what help to expect and from what agency when suddenly faced with the prospect of losing their home, land and livelihood. According to a World Bank study, most impoverishment that occurs can be attributed to the lack of policy on resettlement, 'An extensive review of the anthropological and sociological research literature on resettlement, carried out by the task force to assess displacement impacts worldwide, found — and this conclusion bears repeating — that the most frequent and severe cases of impoverishment have occurred in programs unguided by domestic or international policy norms' (World Bank 1994: 4/14).

The World Bank issued its policy statement on involuntary resettlement in 1980. It has since been updated on several occasions, with the October 2001 update being the latest. The World Bank policy has served as a template for several other policies, such as the policies issued by the Asian Development Bank (ADB), the Organisation for Economic Cooperation and Development (OECD), and other international development agencies.

The World Bank policy was meant primarily for its own staff to guide them in dealing with resettlement issues surrounding development projects, but over the years, the whole world (from regional development banks to governments and now even multinationals and private banks) seems to have adopted its basic principles in their own resettlement policies. Cernea (2005b) provides a historical perspective on the rise of this social policy to its present globally influential position, culminating in 2003, in 10 of the largest and most influential investment banks from seven developed countries adopting a social and environmental framework which has come to be known as 'Equator Principles'. Many more banks have since adopted these principles.

Given the disruptive nature of the involuntary resettlement process, the World Bank policy recommendation is to avoid it as far as possible. For people who, despite all efforts to avoid it, must still be resettled, the policy objective is to ensure reestablishment in ways that improve their standards of living, and do not just restore them to pre-project levels. The World Bank policy is also emphatic that for resettlement not to be reduced to the physical relocation of people and reproduction of their pre-displacement conditions, all resettlement operations must be planned and implemented as development programmes.

In India, there was no national resettlement policy until recently on an issue that affects millions of people every year. An exercise to formulate a national policy began a long time ago, but all that came out first in 2004 was a resettlement policy that failed to meet the expectations it had aroused. Hence, NGOs that were critical of the lack of a policy in the first place, continued to be critical of the policy that emerged. In 2007, a new policy was issued, which, in some respects, is an improvement over the 2004 policy; but this too does not go far enough to fully meet the needs of the affected people (Iyer, this volume). In 2006, Orissa issued a comprehensive resettlement policy, becoming the first state in India to do so (Mathur 2007).

Most governments and public sector undertakings appear reluctant to the idea of issuing resettlement policies that conform to international standards, preferring an ad hoc approach instead. In some cases, where resettlement policies have been formulated under donor agency influence, they are owned reluctantly as an imposition, to be applied only when it becomes unavoidable. For example, the Coal India Limited (CIL) operates about 500 mines in different parts of the country, but its resettlement policy formulated in connection with a World Bank loan remained effective only in those 25 mines that were part of the Coal Sector Environment and Social Mitigation Project (CSESMP) (Mathur 2008).

While policies are important, the related issue of compliance with the policies often does not receive adequate attention. There persists a massive gap between resettlement policy and actual practice (Lyla 2009; Padel and Das, this volume). This criticism applies even in cases where the projects are funded by international agencies. While they may be impressive on paper, the resettlement guidelines drafted by international agencies … have been problematic with regard to their consistent application.

The planning of resettlement

Resettlement planning provides the means to mitigate the adverse impacts of displacement, and to create development opportunities for project-affected people. When population displacement is on a large scale, the World Bank and other policies on involuntary resettlement require the preparation of a resettlement action plan (RAP). Until recently, systematic resettlement planning was, however, largely unknown. When undertaken to stem the opposition to projects and such crisis situations, actions that the authorities initiated were purely ad hoc, in which long-term development programmes meant to fully re-establish resettlers seldom figured. This effectively reduced resettlement to relocation, relieving projects of any further responsibility towards the affected people.

The first requirement for planning resettlement is that there be a reasonable estimate of the number of people that will be affected, but even this basic information is often unavailable. While reviewing the Sardar Sarovar Project, Morse and Berger (1992) were dismayed to note that no basis for designing, implementing and assessing resettlement was in place, and no one knew the scale of the displacement that would result from the dam. Resettlement plans can only be as good as the information on which they are based (World Bank 1994, 2004).

As resettlement experience has shown, 'Poor preparation of resettlement plans is the single most important reason for failure of resettlement components in development projects. Poor preparation leads to delays, increased costs, foregone benefits, which negatively impact human communities affected and subvert the development objectives of civil works projects. In particularly difficult instances, poor resettlement preparation leads to unwelcome political backlash, unintentional environmental degradation, and the unanticipated creation of "development refugees"' (Partridge 1993: 351).

In recent years, the resettlement planning process has somewhat improved, but problems remain with implementation. Emphasis on planning alone cannot, however, ensure success in resettlement. Inadequate attention to the plan implementation issues explains unsatisfactory outcomes in most cases. Even the best prepared plans fail to deliver if not implemented well. Yet, planning receives far more attention than implementation. An evaluation study of World Bank-funded projects found this to be the case: 'In the cases examined, planning received disproportionate attention in comparison with results. This is the downside of the otherwise positive progress with planning. While better planning usually translates into better implementation, this assumption has not held up for involuntary resettlement. As a subsidiary operation, resettlement continues to receive inadequate attention during implementation' (Picciotto et al. 2001: 19).

One factor that makes the greatest difference to resettlement outcomes is the top-level commitment, but that is often lacking. A resettlement evaluation study found poor performance in Karnataka and Maharashtra irrigation projects due to 'a failure of commitment at the highest level of government' (World Bank 1998: 58). On the critical importance of management issues in resettlement, this study went as far as to conclude that if countries do not have the capacity and the commitment to handle resettlement well, they better not undertake large projects.

Resettlement is primarily a management issue. Actual relocation — the moving of people, animals, household possessions, etc — is a matter of demanding logistics. For people to be able to live at new sites, basic services have to be in place, water and temporary housing being the most important. Sooner rather than later, a range of civic amenities too should be available, such as medical facilities, schools, bus services, electricity, temples, churches and other public buildings. In addition, the provision of adequate opportunities for reconstruction of livelihood is basic to the sustainability of the entire resettlement process. All this depends a great deal on administrative capacity, flexibility and continuity (Morse and Berger 1992: 132).

There are several resettlement planning and implementation issues, which often fail to receive adequate attention. Some of them are discussed in the following paragraphs.

Social impact assessment

Resettlement is a potentially impoverishing process. A major flaw in resettlement planning is that generally an assessment of potential adverse impacts of projects is not conducted properly. This is also true of projects financed by the World Bank, known for its meticulous methods of researching and documenting the minutest of project details (Scudder 2005). It is not uncommon for large numbers of affected people to go uncounted at the planning stage. When impacts are not fully identified initially, it becomes difficult to fully mitigate them later. For projects funded by the World Bank, a review found the actual number of people to be resettled 47 per cent higher than the estimate made at the time of appraisal (World Bank 1996: 88).

For dams-related displacement, Gill (2006: 178) acknowledges the prevailing deficiency of the planning process:

> The planning process of many dams is based on an inadequate assessment of adverse impacts. There have been instances where entire categories of impacts were not identified. While it is relatively easy to survey those whose land, houses and other assets are taken for the dam, others, who might be using the river and its catchment for collecting forest products, seasonal fishing, grazing and similar activities, are easy to miss.

A narrow definition of the term 'project-affected people' excludes many people who are negatively impacted by dams, especially the landless, downstream communities, and indigenous people. Often, people physically displaced by canals, powerhouses, and by associated compensation measures such as nature reserves, are also not counted (Scudder 1997 and 2006).

WCD provides an example of underestimation of affected people from a project in Thailand.

> In 1991, when construction started on the Pak Mun dam, 241 families were counted as displaced. By the time construction was completed, it was clear that another 1,459 households had to be relocated. The true extent of the social impact only became evident when the impact of the dam on fisheries livelihoods was admitted in response to prolonged agitation by the affected people. By March 2000, the Thai government paid interim compensation — pending a final solution to the permanent loss of fisheries livelihoods — to 6,204 households for livelihood loss during construction (WCD 2000: 4).

Commenting on planning without correct estimates of the affected people, and such considerations, Morse and Berger (1993: 58) observed:

> Despite Bank policies, many projects have commenced without accurate data. Not only are the direct impacts of the project little understood, and plans made that do not take account of what is likely to happen, but also the broader dimensions of the difficulties go unappreciated. The needs of women and the elderly are left out of the calculation. The consequences for host communities — the villages where oustees will be relocated — are ignored, or evaluated much too late in the day. A range of secondary displacements go unconsidered. As a result, at each stage of project development, new emergencies arise. As these accumulate, those affected feel growing indignation, and political opposition begins to mount. The human costs of the projects are thus misrepresented from the beginning, and tend to be understated or avoided as they arise. By the time a project is under way, there are large interests that are best served by minimizing any apparent negative consequences... Each element is at risk if the real human costs of a project are not fully anticipated.

The remoteness of many project sites makes social impact assessment a difficult exercise. The assessment task is further complicated by the fact that not all losses are quantifiable. For example, people often miss their social networks and lament the loss of access to their traditional places of worship in their new locations, but there is no way to either assess or compensate such impacts in any measurable way.

In addition, the resources provided to carry out census, socioeconomic surveys and related studies, including consultant input, are never adequate. The need to analyse social factors that may influence (and are influenced by) a project continues throughout the life of that project. But most agencies consider social impact assessment (SIA) of some use only in the design stage (as without completing the paperwork required, it is not possible to obtain loan from donor agencies). 'While the theory of social assessment may seem to demand multidisciplinary teams of exceptionally gifted individuals working over an extended period, the reality is usually somewhat more prosaic' (Lucas 2000: 102). Surely anthropologists and sociologists are slotted in, but typically their input is too brief, no longer than one or two man-months on projects where the total planning input of several man-years is not uncommon. Social impact assessments based on whistle-stop tours by visiting experts clearly have their own limitations.

While environmental impact assessment of projects has more or less come to be accepted as a norm, the social impact assessment is often carried out as a component of the environmental impact assessment. As a result, it is often not given the same importance that is now generally attached to environmental impact assessment. It is important that social impact assessments are treated as a distinct type of project preparation activity, in much the same way as other assessments.

Participation

The fact that all development projects improve with the active participation of stakeholders is now widely accepted. However, the question often asked is: Is this truism also applicable in the case of projects that involve resettlement? And can the people who are forced to relocate be expected to cooperate with project authorities, whom they hold accountable for all their woes? As Mejia and Namhad (1996: 93) put it: 'At first glance, forced resettlement might be the last place one would expect to find an example of successful people's participation. Yet, there is no way (short of police action) to mobilise and relocate a community other than to organise their participation'.

Horowitz et al. (1993) are among a growing number of resettlement researchers and practitioners who regard participatory approach particularly relevant to resettlement planning and implementation processes:

> It is perhaps oxymoronic to speak of 'participation' in reservoir-driven relocation, since the move is inherently involuntary. Yet, successful resettlement depends in very large part on an active participation of those forced to move. Not only does participation facilitate identification with the move and lessen the dependency common in these projects, it provides management with information critical to sound decision-making. (ibid.: 242)

Participation in decision making as a right of the project-affected people is also gaining wide support on the ground that in giving up their homes and livelihoods for the sake of projects, they make an important contribution to the development process as a whole. No project can ever get off the ground without their sacrifice.

However, the reasons why planners are increasingly tilting towards participatory approaches are of a purely practical kind, not particularly related to any philosophical position. For planners, an important objective is to ensure that the project costs do not go up, putting the project in jeopardy. Reflecting on his experiences with the Mexico Hydroelectric Project, Guggenheim (1996: 71–72) observed:

> Project costs must be weighed against the benefits gained from the new approach. Aguamilpa and Zimapan are among the few large dams ever completed on time in Mexico. Although not every delay in the other projects can be attributed to fractious resettlement, many can be. During roughly the same period that Aguamilpa and Zimapan were being built, two other large dams — not financed by the Bank — were cancelled entirely because of resettlement protests that blossomed into armed confrontations and marches into Mexico City. Because of the enormous costs of dam construction — nearly a billion dollars for the two projects — each year's delay in project commissioning would have implied foregone benefits that exceeded the total cost of our entire participatory resettlement package by orders of magnitude.

Another important consideration is that participation provides project authorities with the perspectives of displaced people, so critical to the planning for their complex long-term reestablishment. Moreover, as experience has shown, when people are consulted in the planning of resettlement package for them, they do not retract later, and even lend a helping hand to the management in implementing those plans. The fact is that participatory approach is working well in resettlement operations in many cases. Identifying the participatory component in the Costa Rican Arenal Hydroelectric Project as a factor contributing to the success of resettlement, Partridge (1993: 367) observed:

> Another outstanding feature was the degree to which the displaced people were informed, consulted, and integrated as participants in the preparation process. The participatory approach served the purpose of combating tendencies toward sullen and resentful dependency, which often beset the people whose lives are autocratically controlled by others. Participation also provided planners with access to the expectations, beliefs, and knowledge system of the people for whom they were planning, which made possible the prevention of design errors by checking proposal details with them.

However, despite the known virtues of participation, the general tendency is to exclude the involvement of project-affected people in resettlement activities as much as possible. Participation seems to lack sufficient support in higher bureaucratic echelons. Senior administrators, apparently in a hurry all the time, have no patience with participatory approaches that require time as well as financial commitment. They want to get on with the job somehow or the other. Horowitz et al. (1993) found project people in the field sympathetic to the advantages of local participation, but they were inadequately supported by the donor and opposed by regional officials of the central administration, who felt that the 'relocatees' should simply follow orders. The Manatali project did seek settler participation in the project, but far more during the planning phase of the cycle than during implementation.

Often, the affected people first learn about the project when one fine morning they are handed a legal notice that their land is being taken over for project requirements. By that time, the project is almost ready for launch, leaving no scope for any design change that may save them from avoidable displacement. All that the people can do at this stage is to beg the authorities to be kind to them in granting compensation for their land. No consultation is done with the people whose lives the project is going to change forever.

Even simple information, which people need to plan their departure to unknown relocation sites, remains inaccessible (MARG 1986). The officials, viewing project information as sensitive, prefer not to part with it. In this respect, international development agencies fare no better. From the coal mining areas of eastern India, Carter (2000: 60–61) reported:

> Essentially, the World Bank has colluded in withholding information about the real effects of the mining from the people whose lives it will actually affect. Villagers often do not know until the very last minute that it is their village which is to be destroyed by mining. As one writer put it, 'Information control is the main weapon by which this development violence is perpetrated. There is little information sharing about the planned mines, and what information exists is jumbled and indeterminate. The fact is that the people whose lives and environment are to be affected have no clear prior information. Why is it treated as a military secret?'

In general, participatory strategies are still aimed at avoiding conflict than at including stakeholders and displaced communities in decision making, and sharing responsibilities central to the project and to people's lives (Mejia 1999).

Vulnerable groups

Vulnerable groups include people who, by virtue of gender, ethnicity, age, physical or mental disability, economic disadvantage, or social status, may be more adversely affected by resettlement than others, and who may be limited in their ability to claim or take advantage of resettlement assistance and related development benefits (IFC 2002). In many ways, the problems of women, indigenous peoples, encroachers, squatters and other such groups are different, and merit special attention in the planning and implementation of resettlement.

Gender

While displacement has severe consequences for all, for women, these are particularly devastating. Regardless of differences in caste, class, religion or region, women everywhere bear the brunt of the forced move a lot more than the male members of their families. Resettlement results in their marginalisation in various ways (Mehta 2009). Generally, women lose their earlier income opportunities, and are forced to the margins of the labour market. The loss of their previous access to food, fodder and fuel-wood, coupled with the difficulties they encounter accessing them in the new place, makes life a hard struggle. Their participation in decision making is next to nothing, although men admit that consulting the women in the process of site selection and other matters can avert many of the hardships that arise in a new place (Mehta 2000). In the new environment, women get virtually nothing in return for what they leave behind (Dewan 2008).

Many problems that women face in resettlement situations stem from gender bias, especially in developing countries. In India, the age-old notions about gender and the gender roles are too deeply rooted for the planning process to overcome easily. In these circumstances, the planning for resettlement tends to be flawed in its approach right from the start (Mathur 2009a). The gender bias is evident in law; it is present in policies as well. Project authorities seldom consult women on their problems and needs while designing resettlement plans. Under the land acquisition law, it is men as owners of land who get the compensation amount, not women (Basu 2006). Some resettlement policies, such as the Orissa water resources development resettlement policy, are patently discriminatory. For purposes of resettlement assistance, the Orissa resettlement policy for the World Bank-aided water resources projects recognises only unmarried women of 30 years of age and above as a separate family; the equivalent age is 18 for a man (Government of Orissa 1994).

The situation appears to have begun changing slowly, thanks to the pressures from feminists' groups and the efforts of international development agencies. For example, the Asian Development Bank has begun associating gender specialists in resettlement plan preparation exercise and has also brought out a Resettlement Gender Checklist to guide resettlement planners (ADB 2003).

Indigenous people

Indigenous people have suffered centuries of exploitation and displacement. Even after half a century of development, they remain outside the pale of any form of visible change in their condition. Currently, large-scale development projects present a major threat to the lives of these peoples in many parts of the world, particularly in India, Peru, Papua New Guinea, Australia, United States, Canada and Brazil (Blaser et al. 2004; Downing 2002). Many areas with a heavy concentration of indigenous peoples happen to be rich in hydrologic, forest, mineral oil and other resources, and this at once makes these areas attractive locations for projects of various kinds. It should then come as no surprise that indigenous peoples constitute a disproportionately large segment of those adversely affected by development projects. In India, 40 per cent of all those who have been displaced are tribal people, who represent barely 8 per cent of the total population (Government of India 1985).

Generally, development projects prove harmful to indigenous people, especially because they often lack legal recognition and a voice in governance issues. They are particularly vulnerable because they have no individual rights on land. In the absence of any legal title, there is no basis on which to prepare a compensation package in lieu of their land (Mathur 2009). Moreover, compensation packages, where provided, have been utterly inadequate to compensate for the loss of land, livelihood, and break-up of their communities and culture (Mathur 2004). The trauma of resettlement is also exacerbated for indigenous communities because of their strong spiritual ties to their land, and their apprehension that once they move, their way of life will be lost forever. For indigenous peoples, displacement is indeed an unmitigated disaster (Padel and Das 2008).

Although policies of the World Bank and the Asian Development Bank exist to protect tribal peoples and their cultures against the harmful effects of development projects, there remain enormous obstacles to their social, economic and political participation in the development process (Gonzalez-Parra 2001). In India, even the constitutional safeguards are proving inadequate to protect their interests (Randeria 2003).

Vulnerable groups, other than women and indigenous people, also face many hardships as projects often tend not to take into consideration their special needs and problems. Efforts are made to provide them assistance, but these generally remain limited in impact.

Compensation

This is a critical issue in any resettlement programme. Resettlement efforts will come to nothing if the affected people are not compensated adequately. 'The loss of even a small plot of farmland can have vital consequences for the household economy, and unless sufficient and appropriate compensation is given, this initial loss may be but the first step in a wider process of impoverishment and marginalisation' (Sorensen 1996: 211).

As compensation is important to the reestablishment process, it will be helpful to first clarify the meanings of compensation and rehabilitation. Shihata (1993: 47) explains:

> Compensation is what the owner of property, unilaterally acquired by the government, receives in lieu of that property. It can be made in cash or in kind, and is usually based on a standard of valuation provided by law....Rehabilitation, on the other hand, constitutes a series of measures, including but not limited to monetary compensation, aimed at affording the affected population the possibility to become re-established and economically self-sustaining in the shortest possible period. Compensation is usually provided only to land and property owners, while rehabilitation measures are to be provided to all those severely affected by the development project.

Traditionally, compensation approaches have revolved mainly around the following four alternatives: cash, land, employment, and self-employment.

Cash

In the past, resettlement simply meant the payment of cash in lieu of land and other properties taken over for project purposes. However, when the affected people are given compensation in cash and then left to their own devices, they often get impoverished. As experience has shown, cash compensation generally fails to assist in the reestablishment process for several reasons (Cernea and Mathur 2008; FAO 2008). Critical of the compensation principle, Cernea (2008: 91) observed: 'compensation alone cannot prevent impoverishment: it must be enhanced to be fairer, and it must be supplemented by investments for development. If used alone, its corollary *is* impoverishment, not development'.

First, compensation is given only to those persons whose properties the project acquires, ignoring others who lack ownership rights but are in occupation of the assets and depend on them for their living. For example, agricultural labourers, sharecroppers, landless workers, tribal people, hunters, nomadic herders and other such people, who often constitute large groups most severely affected by displacement, are not entitled to compensation.

Second, even those who receive compensation are not able to get back to the kind of living that they lose. Land acquisition procedures do not provide compensation amount enough to purchase land and other assets of comparable worth. The fact is that most landowners losing land are rarely able to own land again. The source of much impoverishment associated with displacement is thus the prevailing compensatory approaches to resettlement.

Third, the bureaucratic way in which compensation payment is made, often after a long wait and in instalments over a period of time, prevents the affected people from moving to the new place and resettle as quickly as possible. In the Bisalpur project, disbursement of compensation amount added further to the misery of the people affected. Until they received full amounts, they could not move to the resettlement colonies built for them (Mathur: 1997). A World Bank study reported that at Nangbeto, people waited for three years for the final cash payments for their houses and are still waiting for compensation for trees (World Bank 1998: 8–9).

Fourth, getting the compensation amount is not a simple matter for most poor people. Project authorities are not known for their integrity in seeing that the rightful claimants get their dues promptly, and in a hassle-free manner. Asked how they spend the compensation amount, one person displaced from an industrial development project in Rajasthan wryly remarked, 'A major portion of compensation amount goes in getting it' (Srivastava 1995: 115). Rampant corruption hits the poor the hardest. They rarely get in their hands the full amount of compensation for their properties, meant to aid them in getting back on their feet.

Finally, a major problem with monetary compensation is that most displaced people, especially tribal people and those from remote villages, do not know what to do with cash in quantities that they see for the first time in their lives. In the excitement, they forget that they need the money to rebuild their lives and lose no time in going on a spending spree. Money is thus frittered away in ways least likely to support their reestablishment. In a project in Nepal, the impact of cash compensation on the lifestyle of the affected people turned out to be more serious than that of the loss of land. The sudden inflow of cash gave them a false sense of riches, and changed their entire behaviour. Gambling and drinking increased to an unprecedented level. As a result, some adults developed tuberculosis, and one died in a miserable condition. One young man, who had received a large sum in compensation, went to a casino in Kathmandu to gamble, only to lose all his money. He ended up working as a dishwasher in the city. One or two persons with some entrepreneurial ambition started a trucking business, but due to lack of experience, failed in the venture (Pokharel 1995).

While resettlement studies have repeatedly shown that cash compensation alone does not help the displaced to become economically productive again, yet projects continue to focus on cash compensation, unaware that there are other better ways to assist those in need. Perera (2000) found a clear compensation bias in the resettlement process in the Singrauli region thermal power projects. Even the NGOs there were supportive of cash compensation in the belief that it would help the displaced improve their living standards, and therefore did nothing to help people identify other options for sustainable reestablishment.

Land

Where rural people are involved, programmes that relocate them to agricultural land of comparable size and quality often prove successful.

Thus, land for the displaced people with agricultural background from rural areas remains the best way to compensate them as no occupational change is involved. No wonder this is a form of compensation which is much preferred by those who lose land.

The mere acquisition of a piece of land in a new place does not, however, mean that resettlers get any closer to recovery, let alone complete reestablishment. New hurdles keep coming up. In many places, the quality of land given as compensation is not comparable to that of the land acquired. The Gujarat government's resettlement policy provides for allotment of land to anyone affected by the Narmada dam opting to resettle in the state. But good policy intents alone are not enough. The fact is that good agricultural land is scarce. Caufield (1997) narrates a case where resettlers from Madhya Pradesh were asked to accept land in Gujarat that lacked any resemblance to the land shown to them on an earlier visit to the area. In such circumstances, many prefer not to stay at the resettlement site and move elsewhere.

Land given as compensation is often not free from ownership disputes. As a result, the land continues to be in the possession of some other people, and the allotment in the name of the displaced remains only on paper. This happened to people displaced by the Sariska Tiger Sanctuary project in Rajasthan. Allotment letters were distributed to the displaced by the chief minister at a specially organised function, but they were unable to get possession of the land on the basis of the letters. The local land records official did not help them on the ground that some other people already had farms on the same land, and that according to records, the legal ownership titles to the land were in their names (Sharma 1995).

Also, the land given is generally too far from the original village, and the displaced people do not wish to disconnect completely with their native places. Moreover, some problems arise due to the unavailability of land in areas large enough to accommodate the entire affected population from one village at one place. For this reason, people who would like to move together to one place are instead moved to different places. Thus, they get dispersed due to land availability constraints. This dispersal, however, affects the existing social bonds, social capital built over the years.

Despite the many problems that come with new land, it remains the best resettlement option for people displaced from their land in rural areas. Arguably, no other means of making a living can provide the sense of security that land can. The scarcity of land is, however, a major limiting factor in pursuing land-centred compensatory approaches. There is no easy way in which project authorities can overcome land scarcity. Perhaps the only way they can do it is by buying land from those willing to sell it, but this may result in displacement of the sellers. It remains doubtful if they can manage to meet the demand this way.

Employment

The practice of offering jobs in the projects as compensation for land or other loss has been followed in many projects. Often, people who get permanent jobs are able to resettle themselves even more quickly than those who get land. This explains the never-ending clamour for jobs, especially the permanent jobs in public sector enterprises. In addition, there are several benefits that go with such jobs, such as the cost of living allowance, annual increments, leave and travel concessions, education allowance for children, besides pension after retirement. For the affected people, a job with a public sector organisation means a lot, not only as a permanent source of good income but also as a status symbol.

For long, the CIL, a government of India undertaking, was able to follow the practice of providing jobs in mines to compensate loss of land. This could be done in the past as jobs then were not as scarce as land. With the modernisation of mining operations, the number of available jobs has rapidly come down, and now falls short of the growing demand. The CIL view now is that the entire coal industry in India is groaning under the weight of overstaffing, and time has come to cry a halt to the practice of giving jobs in exchange for land acquired (Mathur 2008; Roy 2006, this volume).

However, CIL is not the only mining company that finds it impossible to provide jobs as compensation for land loss. In an era when the industry is downsizing to survive in a highly competitive world, it is certainly in no position to provide permanent jobs. The challenge for CIL, which once used the jobs-for-land method of compensation, is how to wean people away from the lure of permanent jobs.

Self-employment

Where land and job options are no longer available, self-employment and income-generation schemes are being introduced. CIL, under the World Bank-aided Social and Environmental Mitigation Project (ESMP) — part of a wider project to modernise CIL's mining operations — laid particular emphasis on such schemes. Overall, results from the CIL self-help, income-generation schemes have not been very promising (Mathur 2008). This may be due to a lack of proper planning. In some cases, skill training has been provided, but this has not been followed up with assistance in gaining access to credit and marketing opportunities. Training programmes also failed to take note of the fact that coping with poverty typically involves engaging in many different activities simultaneously, in a constant effort to make both ends meet. In fact, ESMP made no provision in its budget to provide start-up capital to enable people to start their businesses after training. These ill-planned efforts meant that in the absence of start-up capital and marketing assistance, resettlers could not do anything productive with their training. Also, the training was conducted without taking the demand factor into account. For one village, the training programme turned out tailors in huge numbers, making it impossible for all tailors to remain gainfully employed in that small place. Another major planning deficiency was that the monitoring systems were not in place which could track resettlers' progress with income generation (or the lack of it).

The fact is that unless properly organised, skill training programmes fail more frequently than they succeed. Tamondong-Helin (1996: 177–78) provides insightful comments from her study of a project in Philippines that relied on skill training for an income-restoration programme:

> Skills-training programmes were introduced to help people cope in their new setting. Such programmes included sewing, animal-raising, small-scale business, pottery, leadership training, fruit-tree cultivation, auto-repair, welding and cooperatives management. However, many of the training programmes were not planned appropriately, and there were no outlets for their skills once trained. Some of the skills were impractical, such as pig-raising, a water-consuming activity which was inappropriate because water supply was a problem even for people themselves. People ended up butchering the piglets for consumption, since maintenance and the affordability of feeds were problems. Another unsuccessful training

programme was clay-pot making. Trainees were mostly farmers who possessed rough hands for farm work, while pottery required smoother hands. For those trainees who had learned new skills, despite the provision of project loans, few managed to open small businesses. Many of those who managed to secure loans were obliged to spend their money on weddings, baptismal parties and gambling.

As a solution to the problems arising from forced resettlement, self-employment is still an uncharted territory, and in promoting such income-generation options, the CIL planners indeed face numerous constraints. These include:

- Generally, project-affected people are reluctant to accept the self-employment alternative, as it involves a total change in their occupation and lifestyle. The change from being a farmer to a manager operating an enterprise of his own is too drastic. Already traumatised by the displacement experience, the affected people are naturally apprehensive about things they confront in the new environment. A change in occupation carries with it certain risks. It is not without reason that they happen to be reluctant to enter into businesses, the outcome of which may often be unpredictable. Moreover, even the smallest enterprise takes months to get established. This time luxury is something displaced people cannot afford. They are a people in a hurry.
- The fact is that many income-generation schemes — often formulated in a hurry, without adequate consultation with the people whom they are meant to assist — still remain largely untried and cannot guarantee adequate income on a sustainable basis. This inevitably leads to a high rate of failure. Experiences elsewhere in this regard are also not very encouraging. A large proportion of self-employment projects fold up within 2–3 years of their launch.
- The emphasis on self-employment as an income-restoration strategy comes at a time when the current macroeconomic policies of globalisation and liberalisation are generally unfavourable to small and micro enterprises (SMEs) everywhere. Increasingly, 'the odds are stacked against the self-employed in the marketplace. Consumer trends fluctuate nearly as wildly as the economy, which is becoming more prone to external factors as India opens its markets. Aggressive brand

selling and marketing coupled with the strong financial clout of transnational corporations places the poor, especially poor women, at a particularly unfair advantage in the global marketplace' (Singh and Wysham 1997: 42). In terms of quality and price, products of micro-enterprises simply cannot compete with those of multinational corporations.

- Entrepreneur-centred small businesses supported by micro-credit tend to exclude the poor, the people most in need. They generally benefit a handful of people who are already better off. These people have some business sense, understand the importance of profit and investment, realise the need to take calculated risks, and are therefore in a better position to run the enterprise successfully. The poor often lack entrepreneurial skills. Generally, displaced people are not interested in taking loans to start small businesses, fearing this may lead them into a debt-trap. A study of the micro-credit approach cautioned that micro-credit is not the way out of poverty for many of the truly destitute, and the usefulness of credit to many of them may be limited (Pischke, Schneider and Zander 1996).
- Most affected people do not see self-employment schemes as a source of dependable livelihood which could generate sufficient income on a sustainable basis. There is, however, absolutely no doubt in their minds about the superiority of a public sector company job. For example, when basket making as a source of alternative income generation was suggested to the people affected by mining operations in Parez, a village in south Bihar (now Jharkhand), their instant reaction was that they would unhesitatingly accept it, provided it could guarantee them returns equal to a CIL job (Mathur 2008).

Relocation

People resist forced relocation everywhere, and this is a perfectly natural behaviour. The move costs them heavily, not only in material terms but also in ways that remain uncounted. Their living conditions can never be the same again in a new place. Even with somewhat better housing and infrastructure facilities at relocation sites, most people continue to miss their good old days. In Egypt, a long time after resettlement, many Nubians were still feeling unsettled in their new areas and longing for home (Fahim 1983: 116). However, relocation is not always avoidable, although the need for it can be reduced with imaginative project design.

The actual process of moving families and businesses to a new site presents formidable challenges. People do not easily get around to the notion that they have to move, and leave behind their homes, land and kinsmen, forever. They need assistance in moving to the new site, and once they get there, they require strong support in housing, income generation, social services and other areas. Often, people find none of the promised facilities in place at the new site.

If planned well, relocation can be achieved smoothly, without causing further dislocation. Yet, relocation is not always planned with care. Force is freely used in shifting people away from their homes to a different place. In this regard, the WCD (2000: 106) reports a shocking state of affairs: 'For millions of people on all continents, displacement has essentially occurred through official coercion'. The Alamatti dam in Karnataka provides an example of how not to carry out relocation (World Bank 1998). In dam projects, relocation is conducted in step with the advancing water, as people prefer not to move until the last minute. In case of the Alamatti project, in 1996 and 1997, water was released before the new sites were ready to receive the displaced people. Emergency action had to be taken, including pressing boats and helicopters into action, to evacuate a large number of people. This was a clear sign that the construction schedule for the dam was not synchronised with that of resettlement, and the dam took priority. Flooding people out of their homes turned out to be the de facto relocation method used in this case.

The selection of resettlement site is a critical factor in relocation planning. Access to land, employment, business, marketing opportunities, credit, and social support systems are all linked to location. Most failures in relocation stem from poor location, and there is no way to overcome this at a later stage. When people find that the new site lacks access to income-generation possibilities, especially to good agricultural land, they are left with no option but to abandon it and move elsewhere. The WCD (2000: 107) observed: 'Resettlement sites are often selected without reference to the availability of livelihood opportunities or the preference of displaced persons themselves'.

Feasibility studies that provide inputs essential to the site selection process are generally not undertaken. In their absence, the most commonly employed criterion is land availability. This certainly was the only consideration in relocating people displaced by the Pong Dam in Himachal Pradesh to the Thar desert in Rajasthan, a bolt from the blue for people forced to move a long distance away to an area physically, climatically, socially and culturally different from their own. Unable to make a living in the harsh conditions that deterred even Rajasthan's own landless poor from settling in that region, the Pong people gave up the effort and returned home empty-handed (Mathur 1997).

Equally disastrous can be the consequences of failure to take people into confidence while selecting sites for their relocation. Resettlement sites developed at great cost, but without the participation of affected people, have often remained uninhabited. For relocation to succeed, it is necessary to share information with them on all relocation related matters, such as the suitability of the site, the assistance needed in moving, the timing of the move, the income-generation possibilities and other issues (Davidson et al. 1993). The affected groups must be shown the possible sites identified for their relocation, and the one likely to be the most promising should be selected with their explicit consent. Women can provide their perspectives on housing design, civic facilities and other aspects that are important to the entire resettlement process. No relocation planning can fully succeed without their involvement in the selection of the site and its development.

The consultative process should also extend to the host population as the potential for resettler-host conflict always exits in relocation situations. Few resettlement projects have been documented where host-resettler conflict has not appeared. As Scudder (1997) pointed out: 'Even when political leaders among the host population agree to the movement of resettlers into their midst (as was the case at Kariba), sooner or later conflicts between the two can be expected. They arise because of competition of a larger population over a diminished (in terms of per capita) land base, as well as over access to job opportunities, social services and political power'. Yet, planners fail to take into account the already existing pressure on natural resources, as Lassailly-Jacob (1996: 197) elaborates:

> They too often rely on the host populations' traditions of hospitality and solidarity for granting newcomers access to these resources. While generosity often does occur at the time of resettlement, it does not last long at least not in areas with high population densities. Under these conditions, previously available natural resources suddenly become scarce and precious, and customary rights of access to the land are tightened. Previously treated as unfortunate brothers and sisters, relocatees are soon seen as competitors and intruders. Relations are strained, and conflicts break out due to competition over common resources. Planners should not rely on the hosts' hospitality.

While the importance of involving the host population is increasingly recognised in a general way, in practice this remains the most neglected dimension of relocation planning. Salem-Murdock (1993: 308) strongly argues for reversing this prevailing neglect, essentially in the interest of project sustainability:

> Focus on the host populations does not imply that the physical, socioeconomic, and psychological consequences for these groups are equivalent to the consequences for those forcibly relocated. Nor does it imply that relocatees are receiving too much attention. It simply highlights this other dimension of resettlement and argues that the usual treatment of hosts is unjustifiable, not only on equity grounds, but also for project sustainability over time.

Generally, in the beginning, host populations look at newcomers with suspicion that can easily turn into hostility. 'The Dayaks of Kalimantan and the Papuans are hostile to the new comers, whom they see as getting favoured treatment and whose new lifestyle is at their expense' (Keith 2001: 20–24) If hosts get the feeling that outsiders are being pampered, relocatees will find it difficult to adjust in the new environment. 'Overlooked hosts become jealous of government efforts on behalf of relocatees. Envying the improved housing, water supply and new schools or clinics provided to relocatees, they may turn against them and threaten the project's sustainability' (Lassailly-Jacob 1996: 198). Conflicts need not occur in all cases though. Where the relocated and the host populations are from similar ethnic backgrounds, conflicts are often minimised, and a well-integrated community comes into being.

It is often erroneously assumed that the resettlement process ends once the affected people have been moved to the new site. In fact, this is the beginning of the most important phase in resettlement. As Mejia (1999) observed, this phase involves the task of ensuring the resettlers' adaptation to the new site and new housing, maintenance and management of new services, rebuilding social networks and the structure of the community, new relations with the host population, and, above all, the recovery of prior family income level. The challenges go far beyond the mere physical relocation of the population.

Income restoration

Physically removing large number of people displaced from their home and livelihood is a daunting task. The task of putting these people back on their feet in ways that help them recover their former levels of living, that too in as short a time as possible, is even more daunting. There are cases where relocated people have been successful in gaining access to new opportunities and sharing project benefits, but such cases are few and far between. A World Bank study found income restoration to be the weakest part of resettlement planning (OED 1998).

Because projects disrupt livelihoods, restoring incomes of the affected people should ordinarily appear to be a matter of serious concern everywhere. This, however, has not been the case in most places. One observer noted: 'Until recently, income restoration programmes generally were not included in project design. This was due to the prevailing belief that resettlement of the urban poor does not seriously disrupt economic activities, and that with time families adapt and find other ways to subsist' (Mejia 1999: 176–77) Even now, many planners take disruption for granted as a necessary consequence of the development process, a kind of collateral damage which is unavoidable in the nature of things.

Although there is a growing concern over the fate of project-affected people, the track record of income-restoration programmes remains mostly unsatisfactory. Even the modest goal that there should at least be no drop in income levels as a consequence of development activities has remained elusive in most cases. On the contrary, evidence that projects frequently leave behind a trail of impoverishment is overwhelming (Downing 2002; Mathur and Marsden 1998; McDowell 1996). In a critical response to World Bank's much publicised 1994 Review of Resettlement, Oxfam (1994) noted that the World Bank review could not document one case where a population that had been displaced had regained its standard of living.

The World Bank's own studies indicate that its policy goals in regard to income restoration remain largely unmet. In 1994, a major review of projects with resettlement undertaken by World Bank concluded: '...although the data are weak, projects appear often not to have succeeded in re-establishing resettlers at a better or equal living standard and that unsatisfactory performance still persists on a wide scale. Though fragmentary, the weight of available evidence points to unsatisfactory income restoration more frequently than do satisfactory outcomes' (World Bank 1994: x). Another World Bank report is even more candid in acknowledging the continuing lack of progress on income restoration. It concedes that the record on restoring, let alone improving, incomes has been unsatisfactory, adding that while successful interventions are in a minority, 'the core objective of resettlement planning, namely the restoration or improvement of incomes and standards of living, is still not being achieved, except in a few projects' (World Bank 1998: 48). In Khao Laem, Thailand, where improvement did take place, it was due to favourable changes in the economy, not due to any planned effort by the project (Picciotto et al. 2001: 9).

While the track record on restoring the living standards of people displaced by projects remains dismal, the goal is not unattainable. India's resettlement experience, despite the numerous cases of impoverishment, reveals significant instances of adequate post-displacement recovery, including land-based recovery (Mahapatra 1999: 213). Success stories are now coming to light more frequently than before. Though small in number, there are cases where the displaced people have succeeded in achieving living standards even higher than before. A good example is the success achieved by the people of Khandu village displaced by the Mahi Bajaj Sagar Dam in Rajasthan (Mathur 1997). They were relocated to a colony named Khandu Colony (retaining the old village name) about 40 years ago. This move has proved to be a boon to over 1,000 families of this colony situated on the outskirts of Banswara, a large town that is also the headquarters of Banswara district. Proximity to an urban centre has given them opportunities to improve their lot in many ways, through access to more jobs, new business opportunities and better educational facilities. With the spiralling real estate prices in the Banswara area, their properties are now worth many times more than what they actually paid for them. This has given them a sense of real affluence. The people of Khandu Colony also do not miss their former village because the entire village moved as one group to the colony. Thus, the social network has remained intact. In fact, Khandu Colony is now a thriving community.

There is now a growing concern with how to improve, rather than merely restore, the incomes of resettlers as part of the restructuring of their lives. A recent study strongly recommended that the Bank should begin to shift its emphasis from restoration to improvement of income and living standards as an integral part of the project's developmental objectives. Enough benefits should be captured not only to justify local social disruption, but also to help establish a sustainable, progressive income policy for the displaced (World Bank 1998). For the population involved, resettlement must result in a clear improvement of their living standards, because the people directly affected by a project should always be the first to benefit from it (Wickling III 1999).

Resettlement planning, however, continues to be mainly concerned with the duplication of conditions as they were before relocation. Even where improvement in the former living standards and earning capacities of displaced people is a stated resettlement policy goal, project authorities do not regard resettlement as anything other than a mere damage control exercise, intended to neutralise its more visible negative impacts.

New approaches to improving resettlement

Some new approaches to resettlement, aimed at improving the lives of displaced people, are now emerging. These approaches go well beyond the policy of compensation in cash for the land loss, a policy which has only caused much impoverishment (Cernea 2007; Mathur 2008; Venkateswaran 2007; Wicklin III 1999). These novel ways of addressing resettlement include the following:

- Displaced people as project partners: Currently, all that people get is compensation for land loss, which is never enough to regain the lost livelihood, let alone improve their living standards. The fact is that people who contribute land need to be recognised as shareholders; they contribute their share in the form of land, without which no project can get off the ground. Gradually, approaches that involve the displaced people as shareholders, and even as co-project managers, are emerging in many places (Scudder 2005). For example, in India, the new resettlement policy of Orissa provides for equity in case of industrial and mining projects (GoO 2006). Specifically, the policy provides that at the option of the displaced family, the project may issue convertible preference share up to a maximum of 50 per cent of the one-time cash assistance. Such innovative mechanisms should, however, be used with some caution (World Bank: 2004). The project needs to have a sufficient guarantee of profitability. A loss-making project will expose the people to risks best avoided. Although this method is a great innovation, capable of giving incremental benefits to displaced persons, it should be offered as an option, not as a blanket entitlement. Depending on their risk-taking profile, displaced persons may want to use part of their compensation to invest in project equity.

- Benefit sharing: Projects generate many benefits and new income-generation opportunities, but at present, these are seldom shared with the affected people. Contending that benefits need to be shared equitably, Cernea (2008: 67) notes: 'so far the displaced are not commensurately sharing in the benefits, as they receive only compensation, and compensation is not a benefit, it is only restitution. They are therefore entitled to be included — conceptually, financially, and institutionally — among the sharers in the projects' benefits'. Sharing of benefits is also a way to make the development process more inclusive.

By sharing new opportunities, the projects can assist the displaced in regaining their income levels, at a time when everything seems lost to them (Skinner et al. 2009). Benefit sharing is possible in all kinds of projects and can be done in a variety of ways. For example, development of the relocation site is the kind of work that, instead of being given to outsiders, can be done by the displaced people themselves. This may have a double benefit: (*i*) displaced people will get wages during a particularly vulnerable period in the resettlement process; (*ii*) the new site, when fully developed, will reflect the preferences of the resettlers. As a matter of policy, a power project in Karnataka, India, employed only displaced families to do all the manual work in the land preparation process on a daily wage basis (Wicklin III 1999).

Benefit sharing is, however, a resource for income restoration which project authorities do not always utilise effectively, in an organised manner. This is often due to lack of imagination in using the available resources, poorly prepared resettlement plans, and their indifferent implementation. But the absence of any compelling guidelines is the real reason, and, therefore, even those projects that can make a difference make no effort in this regard.

Strengthening management Capacity

Project resettlement units

While the resettlement policy can go a long way in ensuring that people are saved from disruptive displacement impacts, good intentions of the policy may not always fructify (Mahapatra 1998). An implementation agency must also be in place and be in good shape. That alone can translate the policy and planning aims into tangible benefits.

Too often, governments embark on projects that are inadequately equipped to address resettlement issues. Typically, this responsibility is assigned to a project engineer, in addition to his normal duties. Resettlement is then seen as a technical problem of constructing houses, shops, streets, schools and other infrastructure, rather than as a task of both resettling and improving the lives of the relocatees. In many cases, once people are evacuated from the site marked for project work, engineers take it as the end of the resettlement task. In many cases, project developers also lack the capacity to undertake even such activities for resettlement planning as conducting census, socioeconomic surveys and land acquisition assessment. For this reason, the preparation of a resettlement action plan and related tasks continue to be routinely contracted out to external consultants. Project personnel evince little or no interest in the work of consultants to develop resettlement plans, income-restoration strategies etc., often keeping themselves completely out of the preparatory stages. There is no ownership, no commitment to the planning process. Although the quality of planning and implementation processes improves with the involvement of outside expertise, this does not contribute to the development of in-house capacity for project preparation and implementation.

As a separate entity, resettlement units within the overall management structure of the project have come into existence only in the last 10–15 years. Projects, especially those funded by World Bank and Asian Development Bank, are way ahead of others in this respect. In India, the National Thermal Power Corporation (NTPC) Limited and CIL, two major public sector undertakings, took the lead in creating resettlement units within their establishments. Under growing pressures to provide a better deal to project-affected people, resettlement units are now being gradually established for most large projects, to plan, coordinate, implement and monitor the day-to-day implementation of all activities pertaining to resettlement.

Resettlement units that have come into existence lately do not conform to any preset institutional design. Usually they take one of the following two broad forms.

(a) The common practice is to establish a resettlement unit within the department or the agency responsible for the main investment project. The agency, in this case, retains the responsibility to coordinate all resettlement activities, including land acquisition, relocation and income restoration, tasks that are normally carried out by other agencies (district administration, state and central governments, NGOs, etc). This also allows the staff in the resettlement unit to work more closely with the staff in the main project, whose support is vital to the resettlement task.

(b) The other institutional arrangement for departments or agencies implementing the investment project is to have an outside agency charged with the responsibility for the entire resettlement operation. Where resettlement involved is substantial, an independent authority, which has clearly defined legal, administrative and financial powers, would indeed appear to be a better option. This is how the Sardar Sarovar Project is organised, with all resettlement functions assigned to a separate, independent corporation.

There are many who think that the agency whose projects cause resettlement is not in the best position to assist project-affected people. Its main concern, depending on the type of project, is to build a dam, provide irrigation, generate power, produce coal or construct highways. The agency's performance is also judged on the output of goods and services for which the projects are established in the first place. Since the main tasks in the project (building dams or roads, for example) are related to the field of engineering, resettlement naturally gets relegated into the background as it requires expertise of a different kind.

On the other hand, there are some who favour an outside, independent agency. It is argued that a separate agency will be better able to devote attention to planning and implementing the entire range of resettlement functions. Its performance will be judged wholly on how effectively it performs the resettlement task. It will be more professional in its approach, and thus avoid the kind of mistakes that often make things worse for the displaced people.

The problem with outside agencies, however, is that they stop getting much-needed support from the agency tasked with the main project. The main project management thinks that now that there is a full-fledged agency for the resettlement job, they must go on with the task on their own, without involving them. In fact, agencies that have resettlement units of their own would be too willing to dismantle them and hand over their resettlement responsibility to an outside agency. For them, the resettlement job is nothing but a perpetual headache, and they would be only too pleased to get rid of it.

This, however, will not help matters much. Handing over resettlement job to an outside agency will completely divest the agency responsible for the main project of its responsibility to the people hurt by its activities. Moreover, creating a separate unit will not relieve its headache. People will continue to go to the agency whose project is the source of their woes. They want the agency, not some other organisation (even if that be an NGO), to listen to them and be accountable. People expect the agency that displaces them to have an obligation to look after them. Experience so far has not shown that one arrangement is superior to the other.

Though a welcome step, establishing resettlement units at project headquarters is not enough. The field offices, with little capacity to deliver, still remain largely neglected.

Personnel

Displacement is a traumatic experience for project-affected people and, therefore, the resettlement task ought to be handled by personnel who are not only trained but are also sympathetic to the poor. A major reason for the growing dissatisfaction of project-affected people with government resettlement plans is the poor quality of personnel. More often than not, the persons chosen for such sensitive jobs happen to be those least suited for them. In terms of power and perks that go with government jobs, these jobs rank among the lowest. Therefore, officials who are posted to handle resettlement are often those out of favour with the government. They come to the resettlement job with their own frustrations, and even begin to see themselves as displacees of another kind. Under the circumstances, it is unrealistic to expect them to work with zeal and devotion, and be sympathetic to project-affected people. They have no particular compulsion to try and help those in need. And, by being unhelpful, they can extort money from people who are already poor and desperately in need of their help.

Government agencies generally have a limited capacity to handle resettlement. Typically, this task is handled by the project engineer. Engineers see resettlement as mere relocation, which they manage to accomplish somehow because no construction activity can start without first removing people from the land required for the project work. For engineers, relocation is a task of the highest priority; in fact, the attention of the entire management remains focussed on it. Their performance is also judged not by the resettlement accomplished, but by the yardsticks of a different kind, such as irrigation provided, power generated, coal produced, roads built and so on.

In most projects, the staff lack skills needed to help people suffering from stresses and disorders of displacement and rehabilitation. There are several examples of government ministries deciding that people be removed but not saying how this should be done, leaving it to minions in the field who have no relevant capacity or training whatsoever. As resettlement requires expertise, an interdisciplinary team that includes social scientists and community development experts should be in charge of resettlement during the entire implementation phase. The team can operate effectively only when it is an integral part of the project management team, and not just its appendage.

Some projects have attempted to strengthen resettlement units by inducting social scientists on an ad hoc basis. Others have created a separate cadre of officers for resettlement. However, the conditions under which resettlement personnel work are generally not congenial. In Orissa, the resettlement officer is a key link in the chain of responsibilities for resettlement. Yet, he is so severely understaffed, and so overloaded with a myriad of responsibilities, that it is almost impossible to imagine that his job was ever intended to function effectively. The great range of duties, which covers almost all tasks downstream of land acquisition, ensures that an adequate quality of resettlement plan implementation is most unlikely (Rew et al. 2005).

A major flaw in government personnel management decisions is that even before officials begin to understand the situation in the area, they are ordered to proceed to another place. In Rajasthan, two officers responsible for the resettlement task were posted at the Bisalpur dam project when they were on the verge of retirement, perhaps presuming that a reasonable amount of time is not required to do the job properly (Mathur 1997).

The resettlement personnel see no future in the career ahead of them, and are a frustrated lot. For example, there is a feeling among the CIL resettlement officers that they have been dumped into these positions only because of the World Bank pressure. And once the Bank-assisted project comes to an end, they will either revert to their previous units with lower seniority, or simply lose the job if not given permanent status (Mathur 1998). 'Career cul-de-sacs' is an apt description of these jobs. What hurts resettlement officers is that they frequently become objects of abuse from those they are supposed to be helping (who blame them for disfranchising them), as well as from their employers (who blame them for inconclusive results). As a career option, the role of the resettlement officer is one few would choose (Marsden and Mathur 1998).

The need to assign the best development experts in resettlement agencies is now being recognised, but the best officials in most projects tend to wriggle out of such positions. In addition to the image of resettlement as being a thankless job, what turns them away is the stigma attached to it. The job not only provides no incentives for hardships associated with a difficult field job, the posting in a resettlement agency is generally regarded as a kind of punishment. Often, personnel without any relevant qualification, experience or training are, therefore, assigned to such sensitive positions, where they only make things worse for the people they are supposed to help.

Training is not a core element of the capacity building needed for effective implementation, and remains a neglected activity. Until recently, there were no training programmes in resettlement, although the need for them has long existed. A training programme in resettlement management instituted in 1993 by the World Bank's Economic Development Institute (now known as the World Bank Institute) was the first major initiative in this area. This, however, did not last long and was terminated in 1998. The number to be reached is still very large. Marsden (1998: 34) observed:

> The task is enormous. It is not merely imparting a particular set of techniques, but rather changing the mind-set of a whole cadre and generation of engineers who are used to a top-down, hierarchical way of doing business, and who measure success in terms of the completion of physical structures, and are so rewarded.

Thus, building capacity for resettlement management is a major challenge.

Coordination

The resettlement task cannot be carried out by the resettlement agency alone, acting in isolation all on its own. On several issues, it needs to coordinate with other divisions or sections within the project. These may include engineering, environment, finance, personnel and law. For example, during the implementation phase, resettlement activities need to be closely coordinated with the likely timing of civil works. When civil construction works start before people are moved to the new site, their hurried relocation at the last minute inevitably becomes a crash programme, full of stress not only for the people to be relocated but also for the resettlement officials concerned (McAndrew 1995). Such hardships are entirely avoidable through better coordination.

In addition, a resettlement agency needs to coordinate with many other agencies outside the project. These include government agencies with responsibilities for agriculture, small-scale industry, health, education and community development. Without their cooperation, new sites cannot become fully functional. Nicely constructed resettlement colonies, built years ago, exist in many project areas, but often there are no doctors in clinics and no teachers in schools. Many income-generation activities depend on the support of government agencies, and these activities cannot take off if there is no effective coordination between the resettlement agency and the other relevant government agencies concerned.

Despite the fact that resettlement depends on a close relationship of the resettlement agency with many other agencies, inter-agency coordination problems remain a perennial feature in most projects. A strong coordination mechanism needs to be in place to deal with the many issues that arise in harmonising the activities of several agencies, each with its own exclusive sphere of activity.

The way projects usually approach the coordination issue is by setting up a coordination committee, and ordinarily this arrangement should work satisfactorily. Problems, however, arise due to the way the committees are generally formed. A major problem relates to the unrepresentative character of the committee. Not all stakeholders are included in such committees. Often excluded from the committee membership are the affected people and their organisations. The committee is also not sufficiently empowered to take decisions. Worse, it does not even meet regularly, thus failing to take its designated task seriously enough.

Resettlement costs and budget

Resettlement costs are a small percentage of the total project cost in most cases. Studies have shown that even a substantial increase in resettlement costs has minimal effect on project viability. Yet, projects tend to systematically underestimate the budgetary requirements for resettlement costs (Pearce 1999). Resettlement budgets, in many cases, are not able to meet even the cost of land acquisition (Wicklin III: 1999).

Examples of under-financed resettlement plans are not uncommon. Anxious to see that the project gets approval, project authorities often knowingly indicate their requirement for funds on the lower side, as a realistic estimate can jeopardise the project clearance on grounds of financial constraints. But when it comes to implementing resettlement activities, especially making payment for compensation to resettlers, such underestimated budgets create problems. This happened in Indonesia. When appraising the Kedung Ombo project in 1984, assumptions made about the scale of displacement were unrealistic. The proposed compensation, therefore, proved inadequate. Many families then simply refused to move out even in the face of impending submergence. Such plans without adequate budgets were then of little avail in aiding resettlement (Budiman 1989).

The under-budgeting also occurs due to poor planning of resettlement. If planners are not sure what resettlement would involve, and are unable to be precise in their cost estimates at the stage when resettlement plan is being formulated, funding provided in the plan is bound to fall short of the actual planning requirements. Recovery efforts often fail to achieve their goals due to the initial underestimation of resettlement costs. Perhaps the only costs known to budget planners seem to be those related to acquisition of land, compensation for material losses, and construction of housing at new sites. No wonder the estimated costs turn out to be inadequate during implementation. For example, resettlement costs doubled within three years of the budget approval in the Yacyreta Hydroelectric Project. Evidently, not all costs were considered (Mejia 1999).

One consequence of not providing adequate funding for resettlement is that the costs on resettlement, which must be fully met by the project, continue to be borne by the affected people. In India, a study found that only one per cent of the total cost on dam projects has gone towards rehabilitating the displaced (CSE 1989). The underestimation of resettlement costs, leading to insufficient allocation of financial resources, remains a major cause of impoverishment that occurs amongst the displaced people (Cernea 2008).

The World Bank studies have shown that resettlement projects with high financial allocations were free of major difficulties, while virtually all of the projects with a low allocation rate experienced serious implementation difficulties (Cernea 1999). It is essential that resettlement budgets are adequate to provide not just for compensation for properties acquired, but also for the developmental phase of the resettlement process. Cernea (2008: 62) emphatically noted: ‘Even the best managers of a resettlement project-component would not be able to produce miracles and prevent impoverishment that looms over those displaced, if not given adequate financial means’.

Grievance redress

When resettlement is planned and implemented with the involvement of affected people, there should not remain any scope for complaints. Yet, there could be groups or individuals that think that their problems are not being adequately addressed. Howsoever trivial the grievances may appear, it is unwise to ignore them.

If projects fail to resolve grievances at their level, the people have no option but to seek other means for resolution of their problems. And now there are several avenues open to them to vent their grievances. They can mount a protest campaign with the support of activist groups; they can seek intervention of the higher authorities; can go to courts or get their problems raised in Parliament. They can approach the human rights commission or even knock at the doors of the World Bank’s inspection panel.

Although people now have several options to seek grievance redressal, the processes involved are time consuming. The disputes regarding compensation amount are a case in point. Although people often succeed in extracting increases over the earlier awards, the legal disputes take years to get resolved. The legal system in India is known for long delays, but delays in the resolution of grievance can cost the projects heavily.

Establishing a grievance redressal mechanism is, therefore, in the best interests of the project itself. Committees set up for grievance redressal should involve the affected people. The mechanism should be transparent in its working. Projects should not only be accountable, but also appear to be so. People should know that the grievance redressal system exists, and functions efficiently in ways that are transparent and accountable.

The growing number of protests against development projects reflects poorly on the existing system of dealing with grievances. Resettlement managers tend to dismiss the discontentment among the affected people as a product of instigation by NGOs for their own political ends. Project authorities and the others concerned need to devote much more attention to this issue than has been the case so far.

The role of NGOs

Because involuntary resettlement is essentially a disruptive process, it has become a highly contentious issue, and NGOs have not remained undivided on this issue either. The fact is that NGOs are not a homogeneous group (Hilhorst 2003). Perhaps nothing illustrates better the sharp differences in the NGO community than the situation of NGO movements in the Narmada dam project area (Dhagamwar 1997). While some NGOs are supportive of the resettlement plans and are willing to lend a helping hand to such initiatives, there are others whose confrontational stance tends to obstruct the resettlement process, unintentionally hurting the very people whom they wish to help.

Resettlement agencies are now increasingly turning to NGOs for help in dealing with the problems of involuntary resettlement. In India, a large number of NGOs have been contracted to carry out resettlement operations by several major public sector organisations, especially those being funded by the World Bank and other external donor agencies. The last few years have indeed been a boom time for NGOs working in the area of involuntary resettlement (Mathur 2000). Only a decade or so ago, this level of NGO involvement in resettlement activities would have been inconceivable.

For long, NGOs have been generally viewed as troublemakers by government agencies. Partly their campaigns against development projects, often conducted with international support, strengthened such negative perceptions about them. What, then, has brought about this turnaround in the outlook of development agencies? The pressure of external donor agencies is not the whole answer. Other factors have been at work too.

The fact is that government agencies themselves have now become more aware of their limitations in managing resettlement. This is a task that requires live contact with the people to be resettled on an almost daily basis, and NGOs, known for their closeness to the people, definitely appear better suited for it. A major factor that has changed the attitude is, however, the impressive track record of many NGOs in the fight against poverty. Here, resettlement agencies see a useful role for NGOs in the difficult task facing them — the challenge of reconstructing livelihoods of the affected people.

People also trust NGOs. Presence of these organisations in many project areas has made people more vocal in demanding their rightful claims. As Marsden (1998: 24) noted:

> the emergence of large number of organisations of civil society has meant that poor performance is increasingly visible, and more easily translates into pressures for action and change. It is no longer easy for powerful organisations to ride roughshod over the interests of the weak and marginalised, or to impose solutions which have not been publicly debated and agreed to by all the major stakeholders.

On the other hand, where there are no NGOs, the displaced people are often unable to get resettlement assistance, which they are entitled to. Parasuraman (1999) found the absence of NGOs in the Upper Krishna project to be an important factor contributing to the unsatisfactory performance of the resettlement programme. The absence of advocacy groups had serious negative consequences for the displaced people. The multiplicity of castes, the numerical predominance of backward castes, and the strong economic differences within and between the caste groups, prevented the people from organising themselves to bargain for better R&R provisions.

NGOs have been at the forefront in warning governments and international donors against neglecting the human dimension in the development process. NGO campaigns have brought about vast changes in the way the resettlement agencies now see their task-as one of sharing project benefits with the affected people, and not merely returning them to their pre-project poverty level.

The NGO role in resettlement is now being much appreciated. The fact is that many of the constituent activities of resettlement development are better suited to organisations in the NGO sector. As Cernea (1996) noted, many NGOs have proven themselves very effective in designing resettlement plans and realistic options acceptable not only to the people but also to governments, and in mobilising the energies of the resettlers for better implementation and monitoring of these plans. The NGO involvement in resettlement operations can be particularly helpful in areas such as the following:

- Gathering and sharing information with the affected people, avoiding problems that arise in an information vacuum;
- Eliciting participation of people in all resettlement activities;
- Strengthening local organisations and community self-reliance;
- Delivering services to hard-to-reach communities, which are more efficient and cost-effective than those of the official agencies;
- Planning and implementation of income-generation schemes.

The potential for government-NGO collaboration in resettlement is enormous. Much, however, remains to be done. The collaboration has not proceeded on a completely smooth course, but both sides, governments as well as NGOs, are rapidly learning the ways to pool their skills, and to organise their action plans in ways that prove beneficial to those most in need (Bhat 1992). So far the results of this collaboration have been mixed. While NGOs have been helpful in managing relocation, the main resettlement task, namely the restoration or improvement of incomes and livelihoods, is proving to be an uphill one. Morse and Berger (1992: 180) noted: 'it is one thing to persuade people to move, and provide them with a house and some land at a resettlement site; it is another thing to ensure their long-term rehabilitation'.

Monitoring and evaluation

The best of resettlement plans may face problems during implementation, and not stay on track. Timely detection of these problems and their resolution are critical to achieving resettlement objectives. Effective monitoring can help accomplish this task. Yet, monitoring is one resettlement task that is much neglected.

Regular monitoring provides periodic checks to ascertain whether resettlement activities are proceeding according to the plan. It provides an information-management system for project managers as well as a channel for the affected people to make known their needs and their reactions to resettlement implementation. Evaluation, on the other hand, is an exercise usually undertaken towards the end of the project to assess whether the plan achieved its intended goals.

Monitoring is the responsibility of the project management, and generally the task is carried out internally. To be useful, the findings of internal monitoring should be periodically submitted to the project management. This keeps the management in close touch with the progress and problems of resettlement operations. The reports should highlight the problems in implementation that require particular attention of the management, so that corrective action can be initiated. Such reports often contain huge amount of data that may be more useful for research purposes rather than the mundane tasks of management.

Internal monitoring helps improve implementation, but an outsider's perspective is no less important. Projects are, therefore, increasingly hiring independent observers from universities or research and consulting agencies to monitor their resettlement activities. A major task of external monitoring is to verify the results of internal monitoring. External (or independent) monitoring is often needed to periodically assess resettlement implementation and impacts, verify internal reporting, evaluate qualitative aspects of the resettlement program, and suggest adjustments to the delivery mechanisms and procedures as required (World Bank 2004).

Most projects tend to devote more attention to the monitoring of administrative arrangements rather than the socioeconomic aspects of resettlement. Commenting on this bias of project managers, Appleby (2006: 249) observed, 'Socio-economic monitoring is much less well done even in the best of projects'. This was true even for the Shuikou hydroelectric power project in China, widely considered an exemplary resettlement operation in the World Bank portfolio, for its planning, implementation, and income-restoration activities. The administrative aspects are not insignificant, but it is far more important to keep track of socioeconomic conditions of the affected population.

Each project needs to develop monitoring indicators to suit its particular circumstances, but these indicators must cover all major activities that are essential to the task of resettlement management. To get the best results from monitoring, it is important that the selection of monitoring indicators be done with great care. The affected people can make a meaningful contribution to this task.

The association of affected people in monitoring activities is now widely recommended, as it can greatly improve the quality of monitoring, and as a consequence, the overall quality of the implementation process. No other group of people can provide better feedback on resettlement performance.

Monitoring activity is often at its peak during the relocation stage. This, however, is not a task that can be restricted to any particular period in the resettlement planning and implementation process. Problems may arise at the preparatory stage, the relocation stage, or right in the end, at the reestablishment stage. If not nipped in the bud, these can upset the entire resettlement operation.

Finally, as the experience has shown, involuntary resettlement is intrinsically an impoverishing process. Studies have clearly demonstrated that resettlement-related impoverishment negates the high priority poverty-reduction effort, and is, thus, just the opposite of what development aims for. If development is not to add to the number of the poor, it will be unwise to ignore resettlement.

References

Appa, Gautam and Girish Patel. 1996. 'Unrecognised, unnecessary and unjust displacement: Case studies from Gujarat, India', in Christopher McDowell (ed.), *Understanding impoverishment: The consequences of development-induced displacement*, pp. 139–50. Providence and Oxford: Berghahn Books.

Appleby, Gordon. 2006. 'Managing resettlement operations', in Hari Mohan Mathur (ed.), *Managing resettlement in India: Approaches, issues, experiences*, pp. 243–56. New Delhi: Oxford University Press.

Asian Development Bank (ADB). 2003. *Gender checklist: Resettlement*. Manila: ADB.

Basu, Malika. 2006. 'Gender focus in resettlement planning', in Hari Mohan Mathur (ed.), *Managing resettlement in India: Approaches, issues, experiences*, pp. 214–19. New Delhi: Oxford University Press.

Bhatt, Anil. 1992. *From adversary to collaborator: The role of an NGO in rehabilitation and resettlement of tribal oustees.* Brussels: IIAS (mimeo).

Blaser, Mario, Harvey A. Feit and Glenn McRae (eds). 2004. *In the way of development: Indigenous peoples, life projects and globalization.* London and New York: Zed Books, in association with IDRC.

Budiman, Arief. 1989. 'Involuntary resettlement: Lessons from Kedung Ombo'. Paper presented at the 'International Seminar on Advance Planning for Resettlement', 19–27 June, Jakarta.

Carter, Philip. 2000. 'Lie of the tiger'. *The Ecologist*, 30(5): 60–61.

Caufield, Catherine. 1997. *Masters of illusion: The World Bank and the poverty of nations.* London: Macmillan.

Centre for Science and Environment (CSE). 1989. 'The state of India's environment: The second citizen's report'. New Delhi: CSE.

Cernea, Michael M. 1990. *Poverty risks from population displacement in water resources projects.* DDP 355. Cambridge, MA: Harvard University/HIID.

———. 1996. 'Understanding and preventing impoverishment from displacement: Reflections on the state of knowledge', in Christopher McDowell (ed.), *Understanding impoverishment: The consequences of development-induced displacement*, pp. 13–32. Providence and Oxford: Berghahn Books.

———. 1999. 'Why economic analysis is essential to resettlement: A sociologist's view', in Michael M. Cernea (ed.), *The economics of involuntary resettlement: Questions and challenges*, pp. 5–49. Washington DC: World Bank.

———. 2000. 'Risks, safeguards, and reconstruction: A model for population displacement and resettlement', in Michael M. Cernea and Christopher McDowell (eds), *Risks and reconstruction: Experiences of resettlers and refugees.* Washington DC: World Bank.

———. 2002. 'For a new economics of resettlement: A sociological critique of the compensation principle', in Michael M. Cernea and R. Kanbur, *An exchange on the compensation principle in resettlement*, pp. 22–46. Cornell, NY: Cornell University Press.

———. 2005a. '"Restriction of access" is displacement: A broader concept and policy'. *Forced Migration Review*, (23): 48–49.

———. 2005b. 'The "ripple effect" in social policy and its political content: A debate on social standards in public and private development projects', in Michael B. Likosky (ed.), *Privatising development: Transnational law, infrastructure and human rights*, pp. 65–101. Leiden: Martinus Nijhoff.

Cernea, Michael M. 2006. 'Resettlement management: Denying or confronting risks', in Hari Mohan Mathur (ed.), *Managing resettlement in India: Approaches, issues, experiences*, pp. 20–44. New Delhi: Oxford University Press.

———. 2008. 'Compensation and investment in resettlement: Theory, practice, pitfalls, and needed policy reform', in Michael M. Cernea and Hari Mohan Mathur (eds), *Can compensation prevent impoverishment? Reforming resettlement through investments and benefit-sharing*, pp. 10–20. New Delhi: Oxford University Press.

Cernea, Michael M. and Hari Mohan Mathur (eds). 2008. *Can compensation prevent impoverishment? Reforming resettlement through investments and benefit-sharing*. New Delhi: Oxford University Press.

Chandler, W. 1984. *The myth of TVA: Conservation and development in the Tennessee valley, 1933–1983.* Cambridge, MA: Ballinger.

Davidson, F., M. Zaaijer, M. Peltenburg, and M. Rodell. 1993. *Relocation and resettlement manual: A guide to managing and planning relocation.* Rotterdam: IHUD.

Dewan, Ritu. 2008. 'Development projects and displaced women', in Hari Mohan Mathur (ed.), *India social development report 2008: Development and displacement,* pp. 127–38. New Delhi: Oxford University Press/ Council for Social Development.

de Wet, Chris. 1999. 'Displacement, resettlement, rehabilitation, reparation and development (DRRRD): Regional paper on Africa'. Thematic review 1.3. Cape Town: World Commission on Dams.

———. 2005. *Development-induced displacement: Problems, policies and people.* New York and Oxford: Berghahn Books.

Downing, Theodore E. 2002. *Avoiding new poverty: Mining-induced displacement and resettlement.* London: International Institute for Environment and Development.

Fahim, H. M. 1983. *Egyptian Nubians: Resettlement and years of coping.* Salt Lake City, UT: University of Utah Press.

Food and Agriculture Organization (FAO). 2008. 'Compulsory acquisition of land and compensation (Land tenure studies no. 10)'. Rome: FAO.

Gill, Maninder. 2006. 'Large dam resettlement: Planning and implementation issues', in Hari Mohan Mathur (ed.), *Managing resettlement in India: Approaches, issues, experiences*, pp. 173–94. New Delhi: Oxford University Press.

Gonzalez-Parra, Claudio. 2001. 'Indigenous peoples and mega-projects: Hydroelectric dams in the land of Pehuenches in the highlands of the Bio Bio river, Chile, utopia of development and human rights', in Willem van Genugten and Camilo Perez-Bustillo (eds), *The poverty of rights: Human rights and the eradication of poverty,* pp. 71–86. London and New York: Zed Books.

Government of India. 1985. 'Report of the Committee on Rehabilitation of Displaced Tribals due to Development Projects'. New Delhi: Ministry of Home Affairs.

———. 2004. 'National Policy on Resettlement and Rehabilitation for Project-Affected Families'. New Delhi: Department of Land Resources, Ministry of Rural Development.

———. 2007. 'National Rehabilitation and Resettlement Policy, 2007'. New Delhi: Department of Land Resources, Ministry of Rural Development.

Government of Orissa. 1994. 'The Orissa Resettlement and Rehabilitation of Project-Affected Persons Policy, 1994'. Bhubaneswar: Department of Water Resources, Government of Orissa.

———. 2006. 'Orissa Resettlement and Rehabilitation Policy, 2006'. Bhubaneswar: Revenue Department, Government of Orissa.

Guggenheim, Scott. 1996. 'Mexico Hydroelectric Project', in World Bank, *The World Bank Participation Sourcebook*, pp. 71–72. Washington DC: World Bank.

Hilhorst, Dorothea. 2003. *The real world of NGOs: Discourses, diversity and development.* London and New York: Zed Books.

Gupta, Amita and Sebastian Morris. 2000. 'How much more of this infliction: The case of Ahmedabad–Vadodra Expressway', in Morris Sabastian (ed.), *India infrastructure report 2001: Issues in regulation and market structure,* pp. 77–80. New Delhi: Oxford University Press.

Horowitz, Michael M., Dolores Koenig, Curt Grimm and Yacouba Konate. 1993. 'Resettlement at Manantali, Mali: Short-term success, long-term problems', in Michael M. Cernea and Scott E. Guggenheim, *Anthropological approaches to resettlement: Policy, practice, and theory,* pp. 229–50. Boulder, CO and Oxford: Westview Press.

International Finance Corporation (IFC). 2002. 'Handbook for preparing a resettlement action plan'. Washington DC: IFC.

Keith, Suter. 2001. 'Inside or outside?'. *The World Today*, 57(4): 23–24.

Lassailly-Jacob, Veronique. 1996. 'Land-based strategies in dam-related resettlement programmes in Africa', in Christopher McDowell (ed.), *Understanding impoverishment: The consequences of development-induced displacement,* pp. 187–99. Providence and Oxford: Berghahn Books.

Likosky, Michael B. (ed.). 2005. *Privatising development: Transnational law, infrastructure and human rights.* Leiden and Boston, MA: Martinus Nijhoff.

Lucas, Henry. 2000. 'What do you mean, "social policy analysis"? Reflections on concepts and methodology'. *IDS Bulletin*, 31(4): 98–106.

Mahapatra, L. K. 1998. 'Good intentions or policies are not enough: Reducing impoverishment risks for the tribal oustees', in Hari Mohan Mathur and

David Marsden (eds), *Development projects and impoverishment risks: Resettling project-affected people in India*, pp. 217–36. New Delhi: Oxford University Press.

———. 1999. *Resettlement, impoverishment and reconstruction in India.* New Delhi: Vikas Publishing House.

Marsden, David. 1998. 'Resettlement and rehabilitation in India: Some lessons from recent experiences', in Hari Mohan Mathur and David Marsden (eds), *Development projects and impoverishment risks: Resettling project-affected people in India*, pp. 22–41. New Delhi: Oxford University Press.

Marsden, David and Hari Mohan Mathur. 1998. 'Introduction and overview', in Hari Mohan Mathur and David Marsden (eds), *Development projects and impoverishment risks: Resettling project-affected people in India*, pp. 1–21. New Delhi: Oxford University Press.

Mathur, Hari Mohan. 1997. *Managing projects that involve resettlement: Case studies from Rajasthan, India.* Washington DC: World Bank and Economic Development Institute.

———. 1999. 'The impoverishing potential of development projects: Resettlement requires risk analysis'. *D+C Development and Cooperation*, 6: 24–26.

———. 2000. 'Involuntary resettlement and voluntary organisations: A view from India'. Paper presented at the 'Fourth International Conference of the International Society for Third-Sector Research'. 5–8 July, Dublin.

———. 2004. 'Indigenous peoples, communal land management and development-induced displacement: A view from India'. Paper read at the 'Regional Workshop on Indigenous Peoples and Communal Land Management', 8–9 December, Manila.

———. (ed.). 2006. *Managing resettlement in India: Approaches, issues, experiences.* New Delhi: Oxford University Press.

———. 2007. 'Involuntary resettlement policy of Orissa, India: A new deal for the displaced in a globalizing world'. Paper presented at the 'Workshop on Involuntary Population Displacement and the Evolving Policy Response', at the '12th International Metropolis Conference on Migration, Economic Growth, and Social Cohesion', 8–12 October, Melbourne.

———. 2008a. 'Mining coal, undermining people: Compensation policies and practices of Coal India', in Michael M. Cernea and Hari Mohan Mathur (eds.), *Can compensation prevent impoverishment? Reforming resettlement through investments and benefit-sharing*, pp. 260–85. New Delhi: Oxford University Press.

———. 2008b. 'Managing the consequences of development-induced development', in Hari Mohan Mathur (ed.), *India social development report 2008: Development and displacement*, pp. 179–95. New Delhi: Oxford University Press/Council for Social Development.

Mathur, Hari Mohan. 2009a. 'Gender biases in resettlement planning', in Lyla Mehta (ed.), *Displaced by development: Confronting marginalisation and gender injustice,* pp. 166–94. New Delhi: Sage Publications.

———. 2009b. 'Tribal land issues in India: Communal management, rights, and displacement', in Jayantha Perera (ed.), *Land and cultural survival,* pp. 162–92. Manila: Asian Development Bank.

Mathur, Hari Mohan and David Marsden (eds). 1998. *Development projects and impoverishment risks: Resettling project-affected people in India.* New Delhi: Oxford University Press.

McAndrew, John P. 1995. 'Nabaccan no more: Dispersion of Japanese industrialisation leads to the forced relocation of a Philippine community', in Hari Mohan Mathur and Michael M. Cernea (eds), *Development, displacement and resettlement: Focus on Asian experiences,* pp. 151–67. New Delhi: Vikas Publishing House.

McDowell, Christopher (ed.). 1996. *Understanding impoverishment: The consequences of development-induced displacement.* Providence and Oxford: Berghahn Books.

Mehta, Lyla. 2000. 'Women facing submergence: Displacement and resistance in the Narmada valley', in Vinita Damodaran and Maya Unnithan-Kumar (eds), *Postcolonial India: History, politics and culture*, pp. 267–287. New Delhi: Manohar.

Mehta, Lyla. 2009. 'Introduction', in Lyla Mehta (ed.), *Displaced by development: Confronting marginalisation and gender injustice*, pp. xxv–xliii. New Delhi: Sage Publications.

Mehta, Lyla and Bina Srinivasan. 2000. 'Balancing pains and gains. A perspective paper on gender and large dams'. *Thematic review* 1.1 (Social impacts). Prepared as an input to the World Commission on Dams, Cape Town.

Mejia, Maria Clara. 1999. 'Economic dimensions of urban resettlement: Experiences from Latin America', in Michael M. Cernea (ed.), *The economics of involuntary resettlement: Questions and challenges*, pp. 147–188. Washington DC: World Bank.

Mejia, Maria Clara and Salamon Namhad. 1996. 'Participation in the resettlement operations of the Zimapan hydroelectric project, Mexico', in Jennifer Rietbergen-McCracken (ed.), *Participation in practice: The experience of the World Bank and other stakeholders,* pp. 93–97. Discussion Paper No 333. Washington DC: World Bank.

Morse, Bradford and Thomas Berger. 1992. *Sardar Sarovar: The report of the independent review*. Ottawa: Resource Futures International (RFI).

Multiple Action Research Group (MARG). 1986. *Sardar Sarovar oustees in Madhya Pradesh: What do they know.* New Delhi: MARG.

Operations Evaluation Department (OED). 1998. *Recent experiences with involuntary resettlement-India-Upper Krishna Project (Karnataka and Maharashtra)*. Washington DC: World Bank.

OED. 1996. *The World Bank's experience with large dams: A preliminary review of impacts.* Washington DC: World Bank.

Oxfam. 1994. *Response to resettlement and development review of the World Bank* (Processed).

Padel, Felix and Samrendra Das. 2008. 'Cultural genocide: The real impact of development-induced displacement', in Hari Mohan Mathur (ed.), *India social development report: Development and displacement,* pp. 103–15. New Delhi: Oxford University Press and Council for Social Development.

Parasuraman, S. 1999. *The development dilemma: Displacement in India.* London: Macmillan.

Partridge, William L. 1993. 'Successful involuntary resettlement: Lessons from the Costa Rican Arenal hydroelectric project', in Michael M. Cernea and Scott E. Guggenheim (eds), *Anthropological approaches to resettlement: Policy, practice, and theory*, pp. 351–74. Boulder, CO and Oxford: Westview Press.

Pearce, David W. 1999. 'Methodological issues in the economic analysis for involuntary resettlement operations', in Michael M. Cernea. (ed.), *The economics of involuntary resettlement: Questions and challenges,* pp. 231–56. Washington DC: World Bank.

Perera, Jayantha. 2000. 'Compensation versus rehabilitation in the Singrauli resettlement projects, India'. *The Eastern Anthropologist,* 53(1–2): 53–72.

Picciotto, Robert, Edward B. Rice and Warren van Wicklin (eds). 2000. *Involuntary resettlement: Comparative perspectives.* New Brunswick (USA) and London (UK): Transaction Publishers, for World Bank.

Pischke, J. D. Von, Hartmut Schneider and Rauno Zander. 1996. 'Introductory overview: Principles and perspectives', in Hartmut Schneider (ed.), *Microfinance for the poor?* Paris: Development Centre of the Organisation for Economic Co-operation and Development.

Pokharel, Jagdish C. 1995. 'Population displacement and compensation planning in Kulekhani hydroelectric project, Nepal', in Hari Mohan Mathur and Michael M. Cernea (eds), *Development, displacement and resettlement: Focus on Asian experiences*, pp. 139–550. New Delhi: Vikas Publishing House.

Rew, Alan, Eleanor Fisher and Balaji Pandey. 2005. 'Policy practices in development-induced displacement and rehabilitation', in C. de Wet (ed.), *Development-induced displacement and resettlement*, pp. 38–70. Oxford: Berghahn Books.

Ramanathan, Usha. 2008. 'The Land Acquisition Act 1894: Displacement and state power', in Hari Mohan Mathur (ed.), *India social development report 2008: Development and displacement,* pp. 27–38. New Delhi: Oxford University Press and Council for Social Development.

———. 2009. 'A word on eminent domain', in Lyla Mehta (ed.), *Displaced by development: Confronting marginalization and gender injustice,* pp. 133–45. New Delhi: Sage Publications.

Randeria, Shalini. 2003. 'Cunning states and unaccountable international institutions: Legal plurality, social movements and rights of local communities to common property resources'. *Archives of European Sociology,* 156: 27–60.

Roy, M. P. 2006. 'Approaches to reconstructing livelihoods: The CIL experience with self-employment schemes'. *Social Change*, 36 (1): 141–52.

Salem-Murdock, Muneera. 1993. 'Involuntary resettlement: A plea for the host population', in Michael M. Cernea and Scott E. Guggenheim. 1993. *Anthropological approaches to resettlement: Policy, practice, and theory,* pp. 307–20. Boulder, CO and Oxford: Westview Press.

Scudder Thayer. 1997. 'Social impacts of large dams', in Tony Dorcey (ed.), *Large dams: Learning from the past looking at the future,* pp. 41–68. Workshop proceedings, Gland, Switzerland, 11–12 April 1997.

———. 2005. *The future of large dams: Dealing with social, environmental, institutional and political costs.* London and Sterling, VA: Earthscan.

Sebastian, Morris (ed.). 2000. *India infrastructure report 2001: Issues in regulation and market structure.* New Delhi: Oxford University Press.

Sharma, V. D. 1995. 'Problems of resettlement in Sariska Wildlife Sanctuary', in Hari Mohan Mathur (ed.), *The resettlement of project-affected people: Proceedings of a training seminar,* pp. 140–46. Jaipur: The HCM Rajasthan State Institute of Public Administration.

Shihata, Ibrahim F.I. 1993. 'Legal aspects of involuntary population resettlement', in Michael M. Cernea and Scott E. Guggenheim (eds), *Anthropological approaches to resettlement: Policy, practice, and theory,* pp. 39–54. Boulder, CO and Oxford: Westview Press.

Singh, Kavaljit and Daphne Wysham. 1997. 'Micro credit: Band-aid or wound?'. *The Ecologist,* 27(2): 42–43.

Skinner, Jamie, Madiodio Niasse and Lawrence Haas (eds). 2009. *Sharing the benefits of large dams in west Africa.* London: International Institute for Environment and Development.

Sorensen, Brigitte Refuslund. 1996. *Relocated lives: Displacement and resettlement within the Mahweli Project, Sri Lanka.* Amsterdam: V.U. University Press.

Srivastava, Punya S. 1995. 'Population displacement associated with industrial development: The case of Bhiwadi', in Hari Mohan Mathur (ed.), *The Resettlement of project-affected people: Proceedings of a training seminar,* pp. 111–19. Jaipur: The HCM Rajasthan State Institute of Public Administration.

Tamondong-Helin, Susan D. 1996. 'State power as a medium of impoverishment: The case of the Pantabangan dam resettlement in the Philippines', in Christopher (ed.), *Understanding impoverishment: The consequences of development-induced displacement,* pp. 169–83. Providence and Oxford: Berghahn Books.

Udall, Lori. 1995. 'The international Narmada campaign: A case of sustained advocacy', in William F. Fisher (ed.), *Toward sustainable development? Struggling over India's Narmada river*, pp. 201–227. New York: M. E. Sharpe.

van Wicklin III, Warren A. 1999. 'Sharing project benefits to improve resettlers' livelihoods', in Michael M. Cernea (ed.), *The economics of involuntary resettlement: Questions and challenges,* pp. 231–56. Washington DC: The World Bank.

———. 2002. *INDIA: Evaluating Bank assistance for social development in the 1990s: A country assistance evaluation.* Washington DC: The World Bank Operations Evaluation Department (OED).

Venkateswaran, Shankar. 2007. 'Industrial displacement: Looking beyond compensation'. *Economic and Political Weekly*, 42 (22): 2050–51.

World Bank. 1994. *Resettlement and development: The Bankwide review of projects involving resettlement, 1986–1993.* Washington DC: The World Bank/Environment Department.

———. 1996. *Resettlement and development: The Bankwide review of projects involving resettlement, 1986–1993.* Paper No 32. Washington DC: The World Bank Environment Department.

———. 1998. 'Recent experiences with involuntary resettlement: Overview'. Report No 17538. Washington DC: The World Bank Operations Evaluation Department.

———. 2001. 'Operational Policies 4.12 (Involuntary resettlement)', available at http://go.worldbank.org/64J6NBJY90 (accessed 10 April 2010).

———. 2004. *Involuntary resettlement sourcebook: Planning and implementation in development projects.* Washington DC: World Bank.

World Commission on Dams. 2000. *Dams and development: A new framework for decision-making.* London and Sterling, VA: Earthscan.

Part II

Emerging issues in resettlement policy

2

Converting resettlement policy into resettlement law: A welcome initiative but no occasion for celebration yet

Ramaswamy R. Iyer*

In October 2007, the Government of India notified the National Rehabilitation and Resettlement Policy 2007. They have followed that up with two pieces of draft legislation: the Rehabilitation and Resettlement Bill 2007 and the Land Acquisition (Amendment) Bill 2007 have been introduced in the Lok Sabha. Before considering these, a brief recall of the historical background may be useful.

Strengthening resettlement policy

The debate about the displacement of people caused by various developmental projects such as dams, industrial and mining projects, highways and flyovers, and so on, has been going on for over two decades. Several drafts of a National Rehabilitation Policy document have been under discussion since the 1980s. Finally, in February 2004, the NDA Government, shortly before it demitted office, notified the National Policy on the Resettlement and Rehabilitation of Project Affected Families 2003. Much debate followed, conferences were held, comments were offered by various NGOs and by academics, and consultations took place under the aegis of the National Advisory Council (NAC). The outcome was a revised draft policy document that the NAC placed before the Government. That draft

* The author is grateful to Himanshu Thakkar and Shripad Dharmadhikari for comments on the first draft of this paper.

was put aside and a governmental draft was put in the public domain in 2006. This led to further debate and extensive comments, and ultimately the Government of India notified the NRRP 2007. This was no longer a draft but a formal policy declaration. However, perhaps in response to suggestions that there should be a law and not merely a policy, or suo motu, the Government seems to have decided to convert the 2007 Policy into an Act, and also to amend the Land Acquisition Act 1894, correspondingly. That is the background to the introduction of the two Bills in the Lok Sabha. The Parliamentary Standing Committee asked for comments on these by a certain date, and it must now be considering the comments received.

In an article in the *Economic and Political Weekly*,[1] I had traced the evolution of thinking on the subject in this country and had set forth an approach to a just displacement, resettlement and rehabilitation policy in the form of a series of principles, including the following: avoidance or minimisation of displacement; consideration of non-displacing or less-displacing alternatives; no *forced* displacement; the principle of 'free, informed prior consent'; provision of the fullest information from the earliest stages to the people likely to be affected; acquisition under the Land Acquisition Act 1894 to be restricted to 'public purpose', narrowly redefined to cover only ordinary governmental purposes, excluding private sector or public sector (or even governmental) projects, programmes or activities; strict adherence to the Panchayats (Extension to Scheduled Areas) or PESA Act 1996 in tribal areas; granting project-affected people, through legislation, the first claim on the benefits of the project for which they are displaced, preferably resettling them in the command area of the project; the project-affected people to be better off than before, or at least as well off; making the Policy statutory through an Act; and the establishment of a National Displacement and Rehabilitation Commission.

Reasons for scepticism

If we examine the new Bills keeping in mind the statement made in the EPW article, they seem to include a number of elements that many of us have been urging. We wanted a Rehabilitation Act and here is a Bill. The much criticised Land Acquisition Act is being amended, 'public purpose' is being redefined, governmental acquisition of land for private parties is being substantially reduced;

minimum displacement, non-displacing alternatives, consultation, conformity to PESA, and so on, find a place in the Rehabilitation Bill; an Ombudsman is being provided for the redress of grievances; and a National Rehabilitation Commission is envisaged. Can we then conclude that all the points that many of us have been making for years have been accepted and incorporated, and that celebrations are in order? Such a conclusion would be premature. A closer look indicates that the battle has not been won, that there is need for a continuing campaign, and that the critics and the NGOs should not be beguiled by the adoption of their language. The following are some of the principal reasons for a degree of scepticism and wariness.

(i) Let us take the most positive point first. The provision for a Social Impact Assessment seems very good and has been widely welcomed. However, is it really as good as it seems at first sight? The impacts are rather narrowly confined to physical assets (buildings, temples, institutions, facilities, etc). Social impacts must be more broadly understood to include the loss of identity, disappearance of a whole way of life, dispersal of close-knit communities, loss of a centuries-old relationship with nature, loss of roots, and so on. These can at best be mitigated and not remedied, but they must surely be studied as part of the Social Impact Assessment (SIA) study. Access to drinking water is mentioned, but not access to forests for food, fuel, produce, medicinal herbs etc. (The words *inter alia* can hardly be held to cover all this.) Besides, who will conduct the SIA? It is good that the SIA will be *reviewed* by an independent multi-disciplinary expert body, but it should first be *prepared* by a similar body. (It may be added that the SIA, R&R Plans and other documents should be available in local languages at least a month before the public hearing, and the hearing should be under the auspices of a credible independent panel.)

(ii) Section 7 lays down a *Social Impact Assessment clearance*. This is good, but not enough: it should be part of an overall *clearance for displacement*. If the felling of trees and interference with wildlife and nature in general require statutory clearances, should not the displacement of people be subject to a similar requirement? Such a clearance must come from an independent statutory authority and not from the bureaucracy. The clearance must of course be subject to certain conditions, and must be revocable in the event of non-compliance or lapses. The revocation clause should be actually used.

(iii) The terms 'minimum displacement' and 'non-displacing alternative' are music to the ears, but how binding are these? Who will decide this? The application of this criterion, and the consideration of options that it implies, ought to be an integral part of project planning. Instead, it is left to a later stage (when the consideration of options may no longer be possible), and the decision is left to the Administrator for R&R [Section 10(3) i]. In other words, this crucial decision is entrusted to the bureaucracy. Will the civil society play any role? Will the R&R Committees at the project level or the district level have a say in this matter? (As we shall see, the answer seems to be negative.) Will the Monitoring Committees at the State and Central levels and the National R&R Commission have a role here? No clear answer is available.

(iv) An impressive structure of institutions has been specified, but their responsibilities and powers have not been spelt out. Administrator, Commissioner, project-level and district-level R&R Committees, Ombudsman, Monitoring and Oversight Committees, the National R&R Commission: what each will do, how they will be inter-related, what decision-making powers each will have and in relation to what aspects, and so on, are far from clear. Everything is covered by the phrase 'as may be prescribed'. Until that 'prescription' has been done, we can form no idea as to the scope, purposefulness and effectiveness of the institutional arrangements.

(v) Words such as 'wherever possible', or other similar phrases, are scattered throughout the Bill. For instance, group settlement is laid down, but qualified by the phrase 'wherever possible' [Section 26 (1)]; training is to be provided 'wherever necessary' [Section 41 (ii)]; see also 'if government land is available' in Section 49 (4); 'preferably' in Section 49 (7), and so on. They seem innocuous, but all of them involve *decisions*. Who will make them, and on what basis? Such hedged-in requirements can hardly be mandatory. They are likely to become discretionary, with the discretion vesting in the bureaucracy. (The Bill does not provide alternative solutions; for instance, purchases of land, in the event of negative answers to the assumed 'possibility' or 'availability'.)

(vi) The Ombudsman provision (Section 14) is a good one, but 'grievance' has been narrowly defined to cover only the case of 'not being offered the benefits admissible'. Grievances could relate to many other things: non-participatory project decision, failures of consultation, non-compliance with the minimum displacement condition, non-inclusion of a person in the 'affected' category, and so on. How the Ombudsman will be appointed, how the Ombudsman will function, etc., are left to be prescribed.

(vii) Taking the preceding points together, it appears that the precise manner in which this seemingly benign and enlightened legislation will actually work in practice, will be entirely determined by the delegated/subordinate legislation, i.e., the rules that are made under it.

(viii) The National Monitoring Committee (Section 14) seems totally bureaucratic, except for the non-mandatory association of some experts (the operative word is 'may'). No civil society or NGO participation seems envisaged.

(ix) In the case of the Sardar Sarovar Project the basic principle in force (though it may not always be complied with) is: rehabilitation must precede submergence. The present Bill retreats from that position and requires only 'adequate progress in rehabilitation' prior to displacement (Section 29). This is a retrograde step. Besides, who will decide the adequacy of the progress?

(x) The elements of the rehabilitation 'package' seem inferior to the policies already adopted in projects such as Sardar Sarovar and Tehri. For instance, Section 36 limits the allotment of land to the maximum of 1 hectare of irrigated land or 2 ha of unirrigated land. Besides, it talks about cases of loss of *entire* land; partial loss is not mentioned. And as already stated, it adds the qualifying words, 'if government land is available'.

(xi) Cash in lieu of land is envisaged in several places: Section 36 (2) (second provision; and Sections 42 and 48). This is fraught with danger. Eventually, cash may well become the main form of compensation.

(xii) What are the sanctions behind the provisions of the Bill? In the event of deliberate or inadvertent lapses, or non-compliance or deviations, what consequences will follow? The Bill is silent on this. Without such sanctions, how can the provisions be enforced? (Far from sanctions for non-compliance, there is a sweeping indemnity provision in Section 56!)

Additional points that need consideration

In addition to these primary points, the following secondary ones (some of them quite important) need consideration.

- The definition of 'affected persons' (Section 3b) must be widened to include those not resident in the affected area but providing supplies and services to people in that area, and likely to lose their livelihoods in the event of the displacement of the latter; those affected by the construction of colonies and canals; those downstream of the dam and affected by reduced flows; those affected by some of the remedial measures, such as catchment treatment or compensatory afforestation (secondary and tertiary displacements); and so on.
- The conceptualisation and formulation of a project, consideration of options, unavoidability of displacement, and choice of the least-displacing option: all these need to be done in consultation with the people concerned. However, Section 10 (3) (ii) provides for consultations with affected persons only for the formulation of a rehabilitation or resettlement scheme or plan.
- The project-level R&R Committee will evidently begin to function only *after* the project decision (including the displacement decision) has been taken. Section 12 talks only about monitoring, review and post-implementation audit. (Incidentally, the composition of the Committee includes only one NGO representative.)
- While the composition of the project-level R&R Committee has been specified, that of the district-level Committee has been left to be prescribed.

- As already mentioned, the precise relationship between the project-level oversight committees and the R&R Committees is not clear. Similarly, the National R&R Commission's role seems to be rather narrowly envisaged (monitoring and oversight – not initial clearance or subsequent appellate functions).
- In Section 47, relating to 'linear projects', canals are not specifically mentioned.
- There is a slight lack of clarity as to which of the provisions of the Bill will apply to displacements of a lower magnitude (i.e., less than 400 families in plain areas or 200 families in tribal or hilly areas).
- It is obvious that all administrative authorities are generally supported by and function through staff. It is not quite clear why formal and statutory delegations to lower levels are provided for in Section 10 (4). There may be some innocuous practical reason for this provision, but will such a delegation relieve the Administrator of his/her statutory responsibility?

Some progress overall, but more needs to be done

Turning now to the Land Acquisition (Amendment) Bill 2007, it must be noted that this is not the kind of radical overhaul of the Act that many have been urging. There are three main elements in it: the limiting of acquisition for private parties, the substitution of a Dispute Settlement Authority for the Courts, and the establishment of links to the Rehabilitation Bill.

At first sight, the deletion of all references to companies gives us the impression that acquisition for private parties is being eliminated, but that is not the case. The original Act had the wording 'for a public purpose or for a company'; the words 'or for a company' are now being omitted, but the definition of 'public purpose' itself is being changed to include (supplementary) acquisition for 'a person' (including a company). If the private party purchases 70 per cent of the required land through negotiation, the balance 30 per cent can still be acquired by the Government for that party. The rationale of this is not clear.

Incidentally, it will be seen that the definition of 'public purpose', instead of being made stringent and narrow as many had recommended, is being widened.

Moreover, it was necessary not merely to rule out (or limit) the acquisition of land for private parties under the Land Acquisition Act, but also to ensure that rural communities are not taken advantage of by corporate bodies in unequal negotiations. There is no such provision in the Bill.

Judging by its name, The Land Acquisition Compensation Disputes Settlement Authority will apparently deal only with compensation issues. A longstanding criticism of the Land Acquisition Act has been that the 'public purpose' for which land is being acquired is not open to contestation. There seems to be no change in that position. (One wonders whether the bar on the jurisdiction of the civil courts and the establishment of a Dispute Settlement Authority instead is a good thing to do, but I refrain from going into this.)

The conclusion that emerges from this quick examination of the two Bills is that while it is good that the Government is thinking in terms of a National Rehabilitation Act and amendments to the Land Acquisition Act, there are many weaknesses and questionable features in these Bills. The Bills need to be redrafted after further consultations, both within the Government and with experts, NGOs and others outside the Government.

Note

1. 'Towards a just displacement and rehabilitation policy'. *Economic and Political Weekly,* 42(30): 3103–07.

3

Broadening the definition of 'population displacement': Geography and economics in conservation policy

Michael M. Cernea*

The accelerating pace of development in both developed countries and developing countries has vastly multiplied the instances of compulsory population displacement and involuntary resettlement. Such forced displacement processes are imposed not only under state financed projects undertaken in the public interest, but increasingly also by projects financed by private sector corporations driven by profit motives. As industrialisation and urbanisation accelerate and population densities increase, the vast numbers of such forced displacements are not likely to decrease. Unfortunately, they will continue to increase and expand.

At the same time, however, the resistance offered by civil society to the disruptions and deep ill-effects of forced population displacement is also on the increase. Moreover, the volume of scientific social research focused upon such processes has vastly increased: this research consistently highlights their damaging social and economic

* Many important improvements in this study are due to my late wife, Ruth Cernea, herself an anthropologist, who passed away in 2009. She joined in my fieldwork in some of the places explicitly mentioned in this study, and was my first discussion partner in reflecting on lessons from other field experiences. Thanks are also expressed to several colleagues and friends, particularly to David Turton, Kai Schmidt-Soltau, David Simon, Maninder Gill, Warren Van Wicklin Jr, Bruce Rich, Grazia Borrini-Feyerabend, for their stimulating discussions and shared insights on key issues and cases mentioned in, and relevant to this essay.

contents, their inner conflicts, and their long-enduring negative consequences.

Such progress in social knowledge and awareness informs and strengthens the resistance of civil society to development-caused forced displacement and resettlement (DFDR) processes. And indeed, countless events in different countries testify that the clashes between the drivers of such displacement and the civil society forces that resist these mass-scale expropriations and their displacement corollaries are growing in frequency, visibility and political sharpness. Forced population displacement has thus become one of the public policy territories on which a broader battle is being waged: the battle between opposed political philosophies on the role of the state in economic growth and development. The specific clash is around the core issue of eliminating whenever possible, or reducing and regulating such forced displacements. Social sciences recommend and civil societies demand the introduction of policies and legal frameworks that would restrict unfettered laissez faire and would deliberately mitigate or prevent the dire impoverishment effects of forced migration, by instituting increased protection for the populations at risks.

What are the actual outcomes of these growing clashes, in social practice?

The specific outcomes are neither uniform nor linear. They vary in different countries and sectors, and steps forward may also alternate with setbacks. But the clashes continue and have become an indelible characteristic of contemporary development. Such clashes take on a wide and multiplying variety of forms and structures, ranging from violent local physical confrontations causing loss-of-life, to broad mass movements of solidarity and civil disobedience, or to parliamentary debates and manoeuvres for either firmly promoting, or perniciously stalling, resolution and practical measures.

Nonetheless, despite the immense diversity of instances, circumstances, actors, and specific case-by-case outcomes, trends surface and can be discerned. The kaleidoscopic picture should not be allowed to obscure the still slow but gradually strengthening trend toward crafting more effective protective policies, managing risks and restricting the socially pathological effects of population displacement.

The present article analyses one of the significant policy changes, instituted recently, that illustrates this trend. In essence, it is about an important revision in the theoretical definition of forced population displacement, which recognises economic displacement as displacement even when a physical change of place does not occur. This situation frequently occurs in nature conservation projects, e.g., projects that establish 'protected areas' (PAs) and institute restricted access to certain natural resources that previously were part of the livelihood basis of nearby populations. Various agents of displacement, and especially the promoters of parks and biodiversity 'protected areas', have long embraced a narrow definition that limited the concept of population displacement to geography variables alone and overlooked economic variables. In other words, it limited the definition only to the expropriation of dwellings that change the geographic location of a population, but did not recognise displacement if the dwelling and its location were not affected, even though access to prior lands, fruit trees, plants, and water courses was suddenly prohibited, and thus the economic productive basis of a population's livelihood was suddenly taken away. Obviously, such narrowness had enormously restrictive consequences on the entitlements and welfare levels of the affected people.

Why and how this narrow definition was set aside, and how several major international development agencies — such as the World Bank, the Asian Development Bank, the African Development Bank and other similar financial institutions — have formally broadened and refocused their definition of displacement to rest mainly on economics rather than on geography, is analysed and described further in this article.

Researching and conceptualising forced displacement

Among social scientists, the first researchers to systematically study these complex social processes were anthropologists and sociologists. In India, for instance, the original research initiated in the late 1950s by Roy Burman in Orissa on the forced displacement entailed by the Rourkela industries predated, to his merit, the research carried out by European and American social scientists studying cases of displacement in Africa (see Cernea 1997).[1] The knowledge on displacement and resettlement generated by social scientists has been accumulating long before their findings started to be taken into account — haltingly and reluctantly — in actual development projects initiated by governments or private sector corporations.

As research expanded, the body of knowledge generated by social scientists evolved from case-focused, empirical mono-ethnographies to concept formulation and the gradual build-up of general propositions, theories and models. In other words, elements of a specialised subfield of social inquiry have started to gradually emerge and in time coalesce into the building blocks of a field of distinct and recognised expertise. Currently, the studies on population displacement and resettlement have 'exploded' in many countries, primarily in China, India, Brazil, the US, the UK, Ethiopia, Bangladesh, Argentina and several others.

In parallel, the practical needs of the planners of development projects have pushed them to start paying attention to the social scientists' research, and to consider the formulation and adoption of codified guidelines and norms for actual development programmes that confront displacement and resettlement tasks. Absorption of this knowledge, however, has not been smooth and easy; it has occurred through a constant uphill battle against cognitive dissonance. Social scientists have had a direct hand in writing up the first international policies adopted by some development agencies to minimise and mitigate development-induced displacement and resettlement.

During the last two decades, the 'ripple effect' of the initially adopted policies has become wider and wider, through a process too complex to be outlined in this paper (see Cernea 2005a). Suffice to say that this advance could not have happened without the forceful political struggle of civil society organisations, and of the displaced peoples themselves, against the stern resistance of many governments and private sector corporations. Even today, progress in resettlement policy adoption is still opposed in many countries.

At the same time, development agencies not only absorb this knowledge but also test it, and sometimes contribute to it with lessons from experience. We can observe significant situations in which the interaction between sociologists, anthropologists, social geographers and other social scientists, on the one hand, and institutions and practitioners on the others, has resulted in the further codification of this knowledge, and in the refining of prior concepts. This process of knowledge accumulation, codification, correction and refinement continues, as illustrated by the recent instance of such knowledge refinement and policy improvement.

The pivotal importance of the concept of displacement

Since the concept of 'displacement' holds a pivotal position in the general theory of DFDR, broadening and redefining its scope has far reaching relevance and consequences for both practice and theory. Every forced population migration process starts with displacement.

However, not every such process reaches the stage of real population resettlement, as we know from research in India (Fernandes 2008)[2] and in many other countries. Yet, every such process does necessarily include displacement, the stage during which the affected people are dispossessed of their land assets, houses, etc. Unless the nature of displacement is correctly understood from the outset, not just by academic researchers but primarily by policymakers and development practitioners, the entire process of displacement and resettlement is not likely to be properly planned, commensurately financed and adequately implemented.

Nevertheless, even a summary review of concepts used in different countries immediately reveals that the notion of displacement is often defined improperly. In some countries, among which India is the most surprising example, the concept of displacement is diplomatically avoided or directly shunned in official parlance. True enough, when an official must publicly announce a project which will displace many people from their homes and lands, displacement is not a very comfortable term to use. Yet displaced they will be. A spade ought to be called a spade. India's official terminology for development-caused displacement and resettlement has resorted to a locally patented euphemism. It manufactured the expression 'resettlement and rehabilitation' (abbreviated as R&R). As is immediately visible, the key term displacement is prudently left out from this expression and from countless official documents. But the displacement reality is not eliminated by playing with the vocabulary and avoiding inconvenient but truthful words. The impoverishment effects of displacement cannot be wished away or camouflaged simply by deleting the *term* displacement. Avoiding the precise concept of displacement and planting the R&R wording is like putting a band-aid to cover a sore point: the soreness does not disappear. It would be more candid and transparent if the official terminology used the right term.

Unfortunately, many social scientists in India have ended up tolerating and even getting accustomed to employing, non-critically, this euphemistic terminology. They routinely use 'resettlement and rehabilitation' in their work, abbreviated as R&R. To their credit, it must be said that Indian social scientists studying development-induced displacement and resettlement are, as a group, among the world's most outspoken critics of forced displacement and its terrible socio-economic pathologies. It would seem normal and useful for the state and administrative bodies dealing with displacement to adopt concepts developed by India's social scientists, rather than the latter having to adopt terminology used by the former. For inadequate terminology tends to harm practical work by directing less attention to, in this particular case, what is obscured by an incomplete label.

This is why the re-definition of the concept of displacement has immediate relevance for both resettlement theory and resettlement practice. It is important, therefore, to examine and understand it, to identify its operational implications in various categories of projects — primarily in conservation and environmental programs but also in other sectors — and to define effective norms for its application in different country contexts. In time, this redefinition is likely to affect the approaches to creating protected areas worldwide and, thus, have far-reaching operational implications. Countries, in turn, need to ponder on and introduce this fair definition at the national level and institute consistent procedures for its application.

The significant redefinition: Restriction of access as a form of displacement

Two elements must be noted from the outset regarding the redefinition of displacement and the concept of 'restriction of access':

(a) This redefinition was introduced first in the resettlement policy of the World Bank as part of its periodic updating and improvement when the Bank re-issued this policy in a new version as OP/BP 4.12 and activated it from January 2002 for all the subsequent new projects it finances.
(b) Soon thereafter, and most significantly, this redefinition was replicated and introduced in the policies of other multilateral donors such as the Asian Development Bank, the Inter-American Development Bank and the African Development Bank for their programmes. It also affects programmes financed by the Global Environmental Facility (GEF).

Given the leading role of the multilateral development agencies in financing development, conservation and general environmental protection programmes, this change in their policies and its conceptual foundation are likely to be deeply consequential. Obviously, it will have impacts at the level of national policies of many countries as well, particularly when countries and states are to adopt new, or revise existing, resettlement and rehabilitation policies. For instance, the debate currently going on in India around reforming its outdated resettlement policy and adopting adequate legislation on displacement and resettlement has to confront the 'restricted access' issues the specific conditions of Indian law and needed reforms at the national or state-wide levels.

When is 'restriction of access' instituted through development projects? Circumstances justifying the introduction of 'restricted access' to some natural resources or activities tend to occur in several categories of projects: in area development or extractive industry projects, in various agricultural and forestry projects and conservation projects protecting biodiversity resources or cultural heritage endowments and natural monuments.

Development projects may sometimes cause obstructions in local productive and livelihood activities not just because their land is needed for 'right of way', but also for such situations as creating, even without expropriation, safety zones that limit access and such previous local activities. I came across such a situation during my own fieldwork and research at the site of the Tangguh LNG project for extraction and processing natural gas in the Bintuni Bay of West Papua, Indonesia, a large-scale private-sector project of the British Petroleum (BP) Corporation.

During its early preparation stages, the social assessment studies carried out for the BP Tangguh project found out that some clans of the Simuri tribe inhabiting the area around Bintuni Bay had a customary system of sea tenure rights over various parts of the bay's surface, i.e., a system of fishing rights known, respected and self-enforced through inter-clan relationships. This well-defined traditional system regulated the reciprocal rights or limits to fishing for each clan, including the setting of payment obligations between clans for different types of fishing. For instance, when one clan's members fished for self consumption in another's clan area no fees were to be paid; but if the fishing was for marketing purposes, a defined payment was due from that fishing clan to the clan who had tenure over that particular area of the Bintuni Bay's waters. During the construction of the BP Tangguh LNG project it became necessary to institute a 'restricted access' marine safety protection zone over some 20 hectares of sea surface in the Bintuni Bay around the offshore extraction rigs and in the area between the offshore rigs and the onshore port and processing plant. This zone included sea areas that fell under the customary tenure system of several Simuri clans. Such marine 'protected areas' prevent the circulation of local boats to allow for the project's smooth operation as well as for fishermen's own safety, thus pre-empting and limiting access for several local clans that traditionally fish in the bay area, and affecting their food supply and income from fish and shrimp marketing.

As owner of the Tangguh LNG project, the British Petroleum Company correctly recognised the introduction of a marine safety zone as an instance of 'restricting access' to natural resources for the sea-tenure holding clans, and thus saw it as an economic displacement impact of the project.[3] This was done in part also to achieve consistency with the new requirements of the Asian Development Bank which co-financed the Tangguh project, and with the new conceptualisation of displacement in cases of project-induced restricted access that was adopted by the ADB in line with the World Bank's changed definition of and policy on displacement. BP responded to this policy improvement by introducing in its Tangguh Resettlement Action Plan special measures to compensate the affected fishermen's clans for loss of access and income. The project devised and financed a set of innovative measures to help relocate part of people's fishing activities, even though the project's safety zone by itself had not relocated the people's habitat.[4]

The above case helps illuminate the essence of the policy change we discuss in this article as conceptualised and adopted by the multilateral development agencies, reflecting the two key elements of this policy development:

First, it defines the imposition of 'restricted access' to certain resources in protected areas as a cause of economic displacement.

Second, the new policy broadens the definition of 'displacement' beyond its former conventional acceptation as geographic relocation of people's houses, to include occupational and economic dislocation not necessarily accompanied by the physical (geographical) relocation of the local users.

The risks of economic impoverishment and occupational displacement imposed by such restrictions are recognised as having many consequences comparable to physical displacement, although substantive distinctions between the two do exist.

As is rather well known, the World Bank's resettlement policy (with its preventive measures, and compensatory and entitlement provisions) has been historically covering, among many other sectors,[5] also the displacements caused by conservation programmes through the establishment of parks. But it did not cover the projects that introduced 'restriction of access' without imposing people's physical relocation. The recognition of restricted access as a form of economic displacement was introduced by the beginning of 2002, when the Bank's Board decided to replace the previous (1990) version of the resettlement policy, code-named OD 4.30, with an updated resettlement policy, codenamed OP/BP 4.12.

What explains this change? What did this change mean, and why was the modified approach elevated to policy status?

Twin objectives in establishing protected areas

The definition of 'restriction of access' as displacement even when physical uprooting isn't mandated, was arrived at as result of long and in-depth internal discussions between the World Bank social and environmental specialists, grounded in their joint examination of previous worldwide experiences with the use of 'restricted access'.

The key twin reasons for it are the pursuit of *environmental effectiveness* and of *social equity.* Environmental effectiveness requires real and sustainable protection of biodiversity. In turn, social equity requires identifying and preventing the adverse impacts of PAs upon those whose access to some natural resources is suddenly restricted, by offering them alternative options for securing their livelihood sustainably. This way, they will not end up impoverished, worse off. These two goals are seen as interdependent twin goals, which must be pursued concomitantly.

For this to take place, the means necessary are prescribed and provided through the new policy. Such means, which were absent in the past, are specific entitlements, comparable with those prescribed in typical development-caused displacement situations. Sometimes these may include the identification of alternative productive areas accessible to those affected, or support for alternative income generating activities, or various other forms of compensation (Cernea 2008) and technical assistance, etc.[6]

Protected areas are seen by multilateral development agencies as a crucial modality for conserving unique biodiversity resources and areas endowed with major cultural heritage or natural monuments. Restrictions of access to such resources are objectively necessary to prevent total loss, overuse or gradual depletion, since many such resources have global or national importance, beyond their immediate benefits for the local populations. The challenge is to involve local populations in genuinely managing sustainably such resources, either by themselves or in various patterns of co-management. In certain such situations, restrictions become indispensable. This need for reasonable restrictions is not, in itself, at issue.

At issue, however, are two types of recurrent failures of the institution of restricted access, highlighted increasingly by independent research/evaluation studies.

First, in numerous situations, the introduction of restricted access has failed to achieve its environmental objectives. The resource depletion by the former users has continued, rendering the protection ineffective. Therefore, to avoid further environmental failure, the protection regime needs to be introduced with better incentives and additional organisational skills, improving implementation and monitoring.

Second, the practice of simply, and suddenly, declaring some areas and some prior resource-use patterns as 'restricted' and prohibited has imposed heavy opportunity costs on local people, subtracting without restitution from their livelihood. The social outcome has been net de-capitalisation and impoverishment of those affected.

The change in policy is intended to help overcome both types of failures, by creating organisational, economic and social premises conducive to 'double sustainability', that is, protecting people's livelihoods and the environment at the same time.

What is the content of 'forced displacement'?

Forced population displacement caused by development or environmental projects is usually defined as occurring when people lose, through expropriation, either their *house*, or their *land*, or *both* simultaneously. They are compelled to yield the 'right of way' to the project.

However, this broadly accepted definition of forced displacement has given birth to at least two long, simmering conceptual and definitional debates. The debates, not just academic, are loaded with heavy implications for practice.

In the first debate, the definition was opposed by a somewhat more limited definition of forced displacement, which introduced a distinction between loss of home and loss of land. The supporters of the narrow definition contended that displacement occurs only when people lose their dwellings. Loss of cultivated land, or access to it, it was argued, would 'affect' people's productive activities but will not necessarily *displace* them, because they don't lose their 'place', are not forcibly relocated and can remain in their houses.

Upon closer scrutiny, this viewpoint appeared unrealistic. It belittles the core *economic content* of displacement and reduces it to geography. People's 'place' is their land too, not only the roof above their heads. Land is livelihood and identity.

Confronted with vast empirical evidence and robust theoretical response, the narrow definition of displacement as mere house-expropriation lost the debate. Land dispossession, even if occasionally not accompanied by loss of housing, has been vastly recognised as forced displacement. Today, that narrow definition of displacement is virtually forgotten. The debate is basically settled, even if isolated advocates unrepentantly return to the narrow definition.

In the second debate, the issue at stake was more complex. It referred primarily to populations with customary land ownership, not formal title. When protected areas are established, the populations with customary ownership over those areas (most often tribal or other indigenous groups) are often relocated forcibly.

Forced resettlements from park areas, however, have compiled a historical record abundant in well-documented social disasters. Those physically uprooted were not given equitable, realistic and viable alternatives. Specifically, no land title to other sites were allotted as part of such forced relocations; compensations were not paid or were woefully inadequate; people's place-rooted identity was undermined; conflicts with hostile host populations ensued frequently. In turn, the displaced people, lacking an alternative livelihood, kept pressure on the PA from the outskirts, so that the 'displacement-without-proper-resettlement' also detracted from the expected environmental effectiveness of PAs.

Scholars of various specialties have empirically researched and explained these negative impoverishing outcomes in great detail. The deep economic conflict between park-displaced people and park-promoting conservation, so callously discounted by single-issue conservation militants, has been well captured and called to attention by Geisler in the suggestive title of his study, *Your park, my poverty* (2003), as well as by Kaimowitz and his colleagues in their study, *Your Biosphere is my backyard* (2003) about the Bosawas Reserve in Nicaragua. Several volumes and countless studies have reported hard evidence about the impoverishment risks inflicted unmitigated on those displaced – demonstrating how these risks turned into actual impoverishment and tragic destitution occurrences. These studies point to the ethical clouds that the responsibility for causing such pathological transgressions of justice places upon protected areas and their one-sided proponents (Brechin et al. 2003; Brockington and Igoe 2006; Cernea and Schmidt-Soltau 2003a, 2003b, 2006; Chatty and Colchester 2002; Feeney 1998; Ghimire and Pimbert 2000; Turton 2002; Rudd 2004). *Mutatis Mutandis*, the same must be said about the establishment of SEZs without regard for the welfare of those forcibly placed to make space for such profitable zones.

The mounting criticism of socially irresponsible, forced physical relocations has had some impact, and a slight tactical shift was introduced in the establishment of conservation areas. Though the promotion of PA approaches continued to enact 'restriction of access' and create PAs based on restrictions to certain natural resources, in some instances, it delinked such restrictions from imposing the immediate physical displacement of the people so restricted. The assumption was that without imposing forced geographic displacement, the obligation to compensate and soundly relocate those 'restricted' would disappear because they were not physically removed, and thus the enactment of 'restriction of access' would become benign in its socio-economic effects and could be described as benign, thus taking the sting off PAs and off the uncompensated restriction of access.

Facts on the ground, however, have not fulfilled this self-serving assumption. The real situation of the 'restricted populations' inside parks and other types of PAs has become the subject of what I termed the second debate. The responses to the critique of park-caused physical displacements have varied on a broad range.[7]

Invoking the circumstance that no physical removal is forcibly imposed, and that dwellings are not destroyed, takes place, some promoters of protected areas have denied that the displacement concept can be used when populations are subjected to 'only restricted access'. They argued that because there was no physical resettlement, there was no displacement either, and cited cases of populations that are still inside PAs in spite of laws that either made their residence there illegal or restricted their access to resource streams.

This is a fallacious reasoning. What in fact happens is displacement in its economic sense, without even the mitigation, alternatives and the entitlements provided through planned and organised resettlement. People prohibited by access-restricting laws from using the land and resources declared 'protected areas', like those people who elsewhere are declared to be illegal residents, also remain under a constant threat of being physically relocated at any moment.

One case in point illustrates well the complexities of such situations. This is the case of the Mursi in Ethiopia, about whom the continuous research carried out by David Turton over a period of more than three decades has brought deep scholarly knowledge. The territory of the Mursi lies within and between the Omo and Mago National Parks in southwestern Ethiopia (Turton 1987, 2002). The Mursi depend for about 75 per cent of their subsistence needs on land lying within the park boundaries — agricultural land in the Omo Park and dry-season grazing land in the Mago Park. Although these parks were set up, in a practical sense, over 30 years ago, it was only in early 2005 that the Ethiopian government began taking effective steps to have their boundaries legally established. This was in connection with a proposal from the African Parks Foundation (APF), a transnational conservation organisation then based in the Netherlands,[8] to run the Omo Park in a public–private partnership with the government. The implications of this for the customary land rights of the Mursi were potentially disastrous. They faced the likelihood of permanently restricted access to some of their most valuable subsistence resources, without receiving alternative livelihood options from the foundation that would manage the park commercially. The authorities, meanwhile, would have been able to claim that, in denying such access, they would not be 'evicting' the Mursi physically from their territory and would not, therefore, be obliged to provide alternative livelihood opportunities (Turton 2010). The APF took over the management of the Park in January 2006 but in December 2007 their Board announced its intention to terminate its 25-year management agreement with the government, citing, amongst other reasons, the 'unjustified' criticisms it was attracting from human rights organisations.[9] The Park has now reverted to government control but the Mursi still face the threat of (at best) gradually increasing restrictions on their use of vital subsistence resources.[10] This is why the improved understanding and improved policy resulting from the redefinition of displacement and of restricted access is directly relevant to the need to ensure consistent recognition and enduring protection of the Mursi customary tenure rights and entitlements.

Another dramatic case was reported by Feeney (1998) from Uganda a few years ago: the sudden and brutal relocation of inhabitants from the Kibale game corridor. Physical displacement from other PAs, after years of residence endorsed by authorities, are also known.

The denial of the displacing effects resulting from 'restriction of access', without counter-risk measures, implicitly justifies the promoters' refusal to grant the deprived populations compensation and entitlements to alternative land resources or activities, impoverishing them further.

Responding to this view, many social researchers and resettlement specialists, including some conservation specialists too, have argued and documented empirically that the enforcement of 'restricted access' to resources vital for livelihood is tantamount to economic displacement, destitution and impoverishment. I have myself been a participant in this argument, both inside and outside the World Bank. Long before the adoption of the revised Bank policy, OP 4.12, I argued that 'the concept of displacement describes also situations in which some people are deprived of their productive lands, or of other income-generating assets, without being physically evicted from their houses' (Cernea 1999).

Confronted with field findings and critical analysis, the assumption mentioned above was proven precarious and incorrect. The poverty effects of access-restriction and of denying a prior food/income stream remained severe even in the absence of physical relocation. The underlying issue is that as long as the deep consequences of these restrictions on people are not recognised, pre-empted, and countered, they suddenly, and severely, subtract from the livelihood of the local communities. Vulnerable and poor populations are made even poorer. The economic effects on their livelihoods end up being almost the same as if they were physically, forcibly displaced. Moreover, lacking alternatives, such groups soon revert to surreptitious and now illegal use of the restricted areas, sapping the intended conservation as well. Rather than the vaunted 'win-win', a 'lose-lose' situation is created.

This debate, as opposed to the first one, has been long simmering. But accumulating empirical research evidence has revealed the dire impoverishing effects on people inside parks and protected areas, and the failure to ensure sustainable livelihoods. This empirical evidence and lessons from painful experiences with 'restricted access' have led the major multilateral development agencies to new conclusions, that is, to recognising that the practices of restricted access, even without physical relocation, are tantamount to occupational displacement with imposed impoverishment. For the first time, the newly adopted policy provisions and definitions regarding restricted access bring key international actors to an unambiguous position in this debate. This is why the conversion of this research conclusion into explicit policy is a landmark.

New policy conclusions and operational prescriptions

How is this conversion reflected in the texts of the updated policies? The new policy statements explicitly broaden the coverage of the policy from only situations of involuntary 'taking of land' through expropriation, extending it also to situations of imposed and 'involuntary restriction of access to legally designated parks and protected areas, resulting in adverse impacts on the livelihoods of the displaced persons' (World Bank OP 4.12, Article 36).

Further, the policy explains what is understood by 'involuntary restrictions' and to whom it refers. It states: 'For the purposes of this policy, involuntary restriction of access covers restriction on the use of resources imposed on people living outside a park or protected area, or on those who continue living inside the park, or protected area, during and after implementation' (World Bank OP 4.12, Note 9).

In the 25-year history of the World Bank resettlement policy, this is for the first time that 'loss of access' is being explicitly considered as a form of displacement. However, this is consistent with the conceptual definitions and argument developed by the sociologists and anthropologists studying displacement. It is also consistent with the theoretical principle adopted by the World Bank long ago, that the *definitional* characteristic in forced displacements is not only the *physical geographic removal*, but the imposed *loss of assets* and *income* (Cernea 2005a). It is precisely this displacement-caused *loss* that must be compensated by restoring and improving people's livelihoods.

Indeed, these two distinct definitional elements have often been confused, and probably will be for some time to come. In practice, imposed deprivation of assets can take place, and often does take place, *in situ*, without the physical removal of inhabitants. Therefore, this time the policy warns against such confusion. It specifies that, similar to situations of actual 'taking of land', in restricted access situations 'loss of income sources or means of livelihood, whether or not the affected persons must move to another location' (World Bank OP 4.12, para 3aIII) is also covered under the policy.

The World Bank policy also applies to all GEF projects executed by the Bank, as well as to projects by private sector entities that are co-financed by IFC, the World Bank's group arm for private sector projects.

Beyond the World Bank itself, the international response from other major development agencies to the definition of restriction of access as displacement has been rapid and consensual. Inter-agency consultations and replication followed shortly. For Africa, a region where a long history of abuses has marred the creation of many parks and other protected areas, the African Development Bank (AfDB) has included a new clear statement in its 2003 policy on involuntary resettlement, absent in the prior (1995) version of the policy. The revised 2003 AfDB policy states:

> This policy covers economic and social impacts associated with Bank financed projects involving loss of assets or involuntary restriction of access to assets including national parks, protected areas or of national resources; or loss of income sources or means of livelihood as a result of projects, whether or not the affected persons are required to move (AfDB 2003, para 3.4).

The AfDB places the new provisions on PAs in the context of its stand against the impoverishment risks induced by displacement. It emphasises the obligation of operationally identifying, in each project, the impoverishment processes inherent in displacement, listing them verbatim, and the need to apply counter-risk reconstruction strategies. The AfDB policy states:

> the above lessons highlight the need for improvements in the planning and implementation of resettlement components (and) for identifying the key impoverishment processes entailed in the displacement of persons arising from these projects. These are landlessness, joblessness, homelessness, marginalization, food insecurity, loss of access to common property resources, increased morbidity and community dislocation. Therefore, the key to a development-oriented resettlement scheme is to identify the impoverishment risks of a project and attempt to counteract them by adopting a programme with a people-centered focus rather than

a property-compensation approach, e.g. by addressing landlessness with land-based schemes; joblessness with employment schemes; homelessness with home reconstruction schemes; community disarticulation with community reconstruction schemes, etc. (AfDB 2003, para 2.3.6).

In answering the perennial argument that 'there isn't enough money to apply such better provisions', the AfDB policy correctly notes that the costs of *not* applying a good policy in displacement, 'almost invariably outweigh the investments that would have been needed to plan and execute an acceptable resettlement programme'.

In turn, the Asian Development Bank extended its involuntary resettlement policy in 2003 to also address the 'social and economic impacts that are permanent or temporary and are caused by…change in the use of land or restrictions imposed on land as a result of an ADB operation' (ADB 2003, para 3).

An initial poverty and social assessment (IPSA) is required for every development project and should be undertaken as early as possible in the project cycle…It quantifies any land acquisition, land changes, or *restrictions that will necessitate involuntary resettlement planning* (ADB 2003, para 23–24, emphasis added).

Surely, the chain consensus of the multilateral development banks is more than just inter-agency replication; it reflects a self-critical reconsideration of their previous positions, and the intent to plug a loophole that allowed dispossession without planned resettlement to occur under internationally financed projects. Beyond this correction, it institutionalises positive changes materially able to optimise the governance of the protected areas, thus becoming part of what is seen as a broader set of governance changes in this domain (Borrini-Feyerabend 2004).

The policy change by the multilateral banks also recognises and validates the long and increasing resistance of indigenous people and NGOs, in all continents, against the impoverishment and social injustices inflicted upon them during the creation of many parks and protected areas of various forms, such as corridors or game reserves for elephants, tigers and other animals, that in fact do require protection against extinction. Such dispossession also occurs repeatedly under numerous development projects that not only restrict but take away and exclude the tribal groups from their customarily owned land, displacing them physically without offering them sustainable livelihood alternatives. A recent example of such a situation in Orissa (India) gained not only nationwide but also international exposure, as the resistance of tribal groups at Kalinganagar against exclusion from their lands, to be taken by a private sector steel company, was met with a police fusillade killing 12 tribal people at point blank range.[11] Had the international policy standards for displacement and resettlement been implemented in this case, with viable livelihood alternatives being created for the affected tribal population, such a tragedy would not have taken place. This dramatic case demonstrates once again that without equitable policies in place and genuine implementation of these by the private sector corporations, the corporations will be less and less able to obtain the land they need, even if they rely on state implementation of procedures that are intrinsically unfair and impoverishing.

The policy changes adopted by the World Bank and the regional multilateral agencies are setting a model to follow for private sector foundations that pursue not 'development' projects but biodiversity conservation programmes. Commercial corporations, various organisations or private foundations from developed countries which undertake park management roles in developing countries need to assume, in their turn, ethical responsibility for supporting and applying the same moral and economic safeguard standards protecting the livelihood of conservation-affected local people as those embodied in the policy provisions, as described in this paper. Such organisations, often funded also by OECD governments or by donations from the civil society, cannot escape the moral and political responsibility for the destruction and impoverishing displacement carried out with the hands of local governments, when such displacements are in fact the preliminaries for those organisations' projects to establish a new park or to commercially manage a park (F. Pearce 2005). Fairness to resident populations, as well as basic ethics and respect of human and civil rights, require making sure that any displacement, physical or economic, does not leave the affected people worse off, even if technically it occurs 'prior' to the foundations' formal involvement in the management of a given park.

The economic rationale underpinning the policy change

The policy reassessment discussed in this paper has not occurred lightly. It is the result of considerate analysis of factual evidence, and of dialogue between conservation and social specialists. It is also grounded in the fundamentals of environmental economics. David Pearce, one of the founders of environmental economics and among the very few economic scholars analysing population displacement issues, argued that as in conservation, in development projects too—

> the first rule is that all parties to the project should be better off with the intervention than without it. The fundamental justification for this rule is that if any party is made worse off by the intervention, they are likely to act in such a way that the success of the project will be jeopardised. Clear examples exist in the conservation policy area where protected area might restrict access to local communities who previously used the area of various ecosystem services and products — the so-called 'evictions from Eden'. Unless the local community is compensated in some way, restricted access will generate losses and resentment, and this may result in what then becomes illegal activity, threatening the project....Each party must have an incentive to 'sign up' to the project, which in turn means that the benefits of the project to them must exceed the costs of the project to them (D. Pearce 2006: 137).

From the economic viewpoint, therefore, the strategy conclusion is that the economic displacement caused by access-restrictions — even 'displacement *in situ*', *inside* the protected area — must (*i*) help generate benefits that exceed the costs incurred by the affected people and (*ii*) the benefits need to be channelled back to the affected people. These channelled-back benefits may take the form of a package of entitlements, combining compensation, incentives and added investments to cover losses and incremental costs.

It is sometimes pointed out that a protected area, by preserving biodiversity resources, may ultimately generate biodiversity benefits shared by the affected people as well. This is indeed true, but it is crystal clear that the negative impoverishment impacts on the locals, who are poor to begin with and made poorer by displacement, immediately wreck livelihood, long before the locals get any ultimate benefits.

Conservation is undertaken in the name of global interests, and this brings into discussion the relationships between benefits at global and local levels. Economic analysis has convincingly demonstrated that the benefits of biodiversity conservation through protected areas or parks tend to be highest at the global and national levels and lowest at the level of local communities (Wells 1992). In the same vein, economic research has concluded:

> When analysing costs, they are (found to be) highest at the local level and lowest at the national and international levels...At the local level, net benefits may be negative, indicating that there is no local incentive to undertake land conservation. This suggests that not only must the local community be involved in conservation efforts, but that they should also be able to appropriate a fair share of the under values of conservation (Brown et al. 1993).

The benefits from protected areas accrue primarily to stakeholders and groups which are far away, are developed, and are much better off than the poor local population. In other words, costs of conservation are externalised, imposed upon, and are borne by those less able to afford them (Daly 2008). Residents of PAs are not compensated for the substantial opportunity costs/losses incurred, even when they bear them unwittingly. The ethical failure is obvious. In this case, a known syndrome is at work — some get the gains, while others get the pains.

Social analysis, in turn, has demonstrated that displacement and loss of access to common natural resources is closely associated with social disarticulation, loss of income-generating occupation and identity, increased morbidity and mortality, marginalisation (Cernea and Schmidt-Soltau 2003a) — in short, with most of the basic risks identified by the general model of impoverishment risks and reconstruction (IRR) that applies to development-caused displacement/resettlement in other sectors as well (Cernea 2000). The vastly documented body of findings about these impoverishment risks in Africa (Cernea 2005b) raises issues of social justice and equity in conservation strategies too. The general rationale of the IRR framework, when tailored analytically to the case of parks and protected areas, is congruent with the classic rationale about the economic harm and moral injustice of development-induced displacements in all sectors, which must be reversed by organised reconstruction.

Significantly, awareness about these unacceptable social, economic and cultural effects, is also increasing within the conservation community, as a recent paper critical of western environmentalists' biases has stated. Because,

> protected areas have often increased poverty amongst the poorest of the poor, there is now emerging recognition of both an ethical and practical imperative to why we must consider the linkages between protected areas

> and poverty. Ethically, western environmentalists, no matter how well-meaning, have no right to run roughshod over local needs and rights (McShane 2003: 53).

Although this position is not yet generally embraced, and direct reference to forced displacements is still not made, the 2003 World Parks Congress and the 2004 IUCN Congress in Bangkok adopted the recommendation that areas protected for biodiversity conservation should under no circumstance exacerbate poverty.[12] The big conservation organisations still have to issue self-binding 'how to' prescriptions on how to actually accomplish impoverishment prevention in protected areas, and to formally commit themselves to avoid and oppose displacements that ruin livelihoods.

From policy to implementation

How will the multilateral agencies' new policy definition be implemented? The short answer is — it will face substantial difficulties, at least initially. However promising it is for protection and social equity, consistent implementation of the new policy will have to confront serious obstacles, including a wide range of interests vested in repeating old approaches to PAs, shortage of institutional capacity for enforcing the new approach, technical difficulties in measuring costs and allocations, and entrenched biases ready to exploit all these difficulties for subverting the new approach. Yet, successful implementation is of the highest interest, both to the affected people and to the conservation supporters. Both groups gain important new means for promoting sustainable and equitable protection. It is, therefore, indispensable that governments, major international conservation organisations like the IUCN and WWF, and country-based NGOs genuinely join forces in implementing the new policy approach.

Two decisive premises for implementing this policy will be (*i*) increased financial resources, and (*ii*) more detailed socioeconomic planning. To be noted, the World Bank has not simply revised concepts and policies without securing means for making them stick. It has also prescribed new procedures, project tools and resources. Among these is an improved process of project preparation tailored to protected areas, supported by access to certain financing options previously not available.

The correct implementation of the new policy implies that the designation of a certain territory as a new 'protected areas' must be accompanied by financing resources that were not made available at the time of similar designations in the past. Such additional financing is necessary to enable the affected population to develop alternative income sources to replace the productive capacity of the land placed under restriction. Only conservation-correct discourse cannot substitute for the impoverishment of resident populations suddenly deprived of access to a previously used natural productive capacity. The multilateral agencies have learned the hard way — from their own and others' experiences — that such past approaches have produced fake protection and compounded social misery. Instead, the new policy's implementation is bound to place a more solid financial platform under the establishment of enduring PAs. This way, it is apt to increase and improve effective protection. It will secure genuine global environmental good, and more effectively, because it will compel the provision of a more fair and equitable (read higher) restitution of costs imposed on locals through entitlements to the kind of measures and resources granted in recognised development-caused displacements.

A new policy is always more credible when it explicitly states the issuer's self-imposed commitments and obligations and prescribes/allocates commensurate means tailored to the declared goals.

Through its new policy, the World Bank has committed itself to a sequence of 'required measures' tailored to the needs of the affected populations. Governments asking for Bank assistance and Bank staff members are now required to prepare a 'process framework' for all 'projects involving restriction of access to legally designated parks and protected areas' (World Bank OP 4.12, para 7), since the type of resettlement action plan (RAP) usually required when populations are physically relocated would not apply in this case.[13]

What is called 'process framework' is a formal project document which spells out the steps needed to implement the policy in ways germane to specific protected areas. The purpose of this framework is to institute genuine involvement and consultation, through which members of potentially affected communities would participate in designing the project's components. Explicitly, these consultations are not only about measures for biodiversity sustainability, but also about measures for the sustainability of people's livelihoods. The framework will lay the foundation of a resource management plan, which can be, in time, improved through a process of jointly identifying those activities which may be continued sustainably, distinct from those which must be restricted for protection and replaced with other income-generation activities.[14]

The degree of detail in the policy's exacting demands regarding the interactions between project sponsors and affected population is well reflected in the following, rather long but significant, excerpt:

> A process framework is prepared when Bank-supported projects may cause restrictions in access to natural resources in legally designated parks and protected areas. The purpose of the process framework is to establish a process by which members of potentially affected communities participate in design of project components, in determination of measures necessary to achieve resettlement policy objectives, and in implementation and monitoring of relevant activities....The document should briefly describe the project and components or activities that may involve new or more stringent restrictions on natural resource use. It should also describe the process by which potentially displaced persons participate in project design....The document should establish that potentially affected communities will be involved in identifying any adverse impacts, assessing of the significance of impacts, and establishing of the criteria for eligibility of any mitigating or compensating measures necessary.
>
> Measures to assist affected persons in their efforts to improve their livelihoods or restore them, in real terms, to pre-displacement levels, while maintaining the sustainability of the park or protected area will be identified. The (process framework) document should describe the process for resolving disputes relating to resource use restrictions... and grievances that may arise from members of communities who are dissatisfied with the eligibility criteria, community planning measures, or actual implementation (World Bank OP 4.12, Annex A, paras 26 and 27).

The content of this statement is particularly significant as it establishes the requirement of avoiding one-sidedness, or what could be seen as conservation fundamentalism — namely, pursuing the conservation of biodiversity with callous disregard for the sustainability of peoples' livelihood. This is an important principle. In writing about it elsewhere, we conceptualised this principle as the 'pursuit of double sustainability', or just 'double-sustainability', for both natural biodiversity and peoples' livelihoods (for a more detailed discussion of this concept see Cernea and Schmidt-Soltau (2003a, 2003b, 2006). It breaks with the chronic de-linking of the vital interests of 'park people' from biodiversity conservation.

The new revisions to policy do not mean, however, that the policy prohibits physical relocation in all conditions, even when it is unavoidable to relocate some groups to save a unique resource from further risks. Such situations may occur, for instance, when recent encroachers move in, in large numbers, purposively to exploit the wealth of a rare and precious biodiversity resource — an old forest, an area of unique vegetation — threatening its survival. Distinctions must always be made between natives and newcomers of various sorts. The point is that relocation, if unavoidable, is not a punishment tool but a last-resort tool for safeguarding the enduring survival of the resource, while also materially enabling the area's native inhabitants and their children to achieve an alternative, sustainable livelihood.

Constantly pursuing the 'double sustainability' is the just compass for conservation activities. Of course, once the policy position is established, what matters ultimately are not just the statements in the policy documents but whether resources, both financial and human, are provided for on-the-ground implementation.

Additional financing provided for co-management

The redefinition of restricted access as displacement, changes the prior landscape of conservation work in some important ways, apt to prevent inducing impoverishment. It offers those affected, even when they are not being forced to physically move, access to the entitlements provided under multilateral agencies policies for those who are physically relocated. Like the World Bank, in turn, the Asian Development Bank policy similarly prescribes that, 'affected people will be provided with certain resettlement entitlements, dually as land and asset compensation and transfer allowances, prior to their displacement, dispossession, or restricted access' (ADB 2003, para 38).

In the recent past, too, the establishment of PAs has chronically suffered — even in projects supported by major donors or international NGOs — from insufficient financing. This has diminished the effectiveness of the restrictions themselves as the incremental resources needed for alternative income-generation activities have not been supplied. In turn, promoters of PAs (including governments of the countries where PAs were created) explained away the non-payment of just compensation to affected people by citing lack of resources to cover the costs, thus tacitly recognising that the costs of creating PAs were partly or fully externalised on the local populations, compelling the compelling the locals to bear the cost of the land needed foe the project.

Past situations, therefore, teach us that the recent change in definition will have no practical effect, unless it is backed on the ground by delivery of material entitlements, which the resettlement policies of development banks grant to those affected by the restrictions. This policy revision is *not* just a matter of shifting definitional labels; it is a matter of shifting resources. Because, in the first place, resources are shifted away from those restricted, other resources must be shifted back to them. The means of livelihood subtracted from the affected must be replaced with access to alternative and sustainable means of livelihood, and not just with a one-time compensation, which, in all probability, would not last long. This material safeguard is the ultimate meaning of the change in international definitions and policies.

How will this be accomplished, including the use of fair valuation procedures, calculation of amounts, and the design for alternative productive activities? It's certainly not an easy task. Multilateral development banks are now expected to show practically (in the feasibility reports for PAs and project appraisal reports prescribing restricted access) how the restrictions' costs have been realistically calculated and quantified financially. In turn, international conservation organisations cannot, morally, apply lower feasibility standards in their projects. Only terminology changes in artfully written feasibility reports would not change anything in the absence of transparent economic analyses and explicit resource-allocation and without new, instituted NRM patterns, including co-management. In some cases, such artful descriptions depict imposed relocation as voluntary relocation, while in fact the material and cultural prerequisites for such change in the nature of relocation are far from being met. The mechanisms for channelising the incremental resources needed for establishing PAs and protecting livelihoods should be transparent, to ensure that they truly reach the members of the affected communities and are not siphoned off for other uses at intermediate national, regional or local levels.

Details on these entitlements and other compensation and mitigating measures are given throughout the OP/BP 4.12 policy on involuntary resettlement, and also in ADB's policies.[15] In practice, the international agencies, as well as the local agency or NGO responsible for the PA, need to describe realistically and make 'the arrangements for funding resettlement, including the preparation and review of cost estimates, the flow of funds, and contingency arrangements' (OP/BP 4.12, annex A, para 24).

That this is not just discourse language is already suggested by another significant decision. In April 2004, World Bank has also adopted a new land financing policy, which, for the first time, allows use of financing by IDA (International Development Association) and the Bank for land acquisition, within Bank-supported projects.[16] Before 2004, World Bank did not allow its credits to be used to purchase lands, with only case-by-case exceptions. Any land acquisition had to be financed with government funds. Recently, this condition was lifted, in an effort to facilitate realistic ways to pre-empt impoverishment.

Thus, the new policy represents a multifaceted change, and does include added financial backing. Previously, a series of proposals to this respect inside the same institution, including recommendations of a special task force that was convened to examine World Bank's financing of land acquisition in support of better resettlement, had been rejected.[17] With this background, the recent changes are even more significant.

The increased flexibility for using Bank and IDA financing towards land purchase in displacement situations will also help increase capacity for establishing co-management arrangements over natural resources. Despite their intrinsic promise, such co-management patterns have often failed because of lack of material means. The unfavourable cost-benefit ratio for the local communities made the rhetorical calls to 'co-manage' sound vacuous, and alienated the local actors.

Further, park promoters often promised high alternative revenues from eco-tourism in exchange of restriction-induced losses to local resident groups. But such promises were hugely over-inflated. Sometimes, they were employed as a smokescreen to justify, and hide, the welfare losses caused by eliminating past income-streams. An important GEF study (Todd et al. 2006) on the global-versus-local benefits in GEF-financed projects found that eco-tourism benefits were unwarrantedly exaggerated in feasibility studies, and that local communities typically did not get the promised benefits. Hopefully, the new funding mechanisms for PAs with restricted access will create new options and incentives for innovative co-management patterns.

In turn, the traditional agricultural knowledge possessed by local communities may also be more effective while people remain *in situ*, helping balance restriction of access with sustainable use of other resources for personal consumption.

One step, the importance of which must not be underestimated in the planning of PAs in future, is the analytical difficulty of accurately estimating the costs (losses) to be incurred by residents because of restrictions. This will require perceptive socioeconomic work on the ground in preparing new PA projects, using adequate economic tool-kits. The more accurate the cost identification and coverage, the better the protection of natural resources, and the higher the chances of creating PAs without making local population end up worse off.

In sum, realistic economic and financial premises are indispensable for securing people's interested cooperation in genuine co-management. The World Bank's 'process framework' explicitly requires that such cost-assessments be done not by outside conservation specialists alone, but with the direct participation of the local communities. The combination of local knowledge with outside expertise, plus fairness in negotiating agreed estimates and in assessing incremental costs, are indispensable mechanisms for preparing sound and sustainable conservation initiatives.[18]

Focused research on restricted access areas and poverty

The development and conservation communities are explicitly concerned with researching a fundamental question: 'Can protected areas contribute to poverty reduction?' (Scherl et al. 2004). In turn, to further analyse its own past and ongoing experiences with restricted access in more depth, and to derive lessons useful in implementing new policies, World Bank initiated a project portfolio review in 2004. The review identified a large number of projects — over 100 — supporting parks and access-restricted areas, of which 48 were selected for detailed study.

Among its main preliminary findings, the study notes, self-critically, a lack of proper balance. It says that in the reviewed projects, prior to the policy revision, the 'restrictions of access were thought of mainly in terms of how to achieve conservation objectives, not in terms of impact on livelihood', also, 'mitigation strategies in feasibility analysis were more of an optimistic menu of potential options, rather than the results of thorough feasibility analysis: even when feasible, many strategies were inadequately supported by other elements of the designed projects' (van Wicklin III 2005).

This study recommends, among other operational measures, both the strengthening of technical analyses and more material support for sustainable strategies when protected areas are promoted through World Bank, and in GEF-assisted projects. The review, in progress when this paper is submitted for print, will most likely be a valuable knowledge source about alternative approaches to restriction of access, apt to protect both the biodiversity and the needs of the resident native people.

At the 2004 IUCN World Conservation Congress, several research projects on these issues were announced and planned by CARE, branches of IUCN, the WWF and the African Wildlife Federation, in partnerships with academic researchers. These revolve around 'the social and economic costs and benefits of protected areas in East Africa', and their defined objective is 'promoting social justice in conservation' (Franks 2004: 1). A large-scale, worldwide synthesis study was initiated on the 'social impacts of protected areas' (Brockington and Schmidt-Soltau 2004).

Much of the credit for the current new policy definitions of PAs, restricted access and displacement adopted by development agencies should go to the tenacious and prolonged efforts devoted by cohorts of researchers to two classic themes in development social sciences: 'putting people first' in development projects, and 'people and parks'. In more than one way, this is a non-exogenous policy, having emerged not 'from the outside', through a top-down initiative, but an endogenous one, coming bottom-up from the evidence produced through long, patient and candid field research of the conditions of affected populations. It is this work that has generated the empirical evidence revealing the risks and destitution inflicted on vulnerable indigenous populations by imposed physical displacement or by restriction of access decisions.

Some of these studies (Cernea and Schmidt-Soltau 2003b) went further, and made the critical policy recommendation *to stop and discontinue altogether forced physical displacements as the mainstream park-creation strategy*, unless the full complement of titled replacement land, just compensation, productive alternatives and civil rights protection are provided to the relocated populations.[19] The debate continues around this recommendation, which has not been endorsed yet by major international conservation agencies. The supporters of forced displacement are reluctant to embrace it, though they remain unable to disprove the facts that led to it, or to meet the requirements of livelihood protection.

The ability to derive strategy/policy recommendations from such in-depth field studies and analyses shows why this kind of social research must be expanded. Now, the changes in the policies for creating PAs described in this chapter must be tested through research on how consistently the new definition of restricted access is translated in the projects' design. The research must highlight positive experiences and predictable difficulties.

Overall, the need for accountability in development and conservation interventions for the social effects they trigger, the relationships between poverty reduction and conservation work, the risks of impoverishment, and the financing of counter-risk measures, re-emerge, with increased immediacy, as critical priority areas in resettlement and general development research.

Notes

1. Roy Burman's research was continued by L. K. Mahapatra (1991, 1994) and subsequently has inspired much broader research in India on similar processes. See also Parasuraman's (1999) re-analysis of the beginnings of resettlement research in India, in light of the new, considerably larger and more traumatic processes of population displacement and resettlement unfolding in India in recent decades, such as those triggered by the Narmada Sardar-Sarovar dam, by industrial displacements in Orissa and many others. See also Baviskar (1995), Dreze, Samson and Singh (1997), Mathur and Marsden (1998), and Pandey (1999).
2. Walter Fernandes is conducting an all-Indian social and statistical study of the total number of development-displaced people. According to the latest data he has published, after covering the majority but not all Indian states, the number of displaced people reached 60 million over the 1950–2005 period. But he made a special point to underscore that the overwhelming majority of this number was left impoverished after displacement and that a large part of those displaced have not even been resettled by the authorities who displaced them. See Walter Fernandes (2008); they were given no land on which to attempt to live in their impoverished conditions and to try to rebuild their shattered livelihood.

3. This is described in detail in the Land Acquisition and Resettlement Plan (LARAP) for the Tanguh project. See http://www.adb.org/Documents/Resettlement_Plans/INO/38919-01-PS-RP.pdf (accessed 25 May 2010).
4. To provide income-generation alternatives to this restriction, the project implemented creative solutions: among other measures for helping improve the construction of boats used in the project area, the Tangguh project provides an outboard motor, free of charge, to each of the almost 300 fishermen families in the affected clans. This enables them to much extend the radius of fishing beyond and around the restricted safety zone, while the motor-propelled bigger boats that replace the paddle-propelled boats are also capable of increased speed and fishing productivity http://www.adb.org/Documents/Resettlement_Plans/INO/38919-01-RS-RP.pdf (accessed 25 May 2010).
5. The World Bank's initial policy on involuntary population resettlement was issued in 1980, at which time it was the first policy ever adopted by any international organisation for regulating project-caused processes of displacement and resettlement. Its adoption triggered a long series of international efforts for improving the norms and practice of population resettlement, but also opened up a period of recurrent tensions and criticism, both inside the World Bank and between the Bank and its borrowers, resulting from multiple instances of inconsistency between policy principles and project implementation. However, through the difficult up-hill battles and with the ups and downs that followed after 1980, the initial R&R policy was revised and gradually strengthened. Based on new actual experiences and new social science research and its provisions were refined and expanded at several stages in 1986, 1988, 1990 and 1994 (for a detailed examination of landmark moments in the history of this policy and its growing international embrace, see Cernea 2005a.) The revised policy (OP/BP 4.12) updates and broadens the previous policy's coverage, as described in this article: it was formally adopted by the Bank's Board in November 2001, and became effective on 1 January 2002.
6. For a detailed discussion of compensation practices, their basic and persistent flaws and failures, and of available remedies, see Cernea (2008).
7. Some of these responses were so insensitive to the social and moral issues, and so deeply immersed in denial, that they hardly deserve consideration. For instance, one of such responses argued that resettlement is a 'political matter', and poverty reduction is a moral goal, while conservation is a 'scientific matter' and science-based conservation should not be mixed or 'compromised' with social considerations.
8. Now known as 'African Parks Network', it's head office was shifted from The Netherlands to South Africa in 2007, following the death of its first chairman, Dutch businessman Paul Fentener van Vlissingen.

9. A month before making this announcement, the Board received a letter from survival. International , warning that it could be open to a charge of complicity in a 'serious abuse of Mursi human right'. Letter available at http://www.mursi.org/pdf/survival-afp-letter.pdf (accessed 7 June 2010).
10. This information is based on a detailed manuscript paper by David Turton about the complex events related to the shortlived intervention and retreat of AFP. The manuscript is currently under preparation for publication, and was graciously made available by its author for the summary example in the present article, which I acknowledge with particular gratitude.
11. The concept of 'social exclusion', directly relevant to our entire discussion in this paper, has been analysed in depth by Amartya Sen (2000), in the context of his broad, far-reaching theory on entitlements. In our own opinion, the important concept of social exclusion, germane to the impoverishment risks and effects intrinsic in forced displacement, as well as Amartya Sen's theory of entitlements, ought to be employed more broadly, as analytical and conceptualising tools by the students of compulsory displacement and resettlement.
12. IUCN 3rd World Conservation Congress, Bangkok, 2004.
13. For those situations, projects must include a distinct Resettlement Action Plan (RAP).
14. This could be done, for example, through accepted forms of co-management of the restricted access areas.
15. The reader may consult, in addition to OP/BP 4.12, the *Involuntary Resettlement Sourcebook*, arguably the most complete technical manual in existence about how to carry out displacement and resettlement consistent with World Bank policy (see World Bank 2004a and 2004b).
16. World Bank OP/BP 6.00, *Bank Financing*, 2004 (Note: OP and BP 6.00 are based *on Eligibility of expenditure in World Bank lending: A new policy framework* (R2004-0026/1), approved by the Board of Executive Directors on 13 April 2004.
17. I served on such a taskforce on financing land a decade ago, in the mid-1990s. Yet, the context was insufficiently favourable then and, despite a sharp battle of arguments, the taskforce's initial recommendations with regard to supporting land financing were derailed at that time.
18. To be covered by projects aiming to institute protected areas.
19. Studies recommending such de-mainstreaming of forced physical displacements were presented at the Durban World Parks Congress (2003) and at the Bangkok IUCN World Conservation Congress (2004), were they triggered intense discussion, as many participants supported the recommendation, but some prominent conservation and park supporters opposed it; see Cernea and Schmidt-Soltau (2003a, 2003b).

References

African Development Bank (AfDB). 2003. 'Involuntary Resettlement Policy'. PSDU, November. Available at http://www.afdb.org/fileadmin/uploads/afdb/Documents/Policy-Documents/10000009-EN-BANK-GROUP-INVOLUNTARY-RESETTLEMENT-POLICY.PDF (accessed 8 August 2008).

Asian Development Bank (ADB). 2003. 'Involuntary Resettlement Operational Manual'. Available at http://www.adb.org/Documents/Manuals/Operations/OMF02_25sep06.pdf (accessed 8 August 2008).

Baviskar, A. 1995. *In the belly of the river: Tribal conflicts over development in the Narmada valley.* New Delhi: Oxford University Press.

Borrini-Feyerabend, G. 2004. 'Governance of protected areas, participation and equity', in Secretariat of the Convention on Biological Diversity, *Biodiversity Issues for Consideration in the Planning, Establishment and Management of Protected Areas, Sites and Networks*, pp. 100–05. CBD Technical Series No. 15, Canada.

Brechin, Steven R., P. R. Wilhusen, C. L. Fortwangler, and P. C. West (eds). 2003. *Contested nature: Promoting international biodiversity conservation with social Justice in the twenty-first century*. New York: SUNY Press.

British Petroleum (BP). 2005. 'Land Acquisition and Resettlement Action Plan (LARAP) for the Tangguh LNG Project'. Available at http://www.adb.org/Documents/Resettlement_Plans/INO/38919-01-PS-RP.pdf (accessed 8 August 2008).

Brockington, D., J. Igoe and K. Schmidt-Soltau. 2005. 'Conservation, human rights and poverty reduction: An ongoing debate'. *Conservation Biology*, 19(4): 250–52.

Brockington, D. and J. Igoe. 2006. *Protected areas, displacement and the power of virtualism: conservation in a neoliberal age* (processed).

Brockington, D. and K. Schmidt-Soltau. 2004. 'The social and environmental impacts of wilderness and development'. *Oryx*, 38:140–42.

Brown, K., D. Pearce, C. Perrings and T. Swanson. 1993. *Economics and the conservation of global biological diversity*. Washington DC: GEF/UNDP/UNEP/World Bank.

Cernea, M. M. 1995. 'Social integration and population displacement: The contribution of social science'. *International Social Science Journal*, 143 (1): 91–112.

———. 1999. 'Development's painful social costs'. Introductory study to S. Parasuraman, *The Development Dilemma*. London: MacMillan.

———. 2000. 'Risks, safeguards and reconstruction: a model for population displacement and resettlement', in M. M. Cernea and Chris McDowell (eds), *Risks and reconstruction: experiences of resettlers and refugees*, pp. 11–76. Washington DC: World Bank.

Cernea, M. M. 2005a. 'The "ripple effect" in social policy and its political content: A debate on social standards in public and private development projects', in M. Likosky (ed.), *Privatizing development: Transnational law, infrastructure and human rights*, pp. 65–101. Martinus Nijhoff: Leiden-Boston.

———. 2005b. 'Concept and method: Applying the IRR model in Africa to resettlement and poverty', in I. Ohta and Y. D. Gebre (eds), *Displacement risks in Africa,* pp. 195–258. Kyoto: Kyoto UP; Melbourne: Transpacific Press.

———. 2005c. '"Restriction of access" is displacement: a broader concept and policy'. *Forced Migration Review*, 23: 48–49.

———. 2008. 'Compensation and investment in resettlement: Theory, Practice, Pitfalls, and needed policy reform', in M. M. Cernea and H. M. Mathur (eds), *Can Compensation prevent impoverishment? Reforming resettlement through investments and benefit-sharing*, pp. 15–82. New Delhi, London: Oxford University Press.

Cernea, M. M. and K. Schmidt-Soltau. 2003a. 'The end of forcible displacement? Conservation must not impoverish people'. *Policy Matters*, 12: 42–51.

———. 2003b. 'National parks and poverty risks: Is population resettlement the solution?'. Paper presented at the 'Vth IUCN World Park Congress', Durban, 8–17 September.

———. 2006. 'Poverty risks and national parks: Policy issues in conservation and resettlement'. *World Development* 34(1): 1808–30.

Chatty, D. and M. Colchester (eds). 2002. *Conservation and mobile indigenous peoples: Displacement, forced settlement and sustainable development.* New York and Oxford: Berghahn Books.

Daly, H. 2008. 'Forced displacement: Allocative externality or unjust redistribution?, in Michael M. Cernea and H. M. Mathur (eds), *Can compensation prevent impoverishment. Reforming resettlement through investments and benefit-sharing*, pp. 121–28. New Delhi, London: Oxford University Press.

Dreze, J., Meera Samson and Satyajit Singh. 1997. *The dam and the nation: Displacement and resettlement in the Narmada valley*. New Delhi: Oxford University Press.

Feeney, P. [1998] 2004. *Accountable aid: Local participation in major projects.* Oxford: Oxfam.

Fernandes, W. 2008. 'Indian forced displacement policy and practice: Is compensation upto its functions?', in M. M. Cernea and H. M. Mathur (eds), *Can compensation prevent impoverishment? Reforming resettlement through investments and benefit-sharing*, pp. 180–207. New Delhi, London: Oxford University Press.

Franks, P. 2004. 'The social and economic costs and benefits of protected areas in East Africa'. Mimeo circulated at the '3rd World Conservation Congress', 17–25 November, Bangkok.

Geisler, C. 2003. 'Your park, my poverty: Using impact assessment to counter the displacement effects of environmental greenlining', in Steven R. Brechin, P. R. Wilhusen, C. L. Fortwangler, and P. C. West (eds), *Contested nature: Promoting international biodiversity conservation with social Justice in the twenty-first century*, pp. 217–30. New York: SUNY Press.

Ghimire, K. B. and M. P. Pimbert (eds). 2000. *Social change and conservation: Environmental politics and impacts of national parks and protected areas*. London: UNRISD and Earthscan.

Kaimovitz, D., A. Faune and R. Mendoza. 2003. 'Your biosphere is my backyard: The story of Bosawas in Nicaragua'. *Policy Matters*, 12: 6–15.

Mahapatra, L. K. 1991. 'Development for whom?'. *Social Action*, 41(3): 271–87.

———. 1994. *Tribal development in India: Myth and reality*. Delhi: Vikas Publishing House.

Mathur, Hari Mohan and David Marsden (eds). 1998. *Development projects and impoverishment risks*. New Delhi: Oxford University Press.

McShane, T. O. 2003. 'Protected areas and poverty: The linkages and how to address them'. *Policy Matters*, 12: 52–53.

Ohta, I. and Y. D. Gebre (eds). 2005. *Displacement risks in Africa*. Melbourne: Trans Pacific Press.

Oliver-Smith, A. 2010. *Defying displacement: Grassroots resistance and the critique of development*. Austin: University of Texas Press.

Pandey, B., A. K. Patro, C. V. Rao, K. K. Padhi and S. Mallick. 1998. *Depriving the underprivileged for development*. Bhubaneswar: ISED.

Parasuraman, S. 1999. *The development dilemma: Displacement in India*, London: MacMillan; The Hague: Institute of Social Studies.

Pearce, D. 2006. 'Local costs and benefits and the sustainability of GEF-assisted projects: An economics overview', in GEF, *The role of local benefits in global environmental programmes*. Washington, DC: Global Environment Facility (GEF) Evaluation Office.

Pearce, F. 2005. 'Humans losing out to Africa's big game industry'. *New Scientist*, 2495: 21.

Roy-Burman, B. K. 1968. *Social processes in the industrialization of Rourkela*. New Delhi: Census of India.

Rudd, K. E. 2004. *The impoverishment of the Ugandan Batwa associated with Biwindi Impenetrable National Park*. Middlebury, VT: Middlebury College.

Scherl, L. M., A. Wilson, R. Wild, J. Blockhus, P. Franks, J. McNeeley and T. McShane. 2004. *Can protected areas contribute to poverty reduction? Opportunities and limitations*. Gland (Switzerland) and Cambridge (UK): International Union for Conservation of Nature.

Schmidt-Soltau, K. 2003. 'Conservation-related resettlement in central Africa: Environmental and social risks'. *Development and Change,* 34: 525–51.

Schmidt-Soltau, K. 2005. 'The environmental risks of conservation-related displacements in central Africa', in I. Ohta and Y. D. Gebre (eds), *Displacement risks in Africa,* pp. 282–311. Melbourne: Trans Pacific Press.

Sen, Amartya. 2000. 'Social exclusion: Concept, application, scrutiny'. Social Development Paper No. 1. Manila: Asian Development Bank.

Todd, D., L. Risby, M. Cernea and J. Soussan. 2006. *The role of local benefits in global environmental programmes.* Study carried out by the GEF office of Monitoring and Evaluation (in print).

Turton, D. 1987. 'The Mursi and national park development in the Lower Omo valley', in D. Anderson and R. Grove (eds), *Conservation in Africa: Peoples, policies and practice,* pp. 169–86. Cambridge: Cambridge University Press.

———. 2002. 'The Mursi and the elephant question', in D. Chatty and M. Colchester (eds), *Conservation and mobile indigenous peoples: Displacement, forced settlement and sustainable development* (Studies in forced migrations, Vol. 10), pp. 97–118. New York and Oxford: Berghahn Books.

———. 2010. 'In the shadow of Leviathan: river basin development in Ethiopia's lower Omo Valley'. Paper prepared for the Metropolis XV — Conference on Justice and Migration, Section on: Economic and Social Justice, Risks and Ethics in Development-Caused Population Displacement and Resettlement. The Hague, Netherlands.

van Wicklin III, W. 2005. *Restriction of access in parks and protected areas: A review of World Bank assisted projects* (processed). Washington, DC: QUACU, World Bank.

Wells, Michael, Katrina Brandon and Lee Jay Hannah. 1992. *People and parks: Linking protected area management with local communities.* Washington, DC: World Bank: US Agency for International Development.

World Bank. 1980. 'OMS 2.33 (Social issues in involuntary resettlement in Bank-financed projects)'.

———. 2001. 'Operational Policy 4.12 (Involuntary resettlement)'.

———. 2004a. 'OP/BP 6.00 (Bank financing)'.

———. 2004b. *Involuntary resettlement sourcebook: Planning and implementation in development projects.* Washington, DC: World Bank.

4

Involuntary resettlement policy and transport projects

Gordon Appleby

Development projects are undertaken with the general welfare of the population in mind, but, nonetheless, they raise the possibility of adverse impacts on specific segments of the population. Almost any large infrastructure project, be it dams, roads, urban sanitation, requires land, and, therefore, has direct impact on local populations whose land is taken for the general good. The amount of land required will vary with the project, but the fact remains that, almost invariably, land is required. Because this simple fact has not always been recognised and dealt with in project planning, international development agencies have adopted safeguard policies with the express intention of avoiding impoverishment of any group of people for the general good. The logic here is clear: further impoverishing the poor and vulnerable segments of society, and thus exacerbating existing social and economic inequalities, contradicts the basic notion of economic development — improvement in the condition of life of the population.

The World Bank, for example, adopted its policy on involuntary resettlement in 1980 to ensure equitable treatment of project-affected people (PAPs) in development investments. The policy was based largely on the then experience with high dams and reservoirs that often entail extensive regional dislocation. An institution's policy, however, is applicable to all sectors, and such is the case with the Bank policy on involuntary resettlement (Operational Policy 4.12). Developed on the basis of experience with high dams, the policy applies uniformly to any project that requires land, be it rural access roads, urban renewal, or a power plant. Practitioners in these other areas often argue either that the policy is irrelevant to their activities, or that the policy is heavy-handed in that it involves much more work than is necessary.

While there is force to the argument that uniform and complete application of a central policy in different sectors may result in 'overkill,' it is also true that the negative impacts of many investments are not always as few or as minor as some practitioners would argue. In fact, in the transport sector, involuntary resettlement is almost always an issue in infrastructure projects. Therefore, the key question is not whether the policy applies, but how it should be tailored to the sectoral context. The capacity — of the donor agency as well as the national agency — to effectively implement and monitor resettlement operations also needs to be assessed.

To better understand this situation, this paper examines the development of the policy on involuntary resettlement and its application in the transport sector, with particular emphasis on roads. The objective is to assess the relevance of the policy to transport projects, and assess what next steps may be needed.

Involuntary resettlement policy, its development and its objectives

The first environmental and social safeguard policy adopted by the World Bank was the Operational Manual Statement (OMS) 2.33, entitled 'Social issues associated with involuntary resettlement in Bank-financed projects', which came into effect in 1980. The OMS was largely, if not exclusively, based on worldwide experience with high dams. The dams, while necessary for hydroelectricity to power national development, gave rise, as it was then increasingly recognised, to serious, deleterious impacts on the local population (Scudder 1968, 1973 and 1975; also see Quintaro 1997 and Scudder 2005). Thus, the OMS attempted to reconcile two conflicting issues: the necessity for resettling people in order to execute projects that contribute to the general welfare; and the fact that resettlement not only gives rise to special social and technical problems, but may also be politically sensitive. The OMS enumerated the problems that could arise from resettlement, and specified that more systematic procedures were needed to deal with resettlement under Bank-financed projects. The fundamental premises of the OMS were that resettlement be avoided wherever possible and minimised whenever unavoidable, and that any necessary resettlement be carried out in accordance with a well-prepared resettlement plan.

The policies and procedures for involuntary resettlement in OMS 2.23 were re-specified when the policy was reissued in June 1990, as Operational Directive (OD) 4.30. The OD again stated that the objective of the Bank resettlement policy was to ensure that the population displaced by a project received benefits from it. The policy further specified that resettlement should constitute an integral part of project design and must take into account a number of policy considerations, including:

(i) Avoid wherever possible and minimise resettlement where unavoidable.
(ii) Develop resettlement plans where resettlement is unavoidable, and ensure that such plans provide compensation for losses at full replacement cost, as well as assistance and support with the move.
(iii) Ensure community participation in planning and implementing resettlement.
(iv) Integrate resettlers socially and economically into the host communities.
(v) Provide land, housing, infrastructure and other compensation to adversely affected population.
(vi) Define economic restoration measures, to the extent that livelihoods are affected.[1]

Other provisions in the revised policy underscored the importance of grievance resolution, as well as a detailed timeline, budget and monitoring system.

Although the 1990 revision of the OMS as Operational Directive (OD) 4.30 continued the emphasis on issues arising out of dam construction, the 2002 revision of OD 4.30 into Operational Policy 4.12 incorporated a more explicit consideration of experience with resettlement in a broader range of sectors (World Bank 2004). The policy reiterated the Bank objectives of avoiding, or at least minimising, resettlement and of providing all assistance necessary according to the type and extent of impact.

The policy also made a number of clarifications to the OD with regard to the impacts covered, eligibility for benefits, required measures, and assistance to borrowers. For example, on the required measures, the policy requires that the borrower prepare a resettlement plan that covers (i) informed participation and meaningful consultation of affected people, and (ii) provision of assistance, residential housing and agricultural sites. The policy indicates the preference for land-based resettlement strategies for displaced persons whose livelihoods are land-based.[2]

OP 4.12 also created three new instruments in response to newly identified needs. The Resettlement Policy Framework establishes the overall principles for involuntary resettlement when the project is not able to define its social impacts precisely. The Abbreviated Resettlement Action Plan deals with those cases where nobody has to relocate physically and where no land-take constitutes more than 10 per cent of any PAP's total holding (OP 4.12, para 17[a]; OP 4.12, annex A, fn. 6), an explicit recognition of the possibility that some road projects might in fact engender relatively minor impacts on local populations. The Process Framework was added to deal with environmental investments, where local populations might not be physically relocated but might lose access to natural resources if a national park or reserve area was declared.

Despite the rephrasing, clarifications, and creation of new instruments, over the almost 30 years of the policy, the thrust of the involuntary resettlement policy has remained the same: minimise the need for land-taking; when involuntary resettlement in its broad sense of changed land use is unavoidable, ensure that plans are developed to restore people's standards of living, including residences, businesses and livelihoods, to at least the status quo ante; and, preferably, improve the socioeconomic situation of the people affected by putting resettlement in a development context so that they too benefit from the investment.[3]

Involuntary resettlement policy in the transport sector

Although large hydroelectric projects vary tremendously in the extent of their adverse environmental and related social impacts, the variation in the type and severity of impact is at least as large, and probably even greater, in other sectors.[4] This has certainly been the argument in the transport sector, and is the reason why OP 4.12 developed the notion of an Abbreviated Resettlement Action Plan. The argument is essentially that road projects, unlike dams and reservoirs, often take only small strips of land, and therefore do not imperil the lives or livelihoods of those affected by the land-take. The question is whether this position, so seemingly obvious in the abstract, actually describes project actions on the ground.

The critical point for determining whether or not a policy applies to a project is the initial project screening, which is when an assessment is made about probable impact. The purpose of the initial screening is precisely to identify which policies are triggered, and to determine the severity of the impact, so that appropriate remedial measures can be defined during the project development phase. If, for whatever reason, the initial screening misses the possibility of a policy being triggered, planning measures to redress that outcome can be delayed until well into implementation. At that point, implementation of remedial measures may well be much more difficult, time-consuming and expensive.[5]

In the transport sector, determination of whether a policy, such as that for involuntary resettlement, is invoked under a project, often depends on words. Much confusion over the level of environmental category, and the type of environmental and social work required, stems from the lack of clear definition of the works to be undertaken. In road projects, for example, words like maintenance, routine maintenance, upgrading, rehabilitation, delayed rehabilitation, and improvement (or minor improvement) are often used interchangeably, without clear specification of exactly what works are being referred to. The argument typically runs like this: 'X' is simply a road rehabilitation project; it will follow the existing alignment; there will be no land-take and, therefore, there is no involuntary resettlement involved.

The definition of 'rehabilitation,' however, can be, and often is, quite flexible. At a minimum, it will involve routine works, such as resurfacing, line-marking and bridge maintenance or repainting. There might also be the need to improve drainage, slopes or embankments, or to improve the soil substructure in order to strengthen the pavement. In other cases, additional works may be glossed as rehabilitation: slight widening of a lane or shoulder, improvement of curves, or addition of drainage. In still other cases, the road surface might be upgraded — widened and the surface changed from earth to gravel or from gravel to pavement. In practice, 'rehabilitation' has in the past glossed almost every improvement imaginable, with the exception of new construction, and even that exception is not complete.[6]

The World Bank uses a five-fold categorisation of road rehabilitation in order to clarify the nature of the works. (The extent of the works is a separate matter.) This scheme distinguishes maintenance, rehabilitation, improvements, upgrading and new construction. The defining criteria for each level of works are as follows (Quintero 1994: 2–3):

1. Maintenance
   Routine or periodic works to maintain the road in working condition: All of the work is done on the existing platform
   - Routine works, patching potholes, clearing drains
   - Periodic works such as resurfacing, line marking, bridge maintenance
2. Rehabilitation
   Bringing existing deteriorated roads to previous/original conditions: All of the work is done on the existing platform/right of way. No additional land acquisition is needed.
   - Improving drainage/slopes/embankments/other structures
   - Strengthening pavements
   - Complete resurfacing
   - Recuperating civil works
3. Improvements
   Improving road specifications: Most of the work is done on the existing platform or right of way; additional land acquisition may be needed
   - Widening lanes and shoulders
   - Adding extra lanes in steep inclines
   - Improving curves
   - Strengthening bridges
4. Upgrading
   Changing road category (seasonal to all-weather, secondary to primary, or from gravel to paved): Land acquisition is needed in most cases
   - Adding new lanes (2 to 4; 4 to 6)
   - Changing road surface (e.g., from gravel to paved)
   - Widening intersections
5. New Construction
   New projects built on a new alignment: Major land acquisition is needed.
   - New roads
   - By-passes
   - Realignments (change in route)

The advantage of a more detailed categorisation of works is that it specifies the likely extent of land acquisition and, therefore, the probability that the involuntary resettlement policy will be triggered. If the works remain entirely within the existing platform or right of way, no land acquisition should be required, and there is no need to invoke the involuntary resettlement policy. If some of the work is done outside the existing platform, additional land may, or will be, required, and policy on involuntary resettlement will be triggered. For example, adding a passing lane on a steep incline would require additional land, and trigger the policy. Similarly, though less obviously perhaps, improving the slope of the road on a hill might require a deeper cut into the hillside, and, therefore, require more land. Certainly, adding new lanes and widening intersections would entail a larger road surface area, with the implication of land acquisition and policy invocation.

Even the more detailed categorisation of rehabilitation works is, however, subject to interpretation. The critical phrase is 'the existing platform or right of way (ROW).' It is often the case that the legal right of way is much larger than the effective right of way. The legal right of way is the width ceded to the Ministry of Transport or Public Works as per the laws of the country. In the law, the ROW is typically defined as so many metres on either side of the centreline of the road. The number of metres, in turn, is usually defined by the category of road: national roads are wider than provincial roads, provincial roads are wider than district roads, and district roads are wider than rural access roads.

In fact, the effective ROW is usually smaller than the legal demarcation. The effective ROW is the width that is clear of all occupation and, therefore, dedicated to road use only. For example, a rural road with a legal definition of 30 metres on either side of the centreline might in fact be occupied to within five or six metres of the centreline. The law declares that the area from the centreline will be clear for 30 metres, but the law is not enforced, and many people may not even be aware of the legal specifications.[7] Such instances — and they are numerous — can lead to different interpretations of the actual situation, with government agents arguing that the (legal) ROW remains unchanged, so there is no involuntary resettlement, while donor agency staff argue that the (effective) ROW must be widened, so there will be land clearance and impact on livelihoods, which triggers the policy on involuntary resettlement.

Location is another factor that must be taken into consideration in determining whether or not the policy on involuntary resettlement applies. There are major differences between rural and urban projects, and between rural and urban areas within the same project. Road maintenance is the category with the least presumed impact. In rural areas with low population density or dispersed population, and with little or no roadside economic activity, this may indeed be the case. But in urban areas with high population densities and vibrant roadside economic activity, the situation can be completely different. In the latter, even simple resurfacing of the existing road can disrupt businesses along the road and, therefore, require, at a minimum, temporary relocation of the vendors. Permanent relocation may also be required. If this is true for the simplest case of road projects, it is even more true for the other categories with progressively more serious social impacts — rehabilitation, improvement, upgrading and, of course, new construction. The following section will provide some illustrative examples of such cases and of good practice.

Good practice with involuntary resettlement in the transport sector

Maintenance and rehabilitation

From the perspective of involuntary resettlement, the crucial aspect that road maintenance and road rehabilitation share is that both take place within the existing right of way. The presumption is that, because the land involved already belongs to the highway department or municipality, there will be no, or few, social impacts.

Maintenance

Maintenance means routine or periodic works to maintain the road in working condition. All of the work is done on the existing platform or right of way. The expectation is, as has been mentioned, that there will be no involuntary resettlement required.

That expectation is often too sanguine. Even busy roads, especially in cities and commercial towns, can suffer encroachment within the right of way and even within the roadway. Vendors commonly install their tables and kiosks along heavily trafficked roads in order to take advantage of the pedestrian and vehicular traffic. Simple routine maintenance work may require the relocation of these vendors, at least during the period when the works are underway. Whether or not the vendors are allowed to return to their original locations is a separate question. If so, the dislocation is temporary, and an alternative vending locale is needed only for the short term. If not, the dislocation is permanent, and a new vending locale must be identified and prepared so that the vendors can continue their business successfully.

The intricacy of these questions can be illustrated with the example of the urban transport program in Lagos, Nigeria, being undertaken by the Lagos Metropolitan Transport Authority (LAMATA), which includes not only roads but also rail and water transport. The road program involves a large amount of routine maintenance, as well as rehabilitation, and, in some instances, road improvement (e.g. widening and repaving roads between major arteries in order to facilitate access). Even with the simplest operation, i.e., road maintenance, there are issues of whether relocation should be temporary or permanent. Routine road maintenance in urban areas often involves, as it does in the LAMATA program, clearing the drains along each side of the shoulder of the road. In many places, particularly at intersections and traffic circles, as well as near market areas, vendors have built their stalls on or just behind street drains. While the vendors definitely have to vacate these premises when the drains are to be cleaned, the question is whether to allow them to return to their original locations, since the amount of debris that falls into the drains tends to correlate with the extent of occupation above the drains. Where vendors can be allowed to return, temporary selling locales must be provided nearby. But where vendors must be relocated permanently, new selling locales must be provided so they can continue their businesses.

The LAMATA conundrum is not unique. The need for new selling locations arises in many urban projects. To take another example, an identical situation arose in the Dar es Salaam Community Infrastructure Upgrading Project (CIUP), and for the very same reasons. The neighbourhood streets to be paved had drains on either side of the road. Since the sides of many of these roads were occupied by vendors, the question arose whether the sellers could be allowed to continue to sell from their locations. In this instance also, the basic decision was to allow continued occupation wherever possible, recognising that in some locations, particularly where the width of the street was narrowed in order to avoid condemning residential (or business) property, continued occupation at the edge of the road would not be possible for reasons of public safety, as well as for reasons of maintaining the drains.

Rehabilitation

Rehabilitation brings deteriorated roads to their previous, original condition. Resurfacing is always involved; and there may be strengthening of the substructure, improvement in drainage and embankments, as well as restoration of civil works such as bridges. Importantly, again, all of the work is done on the existing platform, that is, within the existing right of way. Therefore, the expectation is that no additional land acquisition is needed.

There can, nonetheless, be a wide interpretation of the works permitted even in the strict sense of repairing existing roads. In the World Bank typology of road projects, rehabilitation is limited to the repair of existing roads, with no additional land-take. From a legal point of view, the right of way is whatever is specified in the law. From this vantage point, since the land already belongs to the government, a number of improvements are possible. The fact is, however, that much of the unenforced 'legal' right of way may be occupied. For that reason, it is almost always necessary to census the type and extent of such occupation. Table 4.1 provides a template for recording resettlement impacts by road segment.

Table 4.1: Template matrix for recording land occupation

	Road Segment 1	*Road Segment 2*	*Total*
Permanent structures Houses			
Permanent structures Businesses			
Other structures (straw buildings, huts)			
Other infrastructure Wood fence			
Other infrastructure Bamboo fence			
Agricultural fields (note crop)			
Market stalls			
Street vendors			
Other			
Total			

Early assessment of land occupation is necessary to avoid difficult compensation issues later. To take one example from a country in West Africa, road maintenance can involve widening the roadway from 5 or 7 to 10 or 20 metres. In the government perspective, the additional land-take is simply not recognised because there is little distinction made between road maintenance and road upgrading. But the fact was that widening the road, under the guise of 'rehabilitation,' meant acquiring numerous small strips of land, as well as relocating several residences and businesses. Usually this lack of distinction goes unnoticed. But, in those instances where road widening is undertaken immediately prior to (and possibly in anticipation of), donor participation in road upgrading, there can be a serious issue. Such instances create a 'legacy' issue for international donors. For, strictly speaking, the losses under the immediately prior project — not only land but other assets (e.g., crops, trees of economic value, vendor stalls, and even residences) — must be compensated, and there is commonly no record available of the status quo ante, so there is little or no basis for determining individual compensation once the road has been 'rehabilitated'.

Road rehabilitation in post-conflict situations

As has already been discussed, it is important to define the levels of 'rehabilitation' closely so that there is no misunderstanding of the nature of the works and the likelihood of involuntary resettlement. Even once that is done, however, it is still important to distinguish between rehabilitation under normal circumstances and rehabilitation in post-conflict situations. For, if road rehabilitation is an ambiguous term in projects in stable countries, it is a misnomer in post-conflict situations. Depending on the duration of the civil strife, roads may have merely deteriorated or may have completely disappeared. It is unfortunately common in civil war for one side or the other to blow up bridges. This not only means that it takes longer to go from one place to another; it also means some routes essentially devolve into bicycle tracks. Rehabilitating roads under these circumstances effectively means new road design.

Another consideration is that emergency regulations allow project approval without the usual safeguard procedures in place. The Environmental Impact Assessment, the Environmental Management Plan, and the Resettlement Action Plan may all be deferred in order to bring the project on line. In theory, no works should be done until the safeguard documents have been prepared for implementation. This stricture is not always observed in practice.

These principles can be illustrated with the experience of a roads project in Mozambique. At the time of project approval, it was believed that the maintenance or rehabilitation of the road segments would not entail land acquisition or resettlement, and the project was approved without a resettlement plan or even a policy framework.[8] Subsequently, three years into the project, it was discovered that the project had taken over 1,300 land parcels within or near the road reserve, including several houses and informal businesses (mostly in Maputo City) and areas for borrow pits, construction camps and drainage. (Table 4.2 gives the extent of property acquisition by road segment.)

This property acquisition followed government procedures, as interpreted by the Autoridade Nacional de Estradas (ANE), without donor knowledge or approval until late 2005.

In order to bring the project into social safeguards compliance, a mission was fielded in December 2005 to undertake a resettlement audit to determine the extent and nature of land acquisition and resettlement under the project. Most acquisition concerned the taking of strips of cropland at the edge of the road reserve. To acquire these areas, the ANE regional representative depended on the construction companies to inventory land and assets to be acquired, value the losses according to the provincial ministry to agricultural unit price lists, negotiate indemnification with the owners, and make payments, which were subsequently reimbursed by ANE.

This procedure raised three considerations: (i) the completeness of the asset inventory, (ii) the adequacy of valuation rates and procedures, as well as of other assistance, and (iii) conflict of interest in delegating responsibility for the asset inventory and valuation, as well as compensation, from ANE to the construction companies. The mission, therefore, recommended that ANE, in consultation and collaboration with the responsible provincial and land officials, take full and complete responsibility for all land acquisition, compensation valuation, negotiation, and payment, as well as for dispute resolution. It was also recommended that ANE seek some way to offset any hardships caused by providing some benefits to the communities as a whole, rather than to individual families, on the grounds that individual PAPs could no longer be identified with certitude (Appleby 2005a).[9]

Table 4.2: Extent and nature of land-taking under Mozambique Roads III, by road segment

	Segment length	*Kilometers Rebuilt*	*Type of Works*	*Number of Houses (People Affected)*	*Number of Businesses*	*Number of Plots of Crops and/ or Trees*	*State of Works*
Maputo – Marracuene	27	21	Maintenance (Rehabilitation)	1,2912 (28 people) (potentially 10 other houses)	6 + 6 boundary walls (potentially 10 businesses, 80+ market vendors and 66 boundary walls more)	—	Ongoing
Marracuene – Manica	48		Maintenance	0	0	0	Ongoing
Manica – Incoluane	51	36	Maintenance	0	0	200	Completed
Incoluane – Zandamela	164	71	Maintenance	0	0	12 families	Completed
Zandamela – Maxixie	177		Maintenance	2	0	c. 750	Ongoing
Maxixe – Junction 520 (Vilanculos)	126		Rehabilitation	0	0	241	Ongoing
Junction 520 – Junction 212	98		Rehabilitation	0	0	78	Ongoing
[Junction 212 – Muxungue]	122	0	Rehabilitation				To be done under Phase 2
Muxungue – Inchope	153	76	Rehabilitation	0	[Potentially (Inchope), 16 authorized and 77 unauthorized vendors]	5–10 fields (strips)	Ongoing
Totals	966			4 houses [Potential total: 14 houses]	6 businesses, 6 boundary walls (Potential total: 16 businesses, 72 boundary walls, and some 175 market vendors)	1,291	

For similar reasons, a review of a road project in Congo Brazaville noted that,

> project activities require closer specification so that the extent of impact can be assessed by activity. To take one example, the term "road rehabilitation" is not defined. This is important in post-conflict countries, for simple maintenance (i.e., repaving) is seldom enough; many roads must be rebuilt, with new substructure, new bridges and other infrastructure (e.g., culverts, which may direct run-off onto farmers' fields). These works can require significant amounts of land. Second, the legal definition of a rural road, within the national classification of roads, must be provided because this defines the legal limit on the right-of-way for rural roads. Further, a notion of the existing ROW for these roads (i.e., how much land might be affected along any road segment) is also needed. And, if the roads run through towns, will the ROW be narrowed to minimize resettlement or maintained; and if the latter, what are the implications for land acquisition (partial or total) and involuntary resettlement? … (Also) there is no discussion of ancillary land acquisition, i.e., quarries, borrow pits, construction camps or the like. These can represent a significant factor in any sub-project and so must be considered as fully as possible. If only existing quarries will be used, that needs to be stated. If borrow pits will be taken only temporarily, the restoration of the area and the process for returning the land to its original owner/users must be detailed. (Appleby 2006: 2)

Improvement, upgrade and new construction

Road improvement, upgrade and new construction all require land additional to what is available in the existing alignment. The difference between these three categories of road works lies in the extent of the works and, therefore, the probability of significant land acquisition. Road improvement entails slight modifications of the existing alignment and relatively little additional land; road upgrading involves more extensive works and, therefore, more additional land and involuntary resettlement; and, finally, new works require land acquisition along the entire length of the road.

Somewhat surprisingly, perhaps, new road construction is relatively uncommon, and mostly concerns construction of rural access roads or road development in new urbanisations. Major road development, by contrast, more often entails upgrading existing alignments: adding lanes, improving curves and correcting slopes. That major arteries are upgraded rather than built anew is, in fact, expected in that roads usually already connect important centres. These roads are upgraded, sometimes with significant changes in alignment and other improvements, rather than laid out afresh, in order to reduce costs and avoid extensive land acquisition and relocation.

New rural road construction

Burkina Faso provides a relatively good example of new rural road construction. The Direction Nationale de Routes has a special department, the Department de Pistes Rurales (DPR), for rural roads. DPR receives applications for new access roads from local authorities. Each application is verified in the field: a DPR agent runs the prospective track on a motorcycle, recording the alignment with a global positioning system (GPS). Furthermore, DPR commissions a preliminary design study, including alternative alignments. The department then reviews the applications and design material received every year, and prioritises a list of new rural roads that will be built, depending upon the budgetary envelope that becomes available from the government or from international donor agencies.

The review process could benefit from an integrated assessment of the rural roads in the district under consideration. The present review process, for example, does not consider whether the segment of access road proposed by local officials connects at either end with existing rural roads, or whether the new access road and any existing roads to which it connects have reasonable access to a trunk road. In other words, consideration of the proposals on their own merits constitutes a rather piecemeal approach to roads development. A more holistic perspective would help ensure that the proposed alignment is not only verified, and its feasibility examined, but also that the proposed new road provides a strategic piece of the overall, integral road system in the local area.

The review process aside, DPR has a strong set of rules for the design of new access roads. First, the new road will generally follow whatever tracks or bicycle paths now exist. Within that constraint, the alignment may vary up to 20 metres on either side of the track, in order to avoid structures and to eliminate costly works such as bridges or major earthworks. Road alignment specifically avoids habited areas. Second, the alignment is discussed with local officials to avoid any sensitive areas, such as local shrines and sacred trees. Third, the right of way for these roads is generally limited to 10 metres, including the shoulders and drainage. These basic design rules serve to limit the extent of land acquisition to an unavoidable minimum, and represent good practice in new rural road design.

New urban road construction

New road construction in urban areas is more problematic than that in rural areas, for the simple reason that population densities are much higher, and places for the poor to relocate are fewer and much smaller.

Several urban roads projects provide good examples of applying resettlement policies in urban initiatives. The Mauritania urban upgrading project undertook construction of neighborhood roads in new urbanisations around Nouakchott. The basic aim of the project, in a practical sense, were to make it possible for emergency equipment such as fire trucks to be able to reach residential areas when need be. Such a basic aim requires a road of at least a minimum width and straightness. But the project minimised land acquisition by following the existing alignment to the extent possible. Where land acquisition and relocation was unavoidable, the project developed a new urbanisation immediately adjacent to the existing one so that relocatees could maintain their social relationships and did not incur significantly higher transport costs, a common issue in urban relocation.

The Tanzania Community Infrastructure Upgrading Program (CIUP) in Dar es Salaam provides another example of sympathetic urban road construction. CIUP drew key lessons from earlier projects that underscored the need for an extensive consultation process. The project designers recognised that Tanzania had gained valuable experience with resettlement in the course of other projects. For example, the lessons learnt from the Morogro road project included the following three points:

> (1) A top-down approach without much consideration for the people affected by the project is likely to result in public resistance instead of cooperation (2) Community consultation may be time consuming but would result in less time needed for legal procedures, complaints and grievances (3) Tenants of affected properties were not considered for compensation or moving assistance (GoT 2004: 5).

The planners also drew the following lessons from the Songosongo gas pipeline project:

(1) Project-affected people find it easier to accept negative consequences of a project if they understand the objectives and the benefits for the community as a whole.
(2) Active involvement in the entire planning process of the project affected people and consultation with the community at large is indispensable.
(3) Existing conditions, such as customary (land) rights, should be respected as much as possible (ibid.: 6).

The planners also noted: 'The Hanna Nassif community infrastructure upgrading project is a good example of how loss of assets and resettlement can be minimised or even completely avoided and compensation costs reduced. Experience in Hanna Nassif shows that this can be achieved by: Intensive community consultation; Negotiation with affected people (only house owners were considered, no tenants); and Application of flexible planning standards' (ibid.: 6).

On the engineering side, the planning team adopted a flexible approach (ibid.: 2–3) that took into account possible social impacts. The principle of minimisation resettlement was pursued by the following steps:

(i) To minimise the extent of involuntary resettlement specific technical options...(were) taken into consideration. Much of the upgrading activity...focus(ed) on footpath, roads and storm water drainage improvements. In order to reduce the number of potentially affected houses in certain cases the CIUP planners/engineers, in close consultation with the communities, opted to adopt levels of service that are technically and financially appropriate (basic and intermediate service levels).
(ii) Rather than opting for rigid technical standards with respect to ROW and more or less straight geometry of new roads the engineers designed meandering road and drainage structures to accommodate existing structures as much as possible, reduced carriageways and rights of way (ROW) to the minimum feasible width (to maintain unhindered traffic flow), and in some sections limited vehicular flow to one-way traffic.
(iii) Partial demolition of built structures has been taken into account. The potentially affected structures have been carefully surveyed by the engineers to determine whether the

affected building would remain structurally integral and safe from collapse after demolition of part of the structure. In case such examination gave doubtful or negative results, full demolition has been agreed.

(iv) Selecting location for new waste collection structures in uninhabited spaces where surrounding impacts would be minimised, in contrast to other reflections that would rather place the waste collection systems in closer vicinity to where (domestic) waste is generated and people would have short distances only to deliver and store their garbage properly.

(v) In order (to) warrant (or signify) meaningful planning (e.g. to ensure safe emergency evacuation lines and trafficable road conditions) each single location was carefully screened against the above principle versus preparing for a functional road and drainage network.

(vi) The planning and final design solutions … have been done in close cooperation with the environmental team who assessed the EIA documented separately as the EMP for CIUP.

In addition to careful adjustment of the technical requirements of the investment in terms of engineering, the CIUP instituted an extensive, and exemplary, consultation process at all levels in the neighbourhoods:

> The community actively participated in efforts to minimise resettlement. In the sub-ward meetings headed by the chairman residents raised numerous concerns that were duly taken into account by the CIUP planners. The result of this consultation was further reduction of potential project-induced impacts. For example, each potentially affected plot has been scrutinized in a joint survey with Community representatives (Community Planning Teams) and PAPs for possible solutions (e.g. options for accommodating the re-arrangement/construction of a new room or house). The technical expert gave, as applicable, advice on how such re-arrangements could be carried out without affecting the integrity and stability of the old structures. As a result, in most cases where only single or annexed rooms, part of rooms, latrines, verandas, kiosks and fences were … to be demolished, solutions that reduced the impact to (as) a short period (as) …possible (were devised). In fact, in most cases if the owners would start building/rebuilding the affected structures by the time of receipt of compensation payment, no temporary resettlement, loss of business or hardship would be encountered… there is a sufficient time between compensation payment and beginning of the upgrading

construction activities to allow for all newly re-arranged/constructed residential rooms or new business annexes (e.g. kiosks) to be ready for occupation before demolition starts. This would result only in minor impacts on the day-to-day life or income situation of the affected household.

No less importantly, CIUP instituted an innovative resettlement training program for ward leaders, who were responsible for resettlement implementation at the local level. This training addressed a common obstacle in resettlement operations: project officers may be aware of the policy stipulations, but local-level officials, whether or not they are sympathetic to the policy, are often unaware of it and, therefore, have to invent their own procedures and policies. To avoid this situation, CIUP organised several workshops for over 300 ward leaders. The workshops presented the project resettlement policy principles, and then focused on eligibility criteria and the compensation packages for each type of impact. The workshops provided project officers the opportunity to present the policy principles, and then explain how those principles defined eligibility criteria and compensation packages. For the participants, the workshops afforded an opportunity to request clarification on definitions, eligibility criteria, compensation packages, and, perhaps most usefully, to pose actually occurring situations and ask how these specific instances would be handled under the project policy.

Summing-up

The World Bank adopted its policy on involuntary resettlement in 1980 in response to serious negative impacts on local populations affected by investments in high dams. Indeed, the policy was developed largely on the basis of experiences with high dams and reservoirs, which typically have the most serious and widespread impacts. Since a central policy would be applicable to all sectors, development practitioners in the Bank began to argue that the strictures of the involuntary resettlement policy were inappropriate in their areas of activity. Transport engineers, in particular, argued strongly for accommodation to their particular situation, which commonly engenders only minor impacts. The 2002 revision of resettlement policy developed a new instrument to take care of such cases, the Abbreviated Resettlement Plan.

Close examination of the actual impacts of transport projects, specifically roads, on local population, documents that roads may have no effects as major as those of dams or urban renewal, but they still have significant impacts that must be redressed if poor and vulnerable populations are not to suffer deleterious consequences because of development projects. Further, despite complaints to the contrary, application of the central policy is in fact quite flexible. Resettlement in road projects is, for example, assessed in terms of the nature of the construction works, and compensation packages are defined in terms of the impacts expected.

Effective implementation depends, first, on a viable Social and Environmental Unit within the agency with access to senior management and their support in coordinating social and environmental actions throughout the organisation. As several of the examples discussed in this chapter underscore, identification and assessment of potential social impacts need to be an integral part of the project cycle, commencing early in the planning process in order to enable a full consideration of impacts and alternatives, and to avoid later delays and complications.

Community involvement is another essential element of road development programmes. Procedures and skills to inform the public and interested parties about road proposals, as well as consultation and participation of the community in the decision-making process, are crucial to the overall success of the programme, for, as is now increasingly recognised, non-technical factors, that is to say non-engineering factors, are as fundamental an aspect of road development as are the engineering and economics of the project. And, as the Tanzania example demonstrates, training is required not only for road agency staff, consultants, and contractors responsible for assessment of impacts and mitigation measures, but also for local officials, who, in the last analysis, are the people basically responsible for implementing the resettlement operation and resolving any difficulties that arise.

All of these elements — a clear and consistent policy, applications tailored to the specific investment and context, social and environmental assessment capacity in the implementing agency, as well as integral community involvement and local-level training — contribute to the success of resettlement operations in road projects, just as in other sectors. As Ian Johnson, a former vice-president for Environmentally and Socially Sustainable Development in the World Bank, wrote in his foreword to the *Involuntary Resettlement Sourcebook*,

> Involuntary resettlement is an essential and historically underappreciated aspect of development. Unsuccessful resettlement has often been the result of both a lack of sensitivity to this issue and a deficiency of operational guidance on the "how to" of resettlement design and implementation. Today, many governments are convinced of the need to adopt a 'resettlement-with-development' approach, and provide affected people with benefits from the projects that displace them (World Bank 2004: xix).

And, it can be added, today by drawing on their own experiences, many countries are now beginning to fill the void of 'how to' design and implement resettlement operations, to the advantage of not only their projects but also, and even more importantly, to that of the project-affected people, who deserve to benefit from the project, as they make way for it.

Notes

1. http://www.ifc.org/ifcext/enviro.nsf/AttachmentsByTitle/pol-Resettlement/SFILE/OD430_InvoluntaryResettlement.pdf (accessed 27 April 2010).
2. Ibid.
3. The term 'involuntary resettlement' sometimes causes confusion in that it is commonly interpreted to mean physical relocation. In fact, the term, as used in international parlance, applies to any loss of land or land-use rights, whether or not physical relocation of residences or businesses is required. It is, therefore, useful to define involuntary resettlement as any instance where the national law of eminent domain can be invoked (whether or not it is in the event).
4. 'For example, the 500-MW Pehuenche Hydroelectric Project in Chile flooded only about 400 hectares of land (with minimal damage to forest or wildlife resources), and has had no water quality problems. By contrast, the Brokopondo Dam in Suriname inundated about 160,000 hectares of biologically valuable tropical rainforest, and is known for serious water quality and aquatic weed problems, while providing relatively little electric generating capacity (only 30 MW)' (Quintero 1997).
5. There are several outcomes possible in those cases where involuntary resettlement has not been recognised as a probable impact during project design. If the oversight is caught before construction begins, it may be possible to reschedule construction so that stretches of the road where

there is no land-take are rehabilitated before those with land-take are started. The situation becomes more complex if the oversight is recognised only after construction has begun. In that instance, the records of property acquisition are apt to be incomplete. If a property inventory is attempted after the fact without good records, the number of project-affected people can increase appreciably, and, there is often no means to determine which claims are valid and which are not. For example, it is impossible to verify what, if any, assets (e.g. fences, trees, crops) were on the land after it has been bulldozed. In such situations, where individual compensation is no longer feasible, the only option is collective compensation, such as community wells or other infrastructure.

6. For example, in one instance involving a regional development bank, a road rehabilitation project involved 16 kilometres of new alignment. The road was nonetheless classified as a 'rehabilitation' project, and no resettlement program was initially contemplated.
7. The author has come upon instances where international NGOs have inadvertently built infrastructure within the legal right of way. In Madagascar, one NGO built public latrines within the ROW of a national highway, which was destined for widening. In Mali, another NGO created market gardens within the ROW of a local road. If international organisations are unaware of the strictures of national law, it is very likely that the local people, who have less access to public information and who may in fact be mostly illiterate, are even less well informed.
8. The original project design assumed that 'for rehabilitation and periodic maintenance projects the direct impacts can be expected to be relatively minor. The most potential for direct adverse effects to have occurred would have been when the road was originally constructed' (EIA: 7–1). While it is true that new construction will entail greater adverse impact than rehabilitation, it does not follow — and certainly in the instance of Roads III is not the case — that project effects of rehabilitation and even more so of periodic maintenance will ipso facto be only minor.
9. On one stretch of road, the construction company has already attempted to resolve grievances over lost assets. Each time the question was reopened, the number of aggrieved parties increased — from 30 to over 100, to finally, nearly 700. In this case, the company paid all of the claims because there were no grounds for determining who owned which parcels, or what assets thereon had been lost. Collective compensation, in this case community wells in an area of severe water scarcity, is recommended, because retroactive remediation commonly causes difficulties in redressing individual loss.

References

Appleby, Gordon. 2005a. 'Mozambique roads III: Resettlement audit'. Report to the Africa Safeguard Protection and Enhancement (ASPEN) Unit, Africa Region, World Bank.

———. 2005b. 'Resettlement action plan: Projet de developpement agricole et de rehabilitation des pistes rurales, Congo Brazaville: ASPEN comments'. ASPEN, Africa Region, World Bank.

Government of Tanzania (GoT). 2004. 'CIUP (Community Infrastructure Upgrading Program) in Dar es Salaam, Stage 3 report: Resettlement action plan'.

Quintero, Juan. 1997. 'Guidelines for environmental screening of road projects'. Washington DC: World Bank (Latin America and Caribbean Region).

Scudder, Thayer. 1968. 'Social anthropology, man-made lakes and population relocation in Africa'. *Anthropological Quarterly*, 41(3): 168–76.

———. 1973. 'The human ecology of big projects: River basin development and resettlement', in Bernard Siegel (ed.), *Annual review of anthropology*. Palo Alto, CA: Annual Reviews.

———. 1975. 'Resettlement', in N. F. Stanley and M. P. Alpers (eds), *Man-made lakes and human health*. London: Academic Press for Institute of Biology.

———. 2005. *The future of large dams: Dealing with social, environmental, institutional and political costs.* London: Earthscan.

Tsunokawa, Koji and Christopher Hoban (eds). 1997. 'Roads and the environment: A handbook'. Technical Paper No 376. Washington DC: World Bank.

World Bank. 1994. 'Roads and the environment: A handbook'. Report TWU 13. Washington DC: World Bank.

———. 2002a. Operational Policy 4.12 (Involuntary resettlement).

———. 2002b. Operational Policy 4.12, Annex A (Involuntary resettlement instruments).

———. 2004. *Involuntary resettlement sourcebook: Planning and implementation in development projects.* Washington DC: World Bank.

5

Resettlement realities: The gulf between policy and practice

Felix Padel and Samarendra Das*

Rival constructions of reality

All over India, especially in the tribal belt in eastern and central India, *adivasis* and non-tribal farmers alike are asking probing questions about the meaning of development, and questioning what has happened to hundreds of thousands of people already displaced:

> We have sought an explanation from the government about people who have already been displaced in the name of development. How many have been properly rehabilitated? You have not provided them with jobs; you have not rehabilitated them, at all. How can you again displace more people? Where will you relocate them and what jobs will you give them? You tell us first. The government has failed to answer our questions. Our fundamental question is: how can we survive if our lands are taken away from us? We are tribal farmers. We are earthworms (*matiro poko*). Like fishes that die when taken out of water, a cultivator dies when his land is taken away from him. So we won't leave our land. We want permanent development (Bhagaban Majhi, one of the leaders of the Kashipur movement against the Utkal alumina project, in an interview to Das and Das, 2005).

* The author would like to express his thanks to Romy Kraemer for comments on an earlier version of this paper. The paper also has significant inputs from Subrat Sahu, Mamata Dash and Surya Shankar Dash.

Glaring discrepancies exist between policies and promises for resettlement and rehabilitation (R&R), as against the reality of what happens.

To start with, the extensive literature on this subject rarely brings out the voices of resettled people, or those facing an imminent threat of resettlement. Yet, these people's perceptions and experiences are a *social fact* more fundamental than any statistics, which depend on the subjectivity of criteria chosen to be measured, and the measurer's perceptions and relationship with what is being measured. A basic problem in the issue of resettlement concerns the way displaced people are 'objectified': turned into objects, using a language that is alienating and dehumanising. *Feedback* from the 'oustees' and project-affected persons (PAPs), though placed at the top of new R&R policies, is not part of the system. To remedy this situation and incorporate displaced people's perspectives, the tables need to be turned as it were, by making the system of displacement, resettlement and rehabilitation into the subject of analysis, and highlighting disjunctions between what is meant to happen and what actually happens.

A main reason for these discrepancies is the failure to analyse properly, or even to acknowledge, the corruption, intimidation and exploitation which occur at every stage of a 'development project', as well as the environmental degradation involved. If people are resisting resettlement because they have observed that the living standards of people displaced by other projects have gone down instead of up, surely we must concede that they are right in calling these projects 'anti-development', and in resisting being displaced themselves? From the viewpoint of displaced people, whose quality of life has deteriorated, or who refuse to be resettled because they see this, we should perhaps call such projects *displacement projects* rather than *development projects*! Displacement is an objective fact. What constitutes development is much harder to agree on, as we shall see.

To understand the strength of resistance to 'displacement projects', it is necessary to analyse the *clash of ideologies* between a belief in development as something based on material constructs, especially mining-based industrialisation, as against village people's belief in their own culture and way of life, measuring development by whether their quality of life gets better or worse. When farming communities are displaced, especially tribal villages, what is involved amounts not only to a new level of *impoverishment*, but also to *cultural genocide*, since every aspect of the social structure is fundamentally altered and undermined, including the economy, political system, material culture, relationship with the environment, religion and system of values. From being self-reliant, rooted to the land, fundamentally egalitarian cultivators growing most of their own food, the displaced farming communities are forced to the bottom of a ladder, dependent on obscure and cruel corporate hierarchies, which undermine their former freedom and control over their labour and environment. The vast drop in displaced people's quality of life is acknowledged in most serious literature, yet remains little analysed, particularly its discrepancy with CSR models of *sustainable development*.

The image of corporate social responsibility (CSR) promoted by Vedanta, Tata, Posco and other mining companies presents an extraordinary contrast to the reality on the ground, as these companies push their projects in various parts of Orissa. Different, incompatible *social constructions of reality* are involved (Berger and Luckmann 1966), with contrasting definitions about what is happening: fantastic opportunities of foreign direct investment (FDI), or an invasion and take-over of cultivators' land and resources? The companies use PR firms — Vedanta employs London firms Finsbury and CO3, while Posco works through Dilip Cherian's top Indian PR company, Perfect Relations. This PR offensive is aimed at *manufacturing consent* (Chomsky and Hermann 1988), winning over a major section of the population (especially the city- and town-dwelling middle class and business sections of society) through media campaigns, and patronage of cultural, religious and even legal gatherings, to build an image of wonderful benefits being conferred that is at variance with, and masks, the grim reality of actual events.

Social Anthropology can offer several tools for understanding this *reality gap* more objectively. One is the contrast between emic and etic modes of analysis (between how a society represents itself, and an independent mode of analysis). Also, the concept of *social structure* itself, applied on the one hand to the village or community or tribal culture (and how it is changed by resettlement); on the other, the social structure of those imposing the displacement-resettlement process. The imposing system we must lay bare involves structured relationships between company directors, government ministers, senior administrators, the banks and metal traders who generate pressure from abroad, the contracts with engineering and construction companies who implement projects, accountancy firms, lawyers and PR firms whose work is to give an aura of legitimacy to the projects, the use of police to force projects through in the face of popular resistance, the workers who gain employment facing the dirt and danger of the manual work required, and the class of mafia or *goondas* who promote a company's interests on the ground.

Orissa's R&R policy 2006

The Orissa Government Resettlement and Rehabilitation Policy announced in 2006 has been claimed to be among the best in India, and it certainly starts off well, with four *policy objectives* aimed at ensuring 'sustained development through a participatory and transparent process'. It aims:

1. to avoid displacement wherever possible and minimise it;
2. to recognise the voices of displaced communities emphasising the needs of the indigenous communities and vulnerable sections;
3. to ensure environmental sustainability through participatory and transparent process; and
4. to (ensure correct) implementation, monitoring, conflict resolution and grievance redressal ('May 2006 draft', printed in *Adivasi*, December 2006).

The process of finalising this policy happened in a 'kneejerk reaction' to the Kalinganagar police firing, in an attempt to counteract the gathering strength of several high-profile movements by people refusing to be displaced. The details of the policy fall far short of campaigners' demands, however, nullifying the positive impact of the opening statement (Mathur 2006b).

This policy started in 2001 from a new industrial policy promoted in Orissa by the World Bank, UNDP (United Nations Development Programme), UNIDO (UN Industrial Development Organization) and DFID (Department For International Development) of the UK government — a policy aimed at drawing foreign investment to the state. Basically, the UNDP drafted a proposal in 2002 for a consultative process to create the R&R policy, funded by the DFID (July 2003–2005). Among the groups that provided inputs to bring in a people's perspective were Action Aid and the Institute for Social & Economic Development (ISED, Bhubaneswar), besides researchers who wrote studies of dam, coal mining and other projects, in addition to three consultation workshops (2004–05). Meanwhile, an all-India R&R policy was issued in February 2004, which included the aims of minimising displacement, taking account of special needs of *adivasis* and women, raising the living standards of PAFs (project-affected families), and creating harmony between the displaced and displacers (Mathur 2008a). A modified version of this policy was released in 2007. Like the Orissa policy, the Government of India policy contains numerous flaws in the eyes of people's groups, whose suggestions were incorporated only to a minimal extent. The main thrust of both policies is to favour the corporations. So, their impact has in no way lessened resistance to resettlement.

The UNDP draft and the studies it commissioned made certain positive suggestions that were not incorporated in the Orissa policy released in May 2006. It should be noted now that even the UNDP–DFID process was seen as top-down, designed to facilitate the industrial policy, and fell far short of the requirement from genuine people's organisations for civil society participation. For example, some studies recommended that the policy should assign more of a role for NGOs (which did not happen). But most NGOs are hierarchical organisations, with many features of corporations and often funded by them, lacking any actual mandate from the people, and suspect for these reasons in the eyes of most people's groups.

Crucial issues where UNDP draft suggestions were not included in the GoO draft include:

i. the difference between the cash paid for land and the current cost of replacement land. For example, in Kalinganagar, the price paid for tribal people's land was only a tenth of the price for which IDCO (Industrial Development Corporation of Orissa) sold the land on to Tata and other companies (Harsha 2006);

ii. tribal cultivators, who have no *patta* (title deeds) for the lands they cultivate, are still classed as 'encroachers on government land', and suggestions that they should be compensated equally to the minority who possess *patta* did not make it to the policy;

iii. the desirability of compensating land losers with replacement land is not mentioned in the policy, even though this is the minimum requirement under the International Labour Organisation Convention signed by India. As a result, the majority of displaced people lose their land without hope of replacing it, and, in practice, are transformed by displacement from tightly knit communities of skilled cultivators to an amorphous body of unskilled industrial labourers, in an increasingly harsh labour market;

iv. the R&R policy should have made reference to tribal people's fundamental rights to keep their land, guaranteed by Schedule V of the

Constitution and laws such as the OSATIP Regulation 1956 (Orissa Scheduled Areas Transfer of Immovable Property).

What follows is point-by-point summary, and critique, of the 22-point policy to outline its strengths and shortcomings:

1. The primary definition invokes the notorious Land Acquisition Act of 1894, which generations of campaigners say should be scrapped, as it forces the sale of private land owned by small-scale farmers on the colonial grounds of 'eminent domain' by the government.
2. A long list of definitions includes 'compensation' as the 1894 Act defined it.
3. The objectives, defined above, aim to minimise displacement, recognise people's voices, ensure transparency and environmental sustainability, and a proper monitoring and grievance process.
4. Arranges for socioeconomic surveys of people to be displaced by independent agencies.
5. Classifies R&R according to industrial, mining, irrigation (dam), or road/railway projects, etc.
6. Asserts the principle of compensation in cash for land acquired, requiring land not used by a project to be returned to the people after a specified period (case in point being Tata's acquisition of land near Gopalpur that has remained unused). There is no recognition here of the principle of land for land or jobs for land, or the notorious dangers of cash compensation for people not used to large sums.
7. Outlines the R&R plan, including the need 'to ensure as far as practicable overall improvement in the standard of living of the displaced families'.
8. Provides crucial definitions of employment and training schemes offered to various categories of displaced families, including who is entitled to a house, and a commitment to 'give preference' in employment to a member of all families fully displaced (i.e., losing agricultural land and homes). Specified sums are laid down for cash compensation for building houses etc. At people's request, 50% of compensation may be given in 'convertible preference shares' — a new provision, making oustees potential shareholders in the companies displacing them.
9. Deals with 'landless and homestead-less encroachers', perpetuating the odious definition of tribal people who have never had generations-old land-rights acknowledged as 'encroachers', further classifying them into those whose encroachment is 'objectionable' or not. The majority of Kalingnagar oustees, for example, have no *patta*, and therefore minimum entitlement to compensation, even though they have mostly been cultivating their present land for at least three generations.

10–14. Specify certain special assistance to 'Primitive Tribal Groups' and others.

15–18. Set up various committees to make decisions regarding compensation, and R&R: a District Compensation Advisory Committee (DCAC), a State level SCAC, a Rehabilitation-cum-Periphery Development Advisory Committee (RPDAC), which 'may [why not must?] include people's representatives', a State Level Council on R&R, headed by the Chief Minister (SLCRR), and a Directorate of R&R.

19–22. Prescribe budget, assessment of implementation and an 'effective grievance redress mechanism', in which 'participation of the displaced communities will be ensured'.

While several UNDP-commissioned studies had called for the incorporation of displaced people in the decision-making process at every stage, the policy outlines an extremely marginal position for them in the various committees set up to oversee the process — a far cry from the participation and transparency required.

In particular, the principle of 'free prior informed consent' is nowhere to be found. This was proposed by the Extractive Industries Review (EIR), which was basically rejected by the World Bank and sidelined for this very reason. FPIC demands that people should only be displaced if they give their consent freely, after receiving proper information. The EIR process was replaced by that of the MMSD (Mining, Minerals and Sustainable Development), which was overseen by the mining companies ultimately responsible for displacement, and contains no such principle. The R&R process, in other words, is not linked to the decision-making process about whether to implement a project. The system of public hearings presently in place, is regularly abused, and people's voices make no difference to whether a project goes ahead (Kalshian 2007).

An attempt was made to win over protestors against displacement by Tata's and Posco's proposed steel plants at Kalinganagar and Jagatsingpur in special Orissa government orders passed in May 2006, offering slightly higher sums for land losers (*Adivasi*, December 2006: Annexure, xiii–xvi). From the start, the Orissa policy was 'dubbed by critics as "pro-industry"...it has failed to win over those spearheading the anti-displacement agitation at Kalinga Nagar' (Mathur 2006b).

Disjunction between policy and practice

A study by social anthropologist David Mosse (2005) finds almost no correlation between policy and practice in a major agricultural project funded by the DFID in Madhya Pradesh, for which he was a consultant. This lack of correlation between what is promised and what actually happens applies in almost every case of resettlement.

The official version of Orissa's modern history tends to reflect the developers' self-image, focusing on the growth rate, the development of roads, railways, airports, sea ports and mobile phone networks, and the exploitation of the state's minerals. Left out of this version, is the reality on the ground. If displaced people suffer, this suffering is often seen as a necessary 'sacrifice' for overall development — the cost of progress. Overall, or eventually, it is believed that most people's standard of living goes up — even though 'trickle-down economics' has been shown to be false, and most people can see clearly that poverty is getting worse. Company officials often say 'there was nothing here before we came — only mud huts'.

Above all, according to R&R policies formulated by World Bank, DFID and UNDP, as well as the governments of Orissa and India, people's *standard of living is supposed to go up, not down.* It is generally acknowledged that this hardly ever happens in practice (Mathur 2008b: 179).

Most projects have no 'social impact assessment', displaced people are not made part of the decision-making process, and there is no proper check on the success of R&R, or even proper ways to assess this, let alone any disciplinary action against officials responsible for failure, which is why this reality gap remains almost completely outside the approved discourse on R&R.

One basic problem is that in most, if not all, project areas, various forms of intimidation and coercion appear to be standard ways to deal with people unwilling to be displaced, by police and administrative authorities, as well as by a mafia network of *goondas*. This intimidation also operates around people once they are living in a resettlement colony. In traditional tribal villages, differences in status are relatively small. Everyone is of approximately equal status and value. Once displaced from their village and land, people find themselves at the bottom of a hierarchy that is often extremely cruel and corrupt.

Corruption is conspicuous by its absence from most models of R&R, and at the heart of the fundamental discrepancies between theory and practice. In the awarding of contracts for constructing a colony, rather at every stage of the project, corruption is rampant (Dash 2008). This starts with the deals mining companies make, but percolates down to the lowest level. Workers often attest that even labouring jobs, which should be theirs by right, can only be had by paying bribes. For example, villagers living below Nalco's bauxite mine told us that they gave bribes of several thousand rupees just to get preferential selection for labouring jobs up the mountain, which paid a mere Rs 68 a day. Often, it seems, large bribes are more or less mandatory even to get standard land title documents, which small-scale farmers need as a basic security, since without *patta*, they are not entitled to compensation for their land. And often, even after bribes, no documents materialise.

Corruption exists among lower officials because it is tolerated at higher levels. In November 2003, the Minister for Environment & Forests was caught on camera receiving a large bribe from an Australian mining company for leases in Orissa and Chhattisgarh, with words that reveal much about modern attitudes to money: '*Paise khuda to nahi, par khuda ki kasam, khuda se kam bhi nahi*'.[1]

Most of Orissa's first wave of industrial projects were notorious for their lack of adequate R&R, such as the Rourkela steel plant, the Hirakud, Upper Kolab and Indravati dam projects; and also Nalco in Koraput, sometimes cited as a model of good practice, but actually, as we shall see, anything but. Many people say, like Bhagaban: '...resettle these people properly before displacing any more. Until you do this, what guarantee do we have that you won't treat us just like you treated them?'

In the present situation, three companies, in particular, face protracted opposition in Orissa, in a series of projects, some of which have already caused displacement or are currently causing agitation, while others (like iron ore mines) have yet to be finalised: Tata at Kalingnagar and Gopalpur (steel plants), Naraj (thermal power plant near Cuttack), Dhamra (port), and north Orissa (iron ore mines); Posco at Jagatsingpur (steel plant and port) and north Orissa (iron ore mines); and Vedanta at Lanjigarh (alumina refinery), Niyamgiri (planned bauxite mine), Jharsaguda district (smelter and giant power plant), near Puri (university-cum-business centre), and Gandhamardan (another bauxite deposit). Several other projects, which have recently displaced people, or where people have taken a strong stand resisting displacement, include the Utkal alumina refinery, numerous steel plants, sponge iron factories and iron ore mines by Bhushan, Jindal, Mittal and other companies, and the Lower Suktel dam.

The resistance to all these projects by people opposing resettlement is of immense significance. From the viewpoint of the companies, and members of the governments of Orissa and India supporting them, the protestors are holding up foreign investment worth crores. From the viewpoint of protestors threatened with displacement, they face a fundamental injustice. The authorities appear not to understand or care that these people's whole lives are being torn apart. What else is the government for, if not to listen to and serve these people? This is the essence of the reality gap: a gulf of understanding between those imposing and those suffering from displacement.

Displacement tends to be seen as a peripheral aspect of a development project, and the officials in charge of overseeing R&R are neither well-trained nor well-motivated to help in what we now understand is a highly traumatic process for nearly everyone undergoing displacement (Mathur 2006a: 48, 69–70). As Bhagaban says of a meeting with the superintendent of police (SP):

> I put a question to the SP. I asked him, 'Sir, what do you mean by development? (*Agya, unnoti boile kono*?) Can you call displacing people development? The people, for whom development is meant, should reap its benefits. After them, the succeeding generations should enjoy its benefits. That is development. It should not be merely to cater to the greed of a few officials (Das and Das 2005).

Since 1995, the Kashipur movement has been at the forefront of questioning what is meant by 'development' (Lingaraj 1995; Pradhan 1995).

Defined in purely material and economic terms, 'development' loses all connection with the original aim of improving people's actual well-being. Education, health, levels of nutrition and employment are among the important indices often used to study people's well-being, and where reliable statistics on these aspects have been collected, they confirm that industrialised tribal areas are among the most impoverished in India. Nalco-dominated Koraput is the poorest of all, with 78 per cent of the population below poverty line (CSE 2008: 254, 322). But collecting statistics is not enough;

not just because we all know how easily statistics can be massaged. People's own perception of their well-being is vital, so the failure to even include people's voices in most studies of resettlement is very disturbing. The perceptiveness and wit *adivasis* display when they speak freely beat anything in written discourse. The trouble is that they know most outsiders have no wish to hear what they say or to learn from them.

The phenomenon of displacement

The number of people displaced by industrial projects in India, as a whole, is estimated at 60 million in the last 60 years (1948–2008); 3 million in Orissa alone, approximately 75 per cent of whom are *adivasis* and 25 per cent Dalits (Fernandes 2008). There is a tendency in social science to give importance only to what can be measured, highlighting *chrematist* (monetary) values, at the expense of a broader sense of well-being. For various reasons, many aspects of displacement are hard to measure and define. With some aspects it is because of an institutionalised attitude of neglect towards displaced people — for example, no reliable statistics have been kept either of the number of people displaced by most projects or of what happens to them in following years (Fernandes 2008: 90).

Many vital aspects of the displacement process can only be understood if people are prepared to open their hearts and minds to other ways of being. Measurement has little importance here. The *social construction of reality* in tribal culture is worlds away from mainstream culture, and it is a real challenge for the bureaucratic, technology-focused mindset which guides development projects to comprehend the enormity of what is involved when tribal people are uprooted from their land and villages to a resettlement colony.

It is precisely because of this reality gap that resistance to projects is so intense. So, the people who manage projects and resettlement would benefit greatly from trying to understand it. Social anthropology could play an important role in this, from the knowledge of tribal people's construction of reality. This is no substitute, however, for hearing from the people themselves.

Often, effects of displacement are especially dire when communities are dislodged from regions of exceptionally rich biodiversity, which they have adapted to and helped maintain over generations, as in many areas of Orissa. Maps of India's mineral deposits, rivers and forests correspond to the most impoverished areas, which are most dense in terms of tribal population (Sunil, in Das and Das 2006; CSE 2008). This exemplifies the *resource curse* thesis: natural resource abundance becomes a curse for inhabitants displaced by mining and dams (Ross 1999).

The resource curse thesis was originally applied to the relative wealth or poverty of countries, measured by their GDP among other things, but it also applies to regions within countries. For example, people in Scotland, Wales and north England frequently observe how their minerals, oil and water have been extracted over centuries for profit in London, leaving them poorer economically, as well as socially, culturally and environmentally. In India, the mineral-rich areas where mining has taken off in Jharkhand, Chhattisgarh, Orissa etc., are among the country's most impoverished regions. The coal fields, iron ore, chromite and bauxite mines in these states have been transformed from regions rich in fertility and tribal cultures, to wastelands (Somayaji 2008, on coalfields in Orissa; Kalshian 2007).

Dispossessing vast numbers of people from their land in the name of development is a phenomenon that has accelerated rapidly since India's independence. Displacement during colonial times has a hidden, unrecorded history. Numerous communities were displaced by tea plantations in Assam, Kerala and present Bangladesh. In Orissa, British demands for increased revenue from the land caused eviction of thousands of tribal people from their territories (Currie 2000; Padel 2000). It is significant that the legal apparatus for displacement was put in place during colonial times, with the Permanent Settlement Act (1793) and the Land Acquisition Act (1894). W. W. Hunter expressed succinctly the set of values which many British rulers saw as their main legacy to India:

> It is by what we have implanted in the living people, rather than what we have built upon the dead earth, that our name will survive. The permanent aspect of British Rule in India is the growth of Private Rights.
>
> By a wise limitation of our state ownership we have raised up a permanent Proprietary Body, composed of mutually hostile classes; but each of which, from the grand seigneurs down to the Resident Husbandsmen, holds its lands under documents issued by British officials (Hunter 1872: 201, 277, quoted in Padel 2001: 80).

This divide-and-rule legacy of British colonialism is bearing fruit now. The ideology of industrialisation sweeping Orissa stems from the same essential belief system that motivated the industrial revolution in Britain, the USA, the USSR, China and other countries. It is important to bear this history in mind. A collective forgetting of what was done, suffered and said in preceding centuries, leads to a compounding of past mistakes and mistaken belief systems.

The modern pattern of displacing people from their land to make it more profitable was set far away from India. European colonialists exterminated indigenous tribes all over America and Australia, and forced survivors to cede their land and move to reservations, where a policy of detribalisation was imposed. This pattern is also embedded in the history of the colonising countries themselves. In Britain, the Enclosure Acts between 1760 and 1840 started a process of privatising land that evicted small-scale farmers in vast numbers all over the British Isles — a precedent for the land-grabs by the already-rich going on in Orissa right now, which are reducing the already-poor to a poverty worse than anything they knew before. Orissa today witnesses the same kinds of injustice, and very similar justifications, to those evident in 18th and 19th century Britain. What is going on throughout east India could be called a *Rape of the fair country*, after Alexander Cordell's novel (1959) about the mining industry in 19th century Wales, which gives details about the clash of cultures and system of exploitation, very similar to Gopinath Mohanty's novels about tribal Orissa.

Britain's remote northern areas suffered a particular trauma known as the Highland Clearances. The Scottish clans lived a highly traditional life based on small-scale crofting in the highlands and islands, characterised by a distinctive culture and an independent spirit. During the 19th century, English rulers persuaded the Scottish lairds (zamindars) to make their land more profitable by expelling these crofters in huge numbers — just as they persuaded Rajas in Orissa around the same time. Intellectuals of the 'Edinburgh Enlightenment' painted a picture of these crofters as sunken in poverty and warfare, their stone houses as dirty hovels, and their lifestyle as backward and uneconomic. Using this justification, hundreds of communities were permanently erased, and thousands of people died from starvation and disease (Prebble 1969). Of those who survived, many had to become factory workers. Thousands migrated to Britain's colonies in America, Australia and South Africa, where they displaced the natives just as they had been displaced themselves. Many served in the army in various outreaches of the British

Empire, including India. The Kond areas of west Orissa, which are now the scene of invasion by aluminium companies, were forced under British rule by a series of Scottish highland officers, named Macpherson, Campbell, MacViccar, and McNeill (Padel 2000).

The Highland Clearances in Scotland erased cultures and communities, but also cleared forests and farmland to make way for sheep and plantations of foreign trees for timber and paper. Another phase of clearances started in the early 20th century, when some of the world's first dams were built to generate hydro-power for aluminium smelters. These reservoirs fill valleys emptied of their people. The water level is low and a sterile gap of at least 30 feet separates the water from land vegetation. Even back in 1910, when about a third of the world's aluminium was being produced in Scotland, a union leader contrasted the British aluminium company's picture of its main smelter enclave as a 'Garden of Eden', with the 'misery and degradation' which workers endured (Perchard 2008/2009). *Children of the dead end* is a novel written from direct experience of this exploitation (McGee 1982). Then, as now, workers in aluminium factories faced a high incidence of industrial diseases, whose true extent has never been revealed (Perchard 2008, 2010).

Aluminium companies entering the Kond region of western Orissa are after the bauxite deposits on the summits of the biggest mountains. Although the planned mines, unlike dams and factories, may not displace people directly, they erode the water-bearing capacity of the mountains, and thereby threaten the local Konds' cultivation of millet, maize, turmeric, ginger, orange, pineapple and dozens of other food crops, which they depend on for sustenance and income. Mining bauxite from these mountain tops is also an assault on their religion. For Kond religion recognises mountains as prime sacred entities and sources of life — a connection which geologists recognised when they named the base rock of these bauxite-capped mountains as Khondalite (Fox 1932: 136; Padel and Das 2007).

In Orissa, as in Scotland, hundreds of communities have ceased to exist, and hundreds more are threatened with extinction. Local tribal and non-tribal politicians, and landlords in Kashipur and Lanjigarh have sold out their communities, just as the Scottish Lairds did (Saroj 2008). There is no 'empire' for Orissa's displaced people to emigrate to. Factory and construction work is every bit as dangerous and degrading as it was in 19th century Britain, but in the present age of mechanisation, permanent jobs are fewer.

Environmental degradation works alongside the decline in living standards, even more than in industrialising Britain. Around the Upper Indravati reservoir, displaced people cut down the remaining forest, because they have lost their land along with their traditional forest-based livelihood system. Selling the timber as firewood is all that saves them from starvation. More dams are being planned. The Lower Suktel project in Balangir District is ostensibly for irrigation, though its main purpose is apparently to provide water to a planned alumina refinery based on mining Gandhamardan. Huge sums have already been spent on this project, though it has been stalled since 1998 due to strong resistance from most of the 16–26 villages threatened with displacement (Agnihotri 2008). One symbol of the reality gap is a cheque for just six rupees, dated 29 September 2007 (we have it photocopied) which was presented as compensation for his house to Umesh Chhatria of Koindapali village by the special land acquisition officer of Balangir. What can be bought for six rupees?

The following are some of the areas of life where displaced people generally see a marked decline:

- Food security lost along with land
- Self employment replaced by humiliating dependency on a supply labouring jobs
- Egalitarian social structure replaced by a low place in an extreme hierarchy
- Splits in the community between people for and against a project/company
- Access to fresh stream water ends replaced by pump water, often polluted and unreliable (residents in many rehab colonies testify to a dire water shortage)
- Deterioration in community values, corruption, and oppression by *goondas*

Offsetting the deterioration in standards, are various schemes of 'sustainable development' and corporate social responsibility (CSR). Vedanta's 2007–08 annual report devotes many pages to SD and CSR. Their main evidence of good work is statistics of money spent on schools, health centres and SHGs (self-help groups), accredited by a London-based accountancy firm. Investigation on the ground, in the Lanjigarh area, reveals that schools and hospitals are functioning barely, if at all, while SHGs are open to the problem that once loans are disbursed, repayment pressure is intense and affords a means of control over the indebted population — problems reported by several researchers from Bangladesh, where the SHG model first took off (Muhammad 2006). It is true that Vedanta gave training to a number of local youths, but the participation by these youths in repeated demonstrations at Lanjigarh, demanding jobs, belies claims that the company offers major opportunities for local people. Local people insist that most well-paid jobs go to outsiders (Dash 2008).

The basic problem with privatised models of development is that they bypass democratic social controls developed through intense campaigns since independence. Officials have been heard saying, like in the Kashipur region, that once the Utkal project is underway, proper development in terms of schools and hospitals will be given by the company. But the companies involved in Utkal have changed: from Indal, Tata and Norsk Hydro, to Alcan and Hindalco, to Hindalco alone. So when officials say 'company *debo'* (the company will give), the actual company involved shifts its form, and this statement is an echo to words that might have been said 200 years ago about the East India Company and its promises. How to ensure that companies keep their promises? What punishments should be meted out to company executives who deceive people with false promises?

What adds insult to injury is the dehumanised discourse that is customary, concerning people who have been or may be displaced. A study commissioned by Tata soon after the Kalingnagar firing, is a case in point (Harsha 2006), giving statistics of DPs (displaced persons) and PAPs (project-affected persons). Meeting with opposition from villagers, whose friends and relations had been killed, the team 'repeatedly emphasised to them that this survey has been initiated only to strengthen the cause of the affected people. Sometimes it worked, paving way for future deliberations' (ibid.: 10). This contrasts strongly with the tendentious assumption that 'The very fact that the displaced persons have spelt-out their options and preferences for their relocation, resettlement and rehabilitation indicates that they are willing to accept the project. It also indicates that they are mentally preparing themselves to get displaced to give way for the project' (ibid.: iv). Posco, like Tata, has spent a lot of money studying the people resisting displacement, and a visit to the Posco office in Bhubaneswar revealed a site map where resisting households were marked with red dots, pro-Posco households with green, and fence-sitters with blue. In other words, the companies keep lists of 'agitators' to be 'targeted'.

In many ways, what is happening to *adivasis* in Orissa now is a repeat of the Highland Clearances, and much of the literature on *adivasis* in 20th–21st century Orissa repeats the same discourse: a view of clansmen and *adivasis* as unruly, uncouth, uneducated, backward, and, above all, uneconomic and standing in the way of progress. Yet, the reality was, and in Orissa still is, that these people grow a large variety of foods on their land, and if the process is labour-intensive, it also involves a huge variety of experience and communication — bathing in the stream, complex songs, dances, myths related to the local landscape, visits between communities, clan feasts — and careful preservation of the natural environment.

Cultural genocide

When company people say, of a tribal area where they have erected a factory, that 'there was nothing here before — only mud huts', this shows how the dominant mindset equates development with modern, material constructs, such as roads and buildings. Most R&R schemes assess traditional tribal houses as having no economic value. For example, an official account of Nalco's R&R at Damanjodi states:

> The Government of Orissa as well as the NALCO have taken the view that the homesteads lost by the tribal families were practically of no value as they were *small mud huts. As no compensation could be paid for loss of such homesteads*, durable houses (partly *pucca*) could be constructed for them at the cost of NALCO. Secondly, the concept of rehabilitation was based on the fact that it was necessary for NALCO alumina project to create certain amount of community relationship with those who have *lost all their assets in the larger interest of the nation* (Muthayya 1984: 2, emphasis added).

The contrast between houses before and after displacement demonstrates a far-reaching difference in values and culture. Traditional tribal villages, without too much outside interference, have a high quality of life in that each man and woman is self-employed on his/her own land. They have clean water, and take a daily bath in a flowing stream — better than the most expensive bathroom! They make their own houses with earth and wood, and though these houses are officially classified as mere 'mud huts' (and on this basis, people receive minimal compensation for the huts when these are destroyed to make way for a project), they are far superior in many ways to *pucca* concrete houses. They remain cool in summer and warm in winter, unlike concrete buildings in resettlement colonies. They are beautifully painted with clay and well-mixed natural glaze, which keep out mosquitoes, and have many secret spaces for cooking, storing things, and for worship of gods and ancestors. Fire hazard is given by government engineers as a reason for the superiority of *pucca* houses, but these usually have asbestos roofing, in apparent ignorance of the health hazard of asbestos, which is now banned in many countries. Traditional houses are an expression of cultural pride, made through villagers' skill and labour. *Pucca* houses cost about ten times more to build, but if they are superior in fire resistance, they are also soulless, inconvenient and alien in culture. Since the people rarely have any design input, these houses lack the spatial arrangement that binds people into a living community. It seems that a main reason is that the contractors make a profit by building them.

Cultural genocide is the least recognised, but perhaps most painful, aspect of the drastic drop in the quality of life of people who are displaced (Padel and Das 2008). This is why so many farmers say 'we'll die rather than give up our land', recognising that all their values are at stake, since these are rooted in their land and physical community. When Bhagaban says a cultivator dies when his land is taken away, he is not referring just to a physical death from hunger or other causes. He means that people die inside, a 'soul death'. The deaths at Maikanch and Kalinganagar are symbolic of a collective death. This is something hard to communicate to people who have no experience of the kind of rootedness at the heart of *adivasi* society. It echoes the decision to die rather than leave their land of many indigenous peoples in America, where physical genocide — meaning the extermination of all members of a tribe — often went alongside cultural genocide: the killing off of cultures (Brown 1975; Padel and Das 2008).

Briefly, social anthropology analyses the social structure of a tribal (or non-tribal) village in terms of several spheres of life, each of which is radically altered and dismantled by displacement:

- The economy is completely changed when people who have essentially been cultivators are removed from the land and turned into an industrial labour force. Food security vanishes, and money assumes far greater importance in defining relationships between people.

- People's identity is also radically altered. From being largely self-sufficient for their basic food wants and material needs (like making their own houses and channelling water to their fields), they become dependent on a hierarchy outside their control for jobs and every aspect of life. Their fields and houses were often made by their parents or remote forefathers, so losing their land and ancestral village creates a traumatic break with previous generations.
- The political system and power structure in traditional tribal villages are remarkably egalitarian. Differences in status and wealth do exist, but are counteracted by a strong tendency towards sharing and equality. These differences were accentuated by colonial rule, and displacement makes them much greater. From being in control of most aspects of their daily life and the area around their village, people find themselves at the bottom of a corporate hierarchy, dependent on a wide range of more powerful people, many of them outsiders to the area. In other words, displacement disempowers the villagers and lowers their status.
- Women's position is often particularly badly affected, even where education, health centres and self-help groups (SHGs) are provided for oustees. The reason for this is that in a tribal village, women often retain a large degree of control over their own labour, working essentially for themselves and their own families, at times of their own choice. Even when they do coolie labour, this tends to supplement work on their own land as they see fit. Losing their land, they become more dependent on their husbands, and often bear the brunt of men's frustration, in a situation where work ceases to be on their own terms. Tribal women who retain their land go to market to sell their own produce. The dignity from this self-sufficiency is destroyed by displacement. SHGs have an ideology of raising women's status that is often contradicted by ground realities, especially once pressure to repay loans kicks in (Das 2000; Muhammad 2006; Saroj 2008). There are frequent testimonies of displaced women being forced into prostitution, even in the colonies built for them.
- A village's material culture is altered beyond recognition by displacement. From making most of their own food, tools and houses, villagers become dependent on factory-made goods. An influx of cars and trucks into their area makes life more dangerous and pollutes the atmosphere, as do the factories that become the centre of the local power structure.
- Religious life is also transformed. Seeing the incomers around them tearing nature apart, and participating in blasting rock formations and cutting down trees to earn money, undermines people's sense of sacredness in nature, which lies at the heart of traditional tribal religion. For example, a woman who had just been removed from

Kinari village to make way for Vedanta's refinery, said to us '*Amoro deveta bi nasht kole*' — 'they even destroyed our deities' — referring to the *darni vali* (earth goddess stones) that form the centre of a Kond village, which had been bulldozed into rubble along with the houses as soon as villagers were evicted. Similar testimony is given by people displaced by the Indravati reservoir, who say their 'deities were drowned'.

- In this context, the dances, songs, stories, and customary ways of behaviour, which are commonly understood as 'culture', also lose their meaning and vitality. Many displaced by the Indravati dam attest that when times were hard before, the better-off would help those in need. Now everyone is struggling to survive.

An easy way to understand cultural genocide is through the original meaning of 'culture', deriving from Latin *cultus*, which links the meaning of culture, cult, and cultivation. In other words, cultures which still retain their own system of cultivation, linked with a cult of nature-based deities, are bound to be undermined by removal from their land. For those of us who lost any sense of being part of a community rooted to the soil hundreds of years ago, it is very hard to understand the cultural genocide implicit in this kind of displacement, which applies to tribal cultures, which differ markedly from mainstream orientation in their lifestyle's rootedness in nature.

When the Balimela dam was being constructed in the 1960s, a team from the Anthropological Survey of India was commissioned to study the small, distinctive Didayi tribe, a large part of which was about to be displaced (Guha 1970). If this is an extreme example, non-tribal farmers also face cultural genocide, such as the betul-vine cultivators resisting Posco, farmers who resisted Tata's Gopalpur steel plant plans in the 1990s (Shiva 1998), and thousands of cultivators in West Bengal resisting takeover of their land at Singur and Nandigram. The village culture these people are defending is the same '*gram swaraj*' which lay at the heart of Gandhi's concept of Indian culture.

Various people in Orissa and other states who are striving to protect their land from corporate takeover are actually campaigning for much more — to preserve India's cultural integrity and independence against the forces of global finance. And even more than this — to preserve India's natural environment that forms the basis of life itself.

There is a widespread recognition now that bio-cultural diversity co-exists with biodiversity in nature — that indigenous cultures preserve many of the world's most important areas of nature, because the values of these cultures differ fundamentally from those of the industrial society that developed in the West 'built on the misconceived and ultimately ruinous belief in humans' separateness from Nature and dominion over it' (Maffi 2008: 10; Kothari and Pathak 2008). The World Conservation Congress promotes the concept of Indigenous Community Conserved Areas (ICCAs).

In Orissa, one such outstanding area is the forested mountain summit in Niyamgiri, where Vedanta plans to mine bauxite. This is an example of a project that may not cause direct displacement, but strikes at the heart of a cultural heritage, which is also the heart of one of Orissa's best preserved forest areas. The reason is the Dongria Konds and their religion, which centres on 'Niyam Raja, 'Lord of the law', whose abode is the mountain summit. The tribe maintains a taboo on cutting trees up there in Niyam Raja's name, out of a recognition that the natural vegetation conserves the fertility of their land through an abundance of streams. Mining bauxite from Niyamgiri and other Khondalite mountains in south Orissa is bound to cause an erosion of Kond spiritual values, as well as an erosion of Orissa's natural environment and fertility (Dash 2008; Padel and Das 2009).

Clash of ideologies

Displacement arises out of a clash of ideologies. On the one side is the value systems of traditional cultures, where relationships with land and community are more important than money; on the other, an ideology of industrialisation-as-development, in which market forces and swift financial profit override other values. The police firings that killed tribal people at Maikanch village in December 2000, and in Kalinganagar industrial area in January 2006, are key symbols of this struggle in Orissa. Cultivators look at industrial projects, which lower their standard of living and destroy their communities, as the opposite of real development, while 'anti-development' is what those promoting industrialisation and their foreign investors call the farmers who take a stand against displacing projects.

As we write, several other calamities are affecting Orissa, which have an extremely close, though hidden, connection with the subject of 'development-induced displacement': terrible floods, violent attacks between Hindus and Christians focused in Kandhamal district, and a number of violent attacks by Maoists and consequent repression. It will be helpful to examine these connections as a way of appraising the causes of displacement. Floods cause temporary resettlement in relief camps, while the Kandhamal disturbance has left an estimated 12,000 people (mainly Christians) in relief camps that are supposed to be temporary. However, these people have no prospect of a quick return, since former neighbours make this conditional on conversion to Hinduism. And thousands more Christians are now dispersed in other parts of Orissa, or have left the state altogether. As for Maoist-related violence, the *Salwa Judum* civil war in south Chhattisgarh has forced between 47,500 (2007 Chhattisgarh government estimate) and 200,000 (other estimates) people out of their villages in Dantewara district, resettling them initially in 20 relief camps; though atrocious conditions in these camps have forced many thousands to flee beyond the borders of Chhattisgarh to Andhra and other states (CPJC, and Afterword to Sundar 2007). 'Development-induced displacement' thus needs to be understood in the context of huge-scale resettlement due to natural disasters and human violence to relief camps which are meant to be temporary, where poor conditions have caused a massive dispersal of displaced people as refugees.

The floods which swept Orissa in September 2008 displaced about 180,000 people, and marooned about 1,500,000. It seems that mismanagement of Hirakud and other dams is a significant factor.[2] Although flood control was given along with irrigation and hydropower as a main reason for building these dams, recent events have shown that supplying water and power to new factories is the dams' main purpose. Far from controlling floods, evidence suggests that the dams have actually compounded them by releasing water inappropriately, and through the ever-present threat of bursting — the main cause of the disastrous 2008 Bihar floods, after a dam was breached on the Kosi river in Nepal, and officials in Bihar failed to act in time (*timesonline*, 28 August 2008; *bihartimes.com*, 12 September 2008). On 7 November 2007, protest by 30,000 farmers in the Hirakud area highlighted the fact of industry taking water at the expense of irrigation for farmers. The farmers drew a '*chashi rekha*' (farmers' line) against factories' further intake of water (POKSSS 2008).

Dams, thus, cause widespread displacement in two other dimensions, in addition to their large-scale direct displacement — first, through catastrophic floods in times of excessive rain, and second, by reducing canal or river flow that thousands of farmers depend on. When Nehru laid the foundation stone for Hirakud, he saw dams as the 'temples of modern India' — a view he later regretted — and his words are a poignant illustration of the reality gap: 'The Hirakud project is a work which will not cause more misery to the people, but which will bring about the end of their miseries'.[3] Chief Minister Nabakrushna Choudhury also promised that the dam would bring an end to poverty in Orissa. After at least 150,000 people had been displaced, and two tehsildars had been murdered by furious villagers, causing severe police repression, Hirakud was a main factor in Choudhury's resignation in 1956 (Dhalo 2007). Sudden release of water by the Hirakud dam caused widespread displacement and loss of life and property in 1980 and 1999, as well as in 2008.

The Hindu–Christian issue was sparked in December 2007 by the application of certain Christian Panos (the main Scheduled Caste) in Kandhamal district to change their status (which was originally Scheduled Caste) to Scheduled Tribe on the basis that they speak the Kond tribal language Kui — an application that angered Konds, and fanned the flames of a double split in society that broke out in violent attacks: SC (Pano) versus ST (Kond); Hindu versus Christian. The latter split broke out with renewed ferocity in August 2008 following the murder by Maoists of the VHP leader Laxmanananda Saraswati, whom they held responsible for instigating communal violence in December. Since August, countless villages and churches have been burnt, and an estimated 50,000 Christians have been hounded from their homes, in a systematic campaign of 'ethnic cleansing' reminiscent of Hindutva campaigns against Muslims in Gujarat and Rajasthan (S. Mathur 2008; Kanungo 2008).

What we are dealing with here is the spread of a *polarising tendency* in society. The primary issue we address in this paper is a polarisation between those who believe in or promote industrial development-cum-displacement, and those resisting it. The Kandhamal violence demonstrates the power of several related polarisations — Hindu–Christian, and SC–ST — and highlights the position of the Maoists in this process.

Increasingly, people who resist displacement are being branded as Maoists, especially in the Kalinganagar and Posco areas (as also at Singur and Nandigram). To what extent Maoist influence is penetrating these areas is often difficult to gauge. What is clear is that these movements against forced displacement are primarily motivated by farmers' wish to retain their land and communities, and if Maoist influence enters, the main reason for this is people's exasperation at the injustice they face and the Maoists' readiness to capitalise on this, since supporting fights against injustice is at the core of their ideology. It is also apparent that labelling protestors as Maoists makes it easier to justify repressive measures against them.

Before examining the ideology of the protestors, or of the Maoists, we need to look more deeply at the mainstream ideology of development that is the prime cause of displacement. By ideology, we mean patterns of values and beliefs that motivate people and form their perception of what is real and right — *social construction of reality*.

As we have shown, the phenomenon of displacement taking place in Orissa now comes out of a history of industrial revolution in a succession of countries; motivated by a nationalistic faith in 'progress' that shows relatively little variation from 18th–19th-century Britain and America, to communist Russia and China, to Orissa/India today. The heart of this belief system is *materialism*: the belief that a high growth rate and increased material production and construction lead to a rise in the general standard of living. In each of the countries mentioned, millions of people were displaced from their land and faced starvation conditions as a result of rapidly imposed industrialisation. In the case of Russia, Stalin's first five year plan caused the death of around 7 million people through starvation in Ukraine in 1932–33, and Mao's Great Leap Forward in 1958–61 caused the death of an estimated 30 million people due to an enforced shift from agriculture to steel production (Chang 1991, 2005; Short 1999: 480–505). In other words, no one seems to have tried to impose industrialisation more swiftly and cruelly than Mao. This fact alone would make Maoism a very strange ally of people who are resisting industrialisation.

It seems that capitalists and Marxists both believe in industrialisation as a necessary stage of development. They also share a belief in violence, as a means to impose their will. No one analysed the inequities of capitalism better than Marx, but he was limited by the belief systems of his own time, when hardly anyone could see the environmental consequences of large-scale industrialisation in catastrophic climate change, etc. — now plainly visible — and when everyone was excited by a new 'scientific' vision of progress through set stages of development.

This view of human societies as developing through certain fixed or necessary stages of development is known as *social evolutionism*. Originally, it was seen as an application to society of Darwin's theory of evolution of natural species, causing Marx to offer to dedicate a volume of *Das Kapital* to Darwin. Unfortunately, the application of the theory of evolution to society by Herbert Spencer and others was misplaced, since thousands of natural species develop on their own unique path in relation to changes in other species, while social evolutionists posit the same path of development for every society, forcing diverse cultures into a single paradigm of unsolicited cultural uniformity (Padel 2000).

So one aspect of social evolutionism and, therefore, of the mainstream values promoting industrial development in India and Orissa today, involves a set of negative stereotypes about tribal people, and other small-scale farmers, terming them 'primitive', 'backward', 'uneconomic', 'unsustainable' etc. This has actually been the dominant view of tribal cultures since European moderns first encountered them (Meek 1976), and causes an immense undervaluation of tribal culture, implicit in the idea that resettlement will aid tribal people's development in the long run, even if it causes pain now.

A core aspect of the ideology of industrialisation relates to a faith in certain economic theories. In particular, the idea that a high growth rate in the overall economy is bound to trickle down to the poor, has continued to find currency, even though it has been repeatedly discredited, and flies in the face of the evidence all around us. Neoliberal economics gives prime importance to a belief in 'market forces', on the view that if everyone follows their own interests, market forces will produce the proper adjustments in society. This belief, promoted by Adam Smith and others in 18th-century Britain, still forms a core belief in the ideology of developers, even though it is clear that it has led to the rich getting richer and the poor getting poorer. It is forgotten that Adam Smith also attacked the power of corporations, the East India Company in particular, warning of their tendency to make a 'conspiracy against the public' (Robbins 2006: 61).

From the perspective of tribal cultures, the idea that everyone should follow their self-interest promotes selfishness on a dangerous scale. Even the idea of private property, which Hunter outlined as the core colonial legacy to India, is seen by indigenous people as a cause of environmental devastation. As a leading Native American leader, Oren Lyons, sees it, 'Private property is a concept that flies in the face...of the reality of life...a human conception, which amounts to greed' (Lopez 2008: 28).

The privatisation of resources such as land, minerals and water going on now is seen by environmentalists as a danger to the fabric of life, and contrasts with the advice in the famous Constitution of the Six Nations of the Iroquois Confederacy, that any important decision should be assessed on the basis of its likely effects on the seventh generation to come (ibid: 29). This kind of long-term planning is also the reason that Adam Smith distrusted corporations: their thinking is confined to extremely short-term calculations of profits and costs. As we would express this now: wider environmental costs, costs to people being displaced by their projects, and costs likely to fall on future generations, are *externalised*, so that they are not borne by the companies who incur them.

In other words, the displacement process involves double standards. A proper cost-benefit analysis of any project would offset financial and employment benefits against environmental and social costs, and consequent costs to future generations. The way these are externalised so that companies have to pay nothing, or at most guarantee a token 5 per cent of profits to compensate for these costs, shows that development projects are defined by the companies and their beneficiaries.

Rule of law

A blatantly dual set of values is apparent in the application of law. While protestors against the Utkal, Posco and Tata projects are harassed by countless 'false cases' that tie them into a drawn-out and highly exploitative process at the local law courts, the big corporations are seen to wriggle out of legal injunctions with ease, e.g. in the notorious bribes paid by mining companies to ministers, and in the way that Utkal and Vedanta proceeded to build their factories without having first acquired proper environmental clearance for the mines they were depending on (IPTEHR 2006; Samantara 2007; Goodland 2007). Vedanta/Sterlite's clearance for mining Niyamgiri came after the Norwegian Government Council on Ethics (2007) released a report that detailed a long list of transgressions of the law by the Sterlite-Vedanta group, and abuse of the environment and human rights in India and other countries.

The use of *goondas* (hired thugs) by mining companies is a particularly blatant example of double legal standards. As 'outrage against displacement spreads',[4] it is clear to observers in Orissa that the orchestration of *goondas* in support of mining companies is a nexus that involves certain politicians and senior administrators, as well as the mining companies they promote (Dash 2008). The murder of gangster Biranchi Das in Bhubaneswar on 13 April 2008 pointed to senior administrators' involvement in campaigns to terrorise displacement protestors. For example, Raja Acharya, who was arrested for this murder, had a close connection with senior IAS officer Priyabrat Patnaik, who, Raja alleged, offered him a contract working for Posco.[5]

In the Kalinganagar area, leading activists of the Bisthapit Birodhi Jan Manch (People's Platform Against Displacement) have been attacked, and one murdered, while another activist was killed in the Posco area. Amin 'Shyam' Banara was gunned down on 1 May 2008 by goons who accosted him near the Tata factory site — a crime for which gangster Arbind Sing was later arrested. A month before, another activist, Jogendra Jamuda, was shot in the back while driving his mother and wife on a motorbike past the Kalinganagar police station. As Chakradhara Haiburu, 60-year-old spokesman for the BBJM, said, 'If Maoists were involved, it would be Arbind Sing lying dead not Amin Banara'.[6] The main Kalinganagar activists have all received death threats for their opposition to Tata.

Anti-Posco activist Dula Mandal was killed by pro-Posco goons in his village of Govindpur on 21 June 2008, after a day's work alongside hundreds of others, dredging the Jetadhari river mouth. Villagers had alerted the authorities to the importance of this task to avert floods, but after huge delays, and offer of a Rs 20-crore contract for the job, the villagers had decided to do it themselves, which angered businessmen who had hoped to get the contract. After completing the dredging on 30 June, they held a memorial for Dula attended by 3,000 villagers and supporters. A few days later, villagers captured several goons who had used violence, along with six boxes of homemade bombs and other weapons, from the school in Govindpur.[7] When serious violence erupted before this, on 29 November 2007, and bombs had been thrown by goons at a crowd consisting largely of women, Priyabrat Patnaik had made a statement on TV that 'those people have been taught a lesson'.

Similar intimidation, by goons as well as police, took place on 10 March 2008 at a public hearing for a Tata thermal power plant at Naraj, near Cuttack, which would displace several villagers.[8] In this instance, villagers entirely new to this kind of intimidation were beaten up, and they began the process of making a stand against displacement.

Another area where intimidation by goons has escalated is around Maliparbat, a mountain in south Orissa threatened with bauxite mining by Hindalco, where most villagers have come together to oppose the project (Patnaik 2008). Here, goons attacked the village of Maliguda on 20 July, seriously injuring ten villagers who had to be taken to a Koraput hospital. Women and girls were molested.

Villagers who maintain a stance against displacement need the utmost strength and courage, not just because the power nexus confronting them links gangsters and mining companies with people in the government who do secret deals with the companies, but also because of a *manufacturing of consent* by the media. Posco's invitation of journalists to Korea, and Vedanta's invitation of journalists to Lanjigarh, and the money on offer to journalists who promote positive news for these companies, is well known. The number of journalists and editors prepared to take a stand for truth and report what is really happening on the ground, or give a voice to the anti-displacement protestors, is relatively few. So in *the social construction of reality* around the issue of displacement, *the manufacturing of consent* by corporate interests making use of the media plays a significant part.

Tata and Posco followed Vedanta's example of trying to construct their factories before getting mining clearance, in order to exert leverage in their bids. The primary object of their desire is the iron ore in the few as-yet untouched mountains in north Orissa, in a race with Rio Tinto and Mittal. The pollution and devastation of large areas of north and central Orissa by existing iron ore, chromite and coal mines, and about 90 sponge iron factories, have already made life hell for countless *adivasis* (Dash 2008). Sukinda, adjacent to Kalinganagar, has been named one of the 10 most polluted spots on earth (Dutta 2007; CSE 2008: 247). Posco at first did not even want to build a steel plant in Orissa, but was persuaded that this was a condition of gaining access to north Orissa's rich iron deposits. Meanwhile, all the bauxite mountains in south Orissa are exposed to imminent threat of mining clearance. BHP Billiton, Alcoa and Dubai

Aluminium are among the companies known to be manoeuvring for bauxite deals.

Among the most important aspects of development is access to equal justice for all — rich and poor alike. A lot of evidence from the ground indicates that far from getting better, the corruption and intimidation are getting worse. Mining companies, in fact, are notorious for spreading not just material pollution, but also a corruption of values and the dividing of communities.

The pattern for this behaviour was set in the age of the 'robber barons' in 19th century USA, when the biggest capitalists often showed contempt for the process of law. Corrupting elected politicians and Supreme Court judges was a basic part of this system. Cornelius Vanderbilt, one of the first 'railway kings', once remarked, 'What do I care about the law? Hain't I got the power?'. In 1866–68, during the ferocious 'railway wars', rival companies bribed SC judges, and one party was exposed as paying over $1 million in bribes, describing it in his expenses as '*extra and legal services*'. There was an established system for purchasing elected politicians and judges. As Collis P. Huntingdon, another of the 'railway kings', put it in a letter of 1877:

> If you have to pay money to have the right thing done, it is only just and fair to do it ....If a man has the power to do great evil and won't do right unless he is bribed to do it, I think the time spent will be gained when it is a man's duty to go up and bribe the judge (Josephson 1962: 15, 352, 354).

The prevalence of this corruption explains why Abraham Lincoln, shortly before he was assassinated in 1865, drew attention to the dangers of company power for America:

> Corporations have been enthroned...An era of corruption in high places will follow and the money power will endeavour to prolong its reign by working on the prejudices of the people...until wealth is aggregated in a few hands...and the Republic is destroyed (Korten 1995: 58).

'Breaking rules at opportune moments' was one of the secrets of Carnegie's success (Josephson 1962: 43), and for the other robber barons too, laying down a pattern of 'dancing with the law', in which politicians and the judiciary were in effect making and implementing the law at the robber barons' bidding — a pattern painfully visible in corporate takeovers today, in Orissa and worldwide.

The difference in values and beliefs between corporate attitudes to law and those of *adivasis* could not be starker. The Kond concept of Niyam Raja as upholder of law unites a universal with human conceptions of law, like the ancient Indian concept of *dharma*. In fact, hearing that a judge in India's Supreme Court was effectively selling Niyamgiri to Vedanta, by asking the company to set aside fixed sums for tribal development and compensatory afforestation, a Kond elder, in our hearing, said something that demonstrates this connection: '*Taro Karma, Amoro Dharms*' (his the sin, ours the *dharma).*

Another example we witnessed took place during a session of the inquiry by Justice P. K. Mishra into the Maikanch firing on 29 May 2002, when Utkal's chief executive officer was in the witness box, and stated that he could not get the balance sheet to explain where an unaccounted-for Rs 70 crore had gone — listed under 'miscellaneous' in Utkal's accounts, and allegedly set aside for bribes. Unable to account for these missing funds, he passed on responsibility to Ola Lie, the head of Norsk Hydro (resident of London), indicating that Lie was in effect his superior in Utkal, which was then a Hindalco-Norsk-Alcan joint venture. The judge made a joke about the appropriateness of Lie's name, given Utkal's reputation for tampering with the truth. After the Utkal executive, two women were called, an *adivasi* and a Dalit, who had witnessed the shooting in Maikanch, and whose relatives were shot. The whole time each stood in the witness box, she kept her palms joined in *johar/namaste*, in a symbolic plea for justice and truth in that alien environment of the courtroom, where the judge kept an impartial aloofness, while the company lawyers pretended friendliness but tried to trip them up with complicated lines of questioning about who had paid for them to come to Rayagada that day, and where they were during the shooting, implying that they couldn't have seen it, or to cow them with scorn. For example, in answer to the question, 'Occupation?', when one of the women answered, '*Chaso*' (cultivation), the lawyers led a round of titters, as if to dismiss her as an illiterate peasant. Before the end of the session, when the witnesses had left, the judge made the whole courtroom stand while he said that lawyers can be more violent than guns, and that treating villagers with such little respect will erode their faith in our courts.

Indeed, if it is true that Maoists' appeal is on the rise, village people's despair of getting justice at the courts should be counted as a significant factor. The call to armed struggle appears as radical and progressive empowerment for oppressed people who lack legal redress for their grievances. To many observers, it seems that at the grassroots level, money usually decides who wins a case, making a mockery of the idea that the law is impartial between rich and poor. There is little question that the police lodge court cases for unreal offences against activists to deactivate them. Over 500 arrests were made against anti-mining villagers in Kashipur up to 1999 alone (Mahapatra 1999), and villagers attending the court every few weeks for these cases say they have to pay fees or bribes to a range of lawyers and court officials.

A summary of Mishra's report was finally released to the media on 10 October 2003, when *Dharitri* published an account under the title 'Maikanch firing was justified'. Basically, according to the extracts released, the report reaches the contradictory conclusion that grossly excessive force was used, but that the firing was justified. It singles out the OIC (officer-in-command) of Kashipur police station 'for continuing with firing beyond requirement' after the Magistrate had given the order to fire, and also admonishes this magistrate, for giving an open-ended order to fire. The excerpts released mention the 19 rounds fired as excessive, and question the prior intent of the police visit to 'investigate' and 'maintain law and order', but they do not highlight the height at which bullets were fired (i.e., with intention to kill), nor the live ammunition in the guns, which implies a prior intention to cause harm. The report accepted the villagers' account that the incident was provoked when police laid their hands on two of the women. But critics of Utkal had hoped Mishra's inquiry would reveal the collusion between politicians and ministers, police, and company officials. The fact that the report did not apparently touch the question of who called out the armed police, or how this decision was reached, implies to critics that the whole exercise was basically a whitewash. Most controversially, the report went beyond its brief, to justify the alumina project, stating that 'the state cannot afford to remain backward for the sake of so-called environmental protection' — an ideological statement.

In an echo of Cordell's classic novel about Wales, opponents of mining projects talk about a rape of Orissa, its resources as well as its people. Indeed, with the sidelining of legislation that protects India's forests, coasts and land rights by the SEZ and other recent Acts, conservationists as well as rights activists are worried that

India's resources are being looted on a scale that even the East India Company could not dream of, and in the violence and manipulation of law and finance, the ongoing corporate takeover of farming and forest land represents a kind of reincarnation of the EIC — an undermining of India's independence, in which members of the ruling class are colluding with foreign-based financial institutions for short-term gain. In effect, it is the very people and communities living most sustainably that are being sacrificed.

American legal expert Cormac Cullinan's book, *Wild law: A manifesto for earth justice,* raises the question of whether systems of law should now make protecting the basic fabric of life a fundamental concern. As he says, 'Most lawyers and legislators do not know enough about natural regulatory systems, and in any case, do not believe they are relevant to humans ... (We need to) recognise that at the moment the governance systems of most countries and of the international "community" actually facilitate and legitimise the exploitation and destruction of Earth by humans' (Cullinan 2002: 30).

Much of what is being called 'development', is essentially destructive: the removal of non-renewable resources (in the case of Orissa's minerals), and dangerous overuse of water, as well as destruction of communities living basically in harmony with nature. And much of this 'development' promotes *over-consumption*: 'while economists look with pride on the fact that the world economy expanded sevenfold between 1950 and 2000, and world trade is expanding more rapidly, ecologists see that these are based on a profligate use of Earth's "natural capital"' (ibid: 38).

Cullinan calls for a swift change in countries' legal systems to protect the fabric of life in a world which most scientists see as entering a period of severe environmental crisis caused by economic growth gone out of control. The irony of displacement in Orissa is that the very tribal people being displaced have been at the forefront of protecting the environment, living sustainably in the true sense of the word.

The threat of accelerating climate change is a case in point. Orissa is a frontline region in climate change causes as well as effects. As it builds new metal factories, deforests its mountains and valleys for mines, depletes its water and food sources, and accepts a virtually uncontrolled increase in pollution in order to service foreign investors, it is heating up its own climate as well as making a major contribution towards pushing the whole planet towards the tipping point of inevitable runaway global heating. What we need is a fundamental shift of consciousness. We should be learning from Orissa's indigenous people, not dispossessing them of the land they have safeguarded over centuries.

Suggestions for reforming resettlement

1. Minimising development-induced displacement is a must, and the main point in the Orissa and all-India R&R policies of 2006 and 2007 is that they at least recognise this and state it clearly. A recent review of the state of human rights in India by the UN Committee on Economic, Social and Cultural Rights (UNESCR) expresses deep concern about the displacement and forced evictions of millions of families, and their inadequate R&R, especially the adverse impacts on *adivasis* and Dalits, and the harassment of human rights campaigners attempting to help people assert their rights. The committee recommends enforcement of laws that prohibit forced evictions and guarantee proper compensation (UNESCR 2008: paras 31, 71).

2. As Bhagaban Majhi says, no more displacement ought to happen in Orissa until already-displaced people have first been properly resettled and their standard of living has improved. At the very least, a much more stringent attempt should be made by the authorities to avoid displacement. The principle of free, prior informed consent should be applied, as set out in the UN Declaration on the Rights of Indigenous Peoples (September 2007), which says they 'have the right to require that States obtain their free and informed consent prior to the approval of any project affecting their lands, territories and other resources'.

3. The process of consulting with people slated for displacement should be a real and equal procedure, far removed from the present scenario of public hearings, where coercion has become the norm and people's voices have no impact on the outcome. The provisions of the 5th Schedule of the Constitution, the PESA, and the Samata Judgement should be applied to protect tribal people's land rights in Scheduled Areas, at the very least. People's voices should be heard and quoted in official discourse to counteract the proliferation of stereotypes.

4. Social impact assessments should be required. R&R should be carried out by properly trained and well-motivated officials in charge of resettlement, who are trained to understand and deal with the

trauma of displacement, and who have a real motivation of serving the people. In the present circumstances, this is almost unimaginable, so officials need to be trained and educated, starting with a correction of existing stereotypes about tribals, and an awareness of the reality gap, along with a collective determination to bridge it. If people are opposing major projects, it needs to be clearly understood that this is because they are trying to save their communities as well as the land that forms the core of their culture and community. If these people are sometimes angry at the injustice and intimidation they meet with, it needs to be widely accepted that their anger is justified, and that their movements against displacement are seen by many people as an attempt to safeguard the fabric of life itself.

5. Several of the researchers for the UNDP R&R draft commented that for resettlement to be implemented properly and actually raise people's living standards, a radical shift in consciousness is required (Mathur 2008c). For this to happen, the stereotypes of tribal people as 'primitive' and 'backward' need to be completely dismantled, and the classification of certain peoples as 'Primitive Tribal Groups' (still unquestioned in *Adivasi* 2007) should be done away with. The Adivasi Mela in Bhubaneswar still collects representatives from these groups, and creates a 'human zoo' for a few days each year — an inhuman and degrading practice that perpetuates the worst features of colonial ethnography from 150 years ago (Padel 2000). *Adivasis* have a lot they could teach mainstream people about the meaning of community and real sustainability, but changing prevailing attitudes and educating the public to be open and show respect will not be easy. Instead of facilitating the human zoo, anthropologists need to take the lead in confronting the stereotypes and making sure that adivasi voices begin to command the authority they deserve.

Notes

1. 'Money isn't God, but by God, it's no less than God'. *Sunday Express,* 16 November 2003.
2. *The Hindu,* 21 September 2008; *Tehelka,* 5(39), 4 October 2008.
3. *Tehelka*, 5(39), 4 October 2008.
4. *Statesman*, Bhubaneswar, 23 May 2006.
5. *Kalinga Times,* 5 May 2008.
6. See Samadrusti TV, 'Tata steel bullets', http://www.youtube.com/watch?v=vJgr3b8P_JA (accessed 8 April 2010).

7. *Statesman*, 26 June 2008.
8. See Samadrusti TV, 'Tata muscle power', http://www.youtube.com/watch?v=4LvvzuckGjk (accessed 8 April 2010).

References

Agnihotri, Anita. 2008. 'Resettlement issues in water resources development: An empirical study of the lower Suktel irrigation project, Orissa'. *Social Change*, 38(4): 645–60.

Berger, Peter L. and Thomas Luckmann. 1966. *The social construction of reality: A treatise in the sociology of knowledge.* London: Penguin.

Brown, Dee. [1970] 1975. *Bury my heart at wounded knee.* London: Pan.

Campaign for Peace and Justice in Chhattisgarh (CJPC). 2007. *Salwa Judum: Civil war in Chhattisgarh.* Delhi: CPJC, available at http://cpjc.wordpress.com/ (accessed 8 April 2010).

Centre for Science and Environment (CSE). 2008. 'Rich lands, poor People: Is sustainable mining possible? State of India's environment: Citizens' report 6'. Delhi: CSE.

Chang, Jung. 1991. *Wild swans: Three daughters of China.* New York: Simon & Schuster.

Chang, Jung. 2005. *Mao, the unknown story.* London: Cape.

Chomsky, Noam and Edward Herman. 1988. *Manufacturing consent.* New York: Pantheon.

Cordell, Alexander. 1959. *The rape of the fair country.* Monmouthshire, UK: Blorenge Books.

Council on Ethics, Norwegian Govt Pension Fund. 2007. 'Report on Vedanta resources'. Oslo: Ministry of Finance.

Cullinan, Cormac. 2002. *Wild law: A manifesto for earth justice.* Totnes: Green Books, with the Gaia Foundation.

Currie, Bob. 2000. *The politics of hunger: A study of democracy, governance and Kalahandi's poverty.* London: Macmillan.

Das, A. and S. Das. 2005. 'Matiro *poko*, company *loko*' (Earth worm, company man). Documentary film.

———. 2006. '*Ladaat jare*' (The struggle). Documentary film.

Das, Samarendra. 2000. '*Dalalanko kobjare Kondhomaloro gramoporibohono byobostha*' (Into the clutches of the brokers: Kondhomal's village transport system). *Dainik Asha*, 7 November, Berhampur.

Dash, Suryashankar. 2008. 'Niyamgiri, the mountain of law'. Documentary film. Bhubaneswar: Samadrusti TV.

Dutta, Madhumita. 2007. 'Sukinda: Top of the dirty thirty heap', available at http://infochangeindia.org/200712016704/Environment/Features/Sukinda-Top-of-the-Dirty-Thirty-heap.html (accessed 8 April 2010).

Dhalo, B. Krishna. 2007. '*Sarkar javaab diantu!*' (Government, explain!). *Dharitri*, 23 October, Bhubaneswar.

Fernandes, Walter. 2008. 'Sixty years of development-induced displacement in India: Scale, impacts, and the search for alternatives', in Hari Mohan Mathur (ed.), *India social development report 2008: Development and displacement*, pp. 89–102. New Delhi: Oxford University Press.

Fox, C. S. 1932. *Bauxite and aluminous laterite: A treatise discussing in detail.* London: Technical Press.

Goodland, Robert. 2007. *Utkal bauxite and alumina project: Human rights and environmental impacts.* Washington, available at http://www.business-humanrights.org/Categories/Individualcompanies/A/AdityaBirlaGroup (accessed 8 April 2010).

Government of Orissa. 2006. 'Orissa Resettlement and Rehabilitation Policy', GoO Revenue Department, No 18040-R and REH.-1/2006R, as published in *Adivasi,* 46(2), and in *Social Change,* 38(4): 733–49.

Guha, Uma, M. K. A. Siddiqui and P. R. G. Mathur. 1970. *The Didayi.* Calcutta: Anthropological Survey of India.

Harsha Trust, Xavier Institute of Management & District Action Group (Jajpur). 2006. 'Empirical study on people affected and displaced due to Tata Steel in Kalinganagar, Orissa'. Bhubaneswar: Harsha.

Hunter, W. W. 1872. *The annals of rural Bengal (Vol II).* London: Smith, Elder & Co.

Indian People's Tribunal on Environment and Human Rights, headed by Justice S. N. Bhargava. 2006. 'Kashipur: An enquiry into mining and human rights violations in Kashipur, Orissa'. Mumbai: IPTEHR.

Kalshian (ed.). 2007. *Caterpillar and the Mahua flower: Tremors in India's mining fields.* Delhi: Panos.

Kanungo, Pralay. 2008. 'Hindutva's fury against Christians in Orissa'. *Economic & Political Weekly,* 43(37): 16–19.

Kothari, Ashish and Neema Pathak. 2008. 'Defenders of diversity'. *Resurgence,* 250: 36–37.

Korten, David C. 1995. *When corporations rule the world.* London: Earthscan.

Lingaraj. 1995. *Kashipur re andolanara swaro: Bikashara chaka na binasharo bulldozer?* (The wheels of development or the destruction of the bulldozer?). *Pragativadi,* Bhubaneswar, March.

Lopez, Barry. 2008. 'Faithkeeper: Interview with Oren Lyons'. *Resurgence,* 250: 26–30.

McGee, Patrick. [1914] 1982. *Children of the dead end.* Pittsburgh: Caliban Books. Maffi, Luisa. 2008. 'Cultural vitality'. *Resurgence,* 250: 10–11.

Mahapatra, Richard. 1999. 'Confrontation'. *Down To Earth,* 15 April.

Majhi, Bhagaban. 2005. '*Bikash banama jana andolan*' (Development versus people's protest). *Samaj,* Bhubaneswar, 4 January.

Mathur, Hari Mohan. 2006a. 'Resettling people displaced by development projects: Some critical management issues'. *Social Change,* 36(1): 36–86.

Mathur, Hari Mohan. 2006b. 'Globalization, displacement and impoverishment risks: Large corporations and tribal peoples in Orissa, India'. Paper presented at 'Working Group on Involuntary Resettlement, Environmental Risks and Sustainable Development', at 'IAPS/Bibalex Conference on Environment, Health and Sustainable Development', 11–16 September, Alexandria, Egypt.

———. (ed.). 2008a. *India social development report 2008: Development and displacement.* New Delhi: Oxford University Press/Council for Social Development.

———. 2008b. 'Managing the consequences of development-induced displacement', in Hari Mohan Mathur (ed.), *India social development report 2008: Development and displacement,* pp. 179–95. New Delhi: Oxford University Press/Council for Social Development.

———. 2008c. 'A new deal for Orissa's displaced people: Orissa's Involuntary resettlement policy'. *Social Change*, 38(4): 553–75.

Mathur, Shubh. 2008. *The everyday life of Hindu nationalism: An ethnographic account.* Gurgaon: Three Essays Collective.

Meek, R. L. 1976. *Social science and the ignoble savage.* Cambridge: Cambridge University Press.

Moody, Roger. 2007. *Rocks and hard places: The globalization of mining.* London: Zed.

Mosse, David. 2005. *Cultivating development: An ethnography of aid policy and practice.* London: Pluto.

Muhammad, Anu. 2006. 'Monga, micro-credit and the Nobel Prize'. *Counter Currents,* 4 December.

Muthayya, B. C. et al. 1984. *Rehabilitation of displaced villages: A study in Nalco Complex, Damanjodi, Koraput district, Orissa.* Hyderabad: National Institute of Rural Development.

Padel, Felix. 2000. *The sacrifice of human being: British rule and the Konds of Orissa.* Delhi: Oxford University Press.

Padel, Felix; Samarendra Das. 2007. '*Agya*, what do you mean by development?', in Kalshian (ed.), *Caterpillar and the Mahua flower: Tremors in India's mining fields*, pp 26–46. Delhi: Panos.

Padel, Felix. 2008. 'Cultural genocide: The real impact of development-induced displacement', in Hari Mohan Mathur (ed.), *India social development report 2008: Development and displacement,* pp. 103–15. New Delhi: Oxford University Press/Council for Social Development.

Padel, Felix. 2008. 'Orissa's highland clearances: The reality gap in R&R'. *Social Change,* 38(4): 576–608.

Padel, Felix. Forthcoming. *Out of this earth: East India adivasis and the aluminium cartel.*

Patnaik, K. Sudhakar. 2008. 'Project at Mali Parbat: How environmentally friendly', available at http://www.merinews.com/catFull.jsp?articleID=132320 (accessed 8 April 2010).

Paschim Orissa Krushak Sangathan Samanyay Samiti. 2008. *Chashi Rekha.* Sambalpur: POKSSS.

Perchard, Andrew. 2008. 'Sculpting the "Garden of Eden": Patronage, community & the British Aluminium Company in the Scottish highlands, 1895–1982'. Paper presented at a seminar on 'bauxite', Paris.

Pradhan, Jagdish. 1995. 'Aluminium *prakalpo birodhare janaa andolaan'. Sarvodaya*, 51(6), 15 March.

Prebble, John. [1963] 1969. *The highland clearances.* London: Penguin.

Robbins, Nick. 2006. *The corporation that changed the world: How the East India Company shaped the modern multinational.* Hyderabad: Orient Longman.

Ross, Michael. 1999. 'The political economy of the resource curse'. *World Politics,* 51: 297–322.

Samantara, Prafulla. 2006. *Niyamgiri: Waiting for justice.* Berhampur: Lokshakti Abhiyan (Orissa unit).

Sarangi, Deboranjan. 2004. '*Odisharo khanija sampada o baurashtriya* company' (Orissa's mineral resources and the transnational corporation). *Samaj*, Bhubaneswar, 6 June.

Saroj. 2008. '*Kashipur andoland'. Bikolpo Bichar,* July-Dec 2007. Boroghoro, Orissa.

SC & ST Research and Training Institute. 2006. *Adivasi (Development, displacement and rehabilitation),* 46(2), December, Bhubaneswar.

———. 2007. *Adivasi (Primitive Tribal Groups),* 47(1–2), June & December, Bhubaneswar.

Shiva, Vandana and Afasar H. Jafri. 1998. *Stronger than steel: People's movement against globalisation and the Gopalpur steel plant.* Delhi: Research Foundation for Science, Technology and Ecology.

Short, Philip. 1999. *Mao: A life.* London: Hoddon & Stoughton.

Somayaji, Sakarama. 2008. 'Man-made disasters: Displacement, resettlement and rehabilitation in Orissa — Reflections from the field'. *Social Change,* 38 (4): 689–704.

Sundar, Nandini. 2007. *Subalterns and sovereigns: An anthropological history of Bastar 1854–2006.* Second edition. Delhi: OUP.

United Nations Committee on Economic, Social and Cultural Rights (UNESCR). 'Concluding observations, India', 40th session, 28 April–16 May 2008, available at http://www.pwescr.org/docs/Concluding%20Observations.pdf (accessed 8 April 2010).

UN Forum for Indigenous Rights. 2007. 'UN Declaration on the Rights of Indigenous Peoples', available at www.un.org/esa/socdev/unpfii/en/declaration.html (accessed 8 April 2010).

Part III

Compensation and the resettlement process

6

Misunderstood and misused: Re-examining the compensation criterion in resettlement

S. Garikipati*

> Involuntary population displacement and resettlement are frequent enough, big enough, complex and consequential enough; to merit the full mobilization of the social science conceptual and operational tools available to address it (Cernea 1996: 1515).

Development projects may benefit very many people, but often, they also entail social disruption and undesirable consequences for some sections of the population. Displacement of populations epitomises one category of disruptive changes that may occur as by products of such projects (Cernea 1997).[1] Estimates suggest that a new cohort of 10 million people is displaced as a result of development programmes each year in the developing world (World Bank 1994).[2] The magnitude of those adversely affected by development

---

* The author is grateful to Michael Cernea for his thought-provoking correspondence and to Hari Mathur for the opportunity to write this paper. The empirical section of this research was supported by the British Council, Cambridge Commonwealth Trust and Cambridge Philosophical Society. The author is deeply indebted to the people of Narmada valley, especially to the enumerators and translators, and to the support-ers of the Narmada Bachao Andolan for their generous hospitality and assistance.

projects is, however, not as shocking as is the fact that compensation arrangements are almost always considered inadequate, and efforts to resettle the affected people are invariably considered failures. The development-induced displacement and resettlement literature of the 1980s and 1990s was besieged with empirical studies that record such failures.[3]

Over time, experiences with development-induced displacement have seen a revival of academic interest in the 'compensation criterion' (Pearce 1999, 2000; Garikipati 2000; Cernea 2002; Kanbur 2002; Daly 2007; Pearce and Swanson 2007; Cernea and Mathur 2008). Most of the contributions in this area are by economists, which, at times, were in direct response to Cernea's criticism of the limited attention paid by economists to the topic of development-induced displacement (Cernea 1999, 2002).

This theoretical discourse resulted in a severe criticism of the 'compensation criterion' or the 'compensation principle' — the governing principle for cost–benefit analysis, which essentially states that if the gainers can compensate the losers and still be better off, then the project is worth implementing. There are at least three distinct points that emerge from the recent dialogue. First, the compensation criterion is deeply flawed in that in its preoccupation with *efficiency*, it disregards any notion of *equity* (Kanbur 2002; Daly 2007; Pearce and Swanson 2007). In fact, this has compelled economists to adopt more 'equity conscious' approaches, like using weighted sums of gains and losses according to an egalitarian scale of weights (Stiglitz 1999, discussed in Kanbur 2007: 9). Second, researchers have been critical of the conceptual tools used to measure gains and losses within the compensation criterion. More specifically, it is contended that 'willingness to accept', not 'willingness to pay', should be the right measure for losses (Pearce 1999; Pearce and Swanson 2007). Third, critics point out that compensation criterion is not concerned with the actual compensation but regards it only hypothetically (Kanbur 2002; Pearce and Swanson 2007). Kanbur (2002: 7) calls this 'compensation in principle'. They argue that this again brings into question the egalitarian or the distributional implications suggested by the criterion.

In this paper, we take a second look at the compensation criterion, with focus on the three points mentioned above. We start by *re-examining* the theoretical genesis of the compensation criterion.[4] This exercise reveals that some of the criticisms of the compensation criterion are partly down to the way economic theory was used to interpret the principle. Our attempt, we believe, helps restore some of the theoretical confidence in the compensation criterion. We argue that although the criterion suggests the use of 'willingness to accept' while evaluating project costs, this suggestion was not acceptable to the practitioners of cost–benefit analysis until recently. We then demonstrate the practical usefulness of the criterion through a case study. More specifically, we explore the possibility of using the 'contingent valuation method' to elicit their willingness to accept compensation from those displaced by the Sardar Sarovar Project (SSP) in Narmada Valley, India. Our data suggest that such an exercise can elicit values that are incentive-compatible, in that the elicited values reasonably reflect the socioeconomic backgrounds of the affected people.

The rest of the paper is planned as follows. The second section examines the theoretical origins of the compensation criterion and traces its evolution into a practical tool for cost–benefit analysis. In the third section I introduce the case study — the SSP with a focus on the resettlement controversy surrounding it. It also describes the survey villages with particular attention to the socioeconomic lifestyle of their people, since it is these lifestyles that are most likely to be challenged by displacement. The fourth section details the design of an exercise that elicits the SSP-affected people's willingness to accept compensation. The fifth section presents an analysis of the survey data. The final section summarises the study with some concluding comments.

The compensation criterion and surrounding controversy

The development of the compensation criterion

In his otherwise insightful overview of the theoretical origins of the compensation criterion, Kanbur (2002) does not discuss issues surrounding the measurement of gains and losses.[5] We believe these issues are central to the controversy surrounding the compensation criterion. We take a second look at the compensation criterion with a focus on these issues.

In deciding whether to implement a project or not, economists usually use some method of comparing costs and benefits. Such an analysis attempts to solve social welfare problems, which arise when individuals pursuing narrow self interest arrive at outcomes inferior to those that could be achieved through collective action. Although there is no consensus regarding the core assumptions of cost–benefit analysis (CBA), we agree with Kanbur that its main points can be derived by considering the history of its origin.

CBA in its rudimentary form was first conceptualised by Nicholas Kaldor, and was based on a fundamental principle in welfare economics given by Vilfredo Pareto — the Pareto criterion. This criterion allows us to compare the welfare implications of two states of affairs. Thus, a 'Pareto optimum' describes a situation such that any change from it will make at least one person worse off, and a 'Pareto improvement' or 'Pareto superior' describes a change in the situation which makes at least one person better off while none are made worse off, i.e., there are no losers. The main attraction of the Pareto criterion was that it avoids any interpersonal comparisons of well being. However, since projects or policies invariably have losers as well as gainers, the Pareto criterion in its pure form was of little use. The practical and more useful criterion is the potential Pareto criterion or the 'compensation criterion'.

The 'compensation criterion' emerged out of discussions regarding repealing of the Corn Laws among some prominent British economists in the late 1930s.[6] Before that, it was generally believed that all individuals possessed an equal capacity for enjoyment, and gains and losses could de directly compared. Towards the late 1930s, however, leading economists, among them Lionel Robbins and Sir John Hicks, began to question the economist's role as a policy advisor, since such advocacy involved interpersonal comparisons of welfare. Economists began to acknowledge the profession's inability to provide a scientific basis for interpersonal comparisons. Kaldor came up with a solution that could make such comparisons irrelevant. His basic argument was that a project is desirable if it causes the aggregate income to increase, because, in *principle,* everyone can be made better off. The point is that if gains exceed losses then, in *principle,* the losers can be compensated. Hicks, one of the prominent economists of the time, accepted Kaldor's position (Hicks 1939), and this principle eventually came to be known as the 'compensation criterion' or the 'Kaldor–Hicks criterion'.

When it came to turning the in-principle compensation (that turns losers into winners) into *actual* compensation, however, Kaldor showed great reluctance. He wrote that whether compensation should *actually* be distributed 'is a political question on which the economist, *qua* economist, could hardly pronounce an opinion' (Kaldor 1939: 550).[7] By separating *efficiency* from *equity*, the criterion precluded any interpersonal comparisons. Kaldor clearly believed that distributional concerns were outside the scope of economics. This preference for the separation of *efficiency* from *equity* considerations seems to arise from a desire to put economics on a firm base as a scientific discipline, with little or nothing to do with decisions that involve some kind of a value judgment. Kaldor (ibid.: 551) observes that with regard to distributional issues, 'the economist should not be concerned with "prescription" at all, but with the relative advantages of different ways of carrying out certain political ends. For, it is quite impossible to decide on economic grounds what particular pattern of income-distribution maximizes social welfare'. This separation was endorsed by Hicks (1939: 712), who noted that 'if measures making for *efficiency* are to have a fair chance, it is extremely desirable that they should be freed from distributive complication as much as possible'. To Hicks (ibid.: 696) it seems a 'rather dreadful thing to have to accept the view that welfare analysis was unscientific'. Such conclusions, he argues, can have no validity since they will depend entirely on the investigator's own perception of what maximises social welfare.[8]

Clearly, this proposition to separate *efficiency* and *equity* is fine if the compensation criterion is used for normative purposes only (this was perhaps intended by Kaldor and Hicks in their 1939 papers). But such a position is untenable as soon as we leave the abstract world of normative analysis and enter the practical world of policy, where the use of some value judgment becomes an imperative. While we shall return to this point a little later, it is, meanwhile, worth staying on with Hicks.

Measuring costs and benefits

Hicks' later work, in fact, suggests that there was a definite shift towards making the compensation criterion more policy-oriented, and this indeed proved seminal in the area of measuring project- or policy-related benefits and costs.[9] In 1943, Hicks went on to define the terms 'compensating variation' (CV) and 'equivalent variation' (EV), and from these the concepts of and 'willingness to accept' (WTA) and 'willingness to pay' (WTP). Hicks' description of the relationship between CV, and WTA and WTP became the standard test for the compensation criterion, and hence for CBA.[10] It is also the test that we need to consider from the viewpoint of development-induced displacement.[11] In order to intuitively appreciate the concept of CV, consider an individual who will be affected by a move from state N (before project) to state P (after project). The individual's CV for the move from N to P is the income adjustment necessary in state P, in order to make him indifferent between N and the income-adjusted P. If he prefers P to N (he benefits from the project), then his CV is positive and gives the maximum amount he would be willing to pay to move to P. If, however, he prefers N to P (he stands to lose from the project), then his CV is negative and gives the minimum amount he would be willing to accept a move to P.[12]

In summary, the move from N to P passes the compensation criterion if and only if the sum of individuals' willingness to pay for the project exceeds the sum of the willingness to accept payment for the change. WTP is the maximum amount of money someone would pay to buy a good or service he does not already possess (like better roads, cleaner electricity and water supply); and WTA is the minimum amount of money someone would have to be paid to make him give up the good or service that he possesses, or indeed to bear some harm as in the case of intangible costs (homes, lands and satisfaction received from living within a neighborhood).[13] In other words, the potential gainer is buying property rights (over a good or service), and the potential loser is selling his property rights (again over a good or service). Figure 6.1 summarises these measurements corresponding to Hicksian CV test for a move from state N (before project) to a state P (after project).

Note here that Pearce's rights-based approach makes a similar point (Pearce 2002; Pearce and Swanson 2007). The essence of his argument is that since potential losers have property rights over the without-the-project situation (our state N), their willingness to accept compensation for the losses is the right measure of preferences, and not their willingness to pay to avoid the losses. Indeed, Pearce here is in agreement with the Hicksian description of the CV test, and its relationship with WTP and WTA.

Figure 6.1: Measuring costs and benefits of moving from N to P

State N (before project) Benefits: Willingness to accept for losses restored from staying at N Costs: Willingness to pay for gains forgone from staying at N
State P (after project) Benefits: Willingness to pay for gains incurred from moving to P Costs: Willingness to accept for losses incurred from moving to P

The timing is right, perhaps, for us to return to the issue of separation of the *efficiency* and *equity* considerations – the basis on which the compensation criterion has been somewhat severely criticised (Kanbur 2002; Daly 2007; Pearce and Swanson 2007). It is easy to see that separating the issues of growth (efficiency) from those of distribution (equity) may have served a normative purpose. Growth must precede distribution — of this there is little doubt. From a project point of view, before considering distribution of gains among losers, it is clearly important to assert that there are enough gains to go around. Clearly, there is some advantage in analysing a project on a purely potential Pareto criterion. Indeed, if work on the compensation criterion had stopped here, it would have been grave. However, as discussed, Hicks' later work on the CV test for the compensation criterion gave us concepts to measure the aggregate costs (WTA) and benefits (WTP) of a project. This turned the compensation criterion from a purely normative tool into a prescriptive tool.[14] The point is that while the compensation criterion itself abstracts away from distributional issues, and hence from any interpersonal comparison of welfare, the concepts of WTA and WTP that emerge from it allow for such considerations.[15]

In practice, the use of WTA and WTP turns out to be far more equitable than is first suggested. Note, that by definition, willingness to pay for benefits must be finite (people are constrained by what they can pay, and most of the benefits have clear market prices), while willingness to accept could be infinite. This 'income effect' works in favour of the poor when project beneficiaries are comparatively richer (state their WTP) than those adversely affected by it (state their WTA).[16] It is empirically well established that those adversely affected by development projects the world over be-long to some of the most disadvantaged communities.[17] Hence the application of WTA and WTP is likely to be more equitable than suggested in theory.

The use of WTA and WTP in practice

Despite these advantages, WTA and WTP were abandoned as measures of costs and benefits, and economists started searching for alternative ways of doing CBA. Two main reasons may have contributed to this trend. First, using WTA and WTP to calculate costs and benefits from a project implies asking people for an evaluation of their losses or benefits. This way of studying preferences is referred to as 'eliciting preferences'. The other method of studying individual preferences involves observing behaviour in the market, and is referred to as the study of 'revealed preferences'. The latter method is preferred by economists mainly because it is 'incentive compatible', i.e., it provides incentives for truthful revelation of preferences. In other words, individuals have no incentive to deviate from their true preferences when they buy or sell in the market place; however, if asked for their preferences, they may have an incentive to either overstate or understate these. For instance, if compensation is based on losses claimed by the affected, it gives them an incentive to exaggerate. This may result in systematic over-reporting of losses, which can place a project in unwarranted financial difficulties.[18] The practical ramification of this is that willingness to pay and willingness to accept must be elicited in a way that is 'incentive compatible'. Second, asking people for their preferences can be extremely resource intensive; and designing and carrying out an elicitation exercise, especially for a large project, may be exceedingly complicated.

For these theoretical and practical considerations, WTA and WTP were abandoned, and economists started relying on discount rates and market prices to compute the costs and benefits from projects.[19] Clearly, a straightforward comparison of market prices would not take into account distributional concerns, and for this reason, it was important to introduce some notion of equity. This was done mainly by means of assigning weights to the gains and losses of different groups of people according to some egalitarian scale. These are sometimes referred to as 'distributional weights' or 'equity weights'. The method for applying socially-sensitive CBA is sufficiently well documented in any standard textbook in the area.[20]

Although economists, more or less, tended to agree with this way of appraising projects, it was hardly ever used in practice except in a few experimental cases. Studies document the pressure factors at the national and international levels that may have contributed to the use of shortcuts in CBA (Little and Mirrless 1990; Roy 1999, as discussed in Kanbur 2002).[21] Distributional weights were abandoned in favour of simpler methods of computing net benefits of the project that relied very much on the prices and discount rates used, which, in turn, relied on the intuitive abilities of planners and policy makers. In such a scenario, it was obviously easier to implement projects that imposed costs on people who were economically poor and politically voiceless. If any compensation was offered to the affected, it was done so as *fait accompli*. There was little incentive to consult the project-affected people and any opposition was easily asphyxiated. In his paper, Daly (2007) refers to this as the transition from an 'exchange economy' (which is characterised by negotiations between the parties involved) to that of a 'threat economy' (where negotiations are replaced by force).

This trend continued more or less unabated till the early 1990s (and is common even now), when the human and environmental costs associated with development projects could no longer be ignored. The methodology of CBA was criticised for being arbitrary in its choice of parameters, and for not including social and environmental costs — which, at times, were substantial enough to overturn the project decision.[22] These costs could not be included in conventional CBA because the value attached to social and environmental goods could not be inferred from behaviour observed in the market. Typically, such goods could not be commoditised because of the externalities involved, like in the case of public goods. These inadequacies with the CBA, prompted studies to experiment with alternative ways of measuring the costs and benefits associated with non-marketable outcomes of a project. One technique that suggested itself readily was that of Contingent Valuation Method (CVM), which was already being used by environmental economists.

CVM is a survey technique used to accommodate environmental 'intangibles' or similar concerns within the framework of project evaluation, either by looking at the surrogate markets or by creating hypothetical ones (Pearce 1983; Krutilla and Fisher 1985; Dasgupta and Mäler 1994; Dinwiddy and Teal 2004).[23] Where hypothetical markets are created, people are asked to directly report their willingness to pay (WTP) to obtain a specified good/service, or their willingness to accept (WTA) to give up a specified good/service, rather than inferring these from observed behavior in conventional markets (FAO 2000). The name of the method refers to the fact that the values revealed by the respondents are contingent upon the constructed or simulated market presented in the survey (Portney 1994). These studies are sometimes referred to as 'elicited' or 'stated' preference studies.

To our knowledge, Pearce (1999) was the first to recommend that the CVM technique should be used to evaluate costs associated with development-induced displacement, and Garikipati (2000) was the first to report such an exercise (also see Garikipati 2002, 2005).

Although Hicks' compensating variation test recognised that WTA is the correct measure for losses, economic theory suggests that there is little actual difference between the measures of WTA and WTP, and the difference, if any, can be explained by an 'income effect'.[24] The essence of this argument is that if income constraints are removed, evaluating losses using WTA or WTP would give us the same money measure of preferences. This is because the only constraint on WTP is that of the individual's ability to pay.[25] The implication of this reckoning is that either of the measures may be used in practice.[26] Indeed, the CVM literature strongly recommends the use of WTP for measuring both gains and losses (Mitchell and Carson 1989; Arrow et al. 1993).

Defying this theoretical opinion, empirical studies using the CVM routinely find that the measures of WTA differ significantly from those of WTP. More specifically, they find that WTA results in considerably higher money measure of preferences than WTP (see Hanemann 1991; Horowitz and McConnell 2002; Amiran and Hagen 2003). Apart from the income effect discussed above, three main reasons have been put forward to explain the disparity between the two measures. First, we have the 'substitution effect', according to which WTA may be considerably larger than WTP when it is rather difficult to find a substitute for the good to be valued (as is usually the case with environmental goods).[27] Second, the 'endowment effect', which contends that WTA and WTP may often depend on perceived or 'moral' property rights (Boyce et al. 1992). The difference between the measures becomes very large if respondents reject the property rights implied by the WTP measure.[28] Finally, we have a psychological line of reasoning, according to which using WTA to measure costs, and WTP to measure benefits, closely correspond with the way people perceive gains and losses.[29] The idea underlying this argument is that from a psychological point of view, a WTA format where people are being asked to state the amount of compensation they need to incur a loss is not symmetric to a WTA format where they are bidding for a gain. 'Losses appear to matter much more than gains to most people, and valuation of goods depends, to a large degree, on...the direction of change...' (Knetsch 1995: 140).

In the case of development-induced displacement, there is a further reason for not using WTP to evaluate losses, because the affected are usually poor and the costs borne by them may well exceed their willingness to pay, which is constrained by their incomes.

As the problem with using WTP to measure both gains and losses became better known, studies began to advocate using WTP for gains and WTA for losses (e.g., Ahlheim and Buchholz 1999; Garikipati 2000; Pearce 2002; Pearce and Swanson 2007). This sees us coming back full circle to the Hicksian CV test for compensation criterion, from which WTA and WTP were derived in the first place. It seems that that the governing principle of CBA was abandoned, only to be re-advocated after all this time. In some sense, the suggestion of reviving the use of WTA to measure losses seems to restore some of the theoretical glory that has been long overdue to the compensation criterion. The resource constraints and the pressure factors present in the days when shortcuts to CBA were adopted are present even today, but the significant intangible costs associated with development projects call for valuation techniques which cannot be based on market prices alone.

From abstract theory to application

In the rest of this paper, we demonstrate the usefulness of designing a CVM exercise to elicit the willingness to accept compensation from people displaced by a development project. Before we proceed to design the CVM study, it is in order to first introduce the case study.

The case study

The Narmada Valley Development Project is one of the largest multipurpose river valley projects in the world. It envisages the construction of 30 large, 135 medium, and 3,000 small dams. Though the idea to dam the river goes back to the 1950s, its implementation became complicated because the river passes through the three states of Gujarat, Madhya Pradesh (MP) and Maharashtra, and they could not agree on the division of the project's costs and benefits (see Figure 6.2).[30]

Figure 6.2: The Narmada River

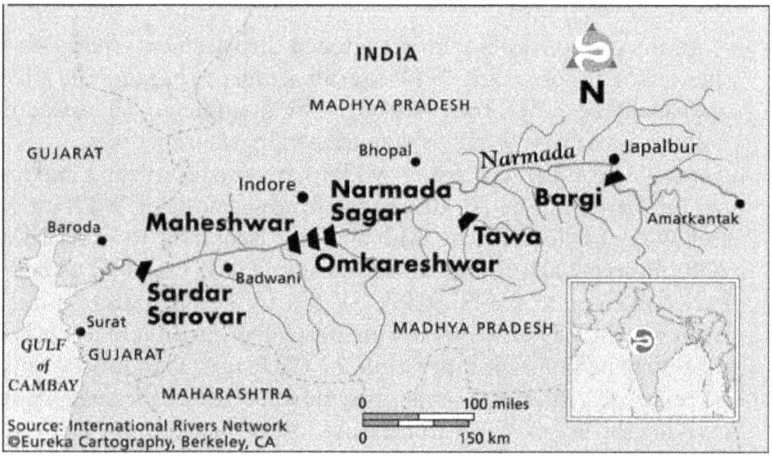

Source: International Rivers Network (IRN) (1999). Copyright Eureka Cartography, Berkeley, CA.

In 1969, the Narmada Water Disputes Tribunal (NWDT) was set up to arbitrate the dispute among the states. The NWDT passed its final judgment in 1978 — the NWDT Award — and the construction of the biggest dam within the project, the SSP, started in 1987.[31] It is this dam around which the resettlement and environmental controversies have centred.

When completed, the dam is expected to be 455 feet high, and its claimed benefits include an installed capacity of 1,450 MW of power and irrigation of 1.8 million hectares of land. Some other benefits are claimed to be the provision of drinking water and irrigation to 40 million people in the drought-prone areas of Kutch and Saurashtra in Gujarat and Rajasthan (Paranjpye 1990). The project was to be completed in the year 2000 (Pathak 1991).

Like any other major dam project, the benefits come with a price tag. It involved a total investment of Rs 6,406 crore, which was revised up to Rs 13,500 crore, at 1986-87 prices (Sheth 1995). The reservoir alone will submerge 37,000 hectares, of which about 11,000 hectares are classified forest. Besides this, it will displace about 40,000 families or 130,000 people in 297 villages (Narmada Control

Authority 1995). Of these, 245 belong to MP, 33 to Maharashtra, and 19 to Gujarat.[32] It is the displacement and resettlement of these people that has become the most controversial issue in the debate surrounding the dam.

Over time, the debate has become extremely polarised. On one side are the pro-dam campaigners who believe that the dam is the 'lifeline of Gujarat', and on the other, there are critics who claim that the costs far exceed the perceived benefits of the dam. Some of the criticisms against the project are that it is not financially viable, will have disastrous environmental consequences, that there is corruption involved in water and electricity distribution, and that better alternatives have not been explored. This paper focuses only on the issues that surround the resettlement aspects of the project.

In a country where dams were eulogised as 'symbols of self sufficiency', and where displacement of people without adequate compensation was justified in the larger 'interest of the nation' (Kothari 1996; also see Mathur 1995), the NWDT Award was hailed as a breakthrough for providing land-based compensation. For the first time in India, 'land for land' compensation was announced for the SSP's reservoir-affected (Morse and Berge 1992).[33] According to the Award, since Gujarat was the prime beneficiary of the project, it was to rehabilitate the affected within its territory, specifically in the command areas of the SSP, and for those unwilling to migrate, bear the entire cost of rehabilitation (NCA 1995). It was also directed to make the provisions one year prior to the actual submergence at any stage. Even though the Award was an improvement over the past policies, it was unsatisfactory in many respects. For instance, it recognised only legal landowners as eligible for land compensation. This was problematic given that land records were poorly maintained in several dam-affected villages (Center for Social Studies 1985, 1990, 1997b). This started a long fight for a just compensation policy. The ARCH-Vahini and the NBA were the two NGOs at the forefront of this agitation.[34] In a bid to speed up the construction of the SSP, the Gujarat government acceded to most of the demands, drawing up one of the most comprehensive resettlement policies, described as 'a model for all the world to follow' (Morse and Berger 1992: 187).[35] With the impressive motive to restore livelihoods, it sought to award each eligible family with a minimum of five acres of irrigable land, a housing site and entitlements to other facilities like community-based resettlement, cattle pastures and common lands, hospitals and schools (NCA 1995).[36]

Despite this ambitious blueprint, there were several difficulties with its implementation. Land allotment, one of its crucial components, ran into severe problems, both on account of quantity and quality (CSS 1991, 1997a; Morse and Berger 1992; TISS 1997). This had also adversely impacted provisions like community relocation and provision of commons. The same studies also reported several problems with other amenities, such as housing, and problems in integrating with host communities. Over time, the resettlement sites became iconic of the 'impoverishment process' that plagues resettler communities worldwide, as illustrated by Cernea's model (1990). The resettlers began to abandon their resettlement sites and their compensatory entitlements, and started returning to their partially submerged original villages, which were still considered much more livable (Garikipati 2002).

A controversy that was largely parochial till the early 1990s came to command unparalleled international attention when growing protests by the affected people compelled the World Bank, SSP's main financer, to review the situation (also see Thukral 1992). The review team (popularly called the 'Morse Committee') returned a 'guilty as charged' verdict against the project authorities (Morse and Berger 1992). This resulted in much introspection at the Bank and in its famous 'Resettlement and Development' report (World Bank 1994), which emphasised the difficulty with implementing resettlement schemes. This also spurred NBA, one of the anti-dam NGOs, into legal action against the project authorities. In 1994, NBA filed a case against the NCA in the Supreme Court of India. A year later, the court passed a stay order that halted dam construction with its lowest part standing at 89 metres. This order has since been rescinded and the dam now stands 110.64 meters high. Furthermore, in May 2006, the Supreme Court declined a stay on the construction to raise its height to 121.92 metres (News Nerve 2006). The controversy in the Narmada Valley that began nearly three decades ago, and instituted a change in global resettlement policy, is, however, far from over. Agitations against the impending increases in the height of the dam and the displacement it is causing have become a way of life for the people of the valley.

The survey villages

A total of nine survey villages were selected for this study such that they represent the various resettlement experiences in the Narmada

Valley. Of these, the villages Kelu, Khera and Kewar (in MP) have not yet been displaced (ND villages); Krit, Kani and Kapi (in Gujarat) and Mati (in Maharashtra) are resettlement sites (R-sites); and Gaman, Mapali (in Gujarat) are partially submerged (PS villages) to which the affected are returning because of their disappointing experiences with resettlement.[37] A total of 847 households were interviewed — this includes every family living in these villages at the time of the survey. The fieldwork was carried out in two stages: between December and June 1998, and April and July 2003.

In the surveyed communities, caste (social) and class (economic) statuses closely correspond. Social status is deeply embedded in the community's psyche; the villagers identify themselves and others as belonging to upper or to lower castes. This also reflects economic status since caste in these communities is firmly linked to the social endorsement to withdraw from labouring for others and, at privileged levels, to withdraw from working on one's own farm. Of the 518 households surveyed in MP (ND villages) 6 per cent belong to the Patidar caste — an upper caste; the rest (94 per cent) belong either to the Bhilala or to the Bhil tribe — lower castes. All the 329 households surveyed in Gujarat and Maharshtra (R-sites and PS villages) are tribal; of these, 37.4 per cent belong to the Tadavi tribe, which is considered a high caste tribe, 59 per cent belong to the Vasava tribe, who are next in the tribal hierarchy, and the remaining 3.6 per cent belong to the Guvar tribe, considered an inferior tribe.

It is useful to analyse community-specific inter-caste interactions in light of their socioeconomic characteristics. The ND villages have large tracts of fertile land with easy access to markets. People have access to very few common property resources and even riverbed cultivation during the dry season is under a highly regulated contract system. Fertile land in Khera and Kewar is largely under the control of a handful of Patidar landlords, which, in the presence of a surplus landless tribal workforce, has helped perpetuate heavily exploitative labour relations. Patidars own between 25 to 175 acres of land each and are hence against relocation, which, under the current resettlement scheme, would leave them with a fraction of their landholdings. Given their economic pre-eminence and caste superiority, the Patidars have imposed their anti-dam politics on entire villages, consisting largely of landless or marginal landholders, who, *subject to their willingness to move to Gujarat*, actually stand to gain from the land awarded under the resettlement scheme. Resettlement officials are not allowed to enter these village and posters proclaiming the village's anti-dam stance can be found everywhere. Kelu is a Bhilala village that has escaped such divisive dam politics because of a much more equitable socioeconomic structure.

In contrast to the economic silhouette of ND villages, the PS villages, located in isolated hilly terrains, are largely non-monetised, subsistence economies with poorly defined property rights, mainly because of access to surplus land. Over 63.4 per cent of the land cultivated is common land and 53.1 per cent of the households cultivate riverbeds during the summer months. Because of easy access to common pastures, the villagers keep large livestock (nine cattle and 13 goats on average). Households also harvest a number of forest products like *mahuda* (madhuca indica), *temru* (diospyros melanoxyplon), timber and bamboo, both for their own use and for the market. The economy relies heavily on an intricate net of couched social contracts. Reciprocal exchanges of labour and other resources (like draught-animal power) are at the heart of such contracts (CSS 1990, 1997; Baviskar 1995; Hakim 1996; TISS 1997). Access to communal labour and resources is determined by social status that delimits a household's economic strategies, creating closely corresponding social and economic statuses. Land cultivated by any household, among other aspects like housing and livestock ownership, is especially limited by its access to communal labour. For instance, the Guvars (traditional herdsmen and a socially inferior tribe) are not allowed to cultivate any land (living by the in-kind payments received for cattle herding), while the village superiors (from the Tadvis or Vasava tribes) may cultivate more land than can be supported by family labour alone. So, although the deep disparities and exploitative relations seen in Khera and Kewar are absent, communal customs have been designed to help perpetuate a repressive class system. These villages are organised in *phalias* or hamlets of 10 to 25 houses, and are nearly self-contained socioeconomic units.[38] The official stance on these PS villages is that they do not exist; the ground reality as elucidated here, however, is very different.[39] Later visits in 2003 suggest that since the time of the survey in 1998, more people have returned to these villages.

The R-sites to which people were relocated between the late 1980s and early 1990s have neither the intense economic divide of the ND villages nor the communal living of the PS villages. These sites are simply a clustered assortment of tin-roof houses, without even the basic sanitation facilities that are associated with the most isolated and backward villages of India. Krit is one of 40 sites used to relocate people of Gaman, and Kani and Kapi are two of the 10 sites used for people of Mapali (Sardar Sarovar Punarvasahat Agency 1997). The distance between a PS village and its R-site is about 100 kilometres, and it takes anywhere between five to nine hours to travel one way. Currently, without irrigation, farming the five acres awarded by the government at Krit is proving to be a challenge and is barely enough to eke out an existence (if completed, the SSP should irrigate Krit). The absence of cattle pastures has also resulted in a decline in cattle numbers (a goat and two cattle on an average), limiting supplementary off-farm incomes. These factors have forced the hitherto communal labour-sharing people of Krit to supplement their incomes by working for landlords from surrounding villages. This is a common experience among resettlement sites. Absence of cattle pastures and cemeteries at Krit also results in frequent clashes between the resettlers and their host community. The future of the Guvars at Krit is also horrifyingly uncertain. As punishment for breaking away from their traditional occupation of cattle-herding, and for challenging tribal hierarchy by cultivating their resettlement lands, the Guvars face severe ostracism. Not only have their lands been confiscated, but they are also not allowed to tend other people's cattle. In pursuing egalitarian aims, relocation, it seems, has led to some unintended consequences. The R-sites of Kani and Kapi are very similar, and the villagers also continue to maintain close ties between these sites. They continue to practise labour sharing, both because of irrigated lands (which require labour throughout the year) and because of their distance from neighbouring landlord villages.

Designing an incentive-compatible consultation process

Before designing the consultation exercise with the displaced, it was important to assess whether to consult individual households or communities. To begin with, the latter approach appeared more practicable. It, however, raised difficult problems, particularly in connection with identifying credible representative institutions for the purpose of bargaining and establishing an effective negotiating framework (Goyal 1996; Singh 1997a). Where representatives could be readily identified, they inexorably wielded considerable socioeconomic ascendancy, and any attempt to include others was frustrated by a social matrix impeding interactions between people from divergent backgrounds. In view of these dynamics, consulting individual households was deemed more appropriate. However, I concede that consulting communities may be the only viable way forward, especially in cases like the SSP where large numbers are involved, and that further research is required into how to constitute more equitable and indigenously acceptable communal institutions.

The consultation experiment was designed using the Contingent Valuation Method (CVM). This study uses the CVM to ask the affected for a valuation of their WTA to give up their homes and lands.[40] Such an exercise would be the first step towards 'voluntary resettlement', which is opposed to 'involuntary resettlement' and has a number of fairly obvious advantages. It helps guarantee that the process of displacement does not adversely affect the displaced people and helps facilitate the implementation of resettlement measures, since all parties involved have an incentive to cooperate (Drèze 1994). Besides this, pending omniscient planners, it has the potential to ensure that compensation reflects the true losses incurred by the affected and can aid in a more sincere cost–benefit analysis (Garikipati 2002, 2005).

Broadly speaking, CVM surveys can adopt an open- or close-ended format. The former requires the respondent to state the value of losses due to the project, while the latter presents the respondent with a pre-formulated compensation package which the respondent then accepts or rejects. Open-ended questions are not only incentive-incompatible (respondents can overstate their losses), but are more difficult to answer as they require independent quantitative estimation of an unfamiliar good (Aprahamian, Chanel and Luchini 2004). Close-ended questions, on the other hand, are more incentive-compatible and are easier to tackle since they frame discrete-choice questions that mimic the decision-making that individuals face in everyday life (Herriges and Shogren 1996). It is for these reasons that the NOAA Panel (Portney 1994) as well as more recent developments of CVM recommend the use of this approach, and hence this study uses the discrete-choice approach to elicit people's WTA to accept displacement.

Before commencing with the household consultation exercise, several village-level meetings were organised. These were mainly designed as unstructured interactive sessions to create an appreciation of the investigation underway, and to inspire mutual trust and understanding.[43] This was important given the polarisation between the anti- and pro-dam views in the Valley, and the general aura of suspicion surrounding outsiders asking resettlement questions.

The consultation exercise had three parts. In the first part, a socio-economic survey was conducted which was used later to understand the resettlement preferences of the project affected. In the second part, the project-affected were asked about their existing compensation package. This was to help with the design of hypothetical compensation to be used in the elicitation part of the survey. In the final part of the exercise, the respondents were offered a set of four hypothetical compensation packages (see Table 6.1). After being told that this was a mere research exercise and would not influence their actual entitlements to compensation, they were asked to either accept or reject these packages. The packages contain varying amounts of cash explicitly in exchange for three important aspects of their pre-displacement lives: commons, community and irrigable lands. The idea was to estimate people's WTA cash in exchange for these qualitative aspects of their lives, since reproducing them elsewhere is difficult if not impossible. In other words, the aim of the CVM survey was to elicit the monetary value that the affected place on each

Table 6.1: Hypothetical Compensation Packages[†]

Short Name	*Package Description*
1. No-Commons	Land and housing as in the original village. Land offer subject to the legal ceiling.[††] Cash offered as compensation for loss of commons.[†††]
2. No-Other-Caste	As No-Commons, but relocation with own tribe only, as opposed to the entire community.
3. No-Community	As No-Commons, but cash offered as compensation for relocating without community.[††††]
4. Only-Cash	Only cash as compensation for displacement.[†††††]

Notes: [†] The packages were not changed for the 2003 surveys, because the resettlement situation and prices remained more or less similar.

[††] Legal land ceiling is 27 acres in rural MP and 55 acres in rural Gujarat (Appu 1996).

[†††] Rs 20,000 were offered after considering the average expenditure on fuel and fodder at the R-sites.

[††††] Equal numbers of respondents were randomly offered either Rs 40,000 or Rs 60,000. These amounts were decided after considering the average labour expenditure at the R-sites.

[†††††] Equal numbers of respondents were randomly offered Rs 200,000, Rs 250,000 or Rs 300,000. These amounts were decided after considering the average price of land and housing at the R-sites.

(significant) dimension of their losses. In order to minimise the influence of 'ordering bias' (Frisch 1993), the evaluation questions were randomly ordered and the sample was also split randomly for packages offering different cash amounts to different respondents.

Respondents were advised that their responses would remain confidential; to emphasise this, interviews were always held within or around their homes and only in the presence of household members. Considerable amount of time was spent in describing the packages, and the respondents were also given ample time to consider the evaluation questions and consult with family members.[41] Respondents were also informed that they were free 'not to make up their minds'. Finally, to check the reliability of the responses, a 'debriefing session' was organised in which the respondents were asked to reconsider their responses and check that they understood their elicited preferences and were serious about these (for why this is important, see Hanemann 1994).[42] This was done by taking them through each of the choices they had made and then questioning them to understand the reasoning behind their elicited preferences. Less than two per cent of the respondents changed their minds during these sessions. Their responses were altered and included in the final analysis.

The resettlement preferences

As a prelude to the CVM survey, the respondents were asked for their perception regarding their resettlements (either as a living experience or as an anticipated one). These were found to be in sharp contrast with official claims. Where displaced, people revealed their acute discontentment with resettlement, and where not yet displaced, they seemed completely ignorant regarding their imminent relocation. For instance, although a large majority (73.3 to 96.4 per cent) of the affected from R-sites and PS villages are unhappy about their resettlements and have repeatedly reported their various grievances to the authorities, official documents claim that the same people have been satisfactorily rehabilitated (SSNN 1995a). Also, according to official documents, 79.8 per cent of the affected from the ND villages are willing to relocate from MP to Gujarat (SSNN 1995b), whereas our survey reveals that 69.7 per cent of them actually prefer to resettle in MP itself, and none of them knew that they were going to be relocated to Gujarat.[44] Interestingly, 81 per cent of the displaced from

R-sites and PS villages and 99 per cent from the ND villages believe that SSP will have no benefits. Also, 97 per cent from the R-sites and PS villages report their compensations as 'not fair' and their living standards to have deteriorated after resettlement. Although this inquiry was primarily designed to work as an icebreaker for the CVM survey, it reveals some very serious problems with the current resettlement situation in the Narmada Valley. The rest of this section discusses the results of the experiment with the CVM survey.

Interestingly, responses for the No-Commons and No-Community package are somewhat similar across the villages, while the No-Other-Caste and Only-Cash packages are more acceptable to the ND villagers. To see why this is so and for an insight into the mechanisms underlying people's elicited preferences, we consider the response to each package in some detail below.

The no-commons package

Table 6.2 presents the response received for the No-Common package by village type. It is apparent from this table that this package was overwhelmingly accepted by the affected irrespective of the village type. This result is in contradiction to the popular belief regarding the resettlement preferences of the SSP-affected. Both the resettlement policy document and the literature (for instance, studies by CSS and TISS; see CSS 1983; TISS 1997) lead us to believe that the affected value their access to commons and, therefore, it may be unlikely that the loss of commons this dimension of their lives can be compensated for with cash. This result is better understood when the relevant socioeconomic information pertaining to the lives of the affected is examined. This exercise reveals the rationale

Table 6.2: Number of Households accepting the compensation packages (percentage)

No.	*Response* / *Package*	*ND-villages*	*R-sites*	*PS-villages*	*All Affected*
1.	No-Commons	482 (93)	160 (88.9)	133 (89.2)	775 (91.5)
2.	No-Other-Caste	399 (77)	157 (87.2)	124 (83.2)	680 (80.3)
3.	No-Community	67 (12.9)	32 (17.8)	23 (15.4)	122 (14.4)
4.	Only-Cash	223 (43.0)	41 (22.8)	28 (18.8)	291 (34.4)

Source: Author's fieldwork.

behind their elicited resettlement preferences, and also helps in verifying the same.[45] In the process, it becomes evident that their revealed preferences reflect their elicited ones. The result on commons is examined first.

Table 6.3 reports dependence on commons, both for the ND villages and the displaced villages, i.e., the R-sites and PS villages. The latter are seen to depend much more on their commons than the former. This is because the not-displaced villages do not have access to any such commons. Even riverbed cultivation in these villages is regularised. It is quite straightforward then to understand why the affected from ND villages accepted cash in lieu of commons. Why others from R-sites and PS villages, which show considerable dependence on commons, have done so, however, needs further investigation.

Table 6.3: Dependence on the commons at the original villages†

Description of the Parameters	*ND Villages*	*R-sites and PS Villages*
Dependence on common land	*Units or source*	
• Share of common land in total land cultivated	Negligible	63%
• Households cultivated riverbed in summer	47%††	54%
Dependence on forest resources	*Units or source*	
• Number of forest labourers per household	–	1
• Fodder for cattle†††	From market	From forest
• Fuel wood collected per month	–	4 quintals
• *Mahuda* (*madhuca indica*) collected per annum	–	2 quintals
• Annual earnings from the sale of *temru* (*diospyros melanoxyplon*)	–	Rs 280

Source: Author's fieldwork.

Notes: † All figures are in averages.

†† Even though riverbed cultivation is seen in the not-displaced villages, the cultivation of the same has been regularised and it cannot, therefore, be construed as a common resource.

††† The number of cattle owned by an average household is a good proxy for the amount of fodder required. An average displaced household held about 13 goats and 10 cattle at the original village. For the not-displaced affected, the same average stood at 8 and 7, respectively.

The R-sites and PS villages, which substantially depended on commons were relocated 5–8 years back. During this period, many at the R-sites have been forced to go without common resources and explore alternatives. Around 60 per cent of them turned to the market to meet such demands. In the process, they sold most of their cattle, retaining only those they could realistically maintain. Table 6.4 lists their expenditure in absence of such resources at the resettlement sites, which was between Rs 4,000 and 5,000 (£70) per annum. This being the case, they no longer view these resources as irreplaceable and can attach an approximate value to them. This is not to say that they put a price tag on forest, but when faced with a sum of Rs 20,000 (£300), they are in a position to say how far in terms of forest resources the amount will take them. To put things in perspective, Rs 20,000, if used to buy forest-based resources, can be expected to last for about four years. It is, thus, a reasonable sum of money for the affected to accept in lieu of commons. Thus, explaining the overwhelming positive response received for the Minus Commons package.

Table 6.4: Corresponding annual expenditure in the absence of forest resources†

Description of the Parameters	*ND Villages*	*R-sites and PS Villages*
Expenditure on fodder††	2,300	3,600
On agricultural tools	1,300	30
On domestic fuel	600	200
On smoke and drink†††	–	100
Total	**31,200**	**3,930–4,930**

Source: Author's fieldwork.

Notes: † All figures are average expenditure in Rupees.

†† The average goat and cattle holding of the displaced households has come down drastically after relocation and is 1 and 2, respectively.

††† At the not-displaced villages, such habits were considered taboo and it was very difficult to get any estimate.

The no-other-caste package

The No-Other-Caste package is also popular, mainly because, except for Khera and Kewar, the survey villages have a more or less homogeneous caste structure. When compared to others, people who rely on members of other tribes for their livelihoods are less likely to accept relocation with their own tribe only. Such inter-tribe dependence is seen in almost all the surveyed communities: in Khera and Kewar, it emanates from disparities in land holdings; and in Krit, Gaman, Mapali and Mati, from disparities in social statuses. To a much lesser extent, it is also seen at the R-sites and in PS villages. In fact, 67 per cent of the people at Khera and Kewar, and all Guvars (whose very survival depends on their communities) rejected this package, while it was popular with the majority of the other households. This includes only those who gave categorical responses.

The no-community package

In sharp contrast to the trend observed for the other packages, only 14.4 per cent said 'yes' to this package, despite a substantial increase in the cash component when compared to the previous packages. It was not only overwhelmingly rejected by the affected, but further discussions revealed that they were sharply critical of it, since it explicitly tried to substitute cash for their community. Evidently, relocation with members of their own community was important for most respondents, and, in general, the marginal rate of substitution of 'commons for cash' is much lower than that of 'community for cash'. The practice of communal labour was seen only in villages with a more or less homogeneous class and caste structure, and was a good proxy for community dependence. A rough estimate of this dependence is constructed in Table 6.5 (panel a).[46] From the estimates presented here, it is easy to see why the affected who practiced communal labour were more reluctant to leave their communities and also less likely to accept cash compensation.

There were communities, however, that were seen to move away from this practice. In the case of one of the resettlement sites surveyed, Krit, such a 'move away' was seen to be a by-product of their relocation. Once again, the affected turned to the market to buy and sell labour. The expenditure incurred by the affected in the absence of communal labour at their resettlement sites is presented in Table 6.4 (panel b). On an average, the affected were seen to spend Rs 7,500 (£100) on labour for construction of house, and Rs 1,350 (£20) per annum on farm labour. It is quite reasonable to imagine that since people had been forced to explore alternatives, and in this process came to associate the practice of communal labour with expenditure

Table 6.5: Significance of community life for the displaced affected[†]

Description	*Units*
Number of hours of labour provided under communal labour sharing[††]	
• Average no. of man-hours required for the construction of a house	540
• Average no. of man-hours required for work on the farm per annum	200
Corresponding expenditure in the absence of labour sharing[†††]	
• Labour expenses incurred while constructing a house	Rs 7,750
• Labour expenses incurred for work on the farm per annum	Rs 1,350
Significance of distance in maintenance of social relations	
• Distance at which men in the village married	14 km
• Average no. of times the women leave their villages in one year	3
• The same average after relocation	1

Source: Author's fieldwork.

Notes: † All figures are in averages and have been approximated to the nearest round figure.

†† Though one of the not-displaced villages, Kelu, used to practice communal labour, this was a long time ago and no reliable estimates could be obtained.

††† These estimates are for the village Krit that used to practice communal labour sharing but no longer does so.

incurred on labour, they were in a position to accept or reject a certain cash offer in lieu of community-based relocation. Since the amount offered in the No-Community package was about 3 to 5 times more than their labour expenses (Rs 40,000 or Rs 60,000), the package was acceptable to most of the affected.

The only-cash package

The Only-Cash package was accepted by 34.4 per cent of the affected, and although this result may seem difficult to reconcile with the responses received for the No-Community package, further inquiry revealed a very interesting implicit understanding among those accepting this package. Their intention was not to take the cash and start life on their own, but to resettle with others from the community accepting this package. Most also demonstrated an understanding of the amount offered and knew approximately what they wanted to do with it.[47]

The implications of these findings for the SSP's resettlement scheme are enormous. We limit comments to the three pivotal features of the scheme that were also the focus of the CVM survey: commons, community resettlement and universal provision of land. Provision of commons at R-sites was envisaged as a means of minimising disruption to the livelihoods of the resettlers; however, converting of this good intention into good practice has been difficult because of non-availability of suitable land. Our findings suggest that alternate provisions like cash transfers or price subsidies would have also been appreciated. These could have mitigated the sudden loss of commons and given people time to explore alternatives.

Community relocation was also expected to facilitate rehabilitation, given that most of the displaced people belonged to closely knit communities. My findings suggest that not all respondents prefer community-based relocation. Victims of exploitative socioeconomic relations, and those who have had an opportunity to interact with people from other communities (via markets), are more willing to accept cash and move out of their communities, while those who practice labour sharing are less willing to do so.

Universal land provision was based on the assumption that all the affected prefer land-based compensation. In direct contradiction to this, one third of the respondents accepted cash compensation. Cash as an alternative to land compensation has some compelling features. For instance, it is not beset with irresolvable quality issues, and if appropriately administered (ensuring timeliness, adequacy and auxiliary help for setting up productive ventures), it is potentially superior to land-based compensation, since, at least in principle, it permits the realisation of a wider set of preferences. There is a danger, however, in inflicting cash on those who are not experienced in the nuances of the market economy (see, for instance, Dhagamwar 1989; Kothari 1996; Singh 1997b). Indeed, a majority of our respondents from the isolated PS villages rejected this alternative.

Consulting the affected for better resettlement

The experiences of people displaced by development project the world over have seen a revival of academic interest in the 'compensation criterion', with several recent studies being severely critical of it. In this article, we attempt to restore some of its theoretical and practical efficacy by tracing its genesis and try to follow its evolution into a practical tool for cost–benefit analysis. The criterion originated out of discussion among British economists in the late 1930s. While at first it was proposed as a normative tool to help decide if a change in policy was efficient (i.e., if net benefits are positive), later work on the criterion suggests that its practical application was considered. In examining the work around the criterion, we are able to establish its relationship with the measures of 'willingness to accept' and 'willingness to pay'. According to the criterion, the former is used to evaluate the losses incurred due to a project and the latter to evaluate benefits from the same. While the compensation criterion remained the fundamental guiding principle of cost–benefit analysis, its practitioners did not adopt the measures of costs and benefits that were derived from it. This is mainly because the measures of willingness to accept and willingness to pay imply asking the project-affected people for a valuation of costs and benefits — an exercise associated with theoretical and practical difficulties.

Alternative project evaluation techniques emerged, and the ones given precedence during the last four decades were primarily based on market prices. While this method was perhaps sufficient to evaluate costs and benefits that had well-established markets, it was entirely inadequate to tackle social and environmental costs that often accompany large development projects. Over time, the costs associated with intangibles intensified, and market-based methods of doing cost–benefit analysis began to be questioned. Mainstream cost–benefit analysts again started to consider the measures of 'willingness to accept' and 'willingness to pay' as given by the compensation criterion. Environmental economists were already using these measures to evaluate environmental intangibles. The technique employed to elicit values was called 'contingent valuation method' — it is a survey-based technique used for the valuation of non-market goods and services. It entailed asking people to value a good or a service, and this value was contingent upon the scenario constructed in the survey. A point that is heavily debated within this literature is whether to use 'willingness to accept' or 'willingness to pay' to evaluate losses suffered due to environmental degradation. The practitioners of contingent valuation, in general, agree that conservative estimates of value were to be preferred, and, hence, surveys should measure willingness to pay to protect the good, not willingness to accept compensation for the loss of the resource. The latter measure of value has been observed to be much higher for environmental goods than the former. Research, however, has established that such an approach is incorrect, especially in the case of development-induced costs, mainly because the costs borne by some may well exceed their willingness to pay, which is heavily constrained by their incomes. Asking people their willingness to pay also implies that they have no property rights over the without-project situation, which is usually incorrect. There is a wider consensus in the current literature that willingness to accept compensation, and not willingness to pay to avoid losses, is the right measure to evaluate losses.

We demonstrate the usefulness of the contingent valuation method to capture the losses suffered by people displaced by a development project. We do this by experimenting with this technique to consult the people of nine villages displaced by the Sardar Sarovar Project in the Narmada Valley (India). In order to design an incentive compatible consultation exercise, we choose to use the close-ended format of eliciting preferences. The close-ended layout confronts the respondent with a 'take it or leave it' scenario as opposed to the open-ended design which asks for a valuation. The former takes away the opportunity to overstate losses, and is hence incentive compatible. Our results suggest that the Sardar Sarovar Resettlement Scheme, which offered a standard package to all the affected, would be better replaced by a more tailor-made scheme, which catered to the various preferences held by the displaced. Not only would such a scheme benefit the affected, but the project authorities may also benefit from not having to live up to ill-conceived promises, like universal land provision, made by pressured politicians. The governments and donor agencies may also benefit from the increased probability of successful resettlement and, hence, a successful project. The paper also demonstrates that the elicited resettlement preferences are influenced by the socioeconomic circumstances of the respondents, suggesting that the respondents were serious about the consultation exercise, and that such exercises are not futile. They are important not only for reasons of being fair to those affected, but also from the viewpoint of a more sincere cost–benefit analysis.

Notes

1. For a discussion on development-induced displacement, among others, see Asthana (1996), Guggenheim and Cernea (1993) and Scudder (1991).
2. Roughly around 40 per cent of the displacement is attributed to large dams, and the rest to urban development and transportation programmes that are started each year.

3. A good overview of these studies is available in Guggenheim and Cernea (1993) and Goldsmith and Hildyard (1984, 1986). This empirical observation was conceptually consolidated in several important theoretical contributions. Among them, the two most significant are, perhaps, Cernea's seminal model of risk and reconstruction (Cernea 1997), which highlights the eight key risks that may be responsible for impoverishing the displaced communities, and the conceptual framework developed by Scudder's to evaluate new settlements (Scudder 1991).
4. Note that we use the word *re-examine* to call to attention the fact that the compensation criterion has already been examined by earlier studies. See especially Kanbur (2002), which first inspired the author into taking a second look at the compensation criterion. We clarify later as to why we think a re-examination is called for.
5. Pearce and Swanson (2007) make a similar observation.
6. For details, see Kanbur (2002).
7. Kaldor (1939: 551) proceeds to say, 'This argument lends justification to the procedure adopted by Professor Pigou in *The Economics of Welfare*, of dividing "welfare economics" into two parts: the first part relating to production, and the second to distribution'. Indeed this suggests that such separation was the preferred opinion of the profession at the time.
8. Cernea suggests an entirely different but eminently plausible explanation for the reluctance shown by economists of the time to consider *actual* payment of compensation (personal communication, 7 March 2007). The compensation principle emerged out of discussion regarding repealing of the Corn Laws — an Act that was to adversely impact upon the 'landlord' class — a class that was by no measure considered wanting. Hence, it was, perhaps, not a matter of great concern that those of this class were not compensated for their losses in reality. Cernea further points out that this is in complete contrast to what happens in cases like development-induced-displacement, where it is precisely the poor and the vulnerable who are most affected, and hence it becomes imperative that we consider the *actual* payment of compensation.
9. None of the papers that discuss the compensation criterion with regards to development-induced costs, which were mentioned in the introduction of this article, pick up this point. We believe this is at least partly responsible for most of the controversy surrounding the compensation criterion.
10. The CV test is related to the Kaldor-Hicks criterion, while the EV test is related to the Scitovsky criterion named after Scitovsky (1941). It states that a project is desirable if the potential losers are unable to bribe the potential winners not to undertake the project.
11. The CV test evaluates project costs by the minimum sum the victim would take to accept it, while the EV test evaluates project costs by the maximum sum the victim would pay to avoid it. For this reason,

it was observed that the difference in the (absolute) magnitude of the CV and EV test was large for projects having significant environmental impact. This was because, although there is no market for the collective good or the accompanying collective bad, the effect on community's welfare was at times substantial. This led to the suggestion that the CV test is used for projects that have significant detrimental effects on the environment, while the EV test is used for projects that are designed to enhance environmental goods. On this point, see Meade (1972) and Mishan (1976).

12. The individual's EV for the move from N to P is given by income adjustment required in state N in order to make him to consider this equivalent to state P. If N is preferred over P, then EV is negative and its absolute value reflects the maximum he would be WTP to avoid the move. If P is preferred over N, then EV is positive and its absolute value reflects the minimum he would be WTA to forgo the move.
13. Kaldor was explicit about including non-pecuniary losses in the analysis of costs. It is not, however, clear whether he wanted to extend the same treatment to gains. He notes that 'an increase in the money value of ...income ...is not ...a sufficient indication of this condition (compensation criterion) being fulfilled: for individuals might,..., sustain loses of a non-pecuniary kind, e.g., if workers derive satisfaction from their particular kind of work, and are obliged to change their employment, something more than their previous level of money income will be necessary to secure their previous level of enjoyment;... Only if the increase in total income is sufficient to compensate for such losses and still leaves something over to the rest of the community, can the project be said to be 'justified' without resort to interpersonal comparisons' (Kaldor 1939: 551, fn 1).
14. Note that interpersonal comparisons of welfare are rendered unavoidable by the usage of WTA and WTP. Indeed, such a proposition may not have been initially envisioned by the proponents of the compensation criterion
15. Note that the very idea of having aggregate welfare measures like WTA and WTP means that we are equating one person's welfare with that of the others which implies comparison.
16. If a project benefits the poor and imposes costs on the rich, the decision on project-worthiness may have to involve some kind of moral judgement or distributional weights.
17. For instance, in India, around 60 per cent of the project-affected are from tribal communities and 25 per cent from scheduled castes (non-tribal socioeconomically backward communities), and evidence suggests that this percentage is on the rise (Central Water Commission 1990; Fernandes 1991; Pinto 1998).

18. For a formal treatment, see Mas-Colell, Winston and Green (1995: 858–62).
19. Note that using market prices to evaluate project benefits might not be as problematic as using them to evaluate losses. The benefits from infrastructural improvements like hydro-electric or road construction projects have well-established markets already, and the prevailing prices can usually reflect the WTP for the good that is being valued (like water supply, electricity or better roads). It is rather more imprecise to rely on market prices to evaluate costs associated with such projects. For instance, in case of project-induced displacement, a complete reliance on the market would give us inaccurate estimates of the true losses incurred by the people. This is because among the goods that people value there may be several intangibles that have no markets, like community-based living, living close to maternal homes, access to common property resources and so on.
20. See, for instance, Dinwiddy and Teal (2004) and Stiglitz (1999).
21. For instance, the critics of the Narmada project in India claim that pressure from powerful lobbies, like the sugar industry and rich farmers, resulted in the implementation of a project that will adversely affect many thousands of poor and vulnerable groups (Aiyar 1989; Paranjpye 1992; Menon 1993).
22. The literature on development-induced displacement is often seen as archetypical of such condemnation.
23. For a review, see Bateman and Willis (1999); for a critical overview of the technique, see Diamond and Hausman (1994) and Hanemann (1994).
24. Economists use the framework of standard utility theory to explain WTA and WTP. Ahlheim and Buchholz (1999) argue that it is incorrect to do so because the absolute values of WTA and WTP or the difference between these values are of no significance within the framework of ordinal utility theory. The only fact that counts is the sign of a welfare change. 'The problem of comparing absolute values arises only if we want to add up individual WTPs or WTAs according to the Hicks-Kaldor criterion, which means leaving the grounds of ordinal utility theory. ...Using aggregate WTPs or WTAs thus implies...entering the world of applied policy' (Ahlheim and Buchholz 1999: 3; also see Garikipati 2000).
25. The seminal paper by Willig (1979) showed that the difference between WTA and WTP crucially depends on the income elasticity of the commodity whose price changes. Willig's analysis is not directly applicable to goods that are not traded in the markets (like in the case of environmental changes). Randall and Stoll (1980) extended Willig's analysis to the case of such goods.
26. This causes the exclusion of the project-affected by default. In eliciting people's preferences for a project, i.e., their willingness to pay for it,

mainstream public-economics assumes a lower bound of reported values as 'zero'. This prevents anyone with high negative valuation from influencing the project decision.

27. The 'substitution effect' was first demonstrated by Hanemann (1991), and the result was later generalised by Flores and Carson (1997). Shogren et al. (1994) report a series of experiments that confirm the existence of the substitution effect.
28. Boyce et al. demonstrate the presence of the 'endowment effect' in an experimental survey.
29. Among others, see Kahneman and Knetsch (1991) and Knetsch (1995).
30. The state of Rajasthan, is also to benefit from the SSP, but it rarely figures in the inter-state dispute.
31. Until, 1985, well after the Tribunal's Award, the Ministry of Environment and Forests held up the clearance of the SSP for want of environmental impact assessment. It was following the intervention by the Prime Minister Rajiv Gandhi that the cabinet gave conditional clearance to the SSP (Singh 1997b).
32. Of the 40,000 families displaced, 12 per cent are from Gujarat, 80 per cent from MP and 8 per cent from Maharashtra. The compensation package is available only to the reservoir-affected, and this figure includes only them. There are other groups, too, that are affected but not recognised as affected. This includes those affected by the canal network, the Kevadia Colony (the administrative field base of the project), secondary displacement, the downstream effect, and so on. Various estimates regarding the total number of the affected, which include these groups, exist. Morse and Berger (1992) place this figure at 175,000 people, Paranjpye (1990) at 300,000 and Fisher (1995) at 100,000 families.
33. Several other affected groups are left out of the compensatory net and their crusade against this injustice continues (see Morse and Berger 1992; Fisher 1995).
34. For an overview of the role of the NGOs, see Sheth (1995) and Thukral (1992).
35. A possible way of comparing 'what the policy was' and 'what it has become' is to refer to the policy as given in Joshi (1983) and later in NCA (1995).
36. This scheme is applicable to all those willing to settle in Gujarat (for the schemes of other states, see Appendix in Drèze, Singh and Samson 1997).
37. The names of the survey villages used in this study are fictitious. The names Gaman and Mapali are due to Hakim (1996).
38. *Phalias* share a common water source and are usually inhabited by members of the same tribe. At times, these were more than 10 kilometres apart and hence it was not uncommon to find women of one *phalia* who

had not visited other *phalias* for years. Most of labour-sharing activities was also contained within a *phalia*.

39. Fifty-nine families registered at the R-sites had actually moved out (this constitutes 32.8 per cent of families still living at these sites). Most of them were found to be living in the PS villages but not officially recognised to be doing so (personal communication, A. B. Chaudhary, resettlement official of the Sardar Sarovar Narmada Nigam, 26 May 1998).
40. Any attempt to study the relationship between WTA and WTP was abandoned very early on in the survey because eliciting WTP to avoid displacement resulted in either 'protest zeros' or nonparticipation.
41. It is likely that, if interviewed separately, women may participate with greater vigour and hold preferences that are different from those of their men. This study, however, did not attempt to interview them separately, because it aimed to capture household's resettlement preferences as would be made given an opportunity, not the gender differences in these preferences, although this in itself is an important issue (see Sparkes 1997).
42. One of the drawbacks of the close-ended CVM approach is that it says little about individual's WTA/WTP (Hanemann and Kanninen 1999). Hanemann (1985) proposed the use of a follow-up question to improve the efficiency of this approach. This is known as the double-bounded model and involves asking the respondent for a second bid. Although second bids were not explicitly asked for, some respondents volunteered this information (see note 47).
43. 'Only-women' sessions were organised in four of the survey villages with very little success. Just a handful of women turned up, but these women typically also turned up for the other village meetings.
44. The fact that officials are not allowed in these villages may be largely responsible for this.
45. A serious objection to surveys is that they cannot be verified. Where CV measures direct use values, it is possible to make a comparison with estimates obtained through indirect methods (Dickie et al. 1987; Bishop and Heberlein 1990). In the current study, the socioeconomic profile of the affected facilitates verification.
46. During my stay at Gaman and Mapali, I had the opportunity to observe the construction of two houses. The figures presented here are based on interviews as well as on observation. Though communal labour sharing was present at a not-displaced village, Kelu, it has long disappeared and no estimates could be obtained.
47. One popular suggestion was that all should pool their money and use a third of it to buy land, a third to construct houses, and deposit the remaining in a bank for their children. About 5 per cent of those who rejected the cash package said they would accept the package if offered more money.

References

Ahlheim, M. and W. Buchholz. 1999. 'WTP or WTA — Is that the question? Reflections on the Difference between "Willingness to Pay" and "Willingness to Accept"'. Working paper, University of Regensburg, Germany.

Aiyar, S. A. 1989. 'The sugar daddies'. *Indian Express*, January 1, Ahmedabad.

Amiran, E. Y. and D. A. Hagen. 2003. 'Willingness To Pay and Willingness To Accept: How much can they differ? Comment'. *The American Economic Review*, 93(1): 458–63.

Appu, P. S. 1996. *Land reforms in India: A survey of policy, legislation and implementation*. New Delhi: Vikas Publishing House.

Aprahamian, F., O. Chanel and O. Luchini. 2004. 'Starting point bias and unobserved heterogeneity in CV surveys: Econometrics with an application to air pollution'. GREQAM Working Paper. France Marseille.

Arrow, K., R. Solow, P. Portney, E. Leamer, R. Radner, and H. Schuman. 1993. 'Report of the NOAA Panel on Contingent Valuation', Federal Register 58(10): 4601–14.

Asthana, R. 1996. 'Involuntary resettlement: International experience'. *Economic and Political Weekly*, 31(24): 1468–75.

Bateman, I. and K. G. Willis (eds). 1999. *Valuing environmental preferences — Theory and practice of the Contingent Valuation Method in the US, EC and developing countries*. Oxford: Oxford University Press.

Baviskar, A. 1995. *In the belly of the river: Tribal conflicts over development in the Narmada valley*. New Delhi: Oxford University Press.

Bishop, C. R. and T. A. Herberlein. 1990. 'The Contingent Valuation Method', in R. L. Johnson and G. V. Johnson (eds), *Economic valuation of natural resources: Issues, theory, and applications*. Boulder: Westview Press.

Boyce, R., T. Brown, G. McClelland, G. Peterson and W. Schulze. 1992. 'An experimental examination of intrinsic values as a source of the WTP-WTA disparity'. *The American Economic Review*, 82(5): 1366–73.

Central Water Commission (CWC). 1990. *Register of large dams in India*. New Delhi: CWC.

Centre for Social Studies. 1985, 1990, 1991 and 1997a. *Resettlement and rehabilitation: Sardar Sarovar Project on the Narmada, various reports*. Surat: Centre for Social Studies.

———. 1997b. 'Resettlement and rehabilitation in Gujarat,' in J. Drèze, M. Samson and S. Singh (eds), *The dam and the nation*. Mumbai: Oxford University Press.

Cernea, M. M. 1997. 'The Risks and Reconstruction Model for resettling displaced populations'. *World Development*, 25(10): 1569–87.

Cernea, M. M. 1999. 'Why economic analysis is essential to resettlement: A sociologist's view', in M. M. Cernea (ed.), *The economics of involuntary settlement: Questions and challenges*, pp. 5–49. Washington DC: World Bank.

———. 2002. 'For a new economics of resettlement: A sociological critique of the compensation principle', in M. M. Cernea and R. Kanbur, 'An exchange on the compensation principle in resettlement', Department of Applied Economics and Management Working Paper 2002–03, Cornell University, New York, Ithaca.

Cernea, M. M. and H. M. Mathur. 2008. *Can compensation prevent impoverishment? Reforming resettlement through investments and benefit-sharing.* New Delhi: Oxford University Press.

Daly, E. H. 2007. 'Externalization of displacement's costs', in M. M. Cernea and H. M. Mathur (eds), *Reforming resettlement: Compensation, investment and benefit-sharing*. New Delhi: Oxford University Press.

Dasgupta, P. and K. G. Mäler. 1994. 'The environment: The environment and emerging Issues', in Layard and Glaiuster (eds), *Cost-benefit analysis.* Cambridge: Cambridge University Press.

Dhagamwar, V. 1989. 'Rehabilitation: Policy and institutional changes required', in Walter Fernandes and Enakshi Ganguly Thukral (eds), *Development, displacement and rehabilitation: Issues for a national debate*, pp. 171–84. New Delhi: Indian Social Institute.

Diamond, A. P. and J. A. Hausman. 1994. 'Contingent valuation: Is some number better than no number?'. *Journal of Economic Perspective*, 8(4): 45–64.

Dinwiddy, C. and F. Teal. 2004. *Principles of cost-benefit analysis for developing countries.* Cambridge: Cambridge University Press.

Drèze, J. 1994. 'Resettlement of Narmada oustees'. *The Economic Times*, February 22, New Delhi.

Drèze, J., M. Samson and S. Singh (eds). 1997. *The dam and the nation.* Mumbai: Oxford University Press.

Fernandes, W. 1991. 'Power and powerlessness: Development projects and displacement of tribals'. *Social Action*, 41: 243–70.

Fisher, W. F. (ed.). 1995. *Working towards sustainable development: The damming of the Narmada river in western India.* New York: M. E. Sharpe.

Flores, N. E. and R. T. Carson. 1997. 'The relationship between the income elasticities of demand and Willingness to Pay'. *Journal of Environmental Economics and Management*, 33(3): 287–95.

Food and Agriculture Organisation (FAO). 2000. 'Application of the Contingent Valuation Method in developing countries: A survey', FAO Economic and Social Development Paper 146. Rome: FAO.

Frisch, D. 1993. 'Reasons for framing effects'. *Organisational behaviour and human decision process*, 54: 399–429.

Garikipati, S. 2000. 'An economic perspective on resettlement of development-induced displacement: A study of the Sardar Sarovar Project displaced', Unpublished Ph.D dissertation, University of Cambridge.

Garikipati, S. 2002. 'Resettlement sites of the Narmada valley — Some revealing insights', *Economic and Political Weekly*, 37(23): 2257–66.

———. 2005. 'Consulting the displaced regarding their resettlement: Is there a way?', *Journal of Refugee Studies*, 18(3): 340–61.

Goldsmith, E. and N. Hildyard (eds). 1984, 1986. *The social and environment effects of large dams*, Vol 1 and 2. Cornwall: Wadebridge Ecological Centre.

Goyal, S. 1996. 'Economic perspective on displacement'. *Economic and Political Weekly*, 31(24): 1461–67.

Guggenheim, S. E. and M. M. Cernea. 1993. *Anthropological approaches to involuntary resettlement policy, practice and theory*. Boulder: Westview Press.

Hakim, R. P. 1996. 'Vasava identity in transition: Some theoretical issues'. *Economic and Political Weekly*, 31(24): 1492–99.

Hanemann, M. W. 1991. 'Willingness to Pay and Willingness to Accept: How much can they differ?', *American Economic Review*, 81: 635–47.

Hanemann, M. W. 1994. 'Valuing the environment through contingent valuation'. *Journal of Economic Perspective*, 8(4): 20–43.

Herriges, J. A. and J. F. Shogren. 1996. 'Starting point bias in dichotomous choice valuation with follow-up questioning'. *Journal of Environment Economics and Management*, 30: 112–31.

Hicks, J. R. 1939. 'The foundations of welfare economics'. *Economic Journal*, 49(196): 696–712.

Hicks, J. R. 1943. 'The four consumer's surpluses'. *Review of Economic Studies*, 11: 31–41.

Horowitz, J. and K. McConnell. 2002. 'A review of WTA/WTP studies', *Journal of Environmental Economics and Management*, 44: 426–47.

International Rivers Network (IRN). 1999. 'The map of Narmada river, available at http://www.riverrevival.org/orgs/NBA.html (accessed 16 July 2001).

Joshi, V. 1983. '*Rehabilitation of submerging villages (Sardar Sarovar Narmada project): General report*. Surat: Centre for Social Studies.

Kahneman, D. and J. Knetsch. 1991. 'Anomalies: The endowment effect, loss aversion and status quo bias'. *Journal of Economic Perspectives*, 5: 193–206.

Kaldor, N. 1939. 'Welfare propositions of economics and interpersonal comparisons of utility'. *The Economic Journal*, 49(195): 549–52.

Kanbur, R. 2002. 'Development economics and the compensation principle', in M. M. Cernea and R. Kanbur, 'An exchange on the compensation principle in resettlement', Department of Applied Economics and Management Working Paper 2002–2033. New York, Ithaca: Cornell University.

Kothari, S. 1996. 'Whose nation? Displaced as victims of development'. *Economic and Political Weekly*, 31(24): 1476–85.

Knetsch, J. L. 1995. 'Asymmetric valuation of gains and losses and preferences order assumptions'. *Economic Inquiry*, 33: 134–41.

Krutilla, J. V. and A. C. Fisher. 1985. *Economics of natural environment studies in the valuation of commodity and amenity resources*. Baltimore: Resources for the Future.

Little, I. M. D. and J. A. Mirrless. 1990. 'Project appraisal and planning twenty years on', in S. Fischer, D. de Tray and S. Shah (eds), *Proceedings of the World Bank Annual Conference on Development Economics, 1990*, pp. 351–82. Washington DC: The World Bank.

Mathur, H. M. 1995. *Development, displacement and resettlement*. New Delhi: Vikas Publishing House.

Meade, E. J. 1972. 'Review of cost-benefit analysis'. *Economic Journal*, 82(325): 244–46.

Menon, M. 1993. 'Narmada waters for Kutch a pipedream'. *Times of India*, June 21, Mumbai.

Mishan, E. J. 1976. 'The use of compensating and equivalent variations in cost-benefit analysis'. *Economica*, 43(170): 185–97.

Mas-Colell, A., M. D. Winston and J. R. Green. 1995. *Microeconomic theory*. New York: Oxford University Press.

Morse, B. and T. Berger. 1992. 'Sardar Sarovar: Report of the independent review'. Ottawa: Resources Futures International.

Mitchell, R. and R. Carson. 1989. *Using surveys to value public goods: The contingent valuation method*. Washington DC: RFF/John Hopkins University Press.

Narmada Control Authority (NCA). 1995. 'Sardar Sarovar (Narmada Project) Master Plan for R&R'. Indore: NCA.

News Nerve. 2006. 'NBA protests supreme court ruling on narmada dam', available at http://www.nerve.in/news:253500704%20%7C%20channel:%20India (accessed 30 August 2002).

Paranjpye, V. 1990. *High dams on the Narmada: A holistic analysis of the river valley projects*. Studies in Ecology and Sustainable Development, 3. New Delhi: Indian National Trust for Art and Cultural Heritage.

———. 1992. 'Final submission made to Mr Bradford Morse, Chairman, World Bank Independent Review, Sardar Sarovar Project'. Pune (Mimeo).

Pathak, M. (ed.). 1991. *Sardar Sarovar Project: A promise for plenty*. New Delhi: Oxford University Press.

Pearce, D. W. 1983. *Cost–benefit Analysis*. London: Macmillan Publications.

———. 1999. 'Methodological issues in the economic analysis for involuntary resettlement operations', in M. M. Cernea (ed.), *The economics of involuntary resettlement, questions and challenges*, pp. 50–82. Washington DC: The World Bank.

———. 2002. 'The role of "property rights" in determining economic values for environmental costs and benefits'. Report to the Environmental Agency, Bristol.

Pearce, D. W. and T. Swanson. 2007. 'The economic evaluation of projects involving forced population displacements', in M. M. Cernea and

H. M. Mathur (eds), *Reforming resettlement: Compensation, investment and benefit-sharing*. New Delhi: Oxford University Press.

Pinto, A. 1998. 'Fillip to land transfers Land Acquisition Bill, 1988'. *Economic and Political Weekly,* 33(49): 3107–09.

Portney, R. P. 1994. 'The contingent valuation debate: Why economists should care'. *Journal of Economic Perspective,* 8(4): 3–17.

Randall, A. and J. R. Stoll. 1980. 'Consumer's surplus in commodity space'. *American Economic Review*, 70: 449–55.

Roy, A. 1999. 'The greater common good', available at http://narmada.org/gcg/gcg.html (accessed 25 August 2002).

Sardar Sarovar Narmada Nigam (SSNN). 1995a. 'Resettlement documents for Krit, Kani and Kapi'. Kevadia Office–Unit II. Vadodara: SSNN.

———. 1995b. 'Resettlement documents for Kewar, Khera and Kelu'. Barwani Office. Khargone: SSNN.

Scudder, T. 1991. 'A sociological framework for the analysis of new land settlements', in M. M. Cernea (ed.), *Putting people first*, pp. 148–87. New York: Oxford University Press.

Scitovsky, T. 1941. 'A note on welfare propositions in economics'. *The Review of Economic Studies,* 8: 78–88.

Sheth, P. N. 1995. 'The Sardar Sarovar Project: Ecopolitics of development', in U. Baxi and B. Parekh (eds), *Crisis and change in contemporary India.* New Delhi: Sage Publications.

Shogren, J., S. Shin, D. Hayes and J. Kliebenstein. 1994. Resolving differences in Willingness to Pay and Willingness to Accept'. *The American Economic Review*, 84(1): 255–70.

Singh, S. 1997a. *Taming the waters: The political economy of large dams in India*. New Delhi: Oxford University Press.

———. 1997b. 'Introduction', in J. Drèze, M. Samson and S. Singh (eds), *The dam and the nation: Displacement and resettlement in the Narmada valley*, pp. 1–23. Mumbai: Oxford University Press.

Stiglitz, J. E. 1999. *Economics of the public sector.* Third edition. New York: W.W. Norton.

Tata Institute of Social Science (TISS). 1997. 'Experience with resettlement and rehabilitation in Maharashtra', in J. Drèze, M. Samson and S. Singh (eds). 1997. *The dam and the nation: Displacement and resettlement in the Narmada valley*, pp. 184–214. Mumbai: Oxford University Press.

Thukral, E. G. (ed.). 1992. *Big dams displaced people: Rivers of sorrow rivers of change*. New Delhi: Sage Publication.

Willig, R. 1979. 'Consumer's surplus without apology'. *American Economic Review*, 66: 587–97.

World Bank. 1994. *Resettlement and development: The bankwide review of projects involving involuntary resettlement 1986–1993*. Washington DC: The World Bank.

7

From Narmada to Nandigram: The never-ending clamour for land as the only route to resettlement

Vasudha Dhagamwar

It has been well said by someone that we walk into the future backwards. This is very true of the entire issue of development-induced displacement. However, perhaps the verb 'stumble' would be more appropriate here. All through the 1980s and 1990s, air was rife with debates on Narmada, Tehri and a score of other dams. Whether they were pro-dam or anti-dam, the thinking members of the public were clear that the Land Acquisition Act was unjust to the displaced people. A few radical changes were made to the lexicon on displacement, mostly due to the efforts of NGOs and activists. First of all, the category of project-affected persons (PAPs) was created. It was recognised that this category was much bigger than the earlier one of project-displaced persons. Consequent to this recognition came the admission that compensation for acquired land was one thing, resettlement or rehabilitation was for loss of livelihood, common property resources and even for loss of community The landless were now seen as PAPs who were also entitled to resettlement and rehabilitation. Loss of livelihood was seen as just as deserving of rehabilitation as loss of land. With more difficulty, women were also admitted as an independent category with their own entitlements.

Circumstances changed, but not ideas on entitlement

Unfortunately, no one was clear what those entitlements should be. Most of the speaking was done by city-bred activists who had little connect with-land based life. No one was clear what one should demand in return for lost livelihood. In some ways, we were muddled in our thinking because the initial struggles in the 1980s were caused by dams. The affected persons were by and large tribal people. They craved for alternate land and forest. As one academic famously, and inaccurately, said, 'We demand a river for a river and a sunset for a sunset'. Like most pithy sayings, it was fraught with problems. With the package came exploitative forest guards and revenue record keepers, and also a lack of roads, schools and health care centres.

Our objections are based on our past experiences. So are the solutions we find to them. This is true of the PAPs and their leaders on the one hand, and of the government on the other. The former oppose acquisition altogether or, as a poor second choice, demand alternate land or jobs. The latter offers more benefits to larger numbers of PAPs. This syndrome continues, without paying the slightest attention to markedly changed factors. Sometimes, the players have changed; at others, it is the larger circumstances, which may include the economy. To test this statement, we can compare the events that have taken place in Orissa with those that have occurred in West Bengal.

The displaced people of Orissa

Let us begin with Orissa, where admittedly not much has changed. This is a state with large mineral wealth and an equally large tribal population which has the advantage of strong support of and leadership from NGOs and activists. Orissa has a big example of a successful resistance by tribals against the Baliapal Army firing range in the 1980s. But the Orissa government appears to have forgotten all about it when it went ahead with other projects nearly two decades later.

In June 2005, it was front page news that Korean steel giant POSCO had offered to set up a new steel plant at Paradip and had signed some agreements with the Orissa government. This development was hailed by the media and the governments as the saviour of Orissa. We were told the amount which would be invested in Orissa ($12 billion), the number of subsidiary projects the steel plant would create (iron mine, port), the amount of steel to be produced (12 million tonnes per year), and the number of jobs it would generate (48,000).

But no one would say how many thousands of square miles of land will be acquired, not just for the industrial areas but also for the huge townships that will inevitably be planned to come up around each one of them. We were not told how many people will lose their homes and livelihoods, how much forest flora, fauna and water resources will be destroyed. Many questions were left unvoiced, let alone answered. This is all too typical of the champions of 'development'. Uncomfortable questions are simply swept under the proverbial carpet!

Much before the POSCO deal, the Tata Iron and Steel Company (TISCO) had entered into an agreement with the Orissa government to set up another steel plant, this time at Kalinga Nagar. Evidently, the land acquisition process was complete, and late in 2005, the company started the process of taking physical possession of the land with the usual police protection. The year 2006 began with determined protests against this move by the local tribals, armed with their bows and arrows. Although one does not know who started the violence, it is admitted that the police opened fire and killed 12 protestors. Apart from resisting the occupation, another grievance that was voiced was that the tribals had not been paid for their land. On their part, TISCO authorities said they had deposited over Rs 3 lakh per acre with the Orissa government, which was responsible for making the payment. However, the tribal people never received this money. Whatever little was paid to them had long been consumed in meeting daily needs. The land was formally acquired several years ago, but the tribals had been cultivating it continually. They were not prepared to vacate the land without getting cultivable land or jobs.

At the same time, tribal protestors also blocked railway lines in Rourkela steel city to bring into focus their demand that lands still unused by the Rourkela steel plant — which is nearly half a century old — be returned to them. This underlined the fact that land was acquired far in excess of the requirement of the projects and left unutilised, while the original owners lost their sole resource.

It seems that TISCO has given up the project in Kalinga Nagar, if not permanently then at least for the time being. POSCO is another matter; it's an ongoing saga.

When the protests first began in 2006, the Koreans must have been completely bemused by them. The protests continued over the months. The government clearly stalled for time. The Korean company has said it has not got possession of even one inch of the 4,004 acres of land promised for its project, but the government would not withdraw the project. The exasperated tribals increased the level of their protests and adopted a new strategy. Thirteen POSCO officials and staff, including some Koreans, were even kidnapped in separate incidents by them in October 2007, and held in confinement for a few hours. POSCO authorities complained that far from helping them, the local police admonished them not to create more trouble by entering the disputed area.

POSCO officials have taken the matter right up to the union government. The Orissa government has suggested that they should begin by constructing transit camps for displaced persons and also training centres, to which the Korean company is said to have agreed. But in the current situation, such a step is unlikely to be of any use. POSCO is fluctuating between moving elsewhere and remaining in Paradip. Chief Minister Navin Patnaik has, however, declared that the project will stay at its approved site.

At the same time, the state government of Orissa was holding a workshop to approve (or may have approved) its draft of a rehabilitation policy that would be more generous to the PAPs in terms of giving cultivable land, jobs and cash. But the government was not willing to view more strictly the quantum of land that would be acquired for any project. It was perceived that such restrictions would drive projects away to other states. The Kalinga Nagar matter was not mentioned at all.

The West Bengal story

Now we come to West Bengal. As we shall see, some key factors are quite different here. But first let's look at the similarities. In Singur, the West Bengal government had entered into an agreement with the Tata Group to set up a car factory. In Nandigram, the plan was for a much larger project; Tata was to set up a large petrochemical hub. At both places, there were determined, even violent, protests against surrendering the possession of land. This occurred when the POSCO project was still facing trouble. So far, the plans and the protests follow a set pattern.

One similarity is in the complaints over compensation. In Kalinga Nagar, the full compensation did not reach the farmers because government servants took the lion's share. In Singur, one hears that the land was mostly tilled by *bargadars* or sharecroppers. Despite Operation Barga, many tracts of land have not been registered in the land records, which meant that their right to a share in the compensation was not recognised by the Land Acquisition Act. The landowners, who were mainly absentee landlords, took it all. At both places, the tillers refused to hand over their land. In Nandigram too, land acquisition was resisted with all the strength the people could muster, although so far there are no complaints related to compensation. There is a rumour that local legislators belonging to the CPM were unhappy about losing their monopoly as the sole providers of any largesse.

Without doubt, in our media, West Bengal gets more space than Orissa and many other states. The two protests in Singur and Nandigram naturally got much more publicity. After all, a national party like the Trinamool Congress was championing the cause of the farmers in Singur. Secondly, the CPM-led government and its cadres were shown up for their anti-poor attitude and their shameless adoption of violence. Some might even say their true colours were revealed.

The outcome of the two protests in West Bengal has been more clear-cut. After Nandigram, the project for establishing a petrochemical hub has shifted to Nayachar, in the Bay of Bengal. Nayachar (literally, a new island) has been created by silt deposits, never mind the warnings about incipient global warming that will raise sea levels by 20 feet in as many years. As for Singur, the West Bengal government has offered a much better resettlement and rehabilitation package.[1] It will provide a wide range of training packages, including training in hardware and software, Which will equip the people to find work in the new industrial set-up. Why did the government wait for violent resistance to devise such forward-looking rehabilitation? Women, however, are still typecast; they will be trained in catering. Equally noteworthy is the news that Tata Motors has agreed to pay the West Bengal government Rs 1,000 crore (10,000 million) as rent over a period of 90 years.[2] Clearly, the company is not going to be losing by this deal. (If they can afford to pay this much of rent. Why don't they provide a better resettlement package, without bloodshed? And why was this not done in Kaliga Nagar? Why couldn't the government show honesty?)

Experiences overlooked

The response of the union government to all these events (especially in West Bengal) was to draft another National Resettlement and Rehabilitation Policy. The 2007 policy seems even grander and more wide-based than the older policies of 2003 and 1998. One cannot help but think that the Indian land mass must be expanding all the way to Africa in the west and to Malaysia in the east to accommodate all the demands for land made not only for rehabilitation, but also for urbanisation, afforestation and industrialisation. Even in the 1980s, when the oustees of Sardar Sarovar project were promised that a village would be resettled as one unit and not broken up, it was proving impossible to find land for an entire village at one place. Agricultural land was even more difficult to find. It is not that these experiences are ignored. No one is even aware of them. The government has simply acted according to old ideas.

The one thing that remains constant is that all promises for land and jobs are subject to availability. Only monetary compensation is unconditional. Of the two categories of land, the promise to provide residential land is more easily met. But here, too, the promise to settle the entire village in one place is proving to be difficult to fulfil. Agricultural land is almost impossible to provide. This is not surprising, given the pressure on land. Promises for farmland are, therefore, most unlikely to be fulfilled, and the result will be increased distrust in the government. It does not need an astrologer to tell us that all this does not augur well for the future.

Apart from the outcome of the protests, much else has changed. Some differences are seen upon comparison with past projects; others are among the four projects. Over the years, opinions and attitudes seem to have become sharper and more polarised. People have learnt the hard way to distrust the promises made so merrily to them. The resistance to land acquisition has hardened to the point of involving bloodshed. Another difference is the increasing acquisition of non-tribal lands. One consequence is that leadership has evolved at the local level; outside activists are no longer necessary to give voice to the people. The affected people are able to express their own resistance. Activists are, however, joining them in the battle. Another factor is that of involvement of political parties from both sides in the fray. Yet another factor is the unwitting involvement of international agencies like the Korean company, POSCO. All these factors may play bigger roles in the future.

A significant fact is that all four projects are industrial. There is not a dam in sight. In this the new projects are different from the old ones. There seems to be a major shift in strategies of development. Dams no longer occupy centre stage. This in itself has, or should have, an impact on the kind of rehabilitation deemed appropriate for the new projects.

Displacement affects tribal people differently

There is another marked difference. The evidence is right there in West Bengal, in Singur and in Nandigram. It is in the nature of the affected population. In Orissa, the affected people were largely tribal. West Bengal has a much smaller population of tribals. To the best of my knowledge, there were tribals neither in Singur nor in Nandigram. Indeed, if there had been any, the protesters would have been quick to highlight their presence.

It is admitted that tribals have entirely different set of problems when they are faced with displacement. Outside their traditional, historical habitat, they are like fish out of water. They hesitate to enter the urban wilderness. They want a river for a river and a forest for a forest. For instance, the Bhils, who were displaced in the 1960s by the Ukai dam on Tapi river, were completely at loss in the new world. In no time, they lost to moneylenders the land given to them in alien Gujarat, and wandered back to their old habitats without anything to do. As a Bhil elder told us, 'all we can do is fish, distil illicit liquor or steal'. They sang a mournful ditty which illustrates their plight so well:

Oh Mother Tapi, what shall we do?
When we go with a shovel they won't give us work
And when we go with a begging bowl they will not give us food
Oh Mother Tapi, what shall we do?

Fortunately, the inter-state dam on Indravati river in Bastar was cancelled, otherwise it would not have hurt the Madia Gonds, who are far more isolated from modern civilisation than the Bhils. Resettlement in the downstream irrigated lands in Andhra Pradesh which was supposed to entice them, was in fact a great threat to their lifestyle, or rather their very survival. For tribal people, we should demand land in their own habitat, and they should be allowed to sell their land when they become urban. We ought not to demand land for all.

It is equally true that non-tribals are different. They are more mobile and adaptable. When they are displaced, they routinely demand irrigated lands elsewhere. This is a point of vital importance. Non-tribals also contemplate a shift to cities much more easily. In fact, villagers from states with little industry are pouring into cities every day. In many states, parents send away the children away to cities to earn and send money back to the family. Mostly, those sent away are sons. This is where the case of the tribal PAPs in Orissa differs from that of PAPs in West Bengal. The tribal people have very few options for survival. True, young tribal men and women are also migrating from Orissa, Chattisgarh and Jharkhand, but they are still fewer in numbers, and one fears they are worse off.

Unsustainability of the land option

This is not all. The brutal truth is that despite keeping their land in Singur and Nandigram, farmers or their sons will keep migrating to cities in search of unskilled jobs. Why should this be so? We are told that these lands are fertile and yield three crops a year. But can they sustain the Bengali farmer? Can he feed his family or his state? Punjab is the bread basket of India. What about West Bengal? The land in Maharashtra and even Gujarat is not half as good as that in the first three states (Uttar Pradesh, Bihar and West Bengal) that lie in the Gangetic plain. Yet Maharashtra and Gujarat are more often hosts to inter-state migrant labour. It is almost as if the farmers of Bengal are saying 'don't take my land, but take my sons and provide them employment'. The migrants are not particularly welcome either. They are made to feel that they have come because their states cannot provide them with livelihood.

Even children are sent to faraway cities to do manual work, or work at sweat shops, *dhabas* and roadside mechanic shops. Girls are sent away to work as domestic servants. As these lines are written, newspapers carry reports about young boys between the age of 7 and 15 years rescued from sweat shops in different parts of Delhi. The boys are from West Bengal, Bihar and Jharkhand.[3] They could also have been from Uttar Pradesh or Orissa. Why don't they come from Maharashtra or Gujarat? Even when land in the two states is not as fertile as it is in the Gangetic plains.

The report says the Sub Divisional Magistrate hearing the case of some of the boys from West Bengal has noted them as neglected children rather than as bonded child labour. Although the NGO that rescued the children is understandably upset, they surely are bonded as well as neglected. These boys are not necessarily from project displaced homes. Their fathers are either landless labourers or small peasants. The boys are here to support their families. Some of them said so in as many words that they would like to go back but may not. The family needs their earnings. Their fathers sent them to earn for the family at an age when they should be in school. This pattern continues and men from Bihar, Jharkhand and Orissa, but inexplicably not from West Bengal, toil as manual labourers in the more prosperous states like Delhi and Punjab, and in western India.

The harsh truth is that land holdings are too small to sustain the family even if it is not a large family. Another equally harsh truth is that however much land may be given to PAPs, in one or two generations it will be inadequate, given the growing population. They will need non-land-based skills and education. The time to start down this path was in the 1950s, with the first project in independent India. Let us at least begin now. Rehabilitation is an ongoing process and not a one-time act. Let us also stop harping on 'land for land' as the ideal and only rehabilitation.

But people don't necessarily ask for land as an absolute good. We have not understood their basic question. They want to know why they have to sacrifice their homes. Development planners tell them what they have is not good enough, and that they want to build something better. Naturally, the people then want a share in the fruit that will be borne out of their sacrifice. If the project promoter says the aim is 'to irrigate land downstream', people ask for a share in that land. If the contention is that the project is to construct industry, people want jobs in it. The young want jobs for themselves; the older men want jobs for their sons and daughters. If their land will be used to create infrastructure, they want to be close to it, not sent miles away into the countryside. Shahpur Jat and other urban villages in Delhi have rehabilitated themselves, precisely because they were deprived only of agricultural land. They stayed on in their homes and gradually converted the space into offices shops and even dwellings, all of which they rented out (MARG 1998).

Displaced not all land-dependent

Because ideal rehabilitation is seen as replication of the old lifestyle, no other model is allowed to stand in its way. All PAPs are seen as a homogenous, or if one dare say, faceless group. There is a total failure to distinguish between different categories of PAPs, apart from the standard one of landed and landholders. The innate difference in the rehabilitation requirements of tribal people and the non-tribals, even if the latter are villagers, is not taken into account. Nor is any attention paid to the aspirations of the younger PAPs, which are quite different from those of the older generation. Our experience in Korba was quite clear on this point (Dhagamwar et al. 2003). The young want new skills that ensure them jobs, put money in their pockets, and make them more mobile, more street-smart and freer of the old feudal bonds. This would be true of the girls as well, if they were given a voice.

We must face the fact that land use all over India is changing. From being a predominantly traditional agrarian country living in its villages, it is moving towards becoming one which is urban, industrial and commercial. It is IT-based and futuristic. Life is rapidly becoming non-land-based. Yet, while we are actually converting land to non-agrarian uses, all of us, which includes the government, courts and NGOs, insist that huge quantities of agricultural land should be set aside for rehabilitating all the existing inhabitants, and effectively a greater number should be made dependant on land. The NGOs generally revile the absentee landlords. They can identify them better than the land records keeper, *the patwari*. But even they do not demand their exclusion from the demand of land-for-land for rehabilitation. The tribal people are a special case, and they deserve special treatment. By clubbing everyone together, we deny the tribals their rights. To give one example, in the Sardar Sarovar submergence zone, the tribals desperately needed forest land. To the tail end, as the fertile land in the plains had been in the possession of peasant castes for several generations. Thee peasants' sons had already moved out into a variety of professions. A generous monetary compensation would have been a fair deal for them. To include them in the category of the displaced who should be given land may have been a good strategy, but it was factually incorrect.

If we look back, the whole question of rehabilitation has escalated after Independence. This is because of several reasons: change in population, number of projects and level of awareness about environmental and social justice issues. Before independence, the population of British India was about 400 million. There was sufficient unoccupied land, so the displaced population could easily find land to till and live on. Under British rule, there was almost no development, and there was little acquisition. After all, the colonial masters were only interested in taking away our raw materials and selling us manufactured goods at much higher prices. With the First Five-Year Plan, India went into the development mode, constructing dams and steel plants, and generally concentrating on producing capital goods. It also meant more land acquisition, and more displacement. In the meanwhile, the population was also exploding.

But we are now proudly on our way to self sufficiency. It is a moot point whether we should develop our own industry, or keep exporting our raw materials and buy back finished goods. That way we can decrease the speed and scale of acquisition. But is that what we want?

At the moment, development is completely skewed. More and more resources are ploughed into cities. Less and less attention is paid to villages, where more than 60 per cent Indians still live. We do not even have compulsory universal primary education. Secondary education for all is out of the question. Nor do we have primary health care, sanitation and potable water. We cannot have an economy which concentrates on a few cities, and does not produce a nationwide skilled and healthy population. In no time, our economy will be held up by the lack of skilled workers at all levels. The existing model clearly has serious inherent problems.

Development is the proverbial Pandora's box. Instead of saying no to everything, we have to sort out the options, take both long-term and short-term views. But we must remember that the bird's eye view alone is not enough before taking decisions; the worm's eye view is also significant. At the moment, all resources and benefits are literally swallowed up by cities, which are becoming not just growing into megacities but into monsters. But they offer employment and opportunity to the everlasting inflow of human beings. Development cannot mean urban development alone. It has to think big and small, far and wide. Along with highways, it must remember to keep space for cyclists and pedestrians, who will always far outnumber motorists. The meek still inherit the earth.

Notes

1. *The Pioneer*, 20 June 2007.
2. *The Indian Express*, 23 August 2007.
3. *The Indian Express*, 30 and 31 November 2007.

References

Dhagamwar, Vasudha, Subrata De and Nikhil Verma. 2003. *Development and displacement: The people of Korba.* New Delhi: Sage.

Multiple Action Research Group (MARG). 1988. '*Baste ujadte kal ki talash mein*' (The displaced in search of tomorrow). Film made by MARG on displacement.

———. 1998. *Shahpur Jat: A village displaced — A study In self rehabilitation.* New Delhi: MARG.

8

Reconstructing livelihoods: The CIL experience with self-employment schemes

M. P. Roy

Coal as a source of energy to meet India's growing need gained new importance only in the early 1970s, when oil prices in the world market witnessed a steep increase. It was around that time that the coal industry was nationalised, giving birth to Coal India Limited (CIL) with its subsidiaries, Western Coalfields Limited (WCL), South Eastern Coalfields Limited (SECL), Mahanadi Coalfields Limited (MCL), Northern Coalfields Limited (NCL) and Central Coalfields Limited (CCL). CIL is now a large public sector undertaking of the Government of India, producing nearly 300 million tonnes of coal annually. With 650,000 employees, CIL operates about 520 coal mines scattered in different parts of the country, mainly in Jharkhand, Orissa, Madhya Pradesh and Uttar Pradesh.

In 1993, the Indian government approached World Bank for assistance in modernising CIL's mining operations. The Bank approved a loan for the Coal Sector Rehabilitation Project (CSRP), covering 25 opencast mines. Subsequently, a Coal Sector Environmental and Social Mitigation Project (CSEMP) was approved in 1995, specifically to mitigate adverse social impacts from CSRP (World Bank 1996). Resettling people displaced due to CSRP activities was a major component of the CSESMP.

Jobs in lieu of land

Earlier, coal was extracted mostly through labour-intensive, underground mines. Not only was coal production low, there was also dearth of labourers in mining areas. Bringing outside workers was a common practice. The land requirement then was small, partly because underground mining needed less land, and partly because the production level was low. It was possible to acquire land by giving a job in the mines to the landowner.

The picture changed dramatically as a result of nationalisation. India now produces about 265 million tonnes of coal annually, and is the fourth largest coal producer in the world. The target is to increase annual production level to 300 million tonnes. About two-third of this production now comes from very highly mechanised opencast mines using non-labour-intensive technology. The requirement of land for these opencast mines has increased tremendously, but the capacity of the mines to offer jobs has greatly declined.

This is best illustrated by an example. To produce 3 million tonnes of coal per year from an opencast mine (with a lifespan of 25 years) requires acquisition of 1,000 hectares of land. Experience shows that 60–65 per cent of this land will be tenancy land owned by about 1,200 land-owning families, with nearly 3,600 adult males directly dependent on it. If the indirectly dependent population is added, the affected male population will be about 4,300. But at the existing level of mechanisation, the total requirement of unskilled manpower will not be more than 550. Thus, there will remain a 4000-strong able-bodied male population which will always be looking for a job in the mine, which has affected their traditional economic system. If women are added to this male population, the total affected population looking for jobs will be quite staggering. Women, too, are eager to take up some means of economic activity, as they were equal partners in the agricultural activities that cannot be carried out due to loss of land for mining purposes. If jobs are to be given to acquire the land that CIL needs, the mine will be doomed, as it will be saddled with excessive manpower (Roy 1997).

The entire nationalised coal industry of India is groaning under the weight of overstaffing. The time has come to cry halt to this practice of giving jobs to land-owning families to acquire their land. The landowners, however, do not want to give up their land (despite being required to do so by the provisions of the Land Acquisition Act and the Coal Bearing Areas Act) unless they are given jobs in the mines.

The real challenge facing the coal industry is to make the self-employment option an attractive and viable alternative to jobs.

Although there is no global solution to this problem, CIL has made a modest beginning. It has tried to assist the Entitled Project Affected Persons (EPAPs) of 14 of its 25 opencast projects (OCPs) of the CSESMP in their quest for income restoration through various self-employment schemes. The CIL's lack of experience in this area is proving to be a big stumbling block. Often, people in villages are not convinced that these alternative avenues of income generation can be viable and sustainable, unless it is proved at least in some places. The challenge is to demonstrate that the options are viable and sustainable. The coal industry desperately wants to see this endeavour succeed.

Policies to mitigate adverse impacts

In India, coal projects are usually set up in relatively remote areas. In addition to affecting landowners, this unleashes a profound social change in villages/habitats surrounding the mine. The disparity of monetary incomes created by employment in the mine tends to create inflationary pressures in the economy of villages surrounding the mine. Consequently, existing social ties and local organisational capacities crumble to a great extent.

In order to address adverse impacts of coal mining, CIL recently adopted two major corporate policies (Hasan 2006). One is the resettlement and rehabilitation (R&R) policy, which addresses the direct and severe impact of land acquisition. The other is the Indigenous Peoples Development Policy (IPDP), which provides for community development assistance that CIL's subsidiaries extend to the affected population of villages situated within one kilometre of the mine boundary.

The two laws with the help of which the coal companies acquire land needed to increase coal production, are the Land Acquisition Act (1894) and the Coal Bearing Areas Act (1957). In both these Acts, compensation for the loss of land is prescribed for titleholders only. The vast majority of people lacking title but dependent on land are not considered for any compensation. The resentment of people whose lands are being acquired forced various state governments that have coal mines in their jurisdictions to come out with additional guidelines, which require the mine developers to give further benefits to landowners. Additionally, in order to bring about a certain amount of uniformity in various state government packages, the Ministry of Coal issued guidelines for the benefit of landowners losing land on account of coal mining.

Despite new guidelines issued both by the states concerned as well as the Ministry of Coal, the situation did not improve much. The number of jobs that could possibly be offered to affected people fell far short of their expectations, because of the high degree of mechanisation. To address these problems, CIL formulated a new R&R policy for all its subsidiaries in 1994.

The Resettlement and Rehabilitation of the Coal India Limited was approved by its board in April 1994. In 1995, the Ministry of Coal conveyed its 'no objection' to the policy to be followed by the subsidiary companies, till the Government of India approved the national R&R policy. The significant changes that characterise the new CIL policy on R&R are:

- From recognising only the loss of land in the compensation process, to considering the loss of economic assets
- From considering only landowners/titleholders to be dealt with, to considering the surrounding communities as partners in the R&R process
- From considering land-owning families as the unit of entitlement, to considering every adult individual as unit of entitlement
- From acting on the basis of regional guidelines, to acting on the basis of a corporate policy
- From provision of employment with the coal company as the major vehicle of rehabilitation, to multiple rehabilitation efforts
- From being mainly accountable to the coal company, to being primarily accountable to the PAP
- From not involving PAPs in planning and implementation, to extensive consultation with and participation of PAPs in the process

Resettlement action plan (RAP)

With the adoption of the principle of adult individual being the unit of R&R entitlement assistance, it became necessary to assess the entitled population dependent on land being acquired. For 14 opencast projects (OCPs) of four coal companies belonging to the

Coal Sector Environmental and Social Mitigation Project (CSESMP), the coal companies hired consultants, NGOs and research organisations to conduct baseline socioeconomic surveys. Based on results of the surveys, and after extensive consultations with project-affected people, Resettlement Action Plans (RAPs) were prepared for implementation.

Indigenous people development plan

In the Directive Principles of State Policy, the Constitution of India directs the State to 'promote with special care the educational and economic interests of the weaker sections of the people and in particular, of the scheduled castes and scheduled tribes and shall protect them from social injustice and all forms of exploitation'. The Constitution also makes specific provisions to protect weaker sections of the population from exploitation, and to ensure that they have access to educational and employment opportunities.

State governments have enacted a number of laws to protect the weaker sections, particularly members of the scheduled castes/scheduled tribes (SC/ST). These laws extend to inhabitants of villages situated in and around mines. The villagers living near the mines are, however, sometimes subjected to additional hardships due to the influx of many newcomers to the area as employees of the mine, and also of people working in ancillary industries and service units of the coal mine.

CIL has a history of paying good salaries and providing security of service to its employees. The employees have access to staff quarters that are well served by electricity, water supply and properly functioning educational and health facilities. While these do not directly affect people living of surrounding communities not employed in the mine, it usually introduces a sense of relative deprivation. To supplement efforts of state governments to improve the quality of life in villages near the mines, CIL, as part of the national 20-point programme, undertakes various community development (CD) works in the vicinity of projects. The communities, however, do not perceive infrastructure improvements done as part of the programme as bringing them any direct benefit. The experience gained so far indicates that the weaker sections of the village population, especially tribal people, are at a disadvantage in receiving benefits from such CD works.

The CIL development policy for indigenous people, adopted in September 1995, tries to rectify these shortcomings. This policy stipulates that every coal mine will implement a plan outlining CD assistance that the subsidiaries will provide to the affected population of villages situated within a kilometre of the mine boundary. The Indigenous People Development Plan (IPDP) has the following three main components:

- Community assets (infrastructure)
- Community activities
- Training and capacity building.

Again, for 25 of the OCPs in five coal companies under the Coal Sector Environmental and Social Mitigation Project (CSESMP), CIL commissioned consultants and NGOs to prepare mine-specific IPDPs. Separate meetings were held with tribal communities and women's groups to elicit their needs.

Implementation of RAPs and IPDPs

The RAP and IPDP are new concepts for CIL officials and its subsidiary coal companies. Like any new concept, it is surely going to take some time before the mechanisms are in place and set for smooth implementation. Since project officers are now confronted with the problem of getting physical possession of land required for coal production, the time has come to implement RAPs and IPDPs with due care.

Most inhabitants of villages in the area want a job in the mine to augment their earnings and improve their standard of living. But mines cannot give jobs to everyone. That is beyond their capacity. Therefore, creation of alternative income-generation avenues in coal-mining areas is critical, if the coal industry is to survive. There are many ways to create new income-generation sources. However, the crux of the problem is that in CIL, there is no experience in this area, and unless it is shown to the people that these alterative avenues of generating income are viable and sustainable, they will not come forward. In the coming years, the challenge for CIL will be to demonstrate that this is possible.

The main role of the CIL subsidiary companies is to produce coal. All subsidiaries have a well-staffed organisational set-up for this purpose. But implementing RAPs and IPDPs requires expertise of a different kind. CIL does not yet have the capacity and experience to organise and facilitate mobilisation of PAPs (above the age of 18 and residents of villages of the IPDP command areas) to undertake income-generation activities or jobs not related to coal.

CIL, therefore, decided to invite NGOs and community-based organisations (CBOs) with a proven track record in community development, rural poverty alleviation and income generation, to come forward and assist the project officers of the 25 OCPs in implementing RAPs and/or IPDPs.

About 11 NGOs came forward to assist project authorities with their expertise and their grassroots connections. Each of the 25 mines now had a group of three key persons belonging to these NGOs. As per the terms of contracts signed by their organisations, three key persons were to stay in one of the villages to instill confidence among people about the good intentions of the coal-mining authority. Each project officer of these 25 mines also had one exclusive officer belonging to the CD/R&R cadre to assist him in the implementation of the RAP and IPDP. Committees/councils and village working groups set up for the purpose ensured active participation of PAPs and villagers in the formulation and implementation of yearly action plans under the RAP/IPDP.

Self-employment income-restoration schemes

The R&R policy of CIL has been intensive tested under CESESMP in 14 opencast mines of four subsidiaries since 1998. These are: Gevra, Dipka, Kusumunda, Dhanpuri and Birsampur of SELC; Jagannath, Ananta, Bharatpur, Bepahar, Lakhanpur and Samaleswari of MCL; Parej East and KD Hesalong of CCL; and Jhingurda of NCL.

It is common knowledge that most beneficiaries of the Integrated Rural Development Plan (IRDP), the Jawahar Rozgar Yojana (JRY) and the tribal sub-plans (TSPs) of various state governments have not got the desired results, even though huge amounts of money have been, and are still being, pumped into the schemes. CIL, being a commercial organisation, cannot be expected to bear the burden of the huge funds needed for EPAPs. It has held that if EPAPs are carefully guided, they can be successful in restoring incomes without mine jobs by judiciously utilising opportunities available to them in the coal-mining areas. Organising various effective income-generation schemes for the PAPs is the real challenge, and CIL has endeavoured hard to ensure their success.

The organisation has gained much useful experience in income restoration for PAPs by implementing the R&R policy in these 14 mines. Almost all PAPs regard the provision of a job as the most desirable rehabilitation option, since it results in five-fold increase of income for most of them. At present, the average wage is about Rs 42,000 per year for unskilled labour in coal mines. This is five times the minimum wage rate. In addition, employment in the mine brings other benefits, such as free medical care and subsidised housing.

Against this backdrop, selling the idea that substantial income generation on a sustainable basis is also possible with non-farm self-employment is proving very difficult (Mathur 2006). Even after completing self-employment training programmes under various annual action plans that began in 1998 in 14 projects of the four subsidiaries, a view has emerged that training of EPAPs for self-employment ventures is not enough in itself. Even support to training with loans or grants hardly seems to make a difference. The majority of project-affected people are farmers or agricultural labourers, and transition to another profession will require a great deal of follow-up, involving business planning assistance and extension service.

Despite the poor performance of self employment-based income-generation schemes, the idea of income from non-farm self-employment schemes is gradually beginning to sink in to the minds of some PAPs. When EPAPs were first consulted on their choices for self-employment schemes in 1998, the options indicated were not many, largely due to ignorance coupled with a bit of scepticism about these schemes. In 1999, a perceptible change was noticed, as EPAPs gave a host of new ideas to be taken up by the community development/R&R officers (CDOs/R&ROs), NGOs, and the targeted beneficiaries themselves. The single most crucial factor that emerged from these 14 RAP mines was mobilisation of credit, and a market for consumption of goods and services to be produced by them.

The income-restoration plans, utilising the non-farm self-employment concept under the 1998 and 1999 annual RAPs, could comprise only about 25 per cent of the potential target group, totaling about 7,500 entitled PAPs in 14 projects of MCL, SECL, CCL and NCL. It could not be ascertained if a significantly higher number of entitled PAPs would enroll in non-farm, income-generation activities over the next couple of years. The income level for many EPAPs trained under the Action Plan of 1998 remained low.

By mid-2002 (the year CSESMP closed), 1,724 EPAPs completed skill training under the income-restoration plans (1998–2001), utilising the non-farm self-employment concept. Of these trained EPAPs, 1,006 (58 per cent) have been able to establish an income (whether primary or supplementary) based on assistance received under the project. But due to vast economic opportunities that usually are available in coal mine areas, of the total caseload of PAPs entitled to assistance for income restoration (9,938), a total of 4,152 (42 per cent) are earning an income as a result of various opportunities available.

From the feedback received from 1,724 EPAPs, it is evident that non-farm self-employment does not automatically guarantee sustainable income for PAPs, a majority of whom hail from a background of agriculture or other traditional, land-based activities. The reasons for low performance include:

- Changing the mindset of PAPs as well as the mine officials proved very difficult. The PAPs continued to clamour for a mine job, and thus did not wholeheartedly try to earn through skills newly acquired under the yearly action programme. Most mine officials felt they were being asked to perform the task of poverty reduction, which was the job of state governments. Irrespective of their disciplines, mine officials had traditionally been groomed to assist in production of coal. As a result, their efforts lacked professionalism.
- The lack of clear-cut guidelines about the nature and extent of funding for various types of income-generation schemes proved to be a bottleneck in generating sufficient income for the trained PAPs. The much hoped for dovetailing of different government poverty alleviation programmes for the benefit of PAPs did not come about. Government officials were often reluctant to extend assistance needed in this regard.
- The marketing of the skills and products of trained PAPs was not satisfactory. Whenever there was a clash with a well-established supplier, the PAPs lost.

New focus on land-based income generation

It is time CIL considered other options for income generation for a larger number of affected people on a wider scale. Although not specified in the R&R policy, the most promising options are land-based income-generation activities on OB dumps/reclaimed land/vacant mine land including forested land.

In all, 25 CSESMP mine contracts for plantation work with the Forest Department had a clause to ensure that from January 1999, all activities would have PAP involvement to the extent possible. Since such contracts were usually for three years at a time, and the work mostly of seasonal nature, the involvement of PAPs could not be sustainable. Recognising this drawback, CIL decided to seek the services of an experienced consultant to assist in developing technically feasible income-generation schemes that could be executed on OB dumps/reclaimed land/vacant mine land, involving PAPs on a sustainable basis.

Since involvement of PAPs in such land-based income-generation activities is a new approach, which has not been practised by any organisation in the country, it was considered prudent to have the concept initially tried as a pilot project. The conditions vary from subsidiary to subsidiary, and the transfer of experience from one to the other is less feasible than among mines within the same subsidiary. Therefore, pilot projects were first taken up for EPAPs in each of the four subsidiaries, namely CCL, NCL, SECL and MCL. Since conditions also varied in Talcher and Ib Valley of the MCL, one project for each of these two areas was also proposed. Altogether, five pilot projects would thus be undertaken one each in NCL, SECL and CCL, and two in MCL (separately for Talcher and Ib Valley).

In 2001, Coal India engaged the services of an experienced consultant to successfully develop and implement such a pilot project in Dipka OCP of SECL over a period of five years. The CD/R&R and other existing personnel were to be involved in all stages of these projects to help them gain experience. The main objective was to develop technically feasible income-generation schemes that could be executed on select OB dumps/reclaimed land/vacant mine lands to generate sustainable incomes roughly equal to the existing minimum agricultural wage (about Rs 1,100 per month) within 15–18 months.

The main advantages of this approach are:

- There is no dearth of OB dumps/reclaimed land/vacant mine lands in opencast mines (due to the requirement of about 10 hectare land for producing one million tonnes of coal).

- A substantial number of PAPs come from agricultural backgrounds. They are either farming their own land or other people's land as sharecroppers. The opportunity to continue earning livelihood through land-based activities will be most welcome to them, as they are familiar with the occupation. In SECL, one PAP with a lucrative job in the excavation department bought agricultural land in a nearby locality to practise agriculture with his son, so that they do not lose their traditional farming skills.
- This will avoid the difficulties involved in changing over from the familiar land-based occupation to an unknown occupation for income generation based on self-employment.

One bottleneck in using OB dumps/reclaimed lands/vacant mine lands for generating income is technology. Fortunately, the organisation was already engaged in afforestation on large tracts of barren land. That could prove to be a dependable source of substantial income for people. Since OB dumps/reclaimed land/vacant mine lands are not different from barren lands, it should be possible to successfully implement the land-based income-generation pilot project in Dipka.

The other possible stumbling block could be the type of organisational arrangement to facilitate such land-based income-generation activities for EPAPs. The subsidiaries might prefer that PAPs form their own cooperatives to undertake income-generation activities on land, which the coal mines could formally acquire for them. The spectre of adverse possession of land in favour of PAPs at some point of time was likely to deter many mine officials from supporting such ventures. Moreover, PAPs had no experience of running a cooperative organisation, and some of them might not not have carried out their share of work. A system of incentives to PAPs who show enterprise would need to be worked out.

In July 2001, implementation of the land-based income-generation pilot began in Dipka, SECL, on 50 hectares of land, consisting of 30 hectares of reclaimed OB dump and 20 hectares of unused mine land. The activities, involving 93 PAPs from three villages, comprised cultivation on 37 hectares of paddy, wheat, pulses, castor, vegetables, fodder grass and medicinal plants, together with dairy and fishery. PAPs formed a cooperative society comprising eight sub-groups, of which seven opened a joint bank account. The PAPs managed to save Rs 67,000 from the income of the 2001–02 crops on a joint account, and reported individual monthly incomes from the pilot project at Rs 814 in March 2002 and Rs 920 in September 2002. Since land allocated for the pilot project had scope for involving additional PAPs, interested PAPs from the neighbouring Gevra mine were being invited to participate.

The pilot project was proposed to be run up to 2006, and a withdrawal strategy had been developed to promote sustainability of the activity. One reason for this was to ensure security of tenure through user rights, as there is no transfer of ownership to PAPs of the mine land provided for land-based income generation.

To conclude, Swami Vivekananda once said, 'God must come to a poor hungry man in the shape of a *chapatti* (bread), if He wishes to be listened.' There is also a saying: 'It is very difficult, almost impossible, to really help the poor to eradicate poverty.' The need of the hour is to try any solution that works to assist PAPs in their struggle to regain their lost livelihoods. This is precisely what Coal India is now doing, and the rich experience it has gained has many useful lessons for the extraction industry in other places as well.

References

Hasan, Mohammed. 2006. 'Managing social issues in extractive industry: Lessons from the India coal sector environmental and social mitigation project', in Hari Mohan Mathur (ed.), *Managing resettlement: Approaches, issues and experiences in India*, pp. 284–302. New Delhi: Oxford University Press.

Mathur, Hari Mohan. 2006. 'New Livelihoods for Old: Restoring Incomes Lost due to Involuntary Resettlement', in Hari Mohan Mathur (ed.), *Managing resettlement in india: approaches, issues and experiences*, pp. 67–98. New Delhi: Oxford University Press.

Roy, M. P. 1997. 'Resettlement issues in Coal India Limited (CIL) projects'. Presentation made at the 'World Bank/EDI Training Workshop on Income Generation for CD/R&R Officers and NGOs', 24 November to 8 December, Ranchi.

World Bank. 1996. 'Staff appraisal report'. India: Coal sector environmental and social mitigation project. Washington DC: Energy and Infrastructure Operations Division, Country Department II, South Asia Region.

9

Resettlement in the Tehri dam project: An ethnographic profile

Tulsi Charan Bisht

The state of Uttarakhand comprises 13 districts.[1] Most of these districts lie in mountainous region. Perennial snow-fed rivers and the terrain provide a perfect backdrop for harnessing hydro-electricity, and a large number of hydro-electric projects are already either under construction or are being planned. Buoyed by these developments, the political masters have decided to convert the state into an 'Urja Pradesh' (energy state). The construction of the Tehri dam is one giant step in this direction. But the cost involved in the construction of the dam is no more a secret. The dam has come under criticism for several reasons, such as economic viability, environmental degradation, safety concerns, and population displacement.

The Tehri dam project is located at the confluence of Bhagirathi and Bhilganga rivers in the Himalayan region of the state of Uttarakhand. Since its formation in 1988, as a joint public sector venture between the Central government and the Government of Uttar Pradesh, the Tehri Hydro Development Corporation (THDC) is the agency responsible for the management of the project. The main benefits of the dam are generation of hydro-electricity and ensuring supply of irrigation and drinking water mainly to Uttar Pradesh and Delhi. The installed electricity generation capacity of Tehri dam Hydro Power Plant is 1,000 MW.[2] The project will help irrigate 2.7 lakh hectares of agricultural land and will stabilise existing irrigation for another 6.04 lakh hectare. It will also ensure 270 million gallons of water per day to Delhi and Uttar Pradesh.[3] (Source: THDC website).

The 260.5-metre-high, rock fill dam, with a reservoir size of 42 square kilometres, has been controversial from its very inception. The topography of the region raised major environmental concerns over the dam's construction. Located in the fragile Himalayan ecosystem, it sits precariously close to a seismic fault line, the Srinagar Thrust (Baldia 1994; Paranjpye 1988). Its location in a seismically active zone led experts to raise a number of safety issues. However, despite calls for a cautious approach from a number of committees formed to look into the environmental and safety concerns of the dam, expert opinions were eventually disregarded to construct the dam (Dogra 1990).[4]

Displacement of massive population, both urban and rural, has been another controversial aspect of the Tehri dam. In a rugged, mountainous terrain of Garhwal Himalayas, Bhagirathi and Bhilganga river valleys were some of the most fertile and densely populated valleys. Construction of the dam at such a location has resulted in massive population dislocation.

Based on ethnographic research, this paper deals with the impact of displacement on the rural population, and the problems they face during the resettlement process. Fieldwork was conducted at two resettlement sites, Pashulok and Pathri, in two phases and over a period of seven months between November 2005 and February 2007. Pashulok is located at the fringes of Rishikesh city, while Pathri is located about 25 kilometres from the city of Haridwar. Data collection was based on ethnographic observation and informal semi-structured interviews. Following selection of 'key informants', a total of 60 interviews were conducted, based on the method of snowball sampling. Gender and caste representation in selection of interviewees was ensured. The fieldwork time was divided between the two sites, though slightly more time was spent at Pashulok. While documentation of the post-displacement everyday life is based on both observation and the interviews, the pre-displacement everyday life details are based on peoples' accounts substantiated by secondary literature.

There is no clear-cut data available about the extent of displacement caused by Tehri dam. No benchmark study was conducted prior to the implementation of the project. Absence of such a study makes it difficult to ascertain the exact extent of displacement, and makes it difficult to evaluate the rehabilitation process, as no proper indicators of pre-displacement socioeconomic status of the displaced population are available.

Displacement as a result of the construction of Tehri dam has taken place in two phases. During the first phase, 13 villages were displaced due to the construction process — seven villages for project works, three for establishing project colony and three for establishing New Tehri town (ASCI 1993: 30). The second phase of displacement occurred due to the submergence of villages in the reservoir. According to Hanumanta Rao Committee (HRC 1997), a total of 109 villages were affected by the construction of the dam.[5] Of these, 35 villages were fully affected and 74 villages partially. Fully affected villages are those villages where more than 75 per cent families are treated as fully affected families. In case more than 50 per cent land of a family is acquired, the family is treated as fully affected family; in case of acquired land being less than 50 per cent, a family is treated as partially affected.

With regard to number of affected rural families, the HRC report puts the number of fully affected families at 4,909, while another 3,998 families are treated as partially affected. In addition to these rural families, 5,291 urban families of Tehri town were also displaced by the dam. The estimates of total population displacement differ. An independent study conducted by Indian National Trust for Art and Cultural Heritage (INTACH) puts the number of displaced people at 85,600, from both urban and rural locations (Paranjpye 1988). But as people are still being displaced, almost two decades after the INTAC study, organisations working in the area, such as MATU, have estimated the extent of displacement crossing the mark of a hundred thousand people.

A general understanding about displacement is that it is a momentary experience and takes place at the time people move from one place to another. But in case of development projects like dams, which have a long gestation period, affects of displacement are felt long before the actual displacement takes place (Cernea 2003). Scudder's 'five stage model' to comprehend the process of displacement is a useful tool that emphasises the need to incorporate the temporal aspect of the displacement process. Scudder argues that the whole process, spread over five stages, takes a 'minimum of two generations' (Scudder 1993: 130)

Following the closure of the last of the three tunnels of the Tehri dam on 29 October 2005, inundation of the reservoir area began. It attracted a lot of media attention. But for those affected by the dam, displacement had been a long-term experience. People from affected areas had to live for decades with an uncertain future. Though the work on the dam began in the early 1970s, making it apparent that the affected people would get displaced, the resettlement process moved at a snail's pace; a number of families are yet to be resettled. The slow process of resettlement resulted in community disintegration. Those in a position to, moved out; those who were economically and socially less well off, had to endure decades of uncertainty and neglect. Following the decision to construct the dam, the development activities in the affected areas also came to a halt, as any new expenses on development activities were seen as a waste of resources.[6] As a result, people had to live with the minimum available infrastructure and facilities. '*Gaon ujadene lag gaye the*' (Our villages had started turning into ruins) was a common response to the pre-displacement situation in the affected area.

Government policies affected the people adversely during the pre-displacement phase. Two policies are especially crucial. First, the policy regarding acquisition of land set the date of 8 September 1976 as the cut-off date for deciding the eligibility for land compensation. The policy put a moratorium on any land transaction after the cut-off date, and those who entered into any such transaction risked losing their right to land compensation.[7] This resulted in the affected population facing economic hardships, as the policy restricted peoples' ability to raise money for various requirements by putting land as collateral (also see HRC 1997) or by sale-purchase of land. The second and related policy, or rather lack of policy, is the non-definition of family. Though family is the unit for deciding compensation, the Rehabilitation Policy of THDC (THDC 1995) is ambiguous about what it means by family and treats only the head of the family, on whose name land is registered in the revenue records, as eligible for compensation. In this case, even if a family has grown up into an extended joint family, and grown-up sons have their own families, they are rendered ineligible for compensation, as the land is still held in the name of the patriarch of the family. As the process of resettlement is still continuing, the policy not only ignored the family dynamics, but also, according to the Hindu Succession Act 1956, denied the coparcenary rights of sons in their ancestral property. Resettlers, therefore, see the policy as a violation of their legal right.[8] They also see the policy as inhumane, as it presupposes the death of the household head as a beneficial condition for compensation. In addition to these policy drawbacks, throughout all these years, people had to deal with a corrupt officialdom and pay bribes to obtain their resettlement package.[9] Complaints about various corrupt practices were common throughout the fieldwork.

Resettlers reflecting on displacement see the whole process as a long, enduring and bitter one, which arrested their past and stunted their future. In a breath of helplessness and despair, a 45-year old woman states,

> I had been hearing about displacement since I was a child. We couldn't do anything, couldn't educate children properly; couldn't repair the house. Our house was old and small and children had to grow up in that house. If we had repaired the house, we wouldn't have got compensation for the repaired house as the government had banned construction. So we could not create any facility for our children; we couldn't pay any attention to their education. Our minds were occupied with thoughts of departure and we were not sure that where we would live in the future.

Comprehending involuntariness of dislocation

Displacement as a process referring to the movement of people is invariably concerned with 'place' or the physical environment. The concept of 'place', however, has found little or almost no space in studies of involuntary relocation resulting from development projects.[10] Various scholars (Downing 1996; Sørensen 1996; Oliver-Smith 2001; Feldman, Geisler and Silberling 2003) have pointed to the necessity of inclusion of 'place' as an analytical concept, but it has mostly remained peripheral.

Inclusion of 'place' as a concept to comprehend the involuntary attitude towards displacement is necessary for two reasons. First, the very notion of involuntariness requires an explanation of what makes a place so significant that people are unwilling to leave it and get settled at some other place. Second, the resettlement process that follows displacement involves reconnecting with a new place, and gets affected by the past experiences and memories of the original place.

Wars, natural disasters, environmental degradation, civil strife and large-scale development projects can all produce movement of people. In the case of displacement caused by events such as war, natural calamity, environmental degradation or civil strife, the involuntary nature of displacement is self-evident. However, this is not the same in case of development-induced displacement, where the demarcation line between voluntariness and non-voluntariness of relocation gets blurred. This is because, in case of development projects, it is incumbent upon the concerned government to ensure resettlement and provide compensation to the displaced population. Yet, as Oliver-Smith (2001: 7) points out, the mere acceptance of compensation 'does not necessarily warrant any conclusion about voluntary resettlement', because the unwillingness to leave the place of origin, and the compulsion that 'not moving out' is a non-option, are stark reminders of the involuntary nature of such displacement. This 'involuntary attitude' often manifests itself in form of organised, sustained opposition towards displacement.

In case of Tehri dam, the involuntary attitude towards displacement was evident from the very inception of the dam. Affected people organised themselves, and the Tehri Bandh Virodhi Sangharsh Samiti, TBVSS (an Anti-Tehri dam committee) came into existence in the year 1976. The focal point of this organised opposition was stalling the construction of dam on issues of its adverse impacts on environment, and population displacement. Involuntary attitude towards displacement, too, must be understood in the context of the fact that the land on offer at resettlement sites was of much greater economic value than the land the affected people were going to lose due to the construction of the dam. Therefore, if the relocation was only an economic concern, it could be assumed that people would have happily accepted the resettlement package on offer.

Comprehending involuntariness, therefore, goes beyond the economic principle. Along with socio-cultural aspects of displacement (also see Cernea and Kanbur 2002), it also requires taking into account peoples' attachment to the 'place' (Altman and Low 1992). In case of people displaced by Tehri dam, attachment with the traditional place was very strong. People had strong genealogical, economic, socio-cultural and affective bonds with their villages and the local environment. These places were seen as *pitrabhumi* (ancestral place) and *janmabhumi* (birthplace), where the resettlers' ancestors had dwelled for centuries, and where the resettlers were born. People had a strong sense of ownership, which was substantiated by various traditional rights they held over their local environment. Having lived there for generations and interacting constantly with the local environment, people had turned it into a socially and culturally meaningful landscape. Resettlers, therefore, had a strong sense of being rooted in the place, and displacement was seen as an act of severance or uprooting often expressed in such phrases: '*Humain jad se ukhad kar phaink diya*' (we have been pulled out of our roots).

Socio-cultural profile of the displaced population

The rural population affected by the construction of Tehri dam is Hindu and belongs to three main caste groups—Brahmins, Kshatriyas and Harijans. These caste groups are further subdivided into sub-castes or *jatis*, and most of the villages are multi-caste villages. The village-based society is patriarchal and patrilocal. Along with the caste, joint family and village are two other main modes of social organisation. The resettlers speak Garhwali, an offshoot of Hindi language. Though the people are practising Hindus, their socio-cultural practices differ considerably from their counterparts in the plains of northern India. The local physical environment has played a critical role in shaping the socio-cultural practices of the inhabitants of the region (Berreman 1963; Saklani 1987; Pandit Raturi 2004) and has resulted in people being identified as *paharis* or highlanders.

The pre-displacement socio-cultural life of the villagers was marked by specific characteristics. Though the village society was caste-based, and the rule of purity and pollution was strictly adhered to, this adherence was generally in the cases of marriage and commensality. In everyday life, caste rules were often lax, and people belonging to different castes mixed together both for work and leisure. Similarly, though the society was patriarchal, in day-to-day life, women's role was vital and unlike their counterparts in the villages in the plains, they did not observe the *parda* (veil) system. Women's role in running the household was even more significant in case the husband was away from home. Used to hard work, women were a strong productive force and were able to manage the household on their own. Nestled in the remote mountainous region, the village life was marked by a considerable sense of security and freedom. Till recently, locking the house was not regarded as a good practice. The sense of security was especially important in the case of women, as they could do most of the outdoor work without being dependent on anyone. Everyday social interaction was of high level as a result of people freely visiting one another's households or meeting at community spaces like water sources or riverfront. The sense of community was strong; and collective participation on occasions such as marriage, childbirth or death was a norm.

Pre-displacement economic profile of resettlers

The traditional village economy was subsistence, agricultural economy. Land was the main asset for the villagers. The topography of the region did not allow large landholdings. However, the agricultural land located in the valleys was fertile and productive. Rice and wheat were grown in irrigated lands known as *Sera*. While coarse grains like *koda*, *jhongara* and a number of pulses, such as *bhat*, *gahat*, were grown in unirrigated *Ukhar* land, people also grew various seasonal vegetables, mostly in land patches surrounding the house. The villagers, thus, had access to a variety of food items. However, not every household grew enough food for the entire year, and those with smaller or mainly unirrigated landholdings, bought food grain from ration shops or in the open market.

Agriculture was undertaken manually with the help of oxen. Manure from household cattle was mostly used to fertilise the fields. Agricultural labour was contributed through participation of the household members, though such labour exchange system like *padyalo* did exit and was frequently used at the time of *ropani* (rice transplantation) and harvesting of crops. Women's role was vital in agricultural work, and they did almost everything except ploughing fields.

Agriculture, though, was the main occupation for the people, the smaller size of land holdings and inequitable distribution of land required diversification of occupation. Animal husbandry was the main supportive activity; household animals played a vital role in the economic life of the people. Cows and buffalos were kept for milk and milk-based produces, as well as for the purpose of manure for fields. Dairy products were mostly used for self-consumption, though the sale of such products as milk and ghee, either locally or in Tehri town market, was a useful source of income for the people. Oxen were the mainstay of agricultural activities and were used for ploughing fields and winnowing.

Physical environment, including the riverfront, played a vital role in the local economy, and the villagers relied heavily on the local environment for a number of consumable and non-consumable items, such as fuel wood, fodder, timber, fish, medicinal herbs etc. Seasonal fishing was an important economic activity, especially for people belonging to the Harijan community. The local environment also supported a number of economic activities, such as basket weaving and making of ropes, brooms and agricultural equipments. The villagers had traditional rights (Rawat 1989) on such common property resources as forest, riverfront and pastures.

Another important feature of the resettlers' economic life was that the male population of working age went out to the cities to eke out a livelihood, while women, young children and the elderly remained back in the village. Seeking employment outside, in cities, and sending remittances back home, now characterises the whole of the hill region of Uttarakhand, and the system has come to be known as 'money-order economy' (Joshi 1995). The village life ensured a sense of security and safety, and living within familiar physical and social environment, women could manage the household affairs on their own, allowing men to leave the household in search of employment.

Painchu was an everyday system of exchange that ensured circulation of goods and commodities of everyday use. Hence, if a household ran out of rice, instead of rushing to the market to buy rice, they would go to the neighbourhood and get rice for the day. The system of *Painchu* was not guided merely by economic considerations, rather it was a 'system of total services' (Mauss 1954: 7) and strengthened the village moral economy, which ensured that 'no one in the village went hungry'.

The subsistence economy of the affected villagers was, thus, supported by a number of activities, and the local environment played a crucial role. An important feature of this economic system was that money was not a day-to-day requirement. This is not to claim that the economy was a non-monetary one, rather it means that the absence of money did not affect the everyday life of the people.

Rehabilitation package

The Tehri dam rehabilitation policy recognises displaced peoples' right to land-based resettlement. The rehabilitation package provides a mix of land and cash offers. The fully affected families are given a choice of either land or cash compensation in lieu of land allotment. In the case of land allotment, two options are offered. The resettlers can opt either for two acres of developed irrigated land, or for half acre of developed irrigated land 'adjacent to the municipal limits of Dehradun city or Haridwar city' (THDC 1995). Among resettlers, these two options have come to be treated as 'rural' and 'urban' resettlement options, respectively. These have implications on their resettlement process and lifestyle. The 'urban' resettlement option of half acre of land falls within the fringes of fast developing urban sprawls, where land prices have been spiralling. Land poachers find it easy to entice the rural folks to sell off their lands, and instances of land sale are quite high here. This has given the resettlers a notion of living in urban areas, and they have spent considerable sums in house construction and other ostentatious items. In addition to agricultural land, each resettler family is also being awarded a residential plot of 200 square metres.

The land being offered to the resettlers is not free, and the cost of the allocated land is 'adjusted from the amount of compensation payable to the oustee in respect of acquired land' (ibid). One positive aspect of the rehabilitation policy is that the landless agricultural labourers of fully affected areas are also treated as eligible for the same compensation package and have been allotted land either two acres or half an acre as per their choice. But a family belonging to landless artisan caste, even if it was dependent on the rural agricultural families, has not been treated as eligible for land compensation. The partially affected families, on the other hand, are not eligible for land compensation and are given cash compensation for their acquired land. In addition to the land or cash for land, the compensation package includes compensation for house structures and trees, grant for shifting house, grant for seeds and manure, and an incentive grant to shift to the resettlement sites prior to a set period of time.

A major drawback of the rehabilitation policy, as pointed out earlier, has been the lack of the definition of family. Provision of one single 200–sq. metre residential plot for a large extended family has either led to overcrowding, or it has compelled such families to build houses on agricultural land. This has already resulted in land fragmentation and land sale. Acknowledging this anomaly of resettlement package, the HRC recommended a new definition of family: 'All the sons and unmarried daughters of the entitled fully affected families who have attained the age of 18 years as on 19.7.1990 are recognised as independent families and will be eligible for rehabilitation provisions' (HRC 1997). The committee report, however, realising the scarcity of available land, suggested paying cash compensation of Rs 150,000 for married sons and Rs 75,000 for major unmarried sons and daughters. The report also recommended a 200-square metre residential plot for each married son. The dam authorities, however, ignored these recommendations of the HRC.

Instead, it has opted for paying the grown-up sons and unmarried daughters who have attained the age of 21 years on 19 July 1990, an amount equivalent to 750 times the minimum agricultural wage. The HRC was the only committee that comprehensively looked into issues relating to rehabilitation, and had made some genuine and rational recommendations. Overlooking these recommendations has caused resentment among the resettlers.

The resettlement sites have been developed mostly within Dehradun and Haridwar districts of Uttarakhand. A total of 17 sites have been developed. These sites, located at considerable distances from one another, have resulted in the dispersal of village communities for two reasons. First, though the rehabilitation policy underlines the need to resettle the village communities at one place, in practice, it has not happened. Second, the offer of compensation choices has turned the community-based focus of rehabilitation process into individual family-based process. The individual families, therefore, could analyse the pros and cons of resettling at a particular location, and what appears to be a well-intended aspect of the rehabilitation policy has ultimately resulted into community breakdown.

The resettlement process

This study is focused on people rehabilitated under the second phase, people who were displaced by the submergence of their houses and properties in the reservoir. Those included in the study had moved to the resettlement sites within the last two years. The resettlers were, therefore, still in a transitional phase of their resettlement.

As one visits resettlement sites, the first impression one gets is that the resettlement has been proper, perhaps profitable, for the resettlers. This is more so in case of Pashulok, where most houses have an urban design and look impressive. This has given the established communities in the area a sense that the displaced people from Tehri dam have been awarded a generous compensation package, including land and cash. Though it has not resulted in any explicit confrontation with the established communities, resettlers do feel that this misconception has a negative consequence for them. For example, they feel that they are being overcharged for various services for which they rely on the established communities. They also fear that as a result of such misconception, they have become a possible target for theft and housebreak.

The resettlers argue that though they were villagers, they have not been resettled on a rural resettlement pattern. They see their resettlement based on an urban pattern. At both the sites, the residential plots are clustered together, which has restricted the resettlers within the 200-square metre boundary. The small residential plot does not allow space to construct a shed for cattle and most of the households, especially in Pashulok, do not own any cattle for this reason. Due to the lack of space, the resettlers can neither grow any fruit trees nor can they grow vegetables. Hence, they feel that they have been denied the basic aspects of their village life. They argue that, at least, the residential and agricultural plots should have been merged so that they could have continued their traditional way of livelihood.[11]

Both the resettlement sites lack in a number of civic amenities. At Pashulok, the street-paving is of very poor quality. At Pathri, most of the streets are unpaved, and hardly any work is being done to pave them. Even the residential plan of Colony II in Pathri is so badly laid out that the residential plots are at least two to three feet below street level. The first lot of villagers found their houses almost half submerged in the first monsoon rain. Since, a temporary drainage system has been laid, but as there is no clear outlet for water, a few downpours result in water-logging as problematic as ever. As a result, the new houses are being constructed only once the foundation is raised by two to three feet to reach the street level. This requires filling up the whole residential plot with soil, which adds considerably to the cost of house construction.

The lack of drainage system has also resulted in water-logging on the streets outside the houses, even during times when there are no rains. Wash water flows outside on open streets. In the absence of a sewage system, the latrines are pit-based, and as resettlers mostly rely on bore-pump water for their daily needs, the existence of latrine pit at close vicinity from the bore-pump is seen as a health hazard. Apart from these drawbacks in the layout plans of resettlement colonies, other basic amenities, like schools, hospitals or primary health care facilities, post offices, banks, fair price shops, are also missing in both the localities. Public transport is a major problem for the resettlers of Pathri. Initially, the THDC ran a bus for the residents, but it was discontinued. The lack of transport facilities not only hampers the day-to-day activities, but it also heightens the concerns about any emergency situation evacuation.

Social disarticulation

Social disarticulation, according to Michael Cernea (1995), primarily results from the loss of social capital and breakdown of social networks. In case of resettlers of the Tehri dam, though the instances of community dispersal and breakdown of various social networks are very much evident, social disarticulation is also palpable in case of those village communities which have been resettled as a group. As pointed out above, the affected population had to live with an uncertainty about resettlement for decades. That uncertainty continues even after their resettlement. At their traditional villages, people had legal ownership rights of the land. This had given them a sense of security. But at the resettlement sites, they have not been given any such legal rights. The land is not registered in their names. All they have been given is a *kabja pramanpatra* (possession certificate) that is not recognised for any legal purpose. Hence, if resettlers wish to take a loan from the bank, they cannot do so because their land papers are not recognised by banks. Even to open a bank account, resettlers require someone from the established local communities to stand as a guarantor for them. Similarly, a resettler, if required, cannot become a guarantor of bail in a law court. The lack of land ownership rights, therefore, has been the main reason for the sense of 'social disarticulation' amongst resettlers, who see themselves as being relegated to a secondary social status. As a result of this uncertainty, a lingering fear exists in resettlers' mind that the government might one day displace them from these lands as well. And the case of a group of first phase resettlers of Tehri dam, who are now being displaced a second time for the extension of the Jollygrant airport near Dehradun city, is often cited as an example.

Livelihood challenges

Agriculture remains the main occupation for the resettlers. At Pashulok, there is an ambivalent attitude towards it. The small size of agricultural plots, and considerable expenses involved in cultivating fields have resulted in a number of plots being left uncultivated. Unlike in the past, when practising agriculture did not involve much money, it now requires money at every step. People need to hire tractors for ploughing fields. They also need money to purchase fertilisers and pesticides. Hired labour is required for rice transplantation and harvesting of paddy and wheat crops. As the village communities have dispersed, the traditional modes of labour exchange, like *padyalo,* have become redundant. The irrigation infrastructure is of poor quality and design. For example, the irrigation canals have been laid, but as they have not been properly designed, people are compelled to break open the sidewalls to get irrigation water into their fields. This makes irrigation by canals incredibly cumbersome in case of plots that are located at a distance from the water source, as most of the water seeps through the various holes on the way. This has led resettlers in Pathri to rely mostly on bore-pump water for irrigation, which requires hiring a pump from outsiders.

The constant requirement of money to practise agriculture has raised concerns about the future, and resettlers see that either they would have to look for alternate sources of income to continue the agricultural practice or they would have to give away their lands on contract. Even in Pathri, where the agricultural output from two acres of land is deemed to be enough to meet the family requirements, the instantaneous and frequent need of cash in practising agriculture is seen as a major hindrance.

The land fragmentation and sale of land are other major threats to the resettlers' livelihood. The policy recognising the legal owner of the family land as the only eligible member for land compensation has created a number of problems in cases of extended joint families, and such families are left with no other option but to construct houses on their agricultural land. The other major concern is the high instances of land sale, especially in Pashulok, in most cases due to the cost of construction of house. Resettlers were given compensation for houses on the basis of their houses being traditional *kacha* houses; the fact that they used to get most of the construction material free from the surrounding environment was ignored. At the resettlement site, on the other hand, resettlers need to buy everything required for house construction. This has resulted in the cost of house construction escalating many times, which the compensation money paid for the original house cannot cover. The additional cost is most commonly met by the sale of land.

Various subsidiary economic activities like dairying, fishing, woodcutting, carpentry and masonry are no longer available to the resettlers in the new environment. Even if resettlers attempt to undertake activities like dairying, they find it hard to negotiate the local markets, which are dominated by the established local communities.

The trust that binds different communities together is yet to develop. Another important economic activity of seeking employ-ment in cities by the grown-up male members of the household has been severely compromised, as a heightened sense of insecurity at both the resettlement locations does not allow male members of the family to move out to cities leaving the womenfolk and children behind. In absence of any gainful employment available in surrounding areas, the resettlers are compelled either to take up menial jobs or to remain unemployed.

At both the resettlement sites, common property resources (CPR) are almost non-existent. At Pathri, women do go to the nearby forest to collect firewood, but they are scared of being harassed by the forest officials. Unlike in their traditional villages, they have no rights to the forest here. The absence of such resources has not only affected the livelihood patterns of the resettlers, but has also undermined their customary practices. For example, traditionally, if a death occurred in a village, male members of every household would carry a log to the cremation ground. The bereaved family, thus, did not have to purchase wood. But now, in the absence of access to the forest, in case of death, the affected family needs to purchase wood, and cremating the dead has become an expensive task.

Displacement, therefore, has raised serious livelihood concerns for resettlers. In the absence of any support programmes, the whole idea of rehabilitation as propagated by the authorities is not working in practice. Michael Cernea says the combined use of terms 'resettlement and rehabilitation or R&R' in the Indian context 'suggests that the post-displacement phase consists of two *distinct processes:* 'resettlement' refers only to the physical relocation of displaced people, while "rehabilitation" connotes the restoration of lost economic and social abilities' (Cernea 1999: 3, emphasis in original).

However, in the case of the Tehri dam, only the resettlement part of the process is under implementation, and once the resettlement package is handed over, the process is deemed to be finalised. The schemes which could have helped rehabilitation are non-existent. Though the rehabilitation policy of THDC underlines that preference would be given to dependents of the affected families in employment with THDC, there are complaints of violation of this provision. Given the large scale of displacement, neither is it feasible from a cost-benefit analysis to employ one member of every affected family.[12] Other such income-generation schemes, like poultry farming, floriculture, animal husbandry, which are incorporated in the rehabilitation policy, are also non-existent.

Everyday life challenges

Resettlers' pre-displacement everyday life was largely organised around their local environment; displacement has disrupted their everyday routines and activities. Absence of routines has resulted in disinterest and a sense of ennui. Even undertaking simple everyday tasks has become a challenge. For example, one man explains that to collect fodder for his two buffalos, he needs to cycle every day for one and half hour to the nearby *sabzi mandi* (vegetable wholesale market), and has to spend 15 to 20 rupee to get leftover roots, stems and leaves as fodder. A major problem faced by resettlers is the involvement of money in their everyday life. Unlike the past, money is now essential to meet day-to-day requirements. In the absence of any regular source of income, this has become a real challenge for resettlers. At the moment, daily monetary requirements are either being met through the remaining compensation money or, in some cases, from the sale of the land.

Gender and displacement: Women's perspective

The necessity of engendering 'forced migration studies' (Doreen 1999) is now being vigorously pursued, and there has been an upward surge of a gender-centric approach within the discipline. This perspective is, however, rarely used within the studies of development-induced displacement. Despite the fact the field of development-induced displacement is now fairly established, very few attempts, such as those by Colson (1999), Lyla Mehta (2008) Parasuraman (1993), have been made to understand the impact of displacement on women. These authors have shown the way displacement has affected women's lives in terms of role expectation, income, marginalisation etc, and have argued for inclusion of women as a priority group.

In the case of the Tehri dam, there have been compound effects of displacement on women's lives. Traditionally, women played a vital role in all spheres of life and they were treated as the backbone of the family and society. It meant a lot of hard work; at times, women spent hours to collect water or fuel-wood for daily household requirements. This, in general, has created a sense that displacement has proved a boon for women. There is no doubt that the drudgery of hard work has been reduced considerably at the resettlement sites. But, displacement has also resulted in marginalisation of women. Unlike in the village, where women could organise the household, including the agricultural activities, at the resettlement sites, their role in various household activities has been reduced considerably. Within the agricultural system, their role has become mostly that of an onlooker. As men oversee the agricultural activities, women's task is that that of a support hand, to supply *chai* (tea) and refreshment. Or, they have become part of the labourer team that is hired to work in the fields. Unlike the past, when they could organise the agricultural work on their own, in the changed environs, they find themselves unable to participate in an equally important manner. Traditionally, they considered their labour had *barkat* (strength to prosper); now they feel that their work has lost that essence. The change in the economic role has diminished women's ability to have access to money. In the village, if required, they could earn small sums of money either by working for someone, or by selling fodder, firewood or dairy produces. By virtue of their labour, they also had the ability to raise loans. But as displacement has undermined these abilities, women are now solely dependent on men for money. Displacement has also affected women's abilities to negotiate various day-to-day activities. For example, even to take a sick child to the doctor, they require help of men. Similarly, while in their villages, women spent most of the time out of the house, but now their day-to-day activities are restricted to the household boundaries. This is especially true in case of Pashulok. Here, women's outside activities are now restricted to evening walks or weekly visits to the nearby *haat* (market), and they report that this change is adversely affecting their health and physical well being.

Socio-cultural impacts of displacement

The dispersal of village communities has been a major impact of displacement. Despite the rehabilitation policy underlining the necessity to relocate the village communities as groups, resettlers find themselves with a completely new set of neighbours. At Pathri, 96 residential plots of Colony I have been allocated to resetters from 10 different villages. As a result, various social and community support mechanisms have disappeared. The changed architecture of the houses, the boundary wall and the gate, has further eroded the social interaction. The gates are especially seen as barriers to normal interaction. The feeling of unease with gates is much stronger at Pashulok. Traditionally, places like riverfront, water sources, forests and pastures had played an important role in sustaining social interaction. The absence of such community spaces at both the locations has adversely affected social life of the resettlers. Women's spaces have become severely circumscribed, and so has the level of their social interaction. The number of community practices, such as village-level participation in a marriage ceremony, has been greatly altered. Unlike the past, when such a ceremony would attract an active participation of all villagers, the participation is now limited to the observing the *nyota* (invitation). As a result, the role of money has greatly increased on such occasions, straining resources of the resettlers. Eventually, the traditional sense of community cooperation is being replaced by an individual competitiveness.

The traditional cultural practices of the resettlers are similarly getting affected. A large number of these practices were very specific to the original place, and cannot be transplanted. For example, *ropani* (rice transplantation) was both an economic and socio-cultural activity, whereby people, while transplanting rice saplings, would also sing and produce folk songs. But now, as the *ropani* is done by hired labourers, the associated cultural activities have come to an end.

Loss of various narratives is another cultural loss to the resettlers. These narratives, like other cultural activities, were very place-specific, and have become redundant as a result of displacement. For example, in case of the Laxaminarayan temple that has been transplanted to Pahulok, a number of associated narratives have been lost as at the new location these narratives are out of context. Hence, the temple has eventually lost the cultural heritage status, and has become like any other normal temple in the absence of traditional cultural narratives associated with it. The resettlers see their life increasingly being influenced by urbanisation that, they believe, will eventually erode their culture, including the language.

The whole process of displacement has been a long and enduring one for the resettlers of Tehri dam. Resettlement to new locations has only intensified the uncertainty about the future. However, there are certain positive aspects of the rehabilitation policy, such as recognising displaced people's right to land-based resettlement.

But such intentions are ultimately undermined by provisions like the non-definition of family. The land allocated to the resettlers has much greater market value than the land they had traditionally owned. This has created a false impression that resettlement has been generous; this has made resetters vulnerable to land poachers. The rapidly growing instances of land sale are indicative of land loss and looming impoverishment. Even the better and higher agricultural productivity of the land at resettlement sites is not a guarantee towards a secure future, as the whole process of agriculture has become money-intensive. The situation is further aggravated by the loss of various livelihood support systems. The transitional period through which the resettlers are passing at the moment, is a crucial one, and in the absence of any support system as part of the resettlement package, negotiating this period is more of an act of individual agency. Like in most other cases of dam-induced displacement, in the case of the Tehri dam, too, relocation of the effected population to a new place is seen as an end in itself. This attitude, ignoring the complex nature of the resettlement process, highlights the short-sighted approach of the policy makers.

A commonly forgotten aspect of development-induced displacement is the fact that such displacement, resulting in a separation of people from their traditional way of life, also results in their incorporation within a rapidly spreading, market-oriented, capitalist way of life. For example, in the case of resettlers of the Tehri dam, commercialisation of agriculture and everyday requirement of money are just two instances of such incorporation. Hence, an emphasis on recreating pre-displacement life conditions is not a feasible option. For example, provision of traditional CPR like pasture land would not address many problems that the relocation poses. This is not to state that the community initiatives should become passé; rather, they need to be reformulated and redirected to the new life situations which result from displacement. Resettlement as a process, therefore, needs to be directed towards rebuilding the everyday life capabilities of the displaced people, as resettlement in new settings requires developing new everyday life capabilities.

Notes

1. Uttarakhand, initially known as Uttaranchal, was carved out of the mega state of Uttar Pradesh in 2000.

2. The Tehri Hydro Power Complex includes the Tehri Dam and Hydro Power Plant with an installed capacity of 1,000 MW, Tehri Pumped Storage Plant installed capacity 1,000 MW and Koteshwar Hydro Electric Project with a capacity of 400 MW. Hence, the combined installed capacity of the Tehri project is 2,400 MW.
3. See THDC website. Available at http://thdc.in/Projects/English/Scripts/Prj#Introduction.aspx?vid=132 (accessed 11 January 2008).
4. A number of committees were constituted to look into these issues. The Task Force headed by S. K. Roy in its final report pointed to the dangers related to the construction of the dam. A Standing Committee, known as Bhumbla Committee, to assess the environmental impact of dam construction, recommended that keeping in view the adverse impacts on environment, permission for the dam's construction should not be given. Hanumanta Rao Committee also outlined various environmental and safety hazards in construction of the Tehri dam.
5. Hanumanta Rao Committee was set up in 1996 by the Central government to look into the environmental and population displacement affects of Tehri dam. The committee submitted a detailed report in 1997.
6. The HRC has also noted that no developmental activities were undertaken in the affected areas during all those years of dam construction.
7. The setting of this date was apparently to check the outside infiltration in the project affected areas. However, such sweeping measure should have been followed by a baseline survey to identify the original inhabitants who could have been made exempt from the moratorium on land transactions.
8. For denoting the affected population, different nomenclatures have been used within existing literature on development-induced displacement. In this study I initially wanted to use the term 'displaced' but during fieldwork it was pointed out to me that '*visthapit*' or 'displaced' was a negative term and gives the affected population a negative identity. People claimed that though they were displaced by the construction of the dam, they have been 'resettled' for the sacrifices they have made. So the preferred term was '*punarvasit*' or resettled. Hence, the term resettler is an outcome of this interaction.
9. So rampant were instances of corruption that the HRC had to take special note of it.
10. Place as an analytic concept, however, is gaining importance in refugee research. Malliki, Kibrieb, Stuppart and others have used the concept of place in analysing various policy frameworks with reference to refugee resettlement. For details, see Kibreab (1999) and Stepputat (1994).
11. The official argument for clustering the resettlers is based on two facts – one, to preserve the community character and the second is based on security reasons. The officials argue that in case of first phase of

resettlement, individual plots of two acres were given, which included residential land. This resulted in dispersal of resettlers and they became easy prey for theft and robbery.

12. In a personal communication with a THDC official, it was revealed that only one person could be employed on every one MW of electricity generation for the project to be beneficial.

References

Altman, I. and S. M. Low (eds). 1992. *Place attachment*. New York: Plenum Press.

Administrative Staff College of India (ASCI). 1993. 'An appraisal of rehabilitation and resettlement: A study of Tehri Hydro Development Project, Uttar Pradesh and Sardar Sarovar Narmada Project, Gujarat'. Hyderabad: ASCI.

Baldia, K. S. 1994. *Sankat main Himalay: Unche bahdhon ka paryavaran aur samaj par dusprabhav (The Himalayas in trouble: Ill effects of high dams on environment and society)*. Nainital: Janta Press Sales.

Berreman, G. D. 1963. *Hindus of the Himalayas*. Berkeley: University of California Press.

Cernea, M. 1995. 'Understanding and preventing impoverishment from displacement: Reflections on the state of knowledge'. *Journal of Refugee Studies*, 8: 154–64.

———. 1999. 'Development's painful social cost', in S. Parasuraman (ed.), *The development dilemma: Displacement in India*, pp. 1–31. New York: St. Martin's Press, in association with Institute of Social Studies.

———. 2003. 'The question not asked: when does displacement end?'. *Forced Migration Review*, 17: 1–3.

Cernea, M. and R. Kanbur. 2002. 'An exchange on the compensation principle in resettlement'. Working Paper, Department of Applied Economics and Management, Cornell University, Ithaca.

Colson, E. 1999. 'Gendering those uprooted by "development"', in I. Doreen (ed.), *Engendering forced migration: Theory and practice*, pp. 23–39. New York, Oxford: Berghahn Books.

Dogra, B. 1990. *Tehri dam project — How expert opinion is undermined*. Bharat Dogra: New Delhi.

Doreen, I. (ed.). 1999. *Engendering forced migration: Theory and practice*. Refugee and Forced Migration Studies Volume 5. New York and Oxford: Berghahn Books.

Downing, T. E. 1996. 'Mitigating social impoverishment when people are involuntarily displaced', in C. McDowell (ed.), *Understanding impoverishment: The consequences of development induced displacement*, pp. 33–48. Providence: Berghahn Books.

Feldman, S., C. Geisler and L. Silberling. 2003. 'Moving targets: Displacement, impoverishment, and development'. *International Social Science Journal*, 175: 7–13.

Hanumantha Rao Committee. 1997. 'Report of the review committee on environmental and rehabilitation aspects of the Tehri hydro-electric project'.

Joshi, P. C. 1995. *Uttarakhand: Issues and challenges*. New Delhi: Har-Anand Publications.

Kibreab, G. 1999. 'Revisiting the debate on people, place, identity and displacement'. *Journal of Refugee Studies*, 12: 384–410.

Mauss, M. 1954. *The gift: Forms and functions of exchange in archaic societies*. Glencoe: Free Press.

Oliver-Smith, A. 2001. *Displacement, resistance and the critique of development: From the grass roots to the global*. Oxford: Refugees Studies Centre, University of Oxford.

Pandit Raturi, H. 2004. *Garhwal ka Itihas (History of Garhwal)*. New Tehri: Bhagirathi Prakashan Grah.

Paranjpye, V. 1988. *Evaluating the Tehri dam: An extended cost benefit appraisal*. New Delhi: INTACH.

Parsuraman, S. 1993. 'Impact of displacement by development projects on women in India'. Working papers, Institute of Social Studies.

Rawat, A. S. 1989. *History of Garhwal, 1358–1947: An erstwhile kingdom in Himalayas*. New Delhi: Indus Pub Co.

Saklani, A. 1987. *The history of a Himalayan princely state: Change, conflicts and awakening*. Delhi: Durga Publications.

Scudder, T. 1993. 'Development-induced relocation and refugee studies: 37 years of change and continuity among Zambia's Gwembe Tonga'. *Journal of Refugee Studies*, 6: 123–152.

Sørensen, B. R. 1996. *Relocated lives: Displacement and resettlement within the Mahaweli Project, Sri Lanka*. Amsterdam: YU Press.

Stepputat, F. 1994. 'Repatriation and politics of space: The case of the Mayan diaspora and return movement'. *Journal of Refugee Studies*, 7: 175–185.

Tehri Hydro Development Corporation (THDC). 1995. 'Rehabilitation Policy'. THDC, New Delhi.

———. 2007. 'Tehri dam & HPP (Stage-I) — Introduction', available at http://thdc.gov.in/Projects/English/Scripts/Prj_Introduction.aspx?vid=132 (accessed 11 January 2008).

10

The micro-politics of urban evictions and rehabilitation: Cases from Kolkata

Medha Chandra

Issues of eviction and rehabilitation have been at the core of many political and social frictions in urban India. Evictions in urban India have targeted low-income urban residents living without any legal tenure in shanty towns and informal urban settlements, as well as residential and commercial encroachments on urban land by higher income groups. Over the past few decades, largely middle-class claims about the environmental pollution and degradation caused by informal urban settlements has been used as a major justification for eviction of such settlements in cities like Mumbai, Delhi and Kolkata. Rehabilitation of the evicted persons has been a contentious issue, with little consistency in the way rehabilitation of urban evictees has been treated by different state governments or even by a single state government across different eviction cases.

Many studies have focused on eviction and rehabilitation issues related to large-scale environmental conflicts surrounding dams, national parks and waterways. The focus of many studies on urban evictions, such as those on eviction of squatters from municipal land, from the sides of rail tracks and canals etc, has been on the legality and procedural impacts of the evictions, including on the issue of compensation and rehabilitation for the evicted persons. This paper looks at a different aspect of urban evictions, away from the realm of town planning law and municipal procedures. This study looks at the social and political factors that shape the nature of evictions, that decide who is evicted and who gets compensation in the event of eviction. These factors may bypass what the law says on a particular issue of urban evictions and rehabilitation, and the decision by a municipality to evict a certain group of people from urban land gets coloured by other criteria, which can be unearthed by examining the micro-politics of the entire case. This paper focuses on this realm of the micro-politics behind evictions in urban India.

Here, the focus is on smaller-scale, yet frequent, environmental conflicts, such as those between urban municipalities, informal urban settlement residents and higher-income residents. This paper focuses on the politics surrounding evictions and rehabilitations of low-income urban residents, using two case studies of environmental conflicts in Kolkata. The aim of this exploration of micro-politics is to understand how urban environmental conflicts, which result in evictions, occur, the trajectory these conflicts take, and how different groups who are part of such environmental conflicts influence municipal decision making regarding evictions and rehabilitations. The case studies, described in detail later in the chapter, studied conflicts over access to and control over urban water bodies in two localities in Kolkata, between grassroots urban residents living in informal settlements and the more affluent urban residents living in the surrounding urban area. This paper explores the micro-politics that shaped the outcome of the two environmental conflicts, resulting in eviction with rehabilitation for the informal settlement in one case, and no evictions in the second case.

It is relevant to point out that informal settlement here means settlements that are not planned and lack proper municipal services, such as adequate drainage, sewage, water supply etc. The legality of a settlement is not being used here to term it as formal or informal. For example, the residents of one of the informal settlements in the case study had bought land legally from the original owner of the land and had land deeds. The residents of the other settlement studied did not have any such legal papers. For the purposes of this study, both settlements, irrespective of their legal standing, but based on their physical condition, are being called informal settlements. The sig-nificance of understanding not just municipal laws and procedures on evictions, but investigating the impact of micro-politics of urban evictions, can be understood from the fact that of the two informal settlements in focus here, the one that had no legal standing remained untouched by evictions, despite sustained and strong efforts made for its eviction by surrounding area residents. The informal settlement in the other case, whose residents had legal paperwork such as land deeds, was the one that got evicted. How and why did these seemingly illogical events occur? That is what this paper wishes to explore. The answer lies beyond the realm of legality, in the realm of politics and discourse.

Theoretical background

The study of the micro-politics of the cases revealed that the factors that influenced a group's success in making claims to the municipality about urban evictions included: the discourses used by the claim-makers to present their claims to the municipality, as well as aspects of the political field within which this claim was made.

Discourse is defined here as:

> a specific ensemble of ideas, concepts, and categorizations that are produced, reproduced and transformed in a particular set of practices and through which meaning is given to physical and social realities (Hajer 1997: 44).

Discourses ascribed to by individuals and groups shape their cognitive commitments and the various possibilities of action for them. Hence, the discourse a claim-maker ascribes to shapes how his or her claim is framed, and how it is presented to the claim-accepting body. The discourse dominant in the claim-accepting body shapes what kinds of claims are considered as valid by the claim-acceptors, and hence, the kinds of claims that will have a higher chance of success in accessing the claim-accepting body.

This paper argues that the access that the claims of various conflicting claim-making groups have to formal municipal channels (claim-acceptors like elected and appointed municipal officials), is shaped to a large extent by the degree of discursive affinity between the discourses of the claim-makers and the formal channel members.[1] As a result of discursive affinity, discourse coalitions can be formed between some claim-makers and formal channel members. This may have exclusionary impacts for claims of other claim-makers in accessing the formal channels. However, this access is not only controlled by the discursive field, but also by the political field in which claim-making and -accepting occur. The political field can be understood by analysing the political culture of the field and the distributions of power in it.

A political field includes actors such as the state, political parties, citizens and social movement organisations, tied together by a particular political culture (Ray 1999). Political culture refers to the acceptable ways of doing politics in a society, strongly influenced by the complex web of social relations like class, gender, religion etc that order society (ibid). It describes the attitudes, beliefs and rules that guide a political system, determined jointly by the history of the system, and the experiences and ideologies of its members (ibid). If a system presents a history of elite domination, bureaucratic hegemony and grassroots marginalisation through an organisational culture predicated on hierarchy and authority, then this also affects the ideologies and experiences of its members. Hence, political culture tends to be self-perpetuating, unless conscious efforts are made to alter it.

Political culture is a combination of High Politics, comprising elements of formal party politics such as party organisational structure, party discipline etc; as well as of everyday politics. Here, everyday politics and High Politics are differentiated in the way that 'politics' and 'Politics' are differentiated in political science literature. Everyday politics is the politics behind everyday interactions of formal channel members with the public, and what it reflects about their inherent attitudes towards people from different social and economic backgrounds at times when not controlled overtly by an ideology and in an explicitly Political situation (such as in a political party meeting). Behaviour under the direction of a defined political ideology in a defined political arena, and for a defined political end — in other words, under the framework of High Politics — is different from the behaviour influenced by everyday politics. When present in situations of High Politics, subjects have a *consciousness* of being under the influence of a political ideology. It is not to say that a Political ideology may not be internalised by a party member and start influencing the politics of their everyday interactions. However, the probability of party ideology impacting everyday praxis would depend on the extent to which the ideology is known and understood by the political party member. In this paper, both aspects of the political culture, that emanating from High Politics and that from everyday politics is considered.

Political culture is thus a combination of the formal aspects of institutional behaviour as predicated by High Politics, and the informal aspects of it as seen in everyday politics. Opportunities for accessing the formal channel may be available in theory, but it is often the informal aspects of the relationships between public authorities and non-state actors, which generate trust and norms of reciprocity essential for the non-state actors in accessing the formal channel. It has been shown that where the formal channel members and the non-state actors share similar characteristics and expectations, there is easier 'closure' of issues and opportunities of engagement (Maloney et al. 2000), raising the possibility of discursive coalitions between socially similarly positioned bureaucrats, politicians and the community elites. This can also result in the formal channel having clientalistic or semi-clientalistic relations with non-elite actors unable to break into these coalitions (Fox 1994, 1996).

These elements are explored here to understand how the discursive and political dimensions of the micro-politics of the case studies determined the outcome, i.e., either eviction or the lack of it for the informal settlement dwellers.

This study is based on fieldwork conducted over two years in two adjacent wards in South Kolkata.[2, 3] To be able to reveal the micro-politics of the two cases, qualitative methodologies were used to access and analyse the claims of all the stakeholder groups involved in the conflict, and to understand the factors which determined which stakeholder group's claim-making to the municipality produced success for that group, and the reasons for this success. Of the various actors important for such an analysis in this topic, on the one hand were the municipality and its definition of what constitutes appropriate urban environmental issues. On the other hand, there were the different groups of claim-makers. The qualitative methods used included over 150 in-depth semi-structured targeted interviews with:

- Grassroots groups and surrounding community groups involved in the environmental conflicts leading to the demand for evictions in the case study areas;[4]
- political party members active in the two case study areas;
- employees of the Kolkata Municipal Corporation (KMC) dealing with these conflicts; and
- elected councillors from the two case study areas.

Focus groups as well as document analysis were also used to understand the micro-politics of the cases. In this paper, extracts from actual interviews are used to highlight the arguments made, and to bring to the fore the voices of the people involved in the conflicts.

Two case studies

The two cases being examined were located in adjacent wards of south Kolkata, and dealt with environmental conflicts between low-income grassroots groups with the surrounding community higher income residents in the two locations. The cases dealt with conflicts between these groups over access to and control over urban water bodies.[5] In both areas, the conflict was between grassroots informal settlements on the banks of each of the local water bodies, and the surrounding area residents. In both cases, the surrounding community alleged that the informal settlements polluted the water of the local pond, and demanded their eviction from the area.

In the first case, in B. P. Nagar, the grassroots informal settlement had legal papers showing their ownership or tenancy on the land, but was unable to access the formal municipal channels with their claims and was evicted.[6] In the second case, in K. Gardens, the informal settlement has been able to resist eviction to date even without any legal standing. It is important to better understand the characteristics of the groups that were involved in the conflict, since this had strong implications for their discourses and also impacted the political field in each case, affecting the ultimate outcome of the two cases.

The surrounding community in B. P. Nagar was largely middle class and upper caste; they exhibited strong unity among themselves. An important reason for this unity was that they were from the same region of former East Bengal (now Bangladesh), and had migrated to Kolkata together as refugees in the 1950s. Other than this common regional origin, they had formed a community organisation called the JSC, which spearheaded a community movement for the eviction of the informal settlement from the banks of the pond in B. P. Nagar. The surrounding community in B. P. Nagar had almost unanimous support from the Left Front (LF), the political party coalition that was dominant in the local municipal borough.[7] The grassroots group in B. P. Nagar was largely poor, low caste and had lived by the pond side for over 50 years working in the surrounding area as rickshaw drivers, housemaids and fisher-folk. They had papers showing that a few of the families had bought the land from the original owner of the pond, and the rest were tenants of the families with ownership papers. The informal settlement was evicted, and the pond taken over by the surrounding community for beautification.

In the second case, in K. Gardens, the surrounding community was composed of upper middle class families, who were largely from upper caste backgrounds. Many of them were employed at high posts in the state government. The grassroots informal settlement was composed of low-income low caste persons, several of whom were employed as sweepers in the municipality. These grassroots residents of the area also had high unity among themselves due to their common employment situation, and also because they had a common regional origin, having migrated to Kolkata from the Indian state of Bihar. The informal settlement in K. Gardens did not have any legal paperwork and had squatted on the pond side land.

There was discursive parity (i.e., similarity of discourses) between the formal municipal channels and the surrounding community's discourse in both the cases, making it highly probable that the surrounding community's claims would be successful in accessing the formal channels in both the cases. However, despite there being a discourse coalition between the formal channel and the surrounding community in K. Gardens, the grassroots group there was able to resist eviction. As compared to the grassroots community in B. P. Nagar, the K. Gardens grassroots group had higher success in resisting evictions due to their united resistance to the surrounding community, their larger number as a group, and better political affiliations.

The political field as well as the discursive field were important in deciding the level of access that grassroots claims against evictions had to the formal municipal channels, and the consequent action taken by these channels regarding these claims. The paper examines the discursive field in the two cases to see how the discursive parity between the environmental discourses of the formal channels and surrounding community claim-makers could have forced the side-lining of the grassroots claims, and led to their eviction based on an environmental justification. The paper also examines the political field to explain why the discursive field alone could not decide the outcome of the claim-making efforts of the groups in conflict with each other in the two case studies.

Analysis of competing discourses in the case studies

Hajer's (1997) Argumentative Approach of discourse analysis is used as the framework to analyse the discursive issues. In this approach, the discourse of different actors can be deciphered from the storylines they use and the images they draw upon to make these storylines compelling. Storylines are essential discursive devices that facilitate discursive closure. The discursive practices of the metaphor, analogy, historical reference, cliché, appeals to collective fear or guilt, all come under the umbrella of the storyline. They fulfil an essential role in the clustering of knowledge, the positioning of actors and, ultimately, in the creation of discourse coalitions amongst the actors of a given domain. Understanding the discursive formats and cognitive commitments of various actors helps in pointing to discourse coalitions, which also reflect the power equations between the different actors in the process of environmental claim-making. The approach draws on Giddens' idea of duality of structure, stating that though the discoursing subject has a central role, the actions of this subject are in the context of social structures of various sort that both enable and constraint their agency (ibid). Hence, both the structure and agency aspects of institutional discourse are considered in this analysis.

Since the surrounding community in both case study areas used environmental reasons for demanding eviction of the informal settlements, the following section on discourses focuses on the environmental discourses used by the surrounding and informal settlement communities. It also examines the degree of discursive parity between municipal discourse and the claim-makers' environmental discourses, to understand how far this discursive parity shaped the eviction outcome for the informal settlements.

Storylines of the grassroots group

The environmental discourse of the grassroots group in both the case studies used three storylines — the first, about fulfilling their materialistic needs using the pond water and the pond side location; the second, about their non-materialistic values for the water body; and the third, about the injustice of their evictions based on material as well as non-material reasoning. They used these three storylines to protest any moves for their eviction.

The first grassroots storyline looked at the environment as a material resource, and talked about the livelihood and lifestyle requirements of the grassroots group that were fulfilled using the water from the ponds, and also their locational advantage of living there. The second storyline looked at the actors' relationship with nature on a non-material level, and talked about the long and deep links with the water bodies that the grassroots groups had. This relationship was through their past or current livelihoods, their life patterns, and their attachment to those areas. This highlighted their use of historical reference as a discursive practice. This storyline also talked about how the grassroots group valued non-material aspects like cooling breezes from the water body, visual pleasure from living next to a body of water etc. The third storyline expressed environmental claims of the grassroots group as the injustice they felt at the idea of being evicted from their homes. It linked their environmental discourse with the discourse of social justice. Thus, the storylines used by the grassroots groups for expressing their relationship with the natural environment combined both their material and the non-material link with the water body.

In the following first interview extract, a grassroots person evicted from B. P. Nagar area expresses his anguish at losing his links with the water body, and the pond side land that was his home. This first extract illustrates the combination of the storylines of non-material values for the area, and the injustice of evictions. In the extracts that follow that, the storylines used are non-materialistic values and link with the water body due to locational and lifestyle concerns, respectively. The grassroots groups' questioning of the justice of the eviction attempts, and the resulting antagonism between them and the surrounding community, is also illustrated. The materialistic storyline is the common thread between all these, as the material concerns are closely intertwined with all other concerns in the case of the grassroots group.

> Our *bheeth mati* (foundation mud), our land, our houses, everything was taken away. But no one even asked for our suggestions or advice...they didn't involve us in any decisions or any discussions. Suddenly they told us you have to go, started measuring the land and started threatening us with the bulldozer and used force to remove us (TS, 22 November 2002, B. P. Nagar, Kolkata).

> We lived near the B. P. Nagar pond in difficult conditions, but we were happy. When it used to get very hot we would sleep on the road outside our home. There was no electricity there; the cool breeze from the pond cooled us (DU, 17 December 2002, Sapui Para, Kolkata).

> We don't have any other place to go. We like living there. We have been living here for fifteen years. It is a nice place. We are attached to it. We work here. We have strong local links here (Woman and man from K. Gardens basti, 2 March 2003 Kolkata).

Storylines of the middle class group in general

Before moving to the actual storylines used by the case study actors, it is relevant to examine discourses that the overwhelmingly middle class news media in Kolkata used regarding urban environmental issues and grassroots informal settlements. This will help show that attitudes and discourses seen in the case studies were part of a general trend in the city, and not specific to the cases themselves. For this, newspaper stories over five years from major English and Bengali newspapers were analysed to reveal their discursive position.

The issue of pollution, and protection of the environment from pollution, featured as the dominant discourse in most news-reporting on the environment in Kolkata. In a selection of newspaper articles on environmental issues taken from 1992 and 2000–2003, about 45 per cent had a pollution prevention focus. The discursive format of the reporting presented Kolkata's grassroots settlements as part of the problem, pressing for their eviction to create a 'clean and green Kolkata'.

About 70 per cent of news articles focused on the issue of encroachments on eastern Kolkata's wetland system (in the East Calcutta Wetlands), and the city's drainage canal system, wildlife loss and pond-filling in the Kolkata region. These articles used scientific justifications for warranting legislative action and municipal crackdown on grassroots settlements, for reclaiming land that these settlements had encroached upon. These storylines played on people's fear and panic; stressing that for the 'greater good', the convenience 'of a few' (the informal settlement residents) should be sacrificed. Recourse to the courts and law enforcement agencies to evict them for recreating a 'green Kolkata' was quite common in this reportage. Reportage of the social justice dimension of environmental issues was largely neglected, with only 15 per cent reporting on the plight of low-income groups evicted from marginal lands like canal sides, from next to railway lines etc. The storyline used emphasised the polluting nature of such settlements, and the anti-environment stance of these settlement dwellers in their protest against eviction.

As seen from the above newspaper examples, the reportage on environmental issues in the English and Bengali news media used the storylines of pollution prevention and improving environmental quality using a technical discourse. Grassroots groups were almost uniformly portrayed as illegal, troublesome groups, whose lifestyle caused pollution and who should be evicted for cleaning up Kolkata. Middle class groups in Kolkata equated environmental issues with pollution prevention and environmental management, denying that any other discourse could be considered environmental. The persistent argument was that the grassroots groups were polluting the water bodies by their presence, hence could not be thought to have any environmental values at all, and should be evicted. The material aspect of the grassroots actors' dependence on the water bodies for their livelihood and lifestyle requirements, as well as their non-material attachment to the water bodies, were not considered valid environmental interactions.

Discourses of middle class surrounding community

From the following interview extracts, it is apparent that the middle class groups in both the case study areas, B. P. Nagar and K. Gardens, followed the general pattern of middle class groups in Kolkata in their discourse towards grassroots informal settlements and the quality of the urban environment. Therefore, they desired the eviction of the grassroots informal settlements to ensure a beautiful locality pleasing to the middle class group. The surrounding community groups were concerned with what Inglehart (1977) calls environmentalism born out of post-materialist concerns, in which people value the environment solely for aesthetic and recreational reasons, devoid of any fulfilling of material needs using the environment. Eckersley (1989) further elaborated on these ideas adding the influence of the higher educational experience on creating an environmentalism that is beyond materialist values, is less anthropocentric and provides intrinsic value to the environment.[8] As seen from the following interview extracts, the environmentalism of the middle class surrounding communities in the case studies can be understood from such a standpoint. Their values towards the environment were derived from their objective separation from the environment, where their day-to-day materialist concerns are not dependent on the environment or fulfilled by it. These values shaped their demands for eviction of the grassroots settlements, since the interaction of these grassroots settlements with the urban ponds did not fit into the middle class groups' environmentalism.

In the first interview extract, a middle class resident from the B. P. Nagar area describes the importance of the pond for the area's environmental quality. He draws upon a storyline highlighting the importance of drainage and pollution prevention for the quality of the local environment. In the second extract, two residents of B. P. Nagar area, who were also politically active with the LF, the dominant political party in West Bengal, comment on the middle class community's involvement in and enjoyment of nature for personal and community recreation.

> This pond is this area's life breath. It keeps this area clean and adds freshness to it. It is necessary for breathing (good air), (for a) good environment, fire fighting etc (BCC, 12 November 2002, B. P. Nagar, Kolkata).[9]

> Idol immersion in the pond after Durga Puja and other celebrations attracts and involves many people. Rabindra Jayanti, Poila Baishak, Bijoya Sammelini (various local cultural and social events), Jwalabhumi Diwas (wetlands day) organised by the Morning Walkers Association, all are celebrated next to the pond (TD and DB, 22 November 2002, B. P. Nagar, Kolkata).

The storyline of concern for pollution prevention and environmental quality combines with that of the enjoyment of nature for personal and community recreation in the following statement made by a middle class resident of B. P. Nagar, about the 'enjoyable' pond that was obtained only after evicting the undesirable informal settlement. In this extract, the middle class resident's statement indicates the power equations in the area, through the middle class group's ability to control access to the water body and define rules for anyone who accesses it, all based on what they consider as 'appropriate' and 'good urban environment.'

> The pond has become nice — with a clean pond, nice environment, where people can sit and enjoy, can bathe. No washing of clothes is allowed. Even the evicted persons bathe here (PS, 9 December 2002, B. P. Nagar, Kolkata).

Similar reactions towards the urban environment are seen in the following extract from the middle class group in K. Gardens. A middle class member of the K. Gardens Society (a local organisation), when outlining the community's vision for the development of the lake and park in the area, draws on the storyline of using the urban ponds for recreation for personal and community use, after evicting the 'undesirable' informal settlement.

> We want to make a water park, swimming pool etc after removing these people (the informal settlement). ...Therefore we are trying to get the lake and park back and develop the lake with a coffee house, paddling, a place for people to relax (AK, 17 December 2002, K. Gardens, Kolkata).

The next quote, by a prominent middle class citizen of the surrounding community in K. Gardens, reflects the use of the pollution prevention storyline. This extract also reflects the power equations in the area, which show the frictions between the informal settlement and the middle class community.

> The *basti* (informal settlement) people do create problems for the K. Gardens residents here.... you have seen how they live. They are expanding their houses right there; more people are coming in. They throw garbage right next to their own houses and use the pond banks as a urinal (NH, 5 February 2003, K. Gardens, Kolkata).

The surrounding community in both case studies also strategically used the high impact and visibility that environmental claims had in the municipality and the news media, for achieving other agendas. The surrounding community in B. P. Nagar wanted to evict the grassroots settlement from the area not just to save the water body from pollution, as they stated overtly, but also because of their stated resentment of the presence of an ugly informal settlement in their 'clean, polite neighbourhood'. Similarly, the K. Gardens surrounding community also stated antipathy in their 'upper class' residential area towards the presence of the 'dirty' squatter settlement filled with 'uncouth people'. Thus, the environmental claims were used to achieve the agenda of evicting groups from the urban area towards which the surrounding community had an identity-based antipathy. As seen in both case studies, claims based on environmental justifications can be used to achieve ends other than purely environmental ones.

Thus, storylines used by the surrounding community groups pointed to the grassroots groups as the perpetrators of pollution who deserved to be evicted to create a good urban environment, while the storylines used by the grassroots group positioned the surrounding community as unjust and interested in using the environment for their entertainment at the cost of the livelihood, lifestyle and other needs of the grassroots groups. As Hajer explained in his argumentative approach, storylines help construct a problem, and also act as devices through which actors are positioned and through which specific ideas of blame, responsibility, urgency, etc. are attributed.

Through storylines, actors can be positioned as the victims of environmental oppression, the perpetrators of environmental pollution, as deserving to be evicted to 'save the environment', and so on. From the preceding interview extracts, it can be seen that the storylines used by the surrounding community, as well as the grassroots groups, helped define the environmental problem in the minds of the speakers, and also the roles assigned by the claim-makers to each other and to themselves. This, in turn, reflects the power equations in the area, inherent in the environmental conflict under discussion.

The environmental discourse in the state sphere

In the argumentative approach of discourse analysis, institutions have been characterised as functioning on the basis of specific cognitive commitments, which have a high degree of salience. Analysing the laws and procedures put in place by institutions to deal with issues from a certain realm, helps understand the cognitive commitments of these institutions. The actual implementation of these laws, and the attitude of the actors who are part of the institution, also need to be considered. Another important thing to be remembered is that behaviour of institutional (or any) actors, is not only a function of the structured discourse of the institution, but also derives from the agency of its members, who may have a different personal cognitive commitment and may want to pose a discursive challenge to the routinised discourse of the institution.

Drawing on Giddens' idea of duality of structure, both the structure and agency aspects of institutional discourse are considered in this section. The cognitive commitment of institutions leading to a routinised discourse is the structural factor that constraints as well as enables the agency of the actors who make up institutions; in this case, the political representatives and bureaucrats. The way in which the institutional discourse gets translated into action, with attendant implementation deficits and aspects of individual agency of the members of the institution, illustrates the agency aspect of the analysis.

Hence, whether the informal settlement residents would be evicted or not based on an environmental justification, depended not only on structural factors, which are the laws related to informal evictions, and environmental laws related to urban water bodies; but also on the agency of the bureaucrats and officials concerned, and on how they chose to interpret the laws based on their own cognitive commitment, self-interest or ideological commitment to a particular conflict outcome.

Formal institutional cognitive commitments — the laws

Since the municipality approached the two cases as environmental conflicts over urban water bodies, it is pertinent to briefly outline the legal framework around the water bodies that existed in Kolkata, and influenced the action against any persons polluting the water bodies or encroaching upon them. The laws applicable to urban water bodies are the state government's West Bengal Inland Fisheries Act 1993; the Water (Prevention and Control of Pollution) Act 1974, and the Land Use and Development Control Plan for the Calcutta Municipal Corporation area 1996. The local government's Kolkata Municipal Corporation (Amendment) Act 2001 also delegates some responsibilities to various municipal departments for the water bodies. These numerous laws are based on a techno-centric view of the urban environment, and approach the environment though the lens of administrative rationalism. They allow for the state to take over a water body under threat of being filled up.

The Kolkata Municipal Corporation (Amendment) Act 2001 lays out procedures and rules about the instances in which evictions can take place, the way in which they should occur, and in what cases the evicted persons are eligible for compensation. However, the way the eviction issue was approached in the two case studies illustrated that these rules were not evenly applied, under heavy influence of other political and social factors.

The implementation deficit — aspects of agency in the formal sphere

Other than the discursive frame of the legislations, the actual functioning of these laws and the various municipal departments in relation to each other were also important in determining how claims of certain actors were understood, and what action was finally taken regarding informal settlement dwellers in the two case study areas. In the field, it was observed that there was reluctance on the part of the state government and the local government departments to deal with the different issues related to urban water bodies. There were no clear rules for how environmental claims were to be made. Thus, despite the existence of an institutional cognitive commitment towards urban water bodies, as seen through the multiple layers of laws at state and local levels, the functional domain, as shaped by the agency of its members, exhibited a denial of the institutional discourse towards the urban environment. Further, agency of its members also impacted this acceptance of institutional discourse.

Municipal councillors were observed to favour certain kinds of claims from people over other kinds. The councillors' discursive frame fitted with municipal bureaucratic discursive styles and confirmed to the discourse of administrative rationalism. However, the political party to which the individual councillors belonged, and their party's discourse towards the environment as well as evictions, impacted the stance taken by the councillors. The impact of High Politics was observed in the way party ideology affected the councillors' overt discourse towards the urban environment and evictions based on environmental justifications. However, actual actions of the councillors was dependant on the everyday politics of their interactions with people of their area, as well as on their own agency, shaped often by calculations of personal and political benefit.

Discourse coalitions, power equations inherent in institutional procedures

As seen in the argumentative approach of discourse analysis, discursive dominance is seen as essentially a socio-cognitive product, whereby the social and cognitive are essentially intertwined (Hajer 1997). Hence, the praxis of the municipality is affected by the structuring effect of its institutional cognitive commitments, as well as of the claim-accepting municipal official/councillor's subject position and agency. The possibility of discourse coalitions being formed is very high where there is solidarity between the claim-makers and claim-acceptors from the municipality based on similarity of identity.[10] Complimentary cognitive commitments of the formal channel members and claim-makers, also conditions the formation of discourse coalitions. Comparing the environmental discourse of formal channel members to that of the middle class and grassroots groups outlined in the previous section, coalition formation seems possible between the surrounding community groups and formal channel members in both case study areas, which could have exclusionary effects for the grassroots claim-makers if such discourse coalitions were formed.

This section also illustrates the difficulties faced by grassroots claim-makers in accessing formal channels for environmental claim-making, due to institutional procedures. These problems include procedural complexity, skills required in environmental claim-making that conform to the discursive pattern of the municipality, and, in the case of water bodies, the physical distance of the municipality's department dealing with water bodies from the grassroots claim-makers. All these impeded effective claim-making from grassroots actors, making them more likely to be evicted in the conflict.

The following extract reflects the attitude of the members of the formal channels towards the grassroots actors' environmental discourse and praxis. Grassroots uses of urban water bodies for their lifestyle and livelihood were looked upon negatively, as ex amples of unenlightened behaviour. The official quoted below points out to the irrelevance of ponds to peoples' lifestyles and livelihoods in cities, thus betraying his cognitive commitment, which only accepted middle class behaviour and needs as appropriate in urban areas.

> My personal opinion is that the educated class is more aware (about the environment). In many ponds, people use the same pond's water for washing (clothes and utensils) and drinking, which is bad. Such people don't have any health awareness (CC, WBPCB, 12 December 2002).

Other than discourse coalitions, which reflect the power inequality between the grassroots groups and the official channels, there is an exclusionary impact of the procedures of the municipality regarding environmental claim-making, which are weighed in favour of certain types of discursive practices and understanding.

> The complaint-making procedure is that every zone has an Executive Engineer, people can complain to him. Parks and Gardens (Department) has two zones one is North and other South. For South Zone issues, you can talk to the zone head, talk to the borough-level District Conservancy Officer for solid waste management. It is their responsibility to see that no one throws garbage in the lake (MM, 23 February 2003).

These procedures of environmental claim-making often require skills that grassroots actors may themselves not possess, and may require the assistance of an intermediary. This institutionalises their dependence on a third party, usually political party middlemen, who extract their own costs for this dependence. Thus, making the use of the formal channels becomes difficult for people who do not have the same discourse frame as the municipality. There is little understanding among institutional actors about the degree to which discourse can become structured in institutional arrangements. The procedural complexity and the skills it requires claim-makers to have, can be judged from the extracts that follow this paragraph; they outline how an environmental claim is made to the municipality. This is further complicated by the discursive divide, as seen earlier, between councillors and claim-makers from a background and cognitive commitment different than those of the councillor. This makes dependence on the councillor for advancing claims problematic, as seen in the first extract.

> A complainant can give a letter to the Executive Engineer. That is the procedure. (The complaint letter can) also come through the councillor. If it comes through the councillor, (it is better as) then he reminds (us) repeatedly and follows up (DC, KMC, 15 March 2003).

Further, the responsibility for urban water bodies was given to the Chief Municipal Town Planner and Architect office of the Kolkata Municipal Corporation, which did not have a local presence in every borough, like the other departments did, and was not easily accessible to claim-makers. For accessing this department, grassroots claim makers would necessarily need to make a special trip to the municipal headquarters, taking out time from their daily wage-earning activity, placing them at a disadvantage with the middle class groups, who have more financial resources and are able to devote more time to claim-making without suffering economic hardship.

> The Chief Municipal Town Planners and Architect Department also look after the ponds' issues. The CMTPA department is only present in the central headquarters of the KMC therefore they can't know about local pond cases (RB, Borough X, 13 March 2003, KMC).

Having seen the impact of discourse on claim-making, the fieldwork also showed that there was a strong impact of the political field in deciding the outcome of the eviction claims. This is discussed in the next section.

Impact of the political field: A review of high politics and everyday politics

High Politics and everyday politics demonstrate their impact on the functioning of the formal channels through the political and bureaucratic culture of the formal channel. High Politics comprises elements of formal party politics, such as party ideologies, organisational structure, party discipline etc. High Politics affects the functioning of municipalities, since councillors and the members of the legislative branch of the municipality are politicians affiliated with different political parties. Their political affiliations and resultant political ideological commitments colour the way they approach all municipal issues. However, as Gledhill (2000) explains, power actually rests on the everyday social practices that are the concrete form taken by relations between the governing and the governed. Hence, everyday politics can be understood as the politics behind everyday interactions of formal channel members (bureaucrats and councillors) with the public.

Everyday politics reflects the inherent attitudes of the formal channel members towards citizens from different backgrounds at times when not *overtly* controlled by a political ideology. It is based on attitudes emerging from a person's subject position, as well as on their own agency. High Politics shapes the behaviour of actors under the influence of an overt and stated political ideology in an explicitly Political situation (as in a political party meeting). Everyday politics needs to be analysed to understand the agency aspect of the political culture, which prompts self-serving behaviour from political representatives, which is different from what is dictated by party ideology of High Politics. High Politics and everyday politics together describe the political context within any public authority, and the character of the formal institution through the behaviour and ideologies of its members.

High politics

As seen in the next extract from an interview with a retired senior bureaucrat, most politicians in the Kolkata Municipal Corporation followed the party discourse regarding the environment in their formal interactions with claim-makers and the municipality. Hence, a party's discourse towards the urban environment (and informal settlements) was important in shaping the formal behaviour and practice of the elected representative from that party regarding this issue.

> Elected municipal representatives think it is better to ask their parties and talk to their party bosses about what to do about any issue (KCS, 28 March 2003, London).

Of the two political parties that were involved in the cases, the CPI (M), which leads the LF coalition, has an environmental discourse derived from its Marxist ideology. This looks at nature as a resource to be exploited for human benefit. The value of scientific understanding of the environment is also important for the CPI (M), which prescribes utilising environmental resources with maximum efficiency. The other political party important in the case study areas, the Trinamool Congress (TC), has an ideological schism within its party regarding the environment. One party faction is against the use of environmental justifications for evicting people; the other supports such evictions using the pollution prevention storyline.

The impact of High Politics on the two cases is apparent from the fact that the political parties in both areas formed their strategy towards the claim-making groups based on the party's environmental discourses, their focus on increasing the party's support profile in the areas, and party unity. Other than this, the two parties also showed their attempts to strengthen their support among those claim-making groups, from whom they thought they would obtain the maximum electoral benefit in each area.

Tables 10.1 and 10.2 provide a brief outline of the actors in the two case study areas. Their political affiliations and identity profiles help understand the following discussions on the High Politics and everyday politics of the area.

In B. P. Nagar, the LF coalition supported the surrounding community claims. As seen from Table 10.1, the surrounding community comprised strong supporters of the LF. The grassroots group members in B. P. Nagar did not have such united political affiliation. As a result of their smaller numbers as compared to the surrounding community, and their weaker political 'value' as voters, the LF coalition opposed the grassroots groups' claims against eviction. The TC supported the grassroots group in a muted way, as the party was trying to strengthen its support base in an area that was traditionally not its stronghold, and attracting the surrounding community's support away from the LF was very difficult for it. The LF's influence on the B. P. Nagar pond case is also apparent from the fact that the KMC, which was ruled by the LF at the time of the evictions, supplied unstinting support to the pollution abatement agenda of the surrounding community, and supplied all necessary input in terms of materials, funds and labour for the eviction of the informal grassroots settlement.[11] High-level KMC political officials were involved in this effort.

In the K. Gardens case, as seen in Table 10.1, about 60 per cent of the grassroots informal settlement residents were employed as municipal sweepers, with strong links to a Left Front trade union. This trade union was a distinct arm of the LF, with the main LF political bodies separate from it. The grassroots municipal workers also had good links with their bureaucrat bosses in the local borough. Through these networks and contacts, the grassroots group were able to overcome the structural predisposition of the formal channel members to support the surrounding community. As seen before, the surrounding community had strong discourse parity with the formal

Table 10.1: Identity of claim-makers

	B. P. Nagar: Grassroots Claim-makers	*B. P. Nagar: Surrounding Community Claim-makers*	*K. Gardens: Grassroots Claim-makers*	*K. Gardens: Surrounding Community Claim-makers*
Occupation	Housemaids; Cycle cart drivers	Small business; Salaried jobs	Municipal workers; Employed in private companies	High rank govt officials; Businesspersons
Caste	SC (lowest Hindu castes)	High caste	SC and ST (tribals)	High caste
Regional ID	West Bengal peasant origin	Refugees from East Bengal	Migrants from Hindi-speaking Bihar	High ranking East Bengal migrants
Numbers	13 families = 80 people	100 families = 500 people	90 families = 400 people	2000 + people
Political Affiliation	Mixed	Strongly LF	Municipal workers: LF; Others: varying	Mixed

Table 10.2: Identity of members of formal claim-making channels

	B. P. Nagar Case Councillor	*B. P. Nagar Case Higher Municipal Officials*	*K. Gardens Councillor*	*K. Gardens Higher Municipal Officials*
Caste	Upper caste	Upper caste	Upper caste	Upper caste
Regional ID	East Bengal refugee origin	Mixed; officials of East Bengal origin	West Bengal origin	Mixed origin
Political Affiliation	LF	Borough LF dominated	TC	Borough TC dominated (previously LF)
Sex	Female	All male	Male	All male

channels, and hence, discourse coalitions could have been formed between them, with exclusionary outcomes for the grassroots group. However, the united political affiliation of the majority of the informal settlement to the LF, as opposed to the scattered political affiliations of the surrounding community, gave the grassroots settlement the tacit political support of the LF. This tacit political support was a result of the LF's electoral calculations, where the assured votes of the united informal settlement residents were more valuable than the scattered votes of the more numerous, yet politically less active, surrounding community. In practice, the LF remained neutral, supporting the grassroots group only through its trade union, not through the main party. This tacit support by the LF, despite its overt discourse to the contrary, made the informal settlement more able to access the formal channels with their claims, even if not using regular formal procedures, but using everyday politics connections with municipal officials and bureaucrats.

The K. Gardens surrounding community did not have a united political affiliation, were not united in their claim for the eviction of the grassroots settlement, and had few personal links with the local administration. Similarly, the TC was opposed to the grassroots settlement in the area, but the party made no significant efforts for their evictions as it wanted to gain the support of the grassroots settlement, while not alienating supporters from the surrounding community. Thus, the impact of High Politics ensured that the LF tacitly supported the grassroots settlement in the area, while the TC remained neutral in practice, making some weak threats against the grassroots settlement.

Self-serving agency of political representatives

Despite party ideologies, the councillors and party members — influenced by everyday politics — showed an opportunistic attitude towards the urban environment, as is seen from the following extract.

> Filling up of ponds involves promoters, real estate dealers, local musclemen and influential politicians — both of the Right and Left. It is very difficult to stop this (BCC, 12 November 2002, B. P. Nagar, Kolkata).

This impact of everyday politics was also seen in the way solidarity groupings were formed in the B. P. Nagar area. As seen in Tables 10.1

and 10.2, many of the prominent formal channel members, politicians as well as officials involved in the pond rejuvenation work, had strong links with the surrounding community due to having lived in B. P. Nagar area or due to common identity profiles. This included having a common regional origin and similar class-caste backgrounds. This solidarity did not go against the self-interest of the formal channel members; hence, the solidarity groups were formed in addition to the discourse coalitions to ensure full political and bureaucratic support for the surrounding community. This had an exclusionary outcome for the grassroots residents' claims. The grassroots residents not only had a very different regional origin, but also a caste-class profile that was very dissimilar to that of the formal channel members. This reduced the possibility of solidarity between the formal channel members and grassroots groups.

Referring to Tables 10.1 and 10.2, we see that the K. Gardens surrounding community had a similar identity profile in terms of regional origin and caste-class with the formal channel members, but since this clashed with the political self-interest of the formal channel members, solidarity groupings did not form between formal channel members and the surrounding community. Supporting the grassroots group better fulfilled the self-interest of the politicians in the formal channel. The municipal officials supported the grassroots group as they had daily contact with a majority of the grassroots residents who were employees of the municipality. Further, as the councillors and other political members of the formal channels influenced the bureaucrats, the latter chose to support the group that was supported by the politicians in the formal channels. Hence, the grassroots group members were able to oppose evictions from the area with the support of the formal channel members, even though this was not formalised support.

In this discussion of the agency of the formal channel members, it appears as though this was only influenced by their self-interest agenda. However, this was not true in all cases, as some formal channel members had personal ideological commitments, which overcame their structural predisposition and self-interest. Thus, agency was not always shaped by self-interest, and could be overcome by personal ideology as well.

Thus, on the one hand was the structuring effect of the political party ideology, and on the other was the agency of the individual politicians, which could be at cross purposes with party ideology with respect to the urban environment and evictions using environmental arguments. This played an important role in deciding which group of claim-makers a councillor or party member would support in an environmental conflict, and whether, in these conflicts, the informal settlements would get evicted; and if so, whether they would get any compensation or resettlement. The structuring effect of party ideology, discursive parity and identity-based solidarity may have pointed to supporting one group of claim-makers. However, the self-interest agenda of formal channel members or their personal ideological commitment could point to supporting another group of claim-makers.

Factors shaping the micro-politics

This study looked at nature and environment as socially constructed categories, in contrast to the functionalist approach, where existence of environmental problems are considered a direct result of identifiable, distinctive and visible objective conditions (Hannigan 1995). The social constructionist approach contends that social problems are not simply reflections of objective conditions in society, but rather come to be identified as such only as a result of an interpretative process engaged in by competing claim-makers (Sandweiss 1998). The 'new environmental conflict' is not conceptualised as a conflict over a predefined unequivocal problem with competing actors, but is seen as a complex and continuous struggle over the definition and meaning of the environmental problem itself (Hajer 1997). Constructivism understands discursive constructs of environmental problems, that there can be different 'realities' of the environmental problematic for different people. This view also considers the impacts of the political and social context on definitions of environmental issues, and the questions of power inherent in the processes of legitimatisation of particular views of environmental problems, which, in this case, can lead to eviction for grassroots groups, using environmental justifications.

The ideal-typical environmental policy models used in positivist policy studies categorise state reaction and action shaped by values of objectivity, scientific proof and expert role in managing environmental problems. These shape the discursive frame within which a particular environmental conflict or situation is judged. This 'standard view' of environmental management (Harvey 1996), is a dominant paradigm of most state actors. Its dominance results in it permeating into popular discourse about environmental problems. Thus, even those actors whose own cognitive commitments give rise to an alternate definition of an environmental issue are forced to mould their claims-making efforts into the dominant and popular paradigm of the standard view of environmental management. Positivist policy-making by formal state channels ascribes to the discourse of administrative rationalism, looking towards the 'big talk' of science for discourse validation (Stott and Sullivan 2000). This disadvantages groups who do not 'speak' this language of science, or whose claims are derived from a moral reasoning, not evidence-based rationality. The limitation of positivist approaches to environmental policy making is that, while making the policy, they overlook or give insufficient emphasis on the political field, and also the interests of the actors who are stakeholders in an environmental issue and inhabit that political field.

As a consequence of these cognitive commitments to a particular environmental discourse, there was a denial of alternate discourses as valid *environmental* discourses. In the field, the possibility of opposing discourses, by entering the formal channel's discursive field, was very remote. The discourse coalitions observed in the study reinforced a dominant discourse bolstering the regime of truth accepted by the formal channels.[12] Opposing environmental discourses were unable to break into these discourse coalitions, due to their inabil-ity to challenge the 'rules of the game' that propagated the regimes of truth accepted by the positivist formal channels. The grassroots groups chose not to challenge the 'rules of the discursive game', and worked with their implicit understanding of structured ways of arguing in the discursive spaces provided by the state formal channels. Working strategically, they chose to downplay that aspect of their environmentalism which was at odds with the environmentalism *expected* of them by the claim-accepting channels. Hence, grassroots actors publicly articulated largely materialist claims and stressed upon the material compensations.

A fundamental issue emerging from this discussion is that the environmentalism of claim-makers, and the resultant action towards any claims derived from that environmentalism shape the range of claims that the claim-makers themselves consider valid. It is the same case for claim-acceptors — they are also influenced by their own environmentalism in their judgements about the appropriateness of a claim. It is very difficult to judge the validity of a claim if seen from within a particular environmentalism. For example, claims asking for eviction of the grassroots groups seem justifiable from within the 'middle-class' post-materialist environmentalism's cognitive commitment to pollution prevention. Similarly, the grassroots discourse asking for continued right to live next to and use the pond water seems right from within the boundaries of grassroots environmentalism. Actions taken by people of these groups may be defendable within the parameters of their own environmental paradigm. Then how can one come to grips with such a situation of environmental conflict, where the claim-makers possess such differing cognitive commitments? It is a basic schism between the green agenda and the brown agenda, and the possibility of relativism leading to inaction and confusion.[13] The answer would require adoption of a mode of thinking, i.e., adoption of a discourse by which to assess the conflict. By doing so, the possibility of falling into the trap of relativism due to having adopted a constructivist approach can be set aside.

Further, it was seen in the study that employment of any discourse as the only credible one was a highly ritualistic affair that served to reproduce existing power relations (Harvey 1996). This was seen in the overwhelming sway that the discourse of administrative rationalism held over the formal channels, and the space it created for post-materialist environmentalism in them. This reproduced the power relations that existed between claim-makers at the grassroots and other groups into the discursive field of the formal channel. Formation of discourse coalitions between groups with discursive affinity is an illustration of the role of discourses in not only reproducing power relations but also actively shaping and institutionalising some of them.

However, the fact that discourses were not the sole criteria in shaping access to the municipal channel leads us to the conclusion that discourses do not stand alone, but are continuously affected by other social factors. Hence, what an actor articulates as his or her dis-course is a product of a dialectic relationship between discourses, beliefs, social relations, institutional structures, material practices and power relations. Discourses internalise effects from all of these domains, while reciprocally entering in, though never as a pure mirror image, to all of these domains (Harvey 1996). This was seen in the study as well, where the discursive constructs of the various claim-making groups and claim-accepting groups were seen to have emerged from a relationship between the discourse and these other social factors. The effects of social relations and identity, of history and shared pasts, of material practices, and power relations between different groups and within groups, were seen as shaping the discursive field of the politics of environmental claim-making. This politics was created by and negotiated using different resources and strategies, and by overcoming different obstacles, by different claim-making groups.

This takes the paper towards conclusions that emerged from the study about the political field. High Politics, as seen in the case studies, involves political parties engaged in a political game using their political ideologies, manifestos, members, and formal channel members from the party in strengthening their hold over political power. Everyday politics is called into play for bolstering this effort. The fact that the 'legal citizens' from the surrounding community had state-sanctioned rights, and could approach formal state channels as part of these rights, made it more difficult for grassroots groups to approach the formal channels. The impact of discourse and social relations on the relationship between formal channels and claim-makers can be seen here.

The identities of the surrounding community members derived from their legality, and their particular class-ethnicity combinations that overlap with those of the constituents of the formal channels prompt formation of solidarity groupings between the formal channels and the citizens. These solidarity groupings, similar to the discourse coalitions emerging out of discursive affinity based on similar environmentalisms, kept the formal channels more attuned and receptive to the surrounding community members from backgrounds with more power in comparison to the grassroots groups. However, the diffused nature of power ensured that this was not entirely an unequal situation for grassroots groups, who use their everyday politics interactions with non-formal channels to keep their interests alive in the overall scheme of things. The interactions of the moment of social relations with that of discourse, power and material practices become apparent from this.

It is relevant to revisit the structure and agency debate. Though people's subject positions and identities shape relations of power, their agency has a role in shaping their actions. The agency of actors is shaped not just by their own calculations of benefit and loss, but also through their ideological commitments, which may propel them to overcome their structural predispositions towards supporting a particular action, and instead prompt them to follow a different path.

Thus, having looked at the discursive field and the political field in relation to access of claims of grassroots groups in environmental conflicts, it is apparent that despite the importance of the discursive field in shaping the access of claims to formal channels, it is also strongly affected by the political field. The relative importance of High Politics and everyday politics depends on the balance between the self-interest agenda of the formal channel members and their structural predisposition. These can, however, be overcome by the agency of formal channel members derived from their personal ideological commitments. All these factors are important in shaping the micro-politics of claim-making in urban environmental conflicts, which often propose eviction of urban informal settlements as part of the solution to urban environmental issues.

Notes

* The data and analysis in this Chapter are from the work the author conducted over 2001–06.

1. Members of municipal claim-accepting channels, such as elected and appointed officials, are referred to in this article as 'formal channels' or 'formal channel members'.
2. A ward is an administrative unit in Indian cities. Each city is divided into a number of wards, with an equal distribution of population in each ward. Each ward has a councillor elected by ward residents to represent them in the municipality
3. Kolkata, formerly known as Calcutta, is the capital of the eastern Indian state of West Bengal. It is a dense, populous city with a population of 4,580,544 (2001 Census) and population density of 24,760 persons/sq km (2001 Census). It is bordered by Hooghly river in the west and wetlands to its east, and many ponds and water bodies are scattered throughout the city
4. Urban grassroots actors are defined here taking into account aspects of income, lifestyle and position of power. Hence, they are defined as urban residents dependent on elements of the urban natural environment like water bodies and land for fulfilling their livelihood and/or lifestyle requirements, combined with their position on margins of power in the urban arena. Hence, those who are considered socially marginal and are

forced to live in informal settlements in degraded urban surroundings, because of lack of viable alternative choices, are considered as part of the grassroots group.

5. These water bodies or ponds are an integral part of Kolkata's urbanscape. In 2002, the Kolkata Municipal Corporation recorded 3,668 water bodies spread throughout the city, including in densely populated areas.
6. For the sake of confidentiality, the names of both localities have been changed.
7. Boroughs are the next higher level of urban administration after wards in Kolkata, with 6–7 urban wards making up a borough. Municipal offices are present at the borough level to increase the accessibility of the municipal administration to the general public, and to increase the efficiency of municipal work. The political affiliations of the elected councillors from the wards in a borough determine which political party is dominant in the borough.
8. Anthropocentrism is the idea that human beings are the central element of the universe, and that all things should be judged in their relationship to human experience and livelihood. The environment is considered to be subsidiary to human interests and to be exploited or used only for achieving human needs. The environment, in anthropocentric thought, has value only as far as it meets any human needs.
9. In all interview extracts, the respondents have been identified only through their initials to protect their identities.
10. Solidarity is defined here as unity or agreement among a group or between groups based on similarity in interest, opinion, purpose etc.
11. A total of 10 million rupees ($228,000 approximately — rate as calculated in March 2005) were spent on the pond upgrade and evictions — a large sum of money for the KMC to allocate to a local project with limited regional impact
12. Foucault explained these dominant forms of social knowledge as able to underpin 'technologies of domination' over people, because they could define a field of knowledge accepted as truth. He stressed that the production of these 'regimes of truth' is the positive dimension of power. This production had to be understood before trying to formulate ways to subvert these regimes of truth through social practice (Gledhill 2000).
13. Green agenda proponents focus on environmental sustainability, while brown agenda proponents focus on human health impacts from polluted and poor environmental conditions. The green agenda focuses on environmental quality, with less emphasis on human concerns, while the brown agenda focuses on environmental quality only as far as it meets human health and other needs.

References

Allen, A. and N. You. 2002. *Sustainable urbanisation — Bridging the green and the brown agendas*. London: Development Planning Unit.

Barry, J. 1999. *Environment and social theory*. London and New York: Routledge.

Bryant, R. L. and S. Bailey. 1997. *Third World political ecology*. London and New York: Routledge.

Camacho, D. (ed.). 1998. *Environmental injustices, political struggles: Race, class, and the environment*. Durham, NC and London: Duke University Press.

Cooke, B. and U. Kothari (eds). 2001. *Participation: The new tyranny?* London: Zed Books.

CPI(M). 2001. *Communist Party of India (Marxist) Programme*. Delhi: Hari Singh Kang.

Dryzek, J. S. and J. Schlosberg (eds). 1998. *Debating the earth: The environmental politics reader*. Oxford and New York: Oxford University Press.

Eckersley, R. 1989. 'Green politics and the new class'. *Political Studies*, 37(2): 205–23.

Fox, J. 1994. 'The difficult transition from clientelism to citizenship: Lessons from Mexico'. *World Politics*, 46(2): 151–84.

Fox, J. 1996. 'How does civil society thicken? The political construction of social capital in rural Mexico'. *World Development*, 24(6): 1089–1103.

Giddens, A. and P. Cassell. 1993. *The Giddens reader*. Stanford: Stanford University Press.

Guha, R. and J. Martinez-Alier. 1997. *Varieties of environmentalism — Essays north and south*. London: Earthscan.

Gledhill, J. 2000. *Power and its disguises: Anthropological perspectives on politics*. Second edition. London: Pluto Press.

Hajer, M. A. 1997. *The politics of environmental discourse — Ecological modernization and the policy process*. Oxford: Clarendon Press.

Hannigan, J. A. 1995. *Environmental sociology — A social construction perspective*. London: Routledge.

Harvey, D. 1996. *Justice, nature & the geography of difference*. Oxford: Blackwell.

Inglehart, R. 1977. *The silent revolution: Changing values and political styles among Western publics*. Princeton, Guildford: Princeton University Press.

Kaviraj, S. (ed.). 1997. *Politics in India*. New Delhi: Oxford University Press.

Maloney, W., G. Smith, and G. Stoker. 2000. 'Social capital and urban governance: Adding a more contextualised "top-down" perspective'. *Political Studies*, 48(4): 802–20.

Pinto, M. 2000. *Metropolitan city governance in India*. New Delhi: Sage.

Ray, R. 1999. *Fields of protest: Women's movements in India*. Minneapolis and London: University of Minnesota Press.

Sandweiss, S. 1998. 'The social construction of environmental justice', in S. Camacho (ed.), *Environmental injustices, political struggles, race, class and the environment*, pp. 31–58. London: Duke University Press.

Sarbabharatiya Trinamool Congress. 1999. *Nirbachani istahaar — Trayodasha Lokshabha nirbachan 1999*. Kolkata: S. Bakshi Publication.

Sivaramakrishnan, K. C. 2000. *Power to the people? The politics and progress of decentralisation*. New Delhi: Konark Publishers.

Stott, P. and S. Sullivan (eds). 2000. *Political ecology — Science, myth and power*. London: Arnold; New York: Oxford University Press.

Times Research Foundation. 1996. 'Power to the people: The local government context', in B. N. Singh and S. Maitra (eds), *Urban environmental management, the Indian experience*. New Delhi: HSMI.

Young, I. M. 2000. *Inclusion and democracy*. Oxford and New York: Oxford University Press.

Part IV

Privatising development

11

Development-induced Displacement in the era of privatisation

Walter Fernandes

Many recent events have reopened the debate on development-induced displacement and deprivation. One may mention among them the refusal of the Government of India to even discuss the report of the World Commission on Dams (WCD); the Supreme Court judgement on the Narmada and the POSCO project (Orissa); the plan to build 48 major dams in the Northeast despite their possible negative impact on the biodiversity of the ecologically rich tribal region; the Special Economic Zones (SEZ) Act 2005 and the National Rehabilitation Policy of 2007, which is meant to be an improvement on the 2003 document but does not go much beyond it; besides the governments' failure to rethink many projects. The message given by these moves is that neither the judiciary nor the State is sensitive to the sufferings that displacement causes. More land is being acquired for projects linked to privatisation of water resources, at least in the Northeast. These events are a cause of concern from the point of view of the right of the poor to a life with dignity. This paper deals with the social impact of the displacement they cause.

The numbers involved

To understand the impact on the displaced persons (DPs) or those deprived of livelihood by the project without physical relocation (project-affected persons or PAPs), the debate on their number has to be situated in the context of these issues. That effort seems to confirm the feeling about lack of concern for the sufferings of the DPs/PAPs, because the country does not even have an official database on their number, or the type of persons who have paid the price of development since independence or the first five-year plan. So, people interested in the theme have to depend on estimates that are often inaccurate.

That explains why, a decade ago, Arundhuti Roy (1999) spoke of 56 million people displaced by large dams alone, and why, based on an estimate of the Indian Institute of Public Administration, Surjit Bhalla (2001) countered her by giving a ridiculously low average of 1,360 DPs per large dam or a total of around five million by all of them. Such extreme positions are understandable, because in the absence of an official database, they have to depend on estimates. Both Roy and Bhalla begin with the Central Water Commission (CWC) definition of all dams above 15 metres as 'large'. It is a legitimate definition, but they err in taking all the large dams as a single category. They then take an average number of DPs of each of them and multiply it by the number of large dams.

This approach is inaccurate, because 15 metres is the minimum height for a dam to be called large. But the more than 4,200 large dams in India differ in submergence area, height and capacity. The Irrigation Department defines dams irrigating up to 2,000 hectares as minor, those irrigating up to 10,000 hectares as medium and those above it as major. Thus, what CWC calls large dams have to be divided into medium and major. That, too, does not solve the problem fully, because many of the dams are for hydro-electrical power generation, not for irrigation. To categorise them, one has to go beyond the CWC definition and divide them into major and medium according to their height. By this count, less than 400 of them are major; the rest are medium. A major dam displaces 25,000–350,000 people. At least 15 have displaced over 100,000 each. The Upper Krishna dam in Karnataka has displaced over 350,000. A medium dam affects 800–8,000 persons. Thus, Bhalla's average of 1,360 is too low even for medium dams, while Roy's is an overestimate even for major dams.

Moreover, until the economic liberalisation, dams were the biggest displacing agents, but other schemes also deprived people of their livelihood. Today, many other schemes seem to get priority, though water resource projects continue to displace people. So, one has to go beyond water resource schemes to know the number of DPs/PAPs. In order to arrive at a more or less accurate number of DPs/PAPs of all the projects, this author and other scholars undertook studies of all displacement after independence or since the five-year plan. After completing these studies (1951–1995) in Andhra Pradesh (Fernandes et al. 2001), Jharkhand (Ekka and Asif 2003), Kerala (Muricken et al. 2003) and Orissa (Fernandes and Asif 1997); (1965–95, later updated to 2001) in Goa (Fernandes and Naik 2001), (1947–2000) West Bengal (Fernandes et al. 2006) and Assam (Fernandes and Bharali 2006), (1947–2004) Gujarat (Lobo and Kumar 2007); and gathering preliminary data from three other states, one comes to a total of around 19.7 million DPs/PAPs. In Assam, West Bengal and Gujarat, and in three states of the Northeast where studies are being launched, we began with 1947 because there was much acquisition for refugee rehabilitation and infrastructure immediately after the country's partition.

In Andhra, we gained access to primary data on 80 per cent of the projects, and in Jharkhand, Orissa and Kerala, to 60 percent. From these studies one arrives at a figure of 3.2 million DPs/PAPs in Andhra, 1.4 million in Orissa, 1.5 million in Jharkhand, 600,000 in Kerala, 66,000 in Goa, 7 million in West Bengal, 1.9 million in Assam, and 4.3 million in Gujarat, or a total of 19,810,834 in eight states. These studies are being updated and case studies are being collected from some other states as well. This exercise indicates that the total number of DPs/PAPs (1951–2004) will go up to 3 million each in Jharkhand and Orissa, 5 million in Andhra, 1 million in Kerala, 100,000 in Goa (1965–2004), 2 million in Assam, and 7.5 million in West Bengal (1947–2004). Even excluding the high displacement states like Chhattisgarh, Madhya Pradesh and Maharashtra, these states account for 27 million DPs/PAPs till 2004. These, together with the ongoing studies in three more states and partial data from others, point to an all-India figure of 60 million DPs/PAPs till 2004 from 25 million hectares, including 7 million hectares of forests and 6 million hectares of other common property resources (CPRs) (Fernandes 2008: 91).

Studies also show that most official figures are underestimates. For example, by official count, Assam has used 159,017.37 hectares of land for development projects and has 343,262 DPs/PAPs (1947–2000). The reality is a minimum of 1.9 million DPs/PAPs from not less than 567,281.29 hectares (Fernandes and Bharali 2006: 107). What is said of a whole state is equally true of individual projects. For example, by official count, the Hirakud Dam in Orissa displaced 110,000 people in the 1950s (Government of Orissa 1968), but researchers put the number at 180,000 (Pattanaik et al. 1987). In the 1970s, the Dumbur Dam in Tripura recognised 2,331 *patta*-owning families as displaced, while studies point to 8,000 to 9,000 of them (Bhaumik 2003: 84). According to district records of 2002, the Farakka Superthermal Plant in West Bengal has 47,294 DPs/PAPs, but a decade ago, World Bank (1994) put their number at 53,632. Their number should be more today. Thus, even 60 million may be an underestimate, but this paper will take it as the starting point.

Types of DPs/PAPs

This is the total of DPs/PAPs, but not all of them are of the same type. Their number has to be divided, first, into DPs and PAPs. Apart from displacing people, development projects deprive more people of livelihood without physical relocation. Dams do this to a much bigger number of persons than other projects do, because they use a massive land area, two-third of which is CPR. The past and ongoing studies point to a minimum of 40 millions affected by water resource projects till 2000, 25 million of them DPs and 15 million PAPs (Fernandes 2004). This, too, may be an underestimate, because this figure does not include massive dams like Sardar Sarovar and Upper Krishna that together have over 5 lakh DPs. More and more of such massive dams are being planned. For example, the proposed Polavaram dam in Andhra will lead to 176,000 DPs/PAPs, and Pagladia in Assam to 105,000 (Bharali 2004).

To this number, should be added indirect DPs, caused by environmental degradation, such as fly ash generated by thermal, cement, and alumina plants, and dust pollution and blasts in coal mines. Fly ash renders the land around the plant unusable, and noise and dust make the area near mines unlivable. Together they force the dependants of this land to move out (Ganguly Thukral 1999), but they are considered voluntary emigrants and are not counted among the DPs. Though their number is large, no methodology has been developed to make an estimate. So, they are not included among the 60 million DPs/PAPs.

Then comes the division by project category. Dams are the biggest displacing agents, but there are others as well, like industries, mines, thermal and other non-hydro power plants, defence and security units, environment protection, refugee rehabilitation, education, health, urban and rural development and social welfare projects. Among the 19,810,834 DPs/PAPs identified by studies in eight states till 2007, 7,602,320 (38.37 per cent) are of water resource projects. However, their proportion differs from state to state, depending on the priority given to each category. In Orissa, they are as many as 54.57 per cent of the total, and in Andhra, they are 58 per cent, while in Assam, they are only 23.39 per cent. Transport accounts for more than 25 per cent (of DPs/PAPs) in West Bengal and Gujarat, and mining accounts for as much in Jharkhand; though in these states, too, dams have displaced large numbers (Fernandes 2008: 91).

The final division is by the era. Globalisation has added a new dimension to development. Ongoing studies suggest that there has been massive acquisition in the 1990s in the name of liberalisation. That is bound to intensify displacement, as the extent of land acquired or committed to various companies, particularly private enterprises shows. Kalinga Nagar is one of the examples, which will be discussed in detail in this chapter.

The type of people affected

The next division is by the type of people. The biggest number of DPs/PAPs is tribal. Out of the 19,810,834 DPs/PAPs, the caste-tribe of 16,729,392 is known; 34.5 per cent of them are tribals. The 3,081,442 persons whose caste-tribe is not known are from Assam, West Bengal, Goa and Kerala. There are indications that among them, 30 per cent each are tribals in West Bengal and Goa, 50 per cent in Assam, and more than 10 per cent in Kerala, where they are only around 1 per cent of the population (Muricken et al. 2003). As a result, the tribal proportion among the DPs/PAPs can be easily put at 40 per cent.

Studies also show that more than 20 per cent of DPs/PAPs are Dalits (Mahapatra 1999). Exact data on the backwards is not available till the 1980s. So it is difficult to know their number among the DPs/PAPs. But the little information that is available indicates that they may be another 20 per cent of the total. For example, at least 150,000 of the CPR dependants in Assam belong to the fishing communities (Fernandes and Bharali 2006). Most persons displaced by the Sriharikota Test Firing Range and the Simhadri Thermal Plan on the Andhra coast are from the fishing community or quarry workers (Fernandes et al. 2001). So are most DPs/PAPs of the coastal schemes in Kerala, such as the Vikram Sarabhai Space Centre (Murickan et al. 2003).

The fact that these voiceless communities are dominant among the DPs/PAPs may also explain the extremely poor state of rehabilitation. Orissa has resettled 35.27 per cent of its DPs during 1951–1995, Andhra 28.82 per cent, Goa 40.78 per cent, Kerala 13.8 per cent, Gujarat 23.62 per cent, West Bengal 9 per cent, and Assam has resettled the DPs of fewer than 10 projects. Officials state that compensation is rehabilitation. This assumption is untenable, because compensation paid is inadequate in most cases, even for *patta* land, for which alone it is paid according to the Land Acquisition Act 1894 (LAA). Its basis is the 'market price', interpreted as the average registered price in an area for the last three years. It is a public secret that what is registered is less than 40 per cent of the real price. Besides, much of the land acquired is in the predominantly tribal 'backward' areas, where its price is low, and more than half is CPRs. The DPs/PAPs get no compensation for the CPRs and get a meagre amount for the little *patta* land they own (Fernandes and Raj 1992: 92). Thus, a substantial proportion of them get no compensation. What most others are paid for their private land is too low for them to begin a new life.

In practice, people are resettled only when they agitate, or when the World Bank wants India to do so. The Bank is interested in economic growth and demands rehabilitation to satisfy human rights activists in the West. But 60 years after India's independence, the Bank has to tell those who swear by *swadeshi* to rehabilitate persons displaced in the name of national development. And those who agitate on the side of the DPs/PAPs are called anti-national! Most project officials are insensitive to the plight of the DPs/PAPs. For example, a retired official of Hirakud said at a meeting in Delhi in August 1999, 'What is 25 million displaced? Many more get its benefits. Burla town is built on excess land acquired for Hirakud'.

Displacement and liberalisation

The figure of 60 millions has to be viewed in the context of liberalisation, and possible privatisation of water, mining and other resources that is linked closely to it. Possible privatisation of water resources is symbolised, among others, by the plan to interlink rivers and to build 48 major dams in the Northeast. According to initial estimates, river-linking is to cost Rs 560 trillion (Bandyopadhyay 2003). Studies show that hardly any major dam has been built with less than a five-year time overrun and 500 per cent cost overrun (Singh et al. 1992: 173–74). If it happens to river-linking, its final cost will be higher than the annual GDP of India (Bandyopadhyay 2003). To get this amount, the only alternative will be to 'sell the rivers' to the private sector. The same can be said about most dams in the Northeast.

Also, massive land acquisition is linked to globalisation. In the past, more land than required was acquired for many projects. For example, two-thirds of the land acquired for the HAL-MIG Plant at Sunabeda (Orissa) in 1966 lay vacant for three decades. At least some of it has apparently been sold at a high profit. But its 16,000 tribal DPs were not resettled (Pandey 1998: 35). Excess land acquired on both sides of the Roro irrigation canals in Jharkhand was given to relatives of the officials for housing (Areeparampil 1996: 22–23). As the statement of the retired official of Hirakud mentioned earlier shows, a number of officials term this misuse as an achievement of the state, rather than a failure that impoverishes many more persons than the project would do, if only the amount of land required were taken over.

With liberalisation, higher land acquisition for the private sector has become an official stand. The Union government stated its intention in the 1994 rehabilitation policy draft which began with:

> It is expected that there will be large scale investments, both on account of internal generation of capital and increased inflow of foreign investments, thereby creating an enhanced demand for land to be provided within a shorter time-span in an increasingly competitive market ruled economic structure. Majority of our mineral resources... are located in the remote and backward areas mostly inhabited by tribals (MRD 1994: 1.1–2).

That this intention is taken seriously is seen from the extent of acquisition by most states. Among the projects for which land is being acquired are the 316 SEZs that have been sanctioned and more that are on the anvil; the 48 major dams being studied in the Northeast for implementation during the next decade; massive mining areas being eyed by private companies in central India; the infrastructure being built such as the East-West Corridor; 71 thermal plants on the Andhra coast; and private industries all over India. Among others, West Bengal has committed 93,995 hectares for industries alone (Ray 2006), and more to other projects. Orissa had used 40,000 hectares for industries in 1951–1995, but planned to acquire 40,000 hectares more in the succeeding decade (Fernandes and Asif 1997 69–70). Andhra has acquired, in 1996–2000, half as much for industry as it did in the preceding 45 years (Fernandes et al. 2001: 69–70). Goa had acquired 3.5 per cent of its landmass in the 1965–1995 period. If all its plans go through, it will acquire 7.2 per cent of its landmass in this decade (Fernandes and Naik 2001 37–39). Gujarat has promised to give land for 27 SEZs (Lobo and Kumar 2007).

Efforts are being made to change laws to suit this objective. Its examples are the Highways Act 1995 and the SEZ Act 2005, the proposal to amend the LAA and the Fifth Schedule, and changes being introduced in many state laws. These initiatives are taken even when some question the need for a few projects under consideration. For example, both the Indian Navy, which controls the Goa airport, and a People's Committee that studied the proposed new private airport, say that the present one can be expanded to accommodate future needs for some decades (*Navhind Times* 1998), but the proposal has not been abandoned fully. An economic analysis of the proposed Navsheva seaport in Thane district shows that it can survive only by stealing traffic from the three existing major ports in Maharashtra and Gujarat (Dewan and Chawla 1999). But, instead of abandoning it, it was proposed to be shifted to Gujarat.

Thus, liberalisation will intensify the process of displacement, and of privatising community resources of the poor, mainly tribal and Dalit, to the benefit of another class. It can, thus, have an adverse impact, on the one hand, on food security, and, on the other, on marginalised communities like the tribals and Dalits. To begin with the latter, private companies are eyeing predominantly tribal land for mining in Jharkhand, Chhattisgarh and the rest of central India, and for major dams in the Northeast (IWGIA 2004: 314).

Food security may be affected, because much fertile land will be taken over. The private sector goes where the infrastructure is, and gets fertile land near roads or railway lines even when alternative sites are available elsewhere. For example, the land on one side of the railway track near Kharagpur in West Bengal is rocky and undulating, but the state acquired 200 acres of fertile land on the other side close to the Kharagpur railway station and the highway for Tata Metalliks in 1992. Later, another 96 acres were proposed for a Birla firm, but the project has not yet taken off (Fernandes et al. 2006). In Goa, the agitation in the early 1990s around Konkan Railway was not against its construction but for its realignment. Around 14 per cent of Goa's landmass is on perpetual mining lease to private companies. Some 10,000 ha of it is not viable anymore, and can be abandoned and the land made available for industries. The agitation was to divert the line along this route and save the *kazan* lands, a pre-Portuguese irrigation system on which several thousand fishing families depend for their sustenance. Neither its technology nor its flora and fauna have been studied (Ecoforum 1993). But the line was built along the coast, and the *kazan* lands bifurcated without a drainage system. After its completion, hundreds of hectares of fertile paddy land are being acquired for industry on both sides of it, though mining land is available.

Impact of displacement

Displacement with poor resettlement, and poorer rehabilitation, results in impoverishment and even misery. Landlessness is its first step. For example, in Andhra Pradesh, the proportion of the landless among the DPs/PAPs rose from 10.6 to 36.5 per cent (Fernandes et al. 2001: 112–13), and in Assam, from 15.56 to 24.38 per cent (Fernandes and Bharali 2006: 108). This change may look innocuous until one realises that the average area cultivated declines substantially. For example, in Assam, the average came down from 3.04 to 1.45 acres per family. In every state studied, most landowners had only the homestead land and none for cultivation. When they did not lose all their land, most small and marginal farmers became landless; medium farmers become marginal farmers; and big farmers become medium farmers.

An obvious result of landlessness is joblessness, because the land the DPs/PAPs lose to the project is their sustenance, both in the form of food and work. So its loss deprives them of both. Joblessness takes two forms. The first is lower access to work. For example, in Andhra, 83.72 per cent of the DPs/PAPs worked on their land before displacement. After it, their access to work declined by more than half, to 41.61 per cent (Fernandes et al. 2001: 141). In Assam, it declined from 77.27 to 56.41 per cent, and in West Bengal, from 91.02 to 53.18 per cent. Equally important is downward occupational mobility, even among those who retain some access to work. 45 per cent of the peasants in Andhra and 50 per cent in Assam, who worked on land before displacement, were forced to become daily wage earners or other unskilled workers after it (Bharali 2007).

Impoverishment forces many DPs/PAPs into bondage. For example, some 30,000 of the 150,000 construction workers of the Asiad facilities in 1982 were slave labourers from Orissa and Chatttisgarh, brought by labour contractors with the promise of a job in Baghdad. Once in Delhi, they were kept in concentration camp-like conditions with no hope of ever returning home. They had been displaced by Hirakud and other projects, and not resettled. Impoverished, they followed the labour contractor. Today, such people form a large proportion of construction and brick kiln workers (Fernandes et al. 2001: 176–78).

Child labour, too, is high among them. Often, parents of displaced families are forced to have to push their children into labour, because the parents are denied access to work. For example, 56 per cent of all displaced families in Assam and 49 per cent in West Bengal were forced to pull their children out of school and turn them into child labourers in order to earn an income for the family (Fernandes 2008: 99). Since the parents are without work, they have no choice but to use for the present, children who are a resource for the future.

This is what some call marginalisation that goes beyond impoverishment, which is defined as only the loss of the economic resources. Marginalisation is loss of the psychological and social infrastructure. Once they are deprived of their material sustenance, the oppressed internalise the dominant value system and abandon hope. They begin to view themselves as a community without rights, or a group that is incapable of developing itself. As John Gaventa (1980: 27–30) says, no unequal society can survive without the subalterns internalising the dominant value system. The subalterns accept their subjugation, lose hope in their future, and try to survive in the present with whatever resources they can lay their hands on.

Turning their children into child labourers is one of the modes of giving priority to the present over the future. In the process, the children are deprived, not merely of their present right to childhood but also of hope in a better future. Women, too, internalise their subordinate status and begin to view their body only as a resource for the present. All our studies show that prostitution grows enormously after displacement, because men do not have work, and women are deprived of the land and forests where they found work and became economic assets in the family. Another sign of marginalisation is the new culture of using natural resources that most communities, particularly tribal, treated as renewable. After the alienation of their sustenance, they destroy, for sheer survival or for sale as firewood, the forests that they had preserved for centuries (Bharali 2007).

This situation can be expected to deteriorate after liberalisation, because intrinsic to it is mechanisation that makes employment generation expensive. As a result, those who lose their sustenance to the project may not even get exploitative jobs, and may be marginalised completely. Little wonder then that more schemes than in the past meet with resistance, as one has seen in the Raigad district of Maharashtra, Goa, Singur in West Bengal and Kashipur in Orissa. However, repression follows when the schemes are opposed. Among its examples are criminal activities in Singur, arrest of persons opposing the SEZs in Goa and the POSCO project in Orissa, police firing that killed some tribals agitating against the Kashipur mines in Rayagada district and others at Kalinga Nagar in Orissa on 2 January 2006.

Search for solutions

The situation described till now shows the need to search for alternatives to the projects and the legal system that cause displacement, impoverishment and marginalisation. The first solution the Government of India suggests is a rehabilitation policy. For five decades, people were displaced without any legal right to rehabilitation. A large number of them were not even entitled to compensation, because the LAA recognises and compensates only individually-owned land. Even that compensation is usually inadequate as it is based on the market price, defined as the registered price in the area for three years (Ramanathan 2008: 27–31). It is well known that the registered price is usually between a third and 40 per cent of the real price paid. Moreover, as stated above, the market price is extremely low in the tribal and other 'backward' areas, which is where most land is acquired. The CPR dependants are ignored. As a result, most of those who lose land are unable to begin life anew.

The Rehabilitation Policy 2003 was the solution suggested by the Government of India, but it is extremely inadequate, because it does not deal with the basic issues of livelihood (Fernandes 2005). The government that came to power in 2004 decided to have an alternative to this policy. The National Advisory Council (NAC) prepared one such alternative that seemed to satisfy most critics. But the Government of India gave priority to another document prepared by the Ministry of Rural Development, which is only marginally better than the 2003 policy (Sethi 2006). At present, Parliament is discussing a law on rehabilitation based on this policy. Also, an amended LAA is before Parliament. In practice, this draft is meant to make land acquisition easier than in the past, but the proposed rehabilitation does not provide any solace to the land-losers.

The civil society demands many changes that the NAC draft seems to respond to. For example, it gives minimisation of displacement as its first object: through least-displacing and non-displacing projects, and where they are not possible, by proceeding through prior informed consent. It proposes the principle that DPs/PAPs should be better off within a reasonable period of time, and wants rehabilitation to be integrated with development. It defines as a family every adult male and female, not merely sons, unlike what the Narmada package does. It includes among them persons displaced from forests, national parks, sanctuaries and urban areas. The policy is to apply also to people displaced 10 years prior to its promulgation. It wants the project to obtain clearance after justifying itself from a social and environmental angle. Public interest is to replace public purpose. The project has to establish that displacement is necessary, and has to meet the social demands of DPs/PAPs. The assessment is to be done through a participatory process.

The NAC draft adds that different phases of the project should be staggered in order to minimise the trauma of displacement. All the services should continue in the area after the notification until the acquisition, except those that require major capital investment. Unused acquired land is to be offered to landless families, and not transferred to others without the consent of the PAF. None is to be displaced more than once. Compensation is to include the market value of the material assets and of lost livelihoods. That includes its non-owning dependents. DPs/PAPs should be among the beneficiaries of the project. Community-based organisations are to be involved in planning rehabilitation. A National Rehabilitation Commission is to be formed.

It opts for replacement value in place of market value-based compensation. Replacement includes the market value of private land and the CPRs, compensation for the trauma of forced deprivation, technical training, psychological, cultural and social preparation of DPs/PAPs to begin a new life, and ensuring re-emergence of the social systems and structures in a new form to make it possible for them to adapt themselves to the society they are pushed into. Such components are important, because most DPs/PAPs are from the powerless classes, from whom the project alienates their only sustenance and forces them to move from the informal to the formal sector, which is alien to them. To cope with the new surroundings, society and economy, they need adequate psychological as well as cultural support, and social and technical training. This totality forms the replacement value, and is integral to the right to a life with dignity. It requires much social and economic investment, and all of it has to be included in the project budget and can be considered social investment.

Most civil society groups agree with many principles enunciated by the NAC draft, but insist that the principle that the victims have to be the first beneficiaries of the project has to get priority. One way of doing it is to ensure that they get as many jobs as possible in the project. At present, very few projects make provision for it. For example, data on 266,000 displaced families in Orissa shows that only about 9,000 of them were a given a job each. In Assam, only three projects gave some jobs. In West Bengal, around 20 per cent were given some jobs, most of them in the 1950s and 1960s. Very few jobs were given in Kerala, and none in Goa (Fernandes 2008: 95).

Civil society groups feel that the DPs/PAPs should be trained by the project to take up as many semi-skilled jobs as possible. A large number of DPs/PAPs are illiterate and are not in a position to acquire technical skills required by the project. Therefore, the first priority of the project has to be to render all of them literate and give them technical training for semi-skilled jobs the project requires. In the NALCO project in the Koraput district of Orissa, a voluntary agency trained the displaced tribals in skills such as driving and welding, and many of them got semi-skilled jobs in the project. This experience shows that it is possible for the illiterate to acquire such skills (Stanley 1996).

The basic principle of rehabilitation has to be replacement of the livelihood lost. The laws have to ensure that displacement is minimised, that all dependents of the assets acquired, and not merely *patta* owners, are counted among DPs/PAPs, and that compensation is extended to them. The NAC draft, in spite of its many positive points, does not uphold replacement value in this sense. The draft also suggests that people's consent be obtained before acquisition, but does not say that it has to be unanimous. One can mention many more shortcomings of this draft. A solution probably lies in examining all the drafts in the light of the principles enunciated by the civil society.

This paper has discussed the state of displacement and the rehabilitation policy, which is not satisfactory. The policy's failure to deal with the basic issues shows the need to revisit the civil society alternative and search for other alternatives. Those who pay the price have a right to a better life after the project, and have to get its first benefits. Compensation should be at replacement value, not at market value. The thinking behind these principles and the alternatives was that assets that the project acquires are people's livelihood, and that the policy or law should be changed to reflect this reality. The policy and the proposed amendments to the LAA do not meet this demand, though the changes being suggested by the NAC go in that direction. But then, the NAC alternative has been rejected. Civil society should accept the challenge of conducting a dialogue on the alternatives. Researchers and civil society members need to form an alliance to deal with these questions, create a database on issues such as compensation and better standard of living, and assist in mobilising the affected persons to help deal with the trauma and avoid impoverishment and marginalisation.

References

Areeparampil, Mathew. 1996. *Tribals of Jharkhand: Victims of development.* New Delhi: Indian Social Institute.

Bandyopadhyay, Jayanta. 2003. 'And quiet flows the river project'. *The Hindu Business Line,* 14 March.

Bhalla, Surjit S. 2001. 'Indian poverty: Ideology and evidence'. *Seminar,* 497: 24–28.

Bharali, Gita. 2004. 'Dams a threat to livelihood'. *The Telegraph,* 29 November.

———. 2007. 'Development-induced displacement: A history of transition to impoverishment and environmental degradation'. Paper presented at the 'Seminar on Ecology', 27–28 March, Dibrugarh University.

Bhaumick, Subir. 2003. 'Tripura's Gumti Dam must go'. *The Ecologist Asia,* 11(1): 84–89.

Dewan, Ritu and Michelle Chawla. 1999. *Of Development amidst fragility: A societal and environmental perspective on Vadhavan port.* Mumbai: Popular Prakashan.

Ecoforum. 1993. *Fish, curry and rice: A citizens' report on the Goan environment.* Mapuca: The Other India Press.

Ekka, Alexius and Mohammed Asif. 2000. *Development-induced displacement and rehabilitation in Jharkhand: A database on its extent and nature.* New Delhi: Indian Social Institute.

Fernandes, Walter. 2005. 'Rehabilitation as a right: Where is the policy?'. *Social Action,* 55(2): 123–37.

——. 2008. 'Sixty years of development-induced displacement in India: Impacts and the search for alternatives', in Hari Mohan Mathur (ed.), *India social development report 2008: Development and displacement,* pp. 89–102. New Delhi: Council for Social Development and Oxford University Press.

Fernandes, Walter and Gita Bharali. *Development-induced displacement in Assam 1947–2000* (Unpublished). Guwahati: North-Eastern Social Research Centre (Mimeo).

Fernandes, Walter and Mohammed Asif. 1997. *Development-induced displacement in Orissa 1951 to 1995: A database on its extent and nature.* New Delhi: Indian Social Institute.

Fernandes, Walter, Nafisa D'Souza, Choudhary Goga, Arundhuti Roy and Mohammad Asif. 2001. *Development-induced displacement, deprivation and rehabilitation in Andhra Pradesh 1951–1995: A quantitative and quantitative study of its extent and nature.* New Delhi: Indian Social Institute; Guwahati: North Eastern Social Research Centre.

Fernandes, Walter and Niraj Naik. 2001. *Development-induced displacement in Goa 1965–1995: A study on its extent and nature.* New Delhi: Indian Social Institute; Panjim: INSAF.

Fernandes, Walter and S. Anthony Raj. 1992. *Development, displacement and rehabilitation in the tribal areas of Orissa.* New Delhi: Indian Social Institute.

Fernandes, Walter, Shanti Chhetry, Sherry Joseph and Inchen Lama. 2006. *Development-induced displacement and deprivation in West Bengal 1947–2000: A quantitative and qualitative database.* Guwahati: North-Eastern Social Research Centre (Mimeo).

Ganguly Thukral, Enakshi. 1999. 'Bottom-Up'. *Humanscape,* 6(11): 10–12.

Gaventa, John. 1980. *Power and powerlessness: Quiescence and rebellion in an Appalachian valley.* Oxford: Clarendon.

Government of Orissa. 1968. *Report on the benefits of Hirakud irrigation: A socio-economic study.* Cuttack: Bureau of Economics and Statistics.

International Work Group for Indigenous Affairs (IWGIA). 2004. *The indigenous world 2004.* Copenhagen: IWGIA.

Lobo, Lancy and Shashikant Kumar. 2007. *Development-induced displacement in Gujarat 1947–2004.* Vadodara: Centre for Culture and Development.

Mahapatra, L. K. 1999. *Resettlement, impoverishment and reconstruction in India: Development for the deprived.* New Delhi: Vikas Publishing House.

MRD. 1994. National Policy for rehabilitation of Persons displaced as a Consequence of acquisition of land. New Delhi: Ministry of Rural Development, Government of India (second draft).

Murickan, Jose, M. K. George, K. A. Emmanuel, Jose Boban and Prakash Pillai R. 2003. *Development-induced displacement: Case of Kerala.* New Delhi: Rawat Publications.

Pandey, Balaji. 1998. *Depriving the underprivileged for development.* Bhubaneswar: Institute for Socio-Economic Development.

Pattanaik, S. K., B. Das and A. B. Mishra. 1987. 'Hirakud Dam: Expectations and realities', in PRIA (ed.), *People and dams*, pp. 47–59. New Delhi: Society for Participatory Research in Asia.

Ramanathan, Usha. 2008. 'The Land Acquisition Act 1894: Displacement and State power', in Hari Mohan Mathur (ed.), *India social development report 2008: Development and displacement*, pp. 27–38. New Delhi: Council for Social Development and Oxford University Press.

Ray, Bibekananda. 2006. 'Thus Capital, I and II'. *The Statesman,* 17 and 18 December.

Roy, Arundhati. 1999. *The greater common good.* Bombay: India Book Distributors Ltd. *Navbhind Times*. 1998. 'New BJP-led government holds the key to airport proposal', 25 March.

Singh, Shekhar, Asish Kothari and Kulan Amin. 1992. 'Evaluating major irrigation projects in India', in Enakshi Ganguly Thukral (ed.), *Big dams displaced people: Rivers of sorrow, rivers of change,* pp. 169–86. New Delhi: Sage Publications.

Stanley, William. 1996. 'Machkund, Upper Kolab and NALCO projects in Koraput district, Orissa'. *Economic and Political Weekly,* 31(24): 1533–38.

World Bank. 1994. *Resettlement and development: The bankwide review of projects involving involuntary resettlement, 1986–1993.* Washington DC: Environment Department, World Bank.

12

Special economic zones: The new 'land' mines

Manshi Asher and Yamini Atmavilas*

The most powerful images of globalised economies across the world today appear to make time, space and place irrelevant. In an era of mobile capital, these images give us the illusion that time, space, place and matter are immaterial. It would be hard to imagine then, that land — immovable, concrete, autochthonous — has emerged as among the most contentious issues of our time. The crises and conflicts over land have brought to the fore enduring forms of socioeconomic and political divisions in the drama of contemporary neo-liberal economic development in India: state versus citizen, farmer versus industrialist, farmer versus realtor/developer, urban versus rural, middle class versus working and lower classes, castes and indigenous people. Perhaps, this is a sign of the divide between realities on ground zero, on the one hand, and the visions that emerge from the corridors of power on the other. This paper will attempt to highlight some of the major issues relating to land acquisition in the wake of the special economic zone (SEZ) policy in India, which, in the past three years or so, has symbolised, reflected and intensified these divides.[1]

At the outset, it has to be specified that the state's SEZ policy uses the same old model of land acquisition that has been used in the colonial and postcolonial period to advance the capitalist development agenda. When examined in terms of magnitude and scope, within a

---

* This is a revised version of a paper presented at the national seminar on 'Displacement issues surrounding Special Economic Zones', held at India International Centre, New Delhi, on 7 October 2008.

short span of three years, the expansion of SEZs has only exacerbated ongoing displacement of rural livelihoods, especially those based on natural resources and common properties. Indeed, a close look at the SEZ policy, its design, structure and its timing reveals that land expropriation and enclavisation is the most central aspect in the creation of SEZs, with the State playing a pivotal role in the process. However, in this paper, we review how the story has unfolded within the realm of land issues within the policy, and its implementation and the role played by the government and developers.

Indeed, common sense would suggest that land is the first requirement for the creation of an enclave/industrial cluster, for which the SEZ Act lays down no upper limit. This means not only that land is a non-negotiable requirement, but also that a large area of contiguous land — anywhere from 3–14,000 hectares — is sought for SEZs. However, when we try to locate the term 'land acquisition' (or land transfer or diversion) in the SEZ Act 2005, we do not find it. The Act opens and ends with the assumption that the SEZ developer is already in possession of the requisite land, and makes no provision for the acquisition process. One might speculate that the architects of the policy assumed that land had to (and would be) be made available irrespective of everything else. Also, as repeatedly highlighted by the government as well, the purpose and focus of the Act itself were not to make available land but to put in place a legislative framework that would validate and protect under all circumstances the powers of the new entities called 'SEZs' and their private 'developers'.

The power to acquire 'land' for private parties in the name of public purpose already exists with the government, under the colonial and draconian Land Acquisition Act (LAA) 1894.[2] Within a few months of the passing of the Act, state governments issued land acquisition notices under the LAA for some of the proposed SEZs. With the rampant use of the Act, the Pandora's box flew open, and what followed were a slew of coercive means for the seizure of land, which met with protests. It was evidently highlighted then that the principle of Eminent Domain would be exercised by the State to make available land for SEZs. Several instances of opposition from land owners and farmers, fisher communities, Dalits, and indigenous communities began to be reported. The stories that first hit the national news were from Jhajjar (Haryana), Raigad (Maharshtra) and Nandigram (West Bengal) in May 2006.

What the Ministry of Commerce and the government did not anticipate was that the intensity of the resistance by peasants and rural populations against the acquisition of their lands would reach fever pitch within such a short span of time. After all, people have suffered and coped with displacement for years now, and might well continue to do so in the context of SEZs. What sets apart the present set of struggles, nay battles, over the land issue?

1. *Location of the SEZs*
   Types of land being acquired is fertile land under cultivation, resulting in direct conflict with middle class farmers; grazing and community land, including *panchami* lands received as part of post-independence land redistribution; temple land, forest land, assigned/ceiling land. Also the size of the SEZs; area and the quantum of contiguous land required
2. *Process of land acquisition*
   Continued use of the draconian Land Acquisition Act of 1894, coercive measures, undervaluation, besides private, realtor capitalism
3. *Effect on communities*
   Displacement, livelihood losses, loss of productive assets, besides loss of access to productive resources and activities
4. *Inadequate protection of land losers by the law and judicial process*
   Absence of a just and protective legislation to protect the land and livelihood or the displaced
5. *Implications for agriculture and food security/sovereignty*
   Transfer of agricultural land in the time of food scarcity and rising food prices across the world

This article will provide a brief overview of some of these aspects and the types of struggles they have produced.

Zones of conflict: Type and status of land transferred to SEZs

As of today, the Central government has given formal approval to a staggering 513 SEZs in 19 states; 250 of these have been notified. Reportedly, hundreds more have been proposed to the Board of Approvals, and a majority has received what is known as 'in-principle approval'. The area being acquired by all the SEZs with 'in-principle approval' is close to 200,000 hectares already (2,000 sq km, or greater than the area of Delhi in the National Capital Region).[3]

Devinder Sharma and Bhaskar Goswami (2006) estimated that close to 1.14 lakh farming households (each household, on an average, comprising five members) and an additional 82,000 farm worker families, who are dependent upon these farms for their livelihoods, will be displaced. The total loss of income to the farming and the farm worker families, then, is an astounding Rs 212 crore a year (Sharma and Goswami 2006). These were the estimates in 2006 after the initial SEZ approvals.

If we look at the distribution of the land, we find that 70 per cent of it is concentrated in the hands of the 25 to 30 per cent of medium and large-sized multiproduct zone developers. Most of the SEZs are also concentrated around urban areas, and their peripheries and other infrastructure-wise developed centres in the top five states that are already considered as industrially progressive.

Fertile agricultural land

The bulk of land being acquired for SEZs is fertile, agricultural land, especially in case of the multiproduct zones. As a result, there is great concern of its impact on agricultural economies, particularly in a context where Indian agriculture is languishing, farmers are committing suicides, and India has been transformed from a food-exporter to a food-importer (Sharma 2006). In Karnataka, SKIL SEZ has been proposed in Nandagudi Hobli, the site of vast tracts of fertile, productive land, with active cultivation, sericulture and horticulture, and ironically, the supplier of nearly 30 per cent of Bengalooru's vegetables and dairy. In Punjab, where almost the entire state is irrigated, SEZs are being set up on prime agriculture land. The Punjab government has been using repressive techniques to browbeat agitating farmers near Barnala, opposing the forcible acquisition of land for a private company, Trident. Similarly, farmers have agitated against the government's repressive policies in acquiring fertile land for an SEZ near Amritsar. Other examples are the SEZs in Mangalore and Kakinada. Most of these being large multiproduct SEZ plans. Although the guidelines by the MoC forbid the acquisition of more than 10 per cent of the double-cropped area for SEZs, in reality, a majority of these estates are coming up on fertile land to take advantage of existing infrastructure, rather than creating infrastructure anew for the nation (an expected 'contribution' of the SEZ model for economic development). In the case of SEZs like Reliance's Jhajjar and Raigad projects, and SKIL in Himachal, lands under acquisition are multi- and double-cropped lands. In Mangalore, where one of the promoters is government-owned ONGC, 2,200 hectares of double- and even triple-cropped land is being acquired for setting up an SEZ.

Interestingly, all the areas where strong resistances have emerged, are areas with thriving agriculture economies, with majority of the farmers being middle to small or marginal land holders.

Dry land and single-cropped land

The second and more important concern is of dry land agriculture economies which have always relied on rain, and single-crop lands like in Tamil Nadu. From the point of view of landowners and farmers, even these single-cropped lands are crucial resources for subsistence and livelihood. In many cases, these lands are leased out and rented to pastoralists, or used for grazing in the seasons when they are not cultivated; thus, they continue to support local livelihoods of not just the farmers but also families dependent on animal husbandry and livestock rearing.

Further, the unevenness of expected compensation may also seriously affect the life and livelihood chances of those displaced. For instance, the compensation being provided for fertile lands may be higher than that provided for dry lands. The farmers in Jhajjar may be able to buy new land with the compensation amount, but the same is not possible for dry land farmers; holding on to land might make more sense to them. However, in states like Tamil Nadu, for instance, most of the land being used for SEZ development is dry land, acquired by the government over the years using the LAA (see next section for details).

Wastelands, forest lands and common properties

Land use in India is not confined to cultivation on private lands, but also extends to commons for collective uses that contribute to day-to-day survival of *adivasi* and landless communities. Fuel, fodder and other non-timber forest produce requirements are met from land that could be categorised as common property resource or *charagah*, *gaucher*, *padit bhoomi* in local languages, but is referred to as 'wasteland' by the government. This makes up almost 20 per cent of the total geographical area of the country (Asher 2006). In many states, these lands comprise cultivable wastelands, grazing lands, pastures or scrub forests, and form an integral part of the local village economy.

According to a study, these lands contribute to almost 12 per cent of the income of poor households (Jodha 1992). In states like Maharashtra, Madhya Pradesh and Rajasthan, a huge pastoral community entirely depends on these lands for livestock rearing. The MoC gives no break-up of the types of land that are being acquired for SEZs. Many of these lands, apart from agricultural and wastelands, will be forest lands with some form of vegetation on them, dense vegetation in most cases. In Maharashtra alone, three big SEZ projects are coming up in the Konkan district, which is home to the ecologically sensitive Western Ghats.

Another critical issue is that in many states, these wastelands are also under cultivation, but farmers are yet to get legal titles. In some instances, these lands are ceiling lands under land reform processes but are yet to be distributed to the landless. In Raigarh district, where Reliance is planning to build a massive SEZ, almost 12,000 hectares of what are known as *dali* lands have been under cultivation by the local tribal population for decades.

Most families, though, still await regularisation of these lands under the recent Forest Rights Act 2006, since they fall under the category of 'forest' land. Such is the case in Orissa. For example, in Jagatsinghpur district, the area where the multinational Pohang Steel Company is planning its SEZ, almost 300 families are yet to be allotted legal titles. In the absence of *pattas* or titles, villagers have virtually no bargaining power and get displaced without adequate or any compensation. Rehabilitation in such cases is not even considered by the government.

Also, it is quite difficult to find contiguous wastelands spread over large areas, especially in states like Tamil Nadu, Haryana, UP and Maharashtra, where these zones are coming up. Thus, it would be virtually impossible to locate them only on wastelands. In its myopic view on the land question in SEZ projects, the ministry has failed completely to consider these complexities, which would surely have serious consequences for rural communities and the last of the common property resources in our country.

Assigned lands and temple lands — The case of AP and Tamil Nadu

The most outrageous acquisitions are taking place in Andhra Pradesh, which has the highest number of SEZ approvals. For the Polepally SEZ, the APIIC and the local administration went about acquiring 300 acres of ceiling land assigned to Dalit and tribal communities more than a decade and a half ago. Most of this land has been under cultivation. Since 1966, the AP government claims to have redistributed 42 lakh acres of land under its land reform programme and a full-fledged legislation, the AP Assigned Lands (Prohibition of Transfers) Act, 1977 (known as Act 9 of 1977).

The obvious question that emerges here is — how can any government first redistribute land to the landless under full-fledged legislation, and then contravene its own move and take away the same land from the *very same* grantees? Transfers of land assigned to the poor are actually illegal under Act 9. The government has sought to work around its own restrictions through a controversial amendment, brought about in December 2006 by the Congress-led government, that allows the state to take over assigned land that had been alienated for 'public purposes' (Balagopal 2007).

However, the Dalits and *adivasis* of Polepally have made it amply clear that the acquired land was not 'alienated' at all. Rather, they were completely dependent on this land, growing crops like rice, jowar, horse gram, chillies and vegetables, sufficient to last them through the year. Subject to constant pressure and coercion from the district revenue department, people had to accept the compensation money which was far smaller in amount than that given for regular *patta* land (Asher 2008a).

In Nanguneri, Tamil Nadu, SIPCOT acquired land in 1996 for a 2500-acre industrial park. It was converted into a multiproduct SEZ in 2001. The land acquired for this project belonged not to individual farmers, but to G R Mutt, a Hindu charitable board. The land was classified as temple land. The farmers cultivating the land stand to get no compensation whatsoever. They are now claiming their rights as tenants.

The question of land rights and SEZs is complicated by public discourse surrounding these issues. Every time a 'crisis' has emerged, the most recent one being the withdrawal of the Tatas from Singur, the media has pitted it as an industry-versus-agriculture argument — polarising the issue enough to keep the attention away from the inherent problems within the SEZ model and policy.

The Central government has reiterated that a Rehabilitation Bill is on its way that would purportedly eliminate all problems related to the current land acquisition policy. But various critiques of these Bills have made it clear that as long as development planning does not include considerations of subsistence livelihoods, food security, food sovereignty, ecological stability and sustainable industrialisation, it will fail to address the myriad issues facing sustainable and just development in this country. It is imperative that this exercise involves local communities and institutions of self governance, as a fundamental principle. But the most important aspect is the ownership and control over resources in the hands of the dispossessed sections, and the need to protect this ownership. Unless this fundamental division is dealt with, issues of planning would be irrelevant.

Process of land appropriation: A flawed policy framework

Procurement of land by the state for SEZs has largely occurred under the Land Acquisition Act of 1894, a legislation enacted by the colonial government in India.[4]

To the myriad criticisms of the use of the Land Acquisition Act of 1894 (LAA) to forcibly appropriate people's lands for SEZs, the initial reaction from the Union Ministry of Commerce was to absolve itself of all responsibility by arguing that:

1. land was a state subject, and, hence, it was up to the state governments to decide how to transfer the land; and
2. that there was no need for acquisition considering that the state industrial development corporations (IDCs) already had a lot of the land available with them and that would be transferred to the SEZs.

On the first argument of letting the state governments decide — none of the state governments who were competing for the maximum number of approvals have thought twice before using the LAA for SEZs. In fact many of the states, in their respective SEZ Acts and policies, had provisions for acquiring land *for* the developers. The Gujarat SEZ Act is one such example; it provides for the creation of a SEZ Development Authority which has the power to acquire land by 'consent or under the provisions of the Land Acquisition Act' for these zones. The authority also has the powers to approve the allocation of government land for the purpose.

The Gujarat government and the MoC at the Centre concur on the claim that Gujarat has been a 'hassle free' state for SEZs, as mostly 'wastelands' or non-agricultural private lands have been transferred for SEZs. Farmers are seen as having no grounds for opposition in the state. There have also been statements in the media that the state government has stayed out of the land 'acquisition' process, with private developers taking the lead in purchasing lands directly from farmers. However, the figures on land transfer provided by the government make it clear that almost 80 per cent of the land transfer for SEZs in Gujarat was performed by the state government. Of the land transferred, 40 per cent was under cultivation, another 30 per cent under grazing and revenue wasteland, and the rest transferred by the GIDC (acquired previously) (Asher 2008b).

This brings us to the second argument (of IDC lands being used), which is only partially true. The APIIC in Andhra Pradesh, CIDCO and MIDC in Maharashtra, GIDC in Gujarat, KIADB in Karnataka, and SIPCOT in Tamil Nadu do have their own land banks, which are being tapped through joint projects or through transfers of land to private developers. These lands have previously been acquired in phases for industrial purposes, using the Land Acquisition Act, over the past few decades. The fact that some of the acquired lands had been lying vacant with the IDCs (in some cases, also being cultivated), and were now being transferred to SEZ developers at much higher rates than their original acquisition price, has spurred a whole new set of issues. There have also been cases of court battles for better compensation by original owners.

However, not all the states had IDCs with readily available lands. Also, given the rate at which the SEZ approvals were being granted, it became clear that the IDCs lands would not be sufficient. As a result, the IDCs have also started acquiring fresh land to be transferred to SEZs.

Dealing with land issues: Band-aid remedies

After the Nandigram imbroglio, an Empowered Group of Ministers (EGoM), headed by Pranab Mukherjee, was formed specifically to review the policy. Together, the group and the MoC issued guidelines that the LAA would no longer be used for land transfer for private SEZs. In April 2007, the EGoM took the following additional decisions on the land-related aspects of SEZs:

- The upper limit on land for multiproduct SEZs was set at 5,000 hectares
- The processing area was increased to 50 per cent from 25 per cent for multiproduct SEZs
- The LAA was not to be used for land transfer to private SEZs

Let us look at these in a little more detail.

Upper limit for multiproduct SEZs

Setting an upper limit on the size of SEZs was critical to managing land acquisition and use, thought the EGoM. However, companies found a way of dealing with it by splitting the zones into two or three separate ones. For instance, the Adani group SEZ in Mundra (Kutch, Gujarat) was split into three parts — the port (2,658 ha), the SEZ (4,498 ha) and the Adani Power SEZ (293 ha). Reliance in Jhajjar, Haryana, also adopted a similar strategy. That even 5,000 hectares of contiguous land would cover all land types and categories — including agriculture land — is something that was probably not considered. In addition, in an effort to ape the Chinese SEZ size of more than 100 sq km, the MoC is pressurising the EGoM to remove the cap on the 5,000-ha limit.[5]

Increase in processing area for MP SEZs

The processing area within a SEZ was first pegged at 25 per cent of the acquired land. It was raised to 35 per cent under pressure from critics, and has now, under more pressure from the public, been raised to 50 per cent. The rationale for such a set-aside clause is obviously the uncertainty surrounding the economic attractiveness (and ultimate viability) of SEZs. If adequate productive investment is not forthcoming, the SEZ developer will be able to cash in on the land value through enormously profitable leases (strictly speaking, land is not transferable by sale within an SEZ). Conglomerates like Reliance already own upwards of 100,000 acres of land in the countryside.

However, the guideline on processing area still left substantial scope for housing and entertainment activities. Even today, if we look at the list of approvals, we find that a substantial number of the approvals are to big housing and infrastructure companies like DLF, Unitech, the Rahejas etc. It is, perhaps, for this reason that the Reserve Bank of India issued a notification in September 2006, asking commercial banks to treat SEZs at par with any other real estate project when it comes to lending, which makes borrowing from banks costlier. While there is pressure from the MoC that this notification should be reconsidered, it is yet to go. In the wake of the global financial crisis, the RBI is now considering the MoC's recommendation.

In another recent move that would help developers of special economic zones (particularly of IT/ITeS SEZs) enhance the 'commercial viability' of projects, the government has allowed them to build more and larger housing facilities, offices and other required social infrastructure in the 'non-processing area' and avail tax benefits for it. The ceilings on housing and office space in the non-processing area of SEZs were imposed to prevent SEZs from becoming a pure-play realty business (Arun 2008).

Land acquisition or private purchase: Between the devil and the deep blue sea

The third measure was, perhaps, the most problematic. It suggested that private companies and developers do most (70 per cent) of the purchasing on their own before looking for assistance from the state governments.

On the administrative front, the big hurdle could have been the land ceiling legislations. But since these legislations are being amended and/or companies are obtaining exemptions, they are not really a 'problem' from the corporate point of view. Also, companies have found their own methods of subverting the ceiling laws by floating subsidiaries. According to a news report, DLF (a major SEZ developer) has floated 68 subsidiaries, each of which has further subsidiaries. EMAAR, another infrastructure developing company, has 350. Further, the Export Promotion Council of India has suggested that ceiling exemptions should be provided after an SEZ project has obtained an in-principle approval.

But, despite these mechanisms, this has not been very successful from the corporate point of view. There are various examples — Kakinada, Raigad, the POSCO project — where the companies have not been able to acquire even 10 per cent of the required land, despite using a combination of generosity and stealth in the face of resistance from landowners.

Questions of success aside, the more relevant question is whether private or direct purchase is desirable in the first place. The general response, especially in the media, has been in favour of private purchase. 'Leave it to the market' is the belief being promoted. But case stories from the ground, especially where private purchase has been widespread, indicate that it is a process is dangerous, apart from being completely devoid of transparency and accountability.

Local political representatives, powerful interests and land mafia enter the picture as soon as there is news of an SEZ project (or mega project). Land prices rise soon after initial deals are struck, and aggressive speculation follows. The farmer who may be the first seller only gets a tiny fraction of the price that agents ultimately negotiate for land sold thereafter.

An excellent example is of the proposed Multi-modal International Hub and Airport and SEZ at Nagpur (Mihan), where the price of a plot is a staggering Rs 500 per square feet, which is many times of what the farmers got from the developer. Land rate has soared to Rs 1–5 crore per acre on the outskirts of the city. 'Driven by the hype created by the project, villages around here have seen a sort of land-riot for some time. About a million small and big investors have invested in plots or farmland beyond the city limits with the hope that prices will appreciate. Realtors estimate at least 200,000 individuals to be engaged in land brokering in and around Nagpur. The district collector's office estimates that 30,000 hectare land (330 crore sq ft) has changed hands from farmers to individuals,' says Jaideep Hardikar, a journalist who recently reported on the matter (Hardiker 2008). Similarly, in Nandagudi, after the announcement of the SEZ, the area saw a 200 per cent rise in the land prices.

Such speculative exercises led Kanchiram Rana, Parliamentary Standing Committee member reviewing SEZs, to remark thus:[6]

> Let me tell you, this hike in price of real estate is not a natural event. Developers are utterly commercial-minded, and they are manipulating land prices. At this rate, the common man will never get a house to

> live in. There is heavy land speculation around all the proposed SEZs in India. Land prices in these areas are hitting sky-high levels. There is one village near Mumbai where land developers are blocking land mass by paying Rs 10 crore (Rs 100 million) per acre. How can you accept and allow such a thing?

There could not be a better proof of the real estate objective of SEZs than the present global financial crisis, which has also impacted investments in SEZs. The fizzling out of the financial and real estate sectors the world over has left SEZ developers facing an acute liquidity squeeze. Consequently, many big players have stalled their projects (Mehra 2008).

Coming back to the problems with private purchase and speculation, quoting a study by CEPT (1999) on land transactions, Amita Shah (2007) in her research has found that some of the villages around Ahmedabad city (where many SEZs are now coming up), have lost up to 60 per cent of the land for non-agriculture uses over the last few years. In most cases, land was sold to intermediaries who would eventually sell the land to actual users, including land developers. As a result, a substantial part of the land had remained unutilised for a fairly long time (Shah and Kumar 2006).

Further, the activated land market in a speculative environment gives impetus to *benami* transactions, which escape the official land records. Shah gives the example of Lakhigam village covered by Dahej Industrial Estate, where only 95 out of 1,063 ha of land were officially converted as well as recorded.

Other irregularities include the tendency of companies to acquire more than what is needed — and this is the case whether the purchase is through or by the government, or directly by companies. Experiences of encroachment by private developers have also come to light in areas where they have managed to set up base or have existing units, thus, inducing displacement. This is generally in the form of dumping of wastes on nearby agricultural land or even through other activities like setting up poles/pipes for transmission lines.

Even with the state reportedly stepping back from active land acquisition, and limiting the number of SEZs it owns — at least partially, and this too is unevenly implemented — its role in acquiring land for private companies has remained one of the most controversial dimensions of the SEZ experience. In two instances of SEZ development, in Por near Baroda and in Hazira (Surat), the government stepped in to forcibly acquire land when the developers failed to directly purchase the land from farmers. Since the compensation amounts from the government were not as attractive, the large landowners of the village decided to go back to the company and settle for a compromise.

In another port area, called Pipavav in Rajula, where several SEZs are now in the pipeline, last year, a private company actually issued a 'Land Acquisition Notice' to a panchayat, specifying the *khasra* numbers of the land it proposed to acquire. The 'notice' demanded that the owners of the land be present on the date notified by the company to deal on the land. The farmers took the matter to the press and the district collector, both of whom had no idea that such a notice had been issued by a private company!

Whatever the means, it is undeniable that SEZs have become potential 'engines of commerce and profit' for the Indian and global real estate industry. Real estate developers are developing at least 130 SEZs, constituting nearly 50 per cent of the total area under them. According to a recent report of ASSOCHAM, the real estate market in India is growing at 30 per cent per annum.[7]

Questions also need to be asked on how different farmers respond to land brokers, real estate agents and companies. Are they on a level playing field? Can farmers (whether a big farmer of Haryana or a tribal from Orissa) understand land markets? And even if they did, would they be able to hold on to their asset, or still be forced to sell it for measly compensation? What, then, happens to the landless and marginal farmers who cannot access lands elsewhere?

There have been many critiques of the idea of 'market price' as well. At any given point, the subjective valuation of a piece of land may be higher than the market price, depending on the quality of land and for reason of sentiment (Arun Kumar and Satish Jain 2008). It is either the farmers in distress, or those who have no interest in holding the land (absentee land owners), who are the first to sell. There have been many reports from Mangalore, Maharashtra, Andhra Pradesh and Tamil Nadu, where people who sold their land initially based on the promise of jobs have changed their minds, and are fighting to get their land — their only productive asset — back.

As for the pros and cons of private purchase, at the end of the day, experience indicates that private companies prefer that state governments provide them the land, because it saves them the trouble of long-drawn and oftentimes difficult negotiations with different parties and the possibility of resistance.

State as facilitator for realtor, and continued use of Land Acquisition Act

What is perhaps most worrying is that the Central government is now attempting to institutionalise the concept of private purchase through an amendment in the Land Acquisition Act 1894. Clause 3(f)(iii), refers to acquisition of 30 per cent of remaining land when 70 per cent has already been acquired by a private party, and veritably states that state acquisition should facilitate private acquisition of land in case of any purpose 'useful to the general public'. But practically any economic activity can be construed to be 'useful to the general public'. In the case of SEZs, while overall economic development is the goal, immediate land transfers and the nature of private economic activity suggest that land transfers are really going to benefit a private party. Moreover, read with the Resettlement and Rehabilitation Bill 2007, this implies that in such projects only those who are displaced from this 30 per cent of land area will have the right to rehabilitation and compensation as per that law (CSD 2008).

The Parliamentary Standing Committee looking into the two new Bills has taken the position that acquisition of land should be a state responsibility, and should not be done by a private party, so that the benefits of rehabilitation and compensation can be shared by the other dependents and livelihood losers, apart from land losers. However, this does not deal with the issue that the compensation would be cash based, and that the Bill provides for rehabilitation only if the affected households are more than 400 in plains and more than 200 in the hills. In most cases, as far as SEZs are concerned, the LAA notices are for agricultural lands and not homesteads. As a result, the displacement is not large scale, and, hence, the rehabilitation requirement could be evaded by the state.

As far as rates of compensation are concerned, they are generally way below the market price. In Polepally, which is barely 40 km from the Shashambad International Airport where land prices are about Rs 1 crore an acre, the APIIC acquired lands for rates ranging from Rs 18,000 to Rs 25 lakh an acre. Further, the new proposed R&R Bill speaks about compensation over and above market rate. Yet, there are many issues raised repeatedly by civil society groups and local struggles that remain unaddressed. The most critical one of these pertains to 'prior informed consent'. This would mean providing information to the affected people and gram sabhas at every stage of the decision making, and taking their views and concerns into account in a transparent and just manner. However, this is absent in the proposed Bill.

Further, in states like Tamil Nadu and Andhra Pradesh, the enforcement of urgency clauses to quickly and secretly acquire land for SEZs has posed new challenges. Under these clauses, enquiries into possible alternate sites — required under Section 5A to prevent displacement — are dispensed with, leaving little concern for 'minimising displacement'.

For now, despite the government's stand that the LAA will not be used for SEZs, there are numerous cases where these notices have been issued and are not being withdrawn. Judicial interventions in High Courts and the Supreme Court, challenging the use of 'public purpose for private parties, have been dismissed on the grounds that infrastructure projects and those that earn revenue would be considered 'public purpose' projects.[8]

Re-examining displacement

There is an urgent need to closely re-examine the phenomenon of 'displacement' in the era of privatisation, where all natural or common resources, like land, water, forest and the sea, have been rendered speculative commodities openly accessible for sale and purchase. Leftist economists have described policies like SEZs as 'accumulation by dispossession' under the neo-liberal development paradigm, involving expropriation of resources like land from their owners (Gopalakrishnan 2008).

The initial displacement of the post-independence period for highways, mines, dams, railways, especially in the hinterlands, ripped of their resources the most marginalised groups like *adivasis* and Dalits. For instance, *adivasis* alone constitute nearly 40 per cent of the displaced population in the post-colonial period until the 1990s. But the location of the SEZs in agriculturally rich peripheries of urban centres has affected the middle class and small peasantry, who have been at the centre of the struggles against SEZs, be it in Raigad, Jhajjar, Gagret, Nandigudi, Vizag or Kakinada. While the stakes of agricultural labour, tenants and sharecroppers and other affected communities (like coast-based fish workers) cannot be denied, the middle class land owners have been at the helm of the opposition in many areas.

Regardless, the government has shown itself as more than a facilitator of the expansion of neo-liberal development for India Inc; in state after state, governments have proven themselves to be welcoming hosts and staunch allies. For the citizenry, the peasants, weavers, landless labour, who face displacement, and loss of livelihood and assets, the state stands as a blurry entity riddled with contradiction. On the one hand, it is a veritable broker of land, resources and power for corporations and realtors, and a repressive force ready to issue notices, coerce, evict, arrest, detain, and even use physical force, in order to provide land for SEZs; on the other, it is the guarantor of rights to which all appeals for justice must be made (Asher 2008c). These contradictory images represent our current crisis of democracy, one that has necessitated strong, even extreme, agitations by some communities to preserve their lives and livelihoods.

Earlier this year, the Goa state government was forced to cancel creation of SEZs under pressure from popular and political protests. In September 2008, villagers from 22 villages, which were targeted for acquisition for the proposed Mukesh Ambani-led Reliance Industries' SEZ, participated in the first-ever referendum on the issue. The result of the referendum was a resounding 'No' to the SEZ in Raigad (Koppikar 2008). On 2 October 2008, eight villages in Tiruvanamallai district passed resolutions at their gram sabha meetings against the government move to acquire 2,200 acres — most of it under cultivation — for the expansion of the Cheyyar Special Economic Zone (Jayakumar 2008). In many other areas, *Dalit and adivasi*, communities are now beginning to reclaim land that they see as rightfully theirs. Such examples of political transformations and democracy-in-action at the grassroots appear to be on the rise across the country, regardless of proposed SEZs or other attempts at land grab.

Notes

1. Special economic zones (SEZ) are physical territories within the country delineated for the purpose of integrated development of industries and other commercial purposes. Apart from several tax concessions, exemptions from labour and environmental legislations are granted to the units in these zones under the SEZ Act 2005. The SEZ policy in India is a modified version of the Export Processing Zone policy. The key differences between the EPZ and SEZ policies are that SEZs can be

developed and run by private developers, and space up to 50 per cent of the total area is provided for a non-processing area, where other commercial and social infrastructure is built.

2. The Land Acqusition Act 1894 provides the State power to acquire any piece of private land for 'public purpose' using the power of Eminent Domain. In 1984, developments carried out by private companies were also added in the definition of public purpose.
3. http://sezindia.nic.in/HTMLS/Formal_approvals_granted_under_SEZ_Act.pdf (accessed 4 October 2008); 'SEZ: For Whose Benefit?', *Outlook*, 12 February 2007.
4. The Land Acqusition Act of 1894 provides the state power to acquire any piece of private land for 'public purpose' using the power of eminent domain. In 1984, developments carried out by private companies were also added in the definition of public purpose.
5. 'EGoM to discuss cap on SEZ area', *Business Standard*, 4 February 2008.
6. 'Government policy on SEZs is wrong', *Rediffnews*, 23 February 2007, available at http://im.rediff.com/money/2007/feb/23sez1.htm (accessed 25 May 2007).
7. 'FDI in real estate to touch 26 per cent by March 2007: ASSOCHAM', *Domain-b.com*, 20 November 2006, available at http://www.domain-b.com/industry/associations/assocham/20061120_estate.html (accessed 20 November 2008).
8. 'Land acquisition for public purposes is justified: SC', *Headlines India*, 7 September 2008, available at http://headlinesindia.mapsofindia.com/business-news/industries/land-acquisition-for-public-purpose-is-justified-sc-1246.html (accessed 10 November 2008).

References

Asher, Manshi. 2006. 'Don't call it wasteland'. *The Times of India*, 12 October.

———. 2008a. 'Land from landless'. *Tehelka*, 5(31), 12 August.

———. 2008b. 'Unraveling the Gujarat SEZ model'. Paper presented at the 'IIAS National Conference on Special Economic Zones: Economic and Social Perspective', 18–21 September, Allahabad.

———. 2008c. '...And now Himachal too stuck in the SEZ conundrum'. *Himvani*, 3 October, available at http://www.himvani.com/news/2008/10/03/and-now-himachal-too-stuck-in-the-sez-conundrum/1693/developmenteconomics/himvani/ (accessed 18 November 2008).

Babu Jayakumar. 2008. 'Will Cheyyar be TN's Nandigram?'. *Express Buzz*, 4 October, available at http://www.expressbuzz.com/edition/story.aspx?artid=Q21m0xwRXaQ=&Title=Rs+30+crore+tsunami+donations+unused&SectionID=vBlkz7JCFvA=&MainSectionID=fyV9T2jIa4A=&SectionName=EL7znOtxBM3qzgMyXZKtxw==&SEO= (accessed 1 November 2008).

Balagopal, K. 2007. 'Land unrest in Andhra Pradesh I: Ceiling surpluses and public lands'. *Economic and Political Weekly*, 42(38): 3828–33.

Campaign for Survival and Dignity. 2008. 'Representation in connection with the Land Acquisition (Amendment) Bill 2007 and Resettlement and Rehabilitation Bill 2007', 28 March.

Gopalakrishnan, Shankar. 2008. 'Neoliberalism and Hindutva: Fascism, free markets and therestructuring of Indian capitalism'. *Monthly Review Magazine*, 14 January, available at http://www.monthlyreview.org/mrzine/gopalakrishnan141108.html (accessed 25 October 2008).

Hardiker, Jaideep. 2008. 'Lured to sell, driven to buy'. *India Together*, 26 November, available at http://www.indiatogether.org/2008/nov/eco-mihanland.htm (accessed 10 December 2008).

Koppikar, Smruti. 2008. 'Songs Of dissent'. *Outlook*, 6 October, available at http://www.outlookindia.com/full.asp?fodname=20081006&fname=Reliance+SEZ+%28F%29&sid=1 (accessed 2 December 2008).

Mehra, Vivek. 2008. 'The country's zones of contention'. *The Financial Express*, 2 December, available at http://www.financialexpress.com/news/the-countrys-zones-of-contention/392894/2 (accessed 10 December 2008).

S. Arun. 2008. 'Social infrastructure norms for SEZs eased'. *Financial Express*, 27 November.

Shah, Amita and Animesh Kumar. 2006. *Development-induced displacement and implications for land use policy: Insights from Gujarat and Orissa.* Ahmedabad: Gujarat Institute of Development Research.

Sharma, Devinder and Bhaskar Goswami. 2006. 'The new maharajas', available at http://www.indiatogether.org/2006/dec/dsh-mahasez.htm (accessed 10 November 2008).

13

Special economic zones, land acquisition and civil society in West Bengal

Abhijit Guha*

An article entitled 'Reflections in the aftermath of Nandigram' was published in the *Economic and Political Weekly* in its May 5 issue in 2007. The name of the author was not disclosed in the journal. It was written by a 'CPI (M) supporter'. The author argued, 'it would be factually incorrect to suggest that the government of West Bengal has been the most aggressive in pursuing the SEZ policy compared to Maharashtra, Haryana, or Gujarat'. After two weeks (on 26 May 2007), a rejoinder in the form of a letter was published in EPW by Siddhartha Guha Roy, which quoted the official announcement made by the Secretary of Industries of the Government of West Bengal on June 12 regarding SEZ in the state (memo no. 1825/JS/DC/2003). The West Bengal SEZ Act was passed in the state Assembly in 2003 (two years before the Central Government had enacted the SEZ Act), although there was no concrete move on the part of the state government to create such zones until 2006. In 2006, a vast area in Nandigram in East Medinipur district was earmarked for a chemical industry. A massive peoples' resistance followed, forcing the government to announce that there will be no SEZ in Nandigram. Acquisition of agricultural land for large and medium industries, however, continues in West Bengal with the colonial Land Acquisition Act of 1894.

---

* This is a revised version of a paper presented at the national seminar on 'Displacement issues surrounding Special Economic Zones', held at India International Centre, New Delhi, on 7 October 2008.

It seems that the WB government, for the time being, may not proceed with the creation of SEZ to attract foreign and domestic capital investment, but it is not making any move to enact any resettlement and rehabilitation law. This, despite the fact that the ruling Left Front enjoys a thrashing majority in the state Assembly for the last 30 years. The SEZ Act of the GoWB does not contain any provision for rehabilitation, which means that land for SEZ in the state would be acquired by the colonial law.

Land acquisition in West Bengal: Legal, developmental and policy dimensions

Land acquisition in West Bengal has a special significance in the context of the pro-peasant land reform policies adopted and implemented by the Left Front government in the state since it came to power in 1977. Almost all the studies conducted by the researchers on displacement in other states of India did not take into consideration the dampening effects of land acquisition on small peasants and sharecroppers, who are the real beneficiaries of land reforms.

Agricultural land is not only a socio-cultural and economic category for the peasants in a rural setting, but the rights of the people over such land depend on the functioning of a specific set of legal, administrative and policy apparatus with which a particular state power is endowed in a given period of time. The functioning of the legal, administrative and policy apparatus of the state power do not again operate in a cultural vacuum. The differing, and sometimes quite opposing, perspectives on issues around development form the cultural context within which the state apparatus functions.

According to the Land Acquisition Act, the state can exercise its right of *eminent domain* wherein it is the ultimate owner of all land, which it can acquire for public purposes after paying full compensation calculated on the basis of market value. Despite several amendments in the Act after India's independence, the two basic principles of land acquisition, (i) public purpose and (ii) compensation on market value, remain unchanged. The various criticisms of the LAA in India have also centred around these two cardinal principles. One of the major criticisms of the LAA is that the expression 'public purposs' is nowhere defined in the Act, and, in India, the courts do not have the power to decide whether the purpose behind a particular acquisition was a public purpose. The court can only direct the Collector to hear the objections of a person whose land has been acquired, but the Collector may not always listen to the objections raised by the legal owner of the land.

The second criticism of the Act is anthropological in nature. It says that the calculation of compensation on the basis of market value not only deprives the land owner, but it also hides the various socio-cultural dimensions of land ownership in an agrarian society. Land does not only have a market price at the time of acquisition, but it also serves various social, political and psychological functions of its owner. The ownership of a small piece of land can empower a landless family, and increase the status and prestige of that family in the local milieu. A piece of land supports a family for a number of generations, not just its present members. But these important dimensions of land and its ownership in an agricultural society are not considered for calculation of its value while giving compensation to a land loser.

Beside these two criticisms, there are others which grew out of the lengthy discourse and debate carried out by activists, scholars, legal experts and non-governmental organisations on the various shortcomings of this Act. The criticisms (see Guha 2007a) are as follows:

1. The LAA only deals with compensation and not rehabilitation of project-affected persons whose lands have been acquired. The responsibility of the state towards the affected persons ends with the payment of compensation.
2. The Act considers the payment of compensation to individuals who have legal ownership rights over land. This means that under this Act, no compensation is payable to landless labourers, forest land users and forest produce collectors, artisans and shifting hill cultivators, because they do not have any legal right over land, although these groups of people are also affected when agricultural and forest lands are acquired for development projects. In West Bengal, the state government had to make an amendment in the LAA (it was done in the 1960s) in order to provide compensation to sharecroppers (*bargadars*), who also suffered loss of livelihood because of acquisition of agricultural land.
3. The LAA only recognises individual property rights, but not community rights over land. As a consequence, the *usefructory*

> *rights* of the tribal and non-tribal communities over common land do not find any place in this law. So, when village common lands are acquired, no compensation in any form is provided to the village communities who derive vari-ous types of benefits (e.g, cattle grazing, fuel-wood collection etc.) from these lands. The LAA does not have any scope for this kind of compensation for loss of common pool resources (CPR). Interestingly, in the vast rural areas of India, privately owned agricultural lands are also used as com-mon grazing lands by the villagers in the post-harvest season. The LAA has no provision to compensate the villagers who may not be the owners of a particular piece of agricultural land but enjoy usefructory *rights* of cattle grazing on this land after the harvest of the crops.

Since Independence, besides the colonial Land Acquisition Act of 1894, there existed another state Act, entitled the West Bengal Land (Requisition and Acquisition) Act, 1948. The latter Act is no more applicable in West Bengal since 31 March 1993 by a decision of the West Bengal Legislative Assembly. In fact, when this particular piece of legislation was first enacted in the Assembly, it was stipulated that the Act has to be renewed in the Assembly by a majority decision every five years since this is a very powerful and coercive law. The government opinion was that the state of West Bengal, which had to receive millions of refugees from erstwhile East Pakistan just after independence, needed huge amount of land for various developmental purposes. For this reason, the government was in need of an Act which was more powerful than the colonial Act in acquiring land from private owners. By the West Bengal Land (Requisition and Acquisition) Act, the government could first requisition a particular piece of land for which the payment of compensation may not be made before the land takeover; while in the earlier LAA of 1894, the government could not take possession of any land without payment of compensation. In the absence of any district-by-district published records on the amount of land acquired by West Bengal government using the two Acts, it is not possible to make any assessment of the policy directions of the state government in acquiring land by these two Acts, which vary in their basic approach towards payment of compensation to the project-affected people. But the long period (1948–93), that is nearly 45 years, during which the West

Bengal government has kept this powerful Act alive, is itself an evidence of its frequent application. In terms of political composition, it should be noted that during this long period, both the Congress and Left-ruled governments who were in power continuously renewed the Act of 1948 in the state Assembly.

The debates and discussions that took place in the state Assembly around the West Bengal Land (Requisition and Acquisition) Act 1948, revealed certain interesting points, which are enumerated below:

1. Without any exception, the political party in power (Congress or the Left parties) invariably justified the extension of Act-II for quicker acquisition of land for various development works.
2. Both the Congress and the Left parties criticised the oppressive character of the West Bengal Land (Requisition and Acquisition) Act 1948 whenever they were in opposition, although representatives of the parties in the Legislative Assembly went for vote on the Bill twice only. It seems that whether the parties would go for vote depended on factors other than the immediate issue at hand.
3. The delay in the payment of compensation seemed to be the most commonly accepted issue which was raised in the Assembly, and no substantial improvement seemed to have taken place with regard to the time taken for the payment of compensation.
4. No member ever raised the point that the government has a moral responsibility for rehabilitation of the people displaced due to acquisition of land. It may be noted in this connection that the Report of the Expert Group on Land Acquisition formed by the Ministry of Agriculture, Government of India, which was published in 1967, categorically mentioned rehabilitation of displaced persons as a 'moral responsibility' of the government (Report of the Expert Group 1967). Since 1967, no member of the West Bengal Assembly, irrespective of political affiliation, was found to have made use of the aforesaid report of the committee to demand rehabilitation of displaced persons during debate sessions on Act-II. Incidentally, the report is still available in the library of the West Bengal Assembly.
5. It is only the Left members who have suggested that the rates of compensation for the rich and the poor should also be different, but they did not make any move towards the differential

payment of compensation through amendments in Act-I or Act-II since coming to power in 1977.

6. The speech delivered by the Land and Land Reforms Minister of the Left Front in the 103rd session of the Assembly on 23 February 1994 revealed the pace at which the land acquisition process was in operation in West Bengal (15,000 pending cases under Act-II). One could easily infer from this, the kind of harassment caused to the displaced persons in the districts of West Bengal, although no member (belonging to the Left or the Congress) spoke on this issue in the Assembly. Every political party seemed to have taken the stand that this harassment of the people of West Bengal caused by land acquisition was an inevitable outcome which has to be shouldered by the poor farmers for the sake of development of the state.[1]

Land acquisition in erstwhile Medinipur district: A case study

From the discussion on the Assembly proceedings, it may be noted that acquisition of agricultural land in Medinipur district came up as an important subject in the Assembly. Project specific questions (viz. Haldia port, Haldia petrochemicals project or Kolaghat thermal power project) were raised by the elected representatives of the people, which revealed some scattered quantitative information on the amount of land acquired for a particular type of development project in the district. No systematic and comprehensive database on land acquisition in the district for a particular year or period was available until 1993.

The first systematic attempt towards creating a database on land acquisition for different categories of projects had been made by the Land Acquisition Department of the erstwhile Medinipur district in April 1993. The results of this maiden effort have not yet been published, but a typed copy in the form of a report is available in the Land Acquisition Department of the Medinipur District Collectorate. The report, which was entitled 'Land acquisition cases of Midnapore: Present status, problems, future strategy' (MDC 1993) was prepared to fulfil two important objectives, (i) to create a database for all the pending cases of the LA Department at Medinipur, and (ii) to supervise and monitor the calculation of interests for all the pending cases under Act-II in order to reduce government liabilities.

The findings of this government report presented an 'alarming picture' in terms of pending LA cases, as well as the government's financial burden with regard to the interest incurred due to the delay in the payment of compensation after the acquisition. Under the subsection entitled 'Present status', the report mentioned quite emphatically that '293 cases have not at all progressed after handing over of possession to the requiring body (RB)' (MDC 1993: 2). The LA Department had sent estimates for 80 per cent payment, but the RBs did not show any interest over the land after taking possession of the same. No action has yet been taken by the LA office for many years. The report categorically stated:

> Action is being taken to send estimates to R.B. as the Govt. liability is mounting. In certain cases where estimates have been sent, there is no response from the R.B. and they express their inability to place fund as it is not included in their respective budget for that year. With the increase in the value of land the liability of the Govt. is increasing in a very alarming manner in addition to the deprivation suffered by landlosers due to non-payment (ibid.: 1).

It should be noted in this connection that the compensation money has to be deposited by the requiring body, i.e., the department or company which is in need of the land. It may be a government department (for example, the irrigation or electricity departments), or a private company (for example, a private hotel or industry), which shall be responsible for placing the fund with the LA Department from which payment of compensation would be made. The cases of acquisition of land for various government departments in Medinipur, which were pending at the time of the preparation of the aforementioned report, showed a huge financial burden on the government itself. In Table 13.1, the department-wise fund requirement of the pending LA cases is shown.

The grand total puts the financial burden on the state government for carrying out the completion of the pending cases at around Rs 26 crore. The report revealed that there were at least 418 LA cases for which gazette notifications had been published but award had not yet been made. Assuming a 15 per cent interest every year, the yearly interest to be paid by the government comes to around Rs 151 lakh, and for the district alone, the liability of the government is increased by a staggering amount of Rs 41,000 every day. The report, however, has not been updated yet.

Table 13.1: Department-wise fund requirement of pending land acquisition cases in Medinipur district (up to April 1993)

Name of the Government Department	*Approximate Amount (in rupees)*
Agriculture	52,13,616.15
Agriculture Irrigation	6,13,581.00
Animal Husbandry	1,01,582.13
Co-operative	34,935.00
Development and Planning	4,77,885.73
Fishery	20,38,439.00
Forest	20,38,439.00
Irrigation	14,54,20,607.67
L.G.U.D.	34,62,536.00
P.W.D.	8,19,81,577.29
Power	10,87,362.79
Public Health Engineering	24,14,912.18
Refugee Relief	89,096.00
Relief	73,940.00
South Eastern Railway	1,33,27,441.81
Transport	2,98,700.00
Total	**26,47,54,107.21**

The report considered another grave aspect of the problem of land acquisition in Medinipur. Under a section entitled 'Implications' (ibid.: 3–4), it noted that in case of the pending cases where the RBs did not seem to be interested in their finalisation, most of them had actually constructed a building, road or irrigation channels, which made it impossible for the land to be returned to the PAPs. It is true that there was a provision for de-requisition of land requisitioned under Act-II, but for all practical purposes this rarely happened. To quote from the report:

> for most of the requisitioned lands the land character has been changed to suit the objective for which the acquisition was made. A completed irrigation project or an industrial estate or a hospital project on a requisitioned land cannot be de-requisitioned. (Ibid.: 3)

The report further observed that even if it is assumed that all the RBs have placed their respective funds with the Collector for making compensation payment to the PAPs (in the report, however, this phrase was never used) by 31 March 1994, even then it would not be possible to make a payment of Rs 26 crore, since the Medinipur Land Acquisition Department, with its existing strength of skilled and specialised staff, working at the normal rate, could make an yearly payment of Rs 4 crore only. At this rate, the District Collectorate could complete the pending cases within 5–6 years in an ideal situation.

The version of the district administration on the present status of land acquisition in Medinipur district not only revealed its 'alarming' and 'severe' condition, but it also acted as an 'eye-opener' (a phrase used in the report) for those in the administration. The report, however, was lacking in certain important aspects of land acquisition:

1. It only calculated the burden of the government in monetary terms for making compensation payments under pending Act-II cases. There are no statistics on the total amount of land acquired so far in Medinipur district for any given period or year. There is also no figure on the amount of land acquired under different categories of projects in the district.
2. The report never made any attempt to estimate the number of persons or families who have been affected by land acquisition under the pending Act-II cases in different areas of the district. Except for mentioning the plight of the owners who turned into land losers in the pending cases, nowhere in the report was found any estimate or statistics about the number of PAPs in Medinipur.
3. It did not also give any list of pending cases of land acquisition for private companies or joint sector business enterprises in Medinipur district. It only dealt with cases of land acquisition for various government departments.

The government report on land acquisition prepared by the Medinipur District Collectorate in 1993 meticulously recorded land acquisition in terms of its constraints and shortcomings. Despite its various lacunae, which have been described in this chapter, the report revealed how difficult and complicated it was to acquire land for development projects. It also gave an indication about the fact that there was very little hope to arrange for all the compensation payment within five to six years. Under these circumstances, one can only imagine the kind of harassment caused to the project-affected families, who have neither received compensation for the acquisition of their cultivable land, nor been allowed to cultivate the land requisitioned by the government but lying unutilised.

Land acquisition for century textiles and industries in Paschim Medinipur district

The land acquisition for Century Textiles and Industries Limited is a typical example of a pending case where a huge chunk of acquired agricultural land remained unutilised for more than five years (Guha 2007). The first reference of land acquisition for this industry was found in a letter dated 3 December 1992 (No 518-C1/b) from the Assistant Secretary to the Government of West Bengal addressed to the Collector of the Medinipur district. In his letter, the Assistant Secretary informed the District Collector that he had received a proposal from the WBIDC for the acquisition of 1137.78 acres of land in 18 mouzas under Kharagpur police station for setting up a sponge and pig iron industry by M/s Century Textiles and Industries Ltd. From this letter, it was learnt that the decision for the acquisition of this huge chunk of land was approved in a meeting of the Cabinet Committee on 2 July 1992. The Assistant Secretary directed the Collector to initiate land acquisition proceedings under the West Bengal Land (Requisition and Acquisition) Act 1948 immediately, because the project was 'connected with an incidental increase in employment opportunities in the stats'. Since December 1992, there was no reference in the Land Acquisition Departmental files about the progress of the land acquisition procedures for the Century project until April 1995. A letter addressed to the managing director of the West Bengal Industrial Development Corporation (WBIDC) (No. CTI/PI/WBIDC/06, dated 6 April 1995) from Century Textiles Company, was traced, according to which the company agreed with WBIDC to procure 641.86 acres of land, of which 85 acres might be given from the land allocated to Tata Metaliks, which remains unutilised. On 17 May 1995, Century Textiles Company again wrote to the Executive Director of WBIDC to clear certain confusions with the Collector of Medinipur district, as the latter was not aware of acquiring 150 acres of land on the western side of a village road. The company also urged the executive director to hand over the land, since land acquisition might take six months, which seemed to be 'too long a period' for the company to wait. After writing this letter, the company requested the WBIDC MD to release an amount of Rs 50,000 towards payment of contingency expenses for land acquisition, as desired by the Additional District Magistrate of Medinipur. On 14 August 1995 (memo No. 1477/L.A.), the Additional District Magistrate of Medinipur informed the Deputy

Secretary of the Land and Land Reforms Department that Century Textiles Company 'had tried private negotiations for obtaining the said land (818.5 acres) with the landowners and failed'. A copy of this letter was also sent to the executive director of the WBIDC. In less than a month, the Deputy Secretary, Land and Land Reforms Department, directed the Collector of Medinipur to investigate the proposal of Century and send a report so that the case may be started under LA Act 1894. This was owing to the fact that the state government had already decided not to pursue land acquisition case under Act-II. (Letter No. 5354 LA (II) 5C-47/95, dated 4 September 1995). In this connection, we may note that in a recent period, a section of intellectuals (which includes Nobel laureate economist Amartya Sen) have started to argue that an arrangement should be made so that the companies may purchase land from the peasants through bargain. These intellectuals believe that, if adopted, this arrangement would enable peasants to get a higher price for the land than they would have received under the existing land acquisition law. These intellectuals seem to be unaware of the fact that the 1984 amendment of the colonial Land Acquisition Act had already made a provision for land acquisition by the government for a private company, and it had also stipulated that the companies may try to purchase land directly from the peasants. But if the company fails, and this may happen if the peasants do not agree to sell their land to the company, then the government would acquire the land by employing the LA Act. So, the arrangement for so-called fair bargain is neither a novel idea nor does it do justice to unwilling peasants. The land acquisition case of Century at Medinipur revealed how this has happened.

After this, notification under Section 4 of the LA Act 1894 for the acquisition of 526.71 acres of land was published first in *Ganasakti* (a CPI-M daily) on 28 October 1995 and then in *Amrita Bazar Patrika* on 30 October 1995, and subsequently, in the *Calcutta Gazette* on 3 November 1995, for the establishment of sponge and pig iron plant on 10 mouzas of Kharagpur police station under the Kalaikunda gram panchayat. The agreement and declaration notification was published again in *Ganasakti*, on 4 April 1996, and in the *Calcutta Gazette* on 8 April 1996. The district LA Department then proceeded to prepare the rate report of the land acquired for the company, in order to make payment of compensation to the affected persons.

The land acquired for Century came under 10 mouzas of the Kharagpur police station, of which two fell within the Kharagpur municipality. The LA Department considered the sale of land for all those mouzas that took place during 1993–1995 by taking figures from the government land sub-registration office, and arrived at varying market values for all kinds of land in those mouzas. The Additional District Magistrate prepared a rate report on 22 April 1996 for the 8 mouzas under acquisition, which were as given in Table 13.2.

Table 13.2: Rate report of 8 mouzas under acquisition in Kharagpur

	Name of the Mouza	*Land value per acre*
Under Kharagpur Municipality	Malancha	Rs 1,00,000
	Dhekia	Rs 64,000
	Rajpura	
	Chaksonadhar	
Under gram panchayat area	Niranjanbar	Rs 50,000
	Kalikapur	
	Tarabamni	
	Sujatpur	

The reasons for this kind of variation in the valuation of land were stated in the report of the Additional District Magistrate, dated 22 April 1996. The whole chunk of land distributed over the 8 mouzas had little variation in terms of its agricultural potential. The land in all the mouzas were classed under *'Jal'*, which yielded only one crop in a year and did not have any access to irrigation facility. But the area towards the railway line and the National Highway 6, which comprised the Malancha and Dhekia mouzas, had a much greater number of land transactions owing to speculation in view of imminent urbanisation originating from the railway township of Kharagpur. For the affected peasants who have lost their land due to acquisition, this variation in their land value within a distance of less than a kilometre, under almost similar type of agricultural conditions, did not seem to have delivered justice to them. On 24 June 1996, 42 land losers of Rajpura mouza submitted a written petition to the district Collector, in which they stated that the reality was that agricultural production showed higher figures for Rajpura not Malancha. So, the land value for the former mouza should be fixed at a higher rate for the calculation of compensation to land losers. Suffice it to say here that the district land acquisition office had no other option but to reject the petition, since the rates of land values were fixed on the basis of sale data collected from the concerned government office of the district.

From a note prepared by the Land Acquisition Department on the tentative cost of acquisition for Century, we came to know that a rate of Rs 7,000 per acre was fixed for *bargadars* affected by the project.

The payments of compensation for the company started and it continued up to the end of March 1998, after which it came to a halt. Century Textiles Company did not start any construction work for its proposed sponge and pit iron plant, although buildings were constructed by the side of the land acquired for the security guards of the company. The company managing director, B K Birla, in an interview to a reporter of *The Statesman*, said that they would not proceed with the project as 'the national market of pig iron has become very much competitive because of the entry of China and Australia in the field'. He also said that this decision was conveyed to the state government long ago. The state Land and Land Reforms Minister, Surya Kanto Mishra, on the other hand, told the reporter: 'We are not finding any taker for the land'.[2] In another detailed report published seven months later by the same newspaper, it was stated that the state government still seemed to be undecided over the fate of the land acquired for Century Textiles.[3] The individual land owners, who possessed plots of land in this area, also stopped cultivation since they received acquisition notices in 1996. It may be of interest in this context to mention that in one of its recent publications, the WBIDC enlisted the sponge and pig iron plant of Century Textiles as an 'upcoming' industrial unit in the Kharagpur area (WBIDC 1999). From a letter dated 19 April 1999 (memo No. 592/LA), addressed to the MD of WBIDC by the Land Acquisition Officer, it was learnt that the district administration sought advice regarding the fate of the land acquired for Century, for which a payment of Rs 3,48,884.84 was made, but the rest of the compensation payment could not be completed since the company did not place any fund with the district Collector. Table 13.3 sum-marises the series of events that took place for the acquisition of agri-cultural land for the Century project, which ultimately could not be established.

Table 13.3: Succession of events showing the case of land acquisition for Century Textiles and Industries

Date	*Event*
2 July 1992	Cabinet of the Government of West Bengal approved the project for the acquisition of 1137.78 acres of land in 18 mouzas under Kharagpur police station by using the LA Act of 1948
3 December 1992	Assistant Secretary writes to District Collector to proceed
28 October 1995	The first public notification published in newspapers. Acquisition by Act-I was made. Land amount reduced to 526.71 acres in 10 mouzas
29 December 1995	The hearing of objections by the land losers completed
10 January 1996	Peasants prevented soil testing
22 March 1996	Mass deputation by the peasants at District Collectorate. Peasants demanded land-for-land or job and higher compensation
2 April 1996	Publication of agreement between the company and the state government in the *Calcutta Gazette* (see appendix C)
10 April 1996	Peasants submitted memorandum to boycott Parliamentary election
2 May 1996	Poll boycott decision of the land losers published in *The Statesman*
22 May 1996	CTIL got possession certificate over 238.86 acres of land
21 June 1996	The report on the objection hearing at Collector's office completed; all objections overruled
May–July 1996	Farmers were not allowed to cultivate on the acquired land. By this time the payment of compensation started
28 February 1997	Land and Land Reforms Minister announces that state would reclaim unused land leased to industries
11 April 1997	CTIL got possession certificate over another 119.39 acres of land
12 March 1998	*The Statesman* reported about the adverse effects of acquisition in Kalaikunda
21 June 1998	Kalaikunda gram panchayat held meeting with the land losers about the land which remained unused by the company
12 October 1998–15 March 1999	The order sheet of the LA Department reveals non-payment of compensation to land losers, as the company stopped placing funds since December 1996
19 April 1999	Land acquisition office of Medinipur writes to the MD of WBIDC seeking advice over the situation
18 November 1999	The company MD tells a reporter of *The Statesman* that they are not interested to establish the plant; the minister also expresses his helplessness over the matter
7 December 1999	Joint Secretary, Land and Land Reforms Department, writes to District Collector to send report on the acquisition

The whole land acquisition episode for Century Textiles revealed some of the maladies of the land acquisition process of India, which are mentioned below:

1. The project-affected people have not been given any role by the state government in determining the fate of their major means of production, even when they remain unutilised for more than five consecutive years.
2. The failure of the company to purchase the required land through private negotiations showed that the peasants were not ready to part with their agricultural land for the proposed pig iron plant.
3. The reason behind the varying rates for the different plots under the same chunk of land showed the limitations of the prevalent procedure for the determination of market price of land under the purview of the LAA of 1894.
4. It became almost impossible for the administration to return the land to its owners even when the same remain unutilised beyond the stipulated period mentioned in the agreement.
5. The government seemed to be a prisoner in the hands of the bureaucratic machinery in dealing with this kind of problem of land acquisition. The state government virtually suppressed the latest information on Century Textiles when the former enlisted Century's plants as one of the upcoming projects in the state even in January 1999.

One important point about the acquisition of land for Tata Metaliks (a pig iron company which has started production) and Century Textiles deserves mention. Huge chunks of fertile agricultural land were selected by the companies and the Cabinet Committee of the West Bengal government gave approval to this selection. Even a casual travel through this area from Medinipur towards Kharagpur would reveal the presence of a huge tract of undulating lateritic non-agricultural land on the western side of the south-eastern railway track, lying on the north bank of Kasai river. During our fieldwork, the land losers of this area repeatedly pointed out that the government should have acquired the non-agricultural land for the industries instead of taking their agricultural land. When this point was raised before the officers and employees of the Land Acquisition Department of the district Collectorate, they simply stated that it was the decision of the government, which the concerned department at the district level had to execute. One very experienced and veteran Assistant Land Acquisition Officer once said to the author of this article: 'Well, the screening committee at the district level may turn down a proposal coming from the Writers' Building in Kolkata. But I have seen through my experience that whenever Calcutta wants acquisition, Medinipur simply obeys the order. There is hardly any exception' (free translation by the author from Bengali). This comment epitomised the power of the *eminent domain* of the state in case of land acquisition for development projects in a pro-peasant state like West Bengal.

Land acquisition for Tata Metaliks

Tata Metaliks is a heavy industry, which was established within the jurisdiction of the Kalaikunda gram panchayat during 1992. This is a pig iron manufacturing plant which was found to produce about 290 tonnes of pig iron per day in 1995–96. After the establishment of Tata Metaliks, the Kalaikunda gram panchayat built a metal road on the western side connecting the plant with National Highway 6 in a place named Sahachawk. The south-eastern railway station line runs on the eastern side of the industry. The Kharagpur railway station is only about 5 kilometres, and the Medinipur district headquarters is 7 kilometres from this place. In this connection, we can recall that in his answer to a question on 1 June 1992 in the West Bengal Assembly, the land and Land Reforms Minister mentioned that 217.23 acre land was acquired for Tata Metaliks (Guha 2007: 85).

The land acquired for the pig iron industry belonged to '*jal soem*' class according to the system of classification made by the Land and Land Reforms Department. The possessions on these lands were given to the company on different dates in the month of August 1991, and declaration notifications were published from November 1991 to January 1992. The Land Acquisition Department approved a rate of Rs 20,686 per acre. The cases of land acquisition for Tata Metaliks have shown that the Government of West Bengal desired a quick acquisition of land for the company, and that is why Act-II (West Bengal Land Requisition and Acquisition Act 1948) was employed for the said purpose (Guha 2007: 87).

The area lies on the bank of the Kasai, which is the largest river of the erstwhile Medinipur district. Cultivation of paddy (staple food of the district) in the villages under study depends primarily on rainfall, and no systematic irrigation facilities have yet been developed by the government. The villagers residing on the south-eastern bank of the river cultivate a variety of vegetables on the land adjoining their homesteads *(kala jami)* owing to a good supply of groundwater tapped through traditional dug wells. But just west of the south-eastern railway track, the groundwater level is not very congenial for cultivation of vegetables. The main agricultural activity on this side of the railway track is rain-fed paddy cultivation for about four to six months of the year. Land for the two big private industries had been acquired by the government on this side during 1991–96.

BOX 13.1 How a peasant fights acquisition

Phanibhusan Patra is a middle-aged man who inherited 7.20 acre fertile land from his father, of which 3.80 acres was paddy land and 3.40 acres were used for vegetable cultivation. Out of his 7.20 acres, 2.80 acres of his paddy fields had been acquired for Tata Metaliks. He belongs to Sadgop caste and was an active participant in the movement against land acquisition. He saved the compensation money in the bank. He thinks that his one acre of paddy land and 3.40 acres of vegetable land are a blessing for him, because these have not yet been acquired. He cultivates paddy, potato, onion, tomato, cauliflower etc, and sells them in the market. His son studies in Class V and the daughter reads in Class VIII (Majumder 2007).

Table 13.4 shows pre-acquisition and post-acquisition agricultural landholding scenario of the land loser families in Gokulpur. After land

Table 13.4: Pre- and post-acquisition agricultural landholding scenario of the land loser families in the village

Size Category of Landholdings in Acres	*Before Land Acquisition*	*Mean Household Size*	*After Land Acquisition*	*Mean Household Size*
Land less	—	—	5 (5.05)	3.60
≤ 0.5	10 (10.10)	1.90	28 (28.28)	4.21
0.5–1.5	38 (38.38)	3.97	39 (39.39)	6.21
1.5–2.5	23 (23.23)	6.80	19 (19.19)	5.16
2.5–3.5	17 (17.17)	7.80	3 (3.03)	9.66
3.5–4.5	4 (4.04)	8.20	3 (3.03)	9.33
4.5–5.0	—	—	1 (1.01)	14.00
5+	7 (7.07)	9.40	1 (1.01)	11.00
Total	**99**	**5.63**	**99**	**5.63**

Note: Figures in parentheses represent percentage out of column total.

acquisition, 5 families out of 99 became landless, which constitutes 5.05 per cent of the total land loser families. The families having less than 0.5 acres of land dramatically increased from 10 (10.10 per cent) to 28 (28.28 per cent) after land acquisition. It was noticed that even after land acquisition, the number of families having 0.5–1.5 acres of land increased from 38 (38.38 per cent) to 39 (39.39 per cent). But, the families having 1.5–2.5 acres of land decreased from 23 (23.23 per cent) to 19 (19.19 per cent). Similarly, a considerable decline was noticed in the number of families having 2.5 acres to more than 5 acres of land; the number of families decreased from 28 (28.28 per cent) to 8 (8.08 per cent) after acquisition. On the other hand, the number of households within the size category 2.5–5+ acres declined from 6.53 to only four.

From this analysis, we can infer that there was a steep decline in the amount of paddy cultivation land, which consequently brought a decrease in the production of paddy. On the other hand, the decrease in amount of paddy land and paddy production led to an increase in non-agricultural activities and loss of household-level food security.

Socio-economic consequences of land acquisition in Gokulpur

The first and foremost consequence of land acquisition in Gokulpur conforms to the observation of Michael Cernea, which he analytically elaborated in one of his series of publications on the 'eight major risks' *(landlessness, joblessness, homelessness, loss of common property, marginalisation, food insecurity, mortality, social disarticulation)* involved in involuntary displacement caused by development projects all over the world (Cernea 1999). Industrialisation in the liberalisation decade in Kharagpur block has undoubtedly led to dispossession of the small and marginal farmers from their principal means of production. It would be pertinent here to look into the scenario of the utilisation of compensation money by the land loser families in one of the sample villages in our study area. Table 13.5 is an attempt to understand this phenomenon.

In this table, we have made an attempt to quantify the pattern of utilisation of the compensation money received by the land losers in the study village.

Table 13.5: Profile of utilisation of compensation money by land loser households in the study area

	Utilisation Category							
Compensation Category (in rupees)	*Purchase of Agricultural Land*	*Purchase of Shallow Tube Well*	*House Building/or Repair*	*Domestic Consumption*	*Marriage of Family Members*	*Repayment of Loan*	*Bank Deposit*	*Business Investment*
<5000	–	10	–	21	14	7	9	02
5000–10000	–	12	–	8	8	3	6	08
10000–15000	–	14	4	12	–	1	7	–
15000–20000	–	9	6	5	–	–	6	–
20000–25000	1	4	–	2	3	–	2	–
25000–30000	–	9	4	5	2	–	5	–
30000–35000	–	1	–	1	–	–	1	–
35000–40000	2	4	1	3	–	–	3	02
40000–45000	–	1	–	1	–	–	1	–
45000–50000	–	1	1	1	–	–	1	–
50000–55000	–	2	2	2	–	–	2	–
55000–60000	–	–	–	–	–	–	–	–
60000<	–	8	7	8	2	–	7	–
Total	3 (3.03)	75(75.75)	25(25.25)	69(69.69)	29(29.29)	11(11.11)	50(50.50)	12(12.12)

Note: Figures in parentheses represent percentage out of column total.

First, it should be mentioned that all the 99 households have received compensation. Second, all the families have utilised the compensation money in more ways than one. So, under each utilisation category, any row total is a result of the addition of same household more than one time under different categories. As a result, sum of the row total is not equal to the total number of households in our sample. This gives a fair idea as to how the villagers have attempted to compensate their loss of land. The maximum number of affected households has spent some portion of the compensation money for agricultural purposes (for example, purchase of agricultural land, shallow tube wells etc.), while the second highest number of households spent some portion of the compensation money in domestic consumption. Beside these, from this table it is also evident that 50.5 per cent families deposited compensation money in the bank.

BOX 13.2 Food insecurity caused by industrialisation

Murali Santra is a land loser Sadgop farmer. He inherited 8.6 acre fertile land from his father. He used to till the land with his family members and got 20,000 – 25,000 kg paddy per year. He cultivated different traditional verities of paddy, such as *Rupsal, Patnai, Sitasal, Jota*, which were usually planted in the rainy season. During the other times of the year, the land remained uncultivated owing to shortage of water. The paddy yielded by this land was used to feed his family, and if there was any surplus, he sold it in the market.

He came to know about acquisition of the land from a notice, which came from the land acquisition office of Midnapore. After receiving the notice, he attended meetings but never submitted any objection in writing. After a short period of time, like other farmers of Gokulpur, he agreed to give away his land with the hope that a member of his family will get a permanent job in the industry. He got a compensation of Rs 22,000 for his 1 acre (located in Amba mouza), which was acquired for Tata Metaliks. He saved this compensation money in the bank.

His family is now undergoing economic as well as psychological stress. The land which he possesses now cannot supply food for his family throughout the year. Now, he has to purchase paddy from the market for two months of the year. After the acquisition of his land, he bought two ploughs and a pair of bullocks and a shallow tube-well.

Since the acquisition, he did not take any loan from the bank, but received some economic assistance from his relatives. He also sells vegetable grown on his homestead land.

He emphatically stated that the most adverse and immediate effect of land acquisition on his family was the scarcity of food and fodder for the cattle (Majumder 2007).

Civil society movements around land acquisition in West Bengal

The civil society movements around development-caused displacement in West Bengal virtually gained momentum after the incidents in Singur and Nandigram. A good number of Kolkata-based intellectuals and litterateurs have become vocal against the government's policy of industrialisation through land acquisition. A plethora of literature is being published on this issue. But interestingly, this literature rarely dealt with the basic changes needed to reform the colonial law and suggestions on rehabilitation packages. In fact, if one looks back, acquisition of fertile land took place in Kharagpur during the early 1990s as revealed from our case studies, but it hardly attracted the attention of the Kolkata-based intellectuals (Guha 2007b). Another important lacuna of the current civil society movement in West Bengal is its lack of attention on the dampening effects of land acquisition on land reforms and Panchayati Raj institutions, the two most important pillars of the pro-peasant policy of the Left Front government in West Bengal. There is virtually no pressure on the state government by the civil society groups or the opposition parties to enact a humane rehabilitation policy and/or law to deal with development-caused displacement in the state. In sum, the whole scenario of civil society movement around land acquisition in West Bengal lacks long-term vision and foresight, and this makes it vulnerable to being trapped in political jargon for some more time to come.

Notes

1. WB Legislative Assembly proceedings for the years 1956, 1963, 1967, 1970, 1972, 1973, 1978, 1983, 1989, 1991, 1992, and 1994.
2. 'Kalaikunda land unused', *The Statesman*, 18 November 1999, p. 4.
3. 'Hungry tribals pay for unfinished dream plant', *The Statesman*, 5 July 2000, p. 4.

References

Cernea, M. 1999. 'Mutual reinforcement: Linking economic and social knowledge about resettlement', in Michael Cernea (ed.), *The economics of involuntary resettlement: Questions and challenges*, pp. 1–4. Washington DC: World Bank.

Guha, A. 2007a. *The land, law and the Left: The saga of disempowerment of the peasantry in the era of globalisation.* New Delhi: Concept Publishing Company.

———. 2007b. 'Peasant resistance in West Bengal: A decade before Singur and Nandigram'. *Economic and Political Weekly,* 42(37): 3706–11.

Guha Roy, S. 2007. 'West Bengal and SEZ Policy', letter published in *Economic and Political Weekly*, 42(21): 1882.

Majumder, A; and Guha, A. 2008. 'A decade after land acquisition in Paschim Medinipur, West Bengal'. *Journal of the Indian Anthropological Society*, 43: 121–33.

CPI(M) supporter. 2007. 'Reflections in the aftermath of Nandigram'. *Economic and Political Weekly,* 42(18): 1594–96.

Government of India. 1967. 'Report of the Group of Experts on Land Acquisition'. Department of Agriculture, Ministry of Food, Agriculture, Community Development and Cooperation.

Medinipur District Collectorate (MDC). 1993. 'Land acquisition cases of Midnapore: Present status, problems, future strategy'. Unpublished report.

West Bengal Industrial Development Corporation (WBIDC), 1999. 'Destination West Bengal'. Calcutta: WBIDC.

West Bengal Legislative Assembly Proceedings. 1956 (Vol. 35), 1963 (Vol. 31), 1967 (Vol. 44), 1970 (Vol. 50), 1972 (Vol. 52), 1973 (Vol. 54), 1978 (Vol. 69), 1983 (Vol. 80), 1989 (Vol. 92), 1991 (Vol. 98), 1992 (Vol. 99), 1994 (Vol. 103). Calcutta: Government of West Bengal.

14

A blow to tribal life: The impact of privatisation in Orissa

Hari Mohan Mathur*

Beginning from the early 1990s, India's economic policies have undergone a dramatic change. These allow a bigger role for the private sector in the development process, a significant change in a long held position that gave primacy to the public sector. The policy reform proactively seeks to attract foreign direct investment (FDI) by creating investor-friendly conditions, which again is in complete reversal of policies that had been in existence for years to promote self-reliance. The current economic downturn seems to have only whetted appetite for more private investment, as the Government of India has further eased its norms to facilitate the flow of FDI in all sectors (Sinha 2009).

The new policy changes have occurred under the globalising influences from multilateral agencies such as the World Bank group and United Nations agencies. For example, in order to open up natural resources to multinational corporations, in 1994, the government amended its laws and policies on mining and minerals under pressure from the World Bank to facilitate the inflow of private investment, foreign as well as domestic, in the sector, which, until recently, was reserved exclusively for the State sector (Randeria 2003; CSE 2008). Multinational corporations (MNCs) have particularly been at the forefront in promoting the process of globalisation, liberalisation

---

* This is a revised version of a shorter article; earlier published in a special displacement and resettlement issue of *The Asia and Pacific Journal of Anthropology*, 10(4), December 2009, pp. 318–28.

and privatisation, as this opens for them new windows of investment and marketing opportunities.

New focus on privatisation

In line with the changed economic policy scene in India, all state governments are currently competing with one another in attracting investment, especially FDI. A state's success in development matters is now coming to be judged by the amount of investment which it attracts, and increasingly, the number of special economic zones (SEZs) that it promotes. The Orissa government also does not want to lag behind others in this race. Accordingly, it has introduced some new liberal industrial and other policies with the specific aim of attracting private industry, especially foreign direct investment (Barney and associates 2001).

Multilateral agencies have also lent their support to the Orissa government's initiatives in promoting private sector investment in development projects. For example, the UNIDO, UNDP and DFID recently co-financed a project, supporting Government of Orissa's preparation of a new industrial policy (UNIDO 2001). This included a comprehensive analysis of industrial situation, identifying the state's comparative advantages and opportunities, and making specific suggestions for the industrial policy. The recommendations were approved by the government, resulting in promulgation of the Industrial Policy Resolution (IPR) on 3 December 2001. The IPR's objective is to attract investment as a means to accelerate the development process.

More recently, the World Bank (2005) has assisted the Government of Orissa in its ongoing efforts to improve the investment climate. It carried out a study to assess the existing investment conditions, identifying and analysing major bottlenecks that deter investment and productivity. Drawing on the analysis, the report provided spe-cific policy recommendations to assist the government in its efforts to address these constraints, and develop a more investor-friendly policy and regulatory environment to enhance investment and growth rates.

Orissa is a resource-rich state, known for its abundant mineral, hydrologic, forest and other natural endowments, and, for this reason, it has attracted large development projects in irrigation, power, industrial and mining sectors right from the beginning of the planning era in the early 1950s (CSE 2008). It is no coincidence that many among the first major public sector projects undertaken in India were located in Orissa. Most natural wealth in Orissa happens to be concentrated in tribal areas, and such projects have resulted in massive displacement of tribal people. A UNEP (2003) report cites the examples of two projects that displaced mostly tribal people. In the Balimela Hydro Project, 98 per cent of those displaced were tribal people. Equally disastrous were the consequences for tribal people affected by the Upper Kolar Dam. In this project, they constituted 96 per cent of the total affected population.

The rich natural resource endowment and now the new investor-friendly policies have made Orissa a particularly attractive destination for large private corporations, including multinational corporations (MNCs), and they indeed are lining up in numbers to invest in this state, especially in steel, alumina and mining industries. Some of these MNCs are BHP Billiton and Rio Tinto (the two biggest mining companies in the world), POSCO and Arcelor-Mittal (the two steel giants), and Alcan (the second most important integrated aluminium producer). Orissa has indeed seen a rapid growth of projects in recent years, and the pace is set to grow even more rapid.

The Government of Orissa has signed numerous memoranda of understanding (MOUs) with large corporations, authorising them to operate in the state, and this number is increasing by the day. In September 2004, South Korean steel major POSCO, in alliance with Australian mining giant BHP Billiton, made an investment proposal worth over 10 million dollars, the largest so far. Others followed soon, including India's steel major Tata (Barik 2004). Arcelor-Mittal, the world's largest steel company, is the latest to arrive on the scene. A report by Morgan Stanley predicts that the state could draw $30 billion to $40 billion in new investments over the next five years. The process seems to go on and on.

Land for industry in tribal areas

The investment coming to Orissa is now creating a demand for land on a large scale, which is hard to meet. This was not unanticipated. In fact, the Draft National Policy for Rehabilitation of Persons Displaced as a Consequence of Acquisition of Land 1995 had warned that the demand for land, as well as for mineral resources and forest reserves located in areas predominantly inhabited by tribal people, would go up due to economic liberalisation:

> With the advent of the New Economic Policy, it is expected that there will be large-scale investments, both on account of internal generation of capital and increased inflow of foreign investments, thereby creating an enhanced demand for land to be provided within a shorter time-span in an increasingly competitive marked-ruled economic structure. Majority of our resources, including coal, iron ore, and manganese reserves are located in the remote and backward regions mostly inhabited by tribals…The demand for land may exist in terms of thousands of acres for industrial and power mega-projects, large-scale construction of multi-purpose irrigation dams, mining operations, reservation of forests and creation of sanctuaries, and national parks, construction of canals, highways and transmission lines (Government of India 1994).

This demand is mostly for land in tribal areas, and it is rapidly growing. For example, mineral-based industries are eyeing large chunks of land mainly in 15 districts, of which 13 are in Scheduled Areas where tribal people constitute around 68 per cent of the local population (Barik 2004). Over the years, most tribal land has been lost to either non-tribal people or taken over by the government and classified as forest or revenue land. In the Scheduled Areas, three-fourth of the land is State land, and most of it is under the category of forest land. Now, under the increasing pressure of privatisation and industrialisation, the access of tribal people to remaining land, water and forests, which they have previously enjoyed, is shrinking further.

For tribal people, who have already lost much land to government projects, and for whom land and land-based resources are their source of sustenance and the basis of existence as communities, the rising demand for lands from private companies is not good news (Mathur 2009). Globalisation and privatisation are rapidly undermining the access and control of tribal people over natural resources in their areas. Earlier, public sector projects had devoured huge chunks of their lands, but now the process of globalisation is going to accelerate the rate of their land loss even further. One observer noted: 'What a national agency would have taken, say, one hundred years to achieve, is being accomplished in less than a decade by the process of globalization, liberalization and privatization' (Munda 2005: 13).

Violations of tribal rights

Tribal people feel that in plans for development promoted by corporations, whatever land area that still remains in their possession is doomed to disappear. The worrisome aspect is that it is the state which is handing over tribal lands to industry in violation of India's constitution and laws. The tribal people in Scheduled V Areas, as defined in the Constitution of India, enjoy certain rights over land, forests, water bodies and other resources. In September 1997, the Supreme Court delivered a landmark judgment upholding these rights of tribal peoples to life and livelihood and to land and forests in a case on the issue of mining filed by Samatha, an NGO in Andhra Pradesh fighting for tribal rights. The court held that forests and lands in Scheduled Areas, whether government or tribal community-owned, cannot be leased out to non-tribal or to private companies for mining or industrial uses. It restricted mining activity in these areas only by the state mineral development corporation or a cooperative of the tribal people (SETU 1999). All such leases by state governments contravened Schedule V of the Constitution and were declared null and void.

The judgment, known as the Samatha judgment, is a significant check to restrain the state from encouraging indiscriminate exploitation of land, forests, water bodies and other resources for commercial purposes. The federal and state governments, however, chose to file an application in the Supreme Court in early 2000, asking for a review, which the judges dismissed. The efforts to circumvent this decision, which reinforces protective provisions of the Constitution for tribal people, are still continuing. Under pressure from multinational corporations, the Government of India and various state governments, including the Government of Orissa, are still looking for an escape route. In July 2003, the Government of Orissa went as far as constituting a state sub-committee chaired by the Chief Minister to discuss implications of the Samatha judgment, which concluded that it was not binding on the state. The reasoning was that there are enough laws in the state to ensure protection of tribal interests, and, therefore, Orissa could stay outside the purview of the court's ruling. On the basis of its interpretation of the ruling, the government decided to allow transfer of land in areas covered by Schedule V of the Constitution for mining and industrial purposes. This is a patently wrong inference, because the ruling was applicable to all states (Down to Earth 2005).

Moreover, laws favourable to tribal people are often not implemented as intended, with the result that the tribal people lose their legal rights. The Panchayats (Extension to Scheduled Areas) Act 1996, known as PESA, provides for mandatory recommendation of the gram sabha prior to granting lease for a minor mineral. In order to make PESA meaningful, more so after the Samatha judgment, the Government of India issued executive instructions in 1998, describing the modalities of consultation with the gram sabhas, and detailing the procedure for land acquisition in Schedule V areas. While adapting PESA, the Orissa government transferred the gram sabha powers to the zila parishad. Here again, Orissa is trying not to concede the rights of tribal people to be consulted on matters concerning the acquisition of land for project purposes, which PESA has specifically conferred on them (Mahapatra 2005).

Pampering corporations, ignoring people

Despite land scarcity and threat to tribal livelihoods, the government is trying to attract investment by all means possible (Mathur 2009). It is trying to create conditions most conducive to attract investors, and has gone out of the way in conceding several demands of MNCs at the cost of the government exchequer. It is propping up large investment projects by appropriating resources from its own people against their will and handing them over to corporations for the asking (Padel and Das 2010). It is becoming a perfect facilitator for entrepreneurs. It is acquiring land around mining sites, however truculent the population may feel. It manages permission for companies from the Union government (Down to Earth 2005: 27). It has simplified the lease procedure for quick processing, and has committed 18 rivers and reservoirs for exclusive use by industry for its water-intensive activities!

In its dealings with MNCs, the government is unable to conceal its weak-kneed character. In June 2005, the Pohang Iron and Steel Company (POSCO) signed an MoU with the state government for an investment worth $12 billion. Srinivas (2005a: 14) finds the deal flawed on many counts, especially on the lack of government's business sense. In terms of this agreement, POSCO is permitted to export a certain portion of its captive iron ore reserves to its steel works in South Korea, to rid it of its high alumina content. The government agreed to this export subject to an equal import of iron ore with low-grade alumina. Why should POSCO send out iron ore when it can be treated or beneficiated here? Srinivas asks (2005a: 14). Other countries have turned down such a proposal, refusing to open up mineral reserves to foreign investors. The fact is that India's iron ore is in great demand because of its low phosphorus content. Others see in this swap of iron ore, an unfair loophole through which iron ore can be exported before the steel mill is up in 2016 (Viswanath and Catching 2008: 32).

In its efforts to woo investment, government is promoting even those collaborative arrangements from which, while it gets little, MNCs stand to gain a lot. One such arrangement is the joint venture project which the Orissa Mining Corporation (OMC) signed, in which its own stake in this venture is only 26 per cent, and its share of profits is to come only from bauxite mining in Kalahandi district. The clause in the agreement for which the government is under attack, is that in case of increase in the mining costs, it is the OMC that will reimburse the joint venture. In addition, it will pay all taxes, including sales tax and statutory duties. In short, while Vedanta will manage the venture, the OMC will shoulder all revenue obligations (Down to Earth 2005: 28).

The case of the Gopalpur steel plant, now on hold, which the Tata Iron and Steel Company (Tisco) set up in Orissa in the mid-1990s, best illustrates how far the government can go to pamper large corporations. This plant will displace people from 25 villages in Chatrapur-Behrampur tehsils and 12 further villages at Pipalpanka Forest Reserve. In Pipalpanka Forest Reserve, the company plans to build a dam across the river Rushikulya. The reservoir and hydro power plant thus created, will meet energy requirements of the steelworks. Ironically, the people of Saroda, near Pipalpanka, have long sought permission from the government to construct a small dam on Rushikulya river for irrigation purposes. The area was surveyed twice, but permission to construct the dam was refused on both occasions, on the ground that the soil was not suitable for the purpose. Yet, when Tisco proposed a bigger dam, to be built at government expense for its own export profits, the soil suddenly became ideal for dam construction, and the Water Resources Department declared that the Pipalpanka Forest Reserve is ideal for dam building. In sum, what was refused to people, the government offered to Tisco on a platter. Shiva and Jaffri (1998) commented that the government seems to see its duty as the protection of Tisco rather than its own people, and added that the Gopalpur steel plant is an example of how power has moved from the people and their government into the hands of a large corporation. The Orissa government, and especially the Chief Minister, seems to be acting on the dictates of Tisco, and colluding with them to snatch away the people's livelihoods for their own personal and business interest.

The government support to Vedanta Alumina Limited (VAL), a company notorious for its past, including dodgy financial dealings, forced eviction of communities, and stolen government lands, recently created an uproar in the Orissa legislative assembly (Barik, *Down to Earth* 2005) Under attack was the government decision to let VAL, a subsidiary of Sterlite Industries (India) Limited (SIIL), set up an alumina refinery project in Kalahandi district, ignoring social and environmental concerns. In Niyamgiri Hill, the project will involve displacement of one of the most primitive tribes, the Dhongria Khond, of which only about 7,000 people are now left. It will be difficult to resettle these tribal people in an environment not akin to theirs. Recently, the Norwegian government's decision to expel Vedanta from its investment universe, based on the findings of an experts' panel set up by the Supreme Court of India, which the court ignored, created for it a piquant situation.[1] Even in the face of proven government complicity in violating laws of the land, the government, trying to appear impartial, imposed on the company a token fine. This shows how MNCs get away lightly even after committing grave violations of laws.

Some MNCs that have invested in Orissa have a dark history in countries where they have earlier established their shops. In order to attract investment, the government, however, overlooks their background. Therefore, companies with poor human rights record are also receiving a warm reception. One such multinational is BHP Billiton, notorious for its human rights abuses. For example, in Colombia, it holds a one-third interest in a consortium that owns and runs Carrejon Zona Norte, the biggest coal stripe mine in the world in the province of La Guajira in northern Colombia. From the beginning of operations in Carrejon Zona Norte, local communities were forcibly removed. The village of Manantial was simply broken up by violence and dispersed without any compensation to make way for the mining construction. This MNC has been allowed to work with POSCO in Orissa (Sarangi 2004).

The people fight back

In the initial years of planned development, acquiring land for development projects was a relatively simple affair. Land to resettle the displaced people was not so hard to find. Generally, people would then accept compensation without much fuss and move on. But, that is not the case anymore. Sachitanand (2005) explains the reason why: 'The circumstances are vastly different today. Educated by NGOs and radical groups, the tribals are no longer ready to move out of their ancestral habitat. The media tends to be sympathetic to their cause in reporting on their confrontation with state authority in eviction cases which, in turn, brings up embarrassing global attention.'

The demands of displaced people were initially modest, and the manner of protest largely peaceful. The protests were organised around inadequacies of compensation for the loss of land and livelihood, resettlement policies and their implementation. Over the years, the demands have grown, and protests are becoming increasingly aggressive (Das and Narayanan 2009). The amount of land loss and inadequate compensation are not the only issues to protest about.

> Even when the amount of land lost is not too great, displaced people often protest about other inconveniences caused by the newly established industrial plants. For instance, when the National Aluminum Company (NALCO) acquired a fairly long stretch of land to set up its own rail line from the mines to the plant, the company faced allegations from the displaced villager that the new railway tracks were causing waterlogging in the remaining portions of their cultivable fields, adversely affecting their livelihood. Similarly, when NALCO took water from the Brahmani River for its water supply, local people alleged that this had a negative impact on their water supply and demanded compensation. When they were refused extra compensation in both cases the villagers protested by sitting on the railway tracks and stopping water flow by breaking pipes and closing valve (World Bank 2005: 23).

What people find painful and are opposing is the sudden imposition of new projects on their lands, and their forced eviction against their will and knowingly ignoring their genuine concerns. They feel helpless against such thoughtless projects of the state, and now the corporations, and grumble that their lot is only to give up their lands and endure the worst forms of impoverishment, while the MNCs earn huge profits from their mineral-laden lands (Meher 2009).

A tribal leader from Jharkhand, a neighbouring state, expressing the anguish of his people over this iniquitous process of development, observed: 'People are simply pushed aside with a pittance, while the company is likely to make enormous profit. Even the Jharkhand Government is to get Rs 100 crore as royalty. There is such wealth in the land of *adivasis*. But they are deprived of even 0.1 per cent of this profit' (Kujur 2006: 181). Many people have even begun to relate their growing impoverishment to their productive lands.

The tribal people have lost patience with the kind of development model that is being promoted in Orissa, which they think is wholly iniquitous and is only making things worse for them. They are no longer prepared to suffer in silence its continuing onslaught on their lives and culture, and are instead becoming increasingly hostile to the establishment of new projects on their lands, which they expect to do nothing but ruin their lives, leaving them in a condition from which they can never hope to recover. They see no need for more projects, as these only produce more disasters, and are even demanding that they be left alone to determine the best way to use the natural wealth of their lands for furthering the development process.

In recent years, a number of NGOs have come up in Orissa to lend support to the struggles of tribal people against the ongoing industrial and mining development projects. They are based mostly in tribal dominated areas, which are currently the scene of burgeoning industrial and mining activity. The NGOs, like the people whom they support, tend to view large investment projects by MNCs as entirely harmful to the interests of the local population. However, such views are in direct conflict with the way the government sees its development programme. In Rayagada district, where alumina projects were adversely affecting the tribal people, an independent research study found the government agencies and the NGOs neatly ranged in two warring camps, with government personnel supporting the industry and NGO groups fighting for the cause of the poor tribal people (CSD 1999). A situation has now arisen in which the government and the NGOs do not see eye to eye on any development issue. One NGO that initially worked with the government in developing a resettlement plan later disassociated itself from the implementation process (A. Das 2006). They feel disillusioned. The role of NGOs in campaigning against harassment of the tribal people by industry employees is not appreciated in official circles, and they have, in fact, been threatened and blacklisted by the government. Even the financial grants earlier approved have been cancelled in some cases.

The protests against disastrous projects show no signs of a let up. On the contrary, they are gaining strength by the day, and becoming more and more militant. Some resentment against outsider initiatives to set up industries is often observed in natural resource-rich economies, and resource-rich Orissa is no exception. A recent study of investment climate in Orissa reported: 'There is a fairly widespread view that such large-scale investments will result in the exploitation of Orissa's natural resources and will drain away of her wealth, with very modest benefits to the local people either in terms of direct employment or growth of local, small-scale manufacturing units through ancillarization. Local sentiment strongly favours the concept of Bhumiputra (son of the soil) to take the lead in establishing industries' (World Bank 2005: 29). Even companies that offer very liberal packages fail to escape social resistance. However, resistance to new development initiatives is often also rooted in genuine grievances of the displaced people (Srinivas 2005b). People are not necessarily opposed to development, but they do expect the process to bring benefits for all, not for a handful of affluent groups.

Crushing resistance to projects

In Orissa, opposition to development projects is taken as an activity directed against the government, and it is not tolerated. Any sign of resistance, especially to private sector mining, industrial and other projects, is viewed seriously, and the government steps in to nip it in the bud, using any amount of force required. A study team found overwhelming evidence of excessive use of coercive methods by the district authorities against the tribal population in Kacheipadar and Sunger, two villages of Orissa. The team reported: 'In both the villages, hundreds of people, including young boys and girls, were arrested and taken into custody. Teargas shells were fired in Kacheipadar. In the Sunger area, the company let loose goons to harass the villagers. An elderly woman in Sunger village informed the observers that she had never seen police in her life until the recent incident, and now, policemen were frequently knocking on the door' (CSD 1999: 21). Strangely, the attention to the plight of these people by Agragamee, a local NGO, was misunderstood in the government circles, resulting in its blacklisting.

The use of force to crush opposition has often resulted in not only grievous injuries to protestors, but also death. This happened in Gopalpur, for example. 'On December 30th, 1995, the Indian Prime Minister laid the foundation stone of the Gopalpur Steel Plant. The next day, local people demolished it. In August 1996 the Orissa government frustrated by this campaign of resistance, began a 'reign of terror' ... Six platoons of armed police — a total of 6,000 armed men — were sent in to harass the villagers and break up the protests. During four days of protest the police beat the villagers with canes and used tear-gas shells on women and children. Two women died as a result, and many other people were injured, some severely' (Shiva and Jafri 1998: 353).

The police tend to remain on the side of the MNCs. In Lanjigada of Kalaandi, Orissa, where tribals and Dalits are fighting against the Sterlite project, the government has given reserved forest area for mining to Sterlite Corporation, and Sterlite has negotiated with Aloca of US for exporting aluminium. When company goons attacked local people, the Niyamgiri Surakshya Samiti (NSS) went to the police to file cases against the company officials, but the police refused to accept their complaint. On the contrary, when NSS broke the foundation stone just one day after it was set up by the Chief Minister on 8 June 2003, the police promptly arrested and sent them to jail. In 2000, the Prakritik Sampad Suraksha Parishad (PSSP) faced police firing, but the judicial inquiry commission has not held anybody responsible for the incident (Sarangi and associates 2005).

The Kalinganagar incident represents the worst form of brutality by the state against its own citizens. On 2 January 2006, 12 tribal people died on the spot when police opened fire on a crowd protesting over land acquisition for the construction of a steel plant in Kalinganagar industrial complex. The use of force to displace people and acquire their lands for development projects, with little or no compensation, is nothing new in Orissa. For the government, this case is, however, particularly worrisome, as it has occurred when several large corporations have signed MoUs with the government, and are making huge investments especially in steel and alumina industries. There is apprehension that tribal unrest may scare investors, jeopardising the rapid industrialisation programme, which the government has launched with great fanfare in Orissa (Sengupta 2006; Johnson 2006).

This unfortunate incident has again exposed the government's failure on the resettlement front. Whenever new projects come up, tribal people are routinely evicted from lands that they have been living on since times immemorial. With their only source of livelihood gone, they often end up poorer than before. The government's commitment to treating fairly the people displaced by its own development programmes remains weak.

Responding to the crisis

Faced with the widespread anger of people against new projects, and the pressure from international donors to adopt a policy on involuntary resettlement, around 2001, the Government of Orissa began to see the need for a comprehensive policy to address the emerging problems of development-induced displacement. The United Nations Development Programme (UNDP) then came forward to assist the government with a comprehensive resettlement and rehabilitation policy draft conforming to the highest international standards.

The UNDP Orissa Resettlement Policy Project commenced in July 2003 and ended on 30 September 2005. To prepare the policy, the project undertook an in-depth and a wide-ranging research, study and consultative process. The Orissa State Resettlement and Rehabilitation Policy Draft 2005, which emerged from this exercise, also took into account the best elements from resettlement policies everywhere, and, more importantly, it incorporated the people's perspective on problems of resettlement, which often is so sadly missing in most policies and practices (Mathur 2007).

This UNDP resettlement policy draft was submitted to the Government of Orissa when the project terminated, but nothing much happened for a long time. It took the killing of 12 tribal people in Kalinganagar on 2 January 2006 to jolt the government to look at the UNDP draft, and initiate the process required for its adoption as resettlement policy. Within a week of the incident, the government, in a knee-jerk reaction, hurriedly set up a ministerial committee to finalise the policy, and the government quickly came out with its own policy draft (Jena 2006). In May 2006, the government finally announced the much awaited policy to resettle and rehabilitate people who would be displaced by new industries and other development projects (Government of Orissa 2006).

Although the resettlement policy which the government has issued differs in some respects from the UNDP draft policy, and has lost some of its innovative provisions intended to support both investment and equitable benefit-sharing, it is a welcome development (Shankaran 2009; Padel and Das, this volume). In the present context, the policy is definitely a timely and significant intervention. It certainly is a big step forward.

The Orissa government resettlement policy, however, evoked criticism on several counts. It has been dubbed by critics as 'pro-industry'. 'The new policy, which appears to be silent on the questions raised by those resisting displacement, has been welcomed by the industry' (P. Das 2006). For this reason, it has failed to win over those spearheading the anti-displacement agitation at Kalinganagar. The people there are determined to not give up their lands and homes to make way for industries, and the deadlock persists.

The present serious situation in regard to resettlement of those affected by development interventions stems not only from the policy inadequacy, but also from the lack of implementation capacity. Displacement has gone on in Orissa since the beginning of development era in India from the late 1940s, but there is nothing to show that it ever received the attention that it deserves. The World Bank Orissa study (2005) also highlights that the regulatory role of the state to limit negative spill-over has not been discharged effectively because of weak implementation capacity.

A raw deal for the tribal people

Experience suggests that where projects fail to manage resettlement adequately, the affected people face a number of impoverishment risks, which include landlessness, joblessness, homelessness, marginalisation, morbidity, food insecurity, loss of access to common property assets, and social disorganisation (Cernea 1995 and 2000; Mathur and Marsden 1998; Mathur 1999). The Orissa experience with projects involving resettlement is no different. It suggests that the involuntary resettlement impact on tribal people has been overwhelmingly disastrous (Padel and Das 2008). Development projects have only led to their further impoverishment (Mahapatra 1999a; Pandey 1998). An impoverishment risks study by Mahapatra (1999b) found evidence that confirms the loss of income-generating assets, employment, common property, decline in health and nutritional levels, and loss of social and human capital, as risks that widely afflict the project-affected people.

The impact of impoverishment associated with displacement is far more severe for tribal people than for the non-tribal groups. These people have a special relationship with the land and the forest which are their main sources of livelihood. The fact is that what is lost in not a piece of land or a patch of forest, but a way of life, which displacement tends to destroy and which no resettlement effort can ever compensate (Padel and Das 2008; Perera 2009). Tribal people lack skills to change over to any other productive activity for a living. Dislodged from their lands, many simply move to the nearest town to join the burgeoning number of slum-dwellers. A Government of India report noted:

> While the problem of displacement upsets not only the tribal population but also the general population who come within the submergence of acquisition area, there are some basic points of difference in the type of difficulties faced by the two communities. The most important one relates to the cultural aspects of life. While the kinship of the general population is spread far and wide, this is not true of the tribal groups whose habitation may be confined only to certain specific areas. Any unsettlement in the case of the later, therefore, deals a far more crushing blow to their socio-cultural life than in the case of the former. Secondly, on account of low educational level and a tradition of a life of comparative exclusiveness and isolation, the Scheduled Tribes find adjustment more difficult in an alien location. The third important reason for which the displacement is felt more acutely by the Scheduled Tribes than by the general population is that the former depend for their living including trade, profession and calling, on roots and fruits, minor forest produce, forest raw materials, game and birds and the natural surrounding and endowment, far more than the general population. The rehabilitation programmes of the displaced families taken up in various states generally do not take into account this particular aspect of the tribal displacement. Finally, the Scheduled Tribes being economically the weakest of all communities find it harder than others to settle on new avocations on a different site of settlement (Government of India 1984: 178).

There are also other reasons why tribal people face relatively more risks of impoverishment. Even where well-intentioned policies and programmes exist for them, 'they cannot take advantage of the policy or ad hoc rules and they rarely, if ever, venture to go to courts or appellate authorities to vindicate their rights or redress the wrongs done to them' (Mahapatra 1998: 216–17). The Indian legal system is cumbersome, dilatory, expensive and often weighted against them partly due to their poverty, illiteracy and low social status. The unhelpful attitude of officials also contributes to their impoverishment. Officials tend to deny them their due, often on the ground that the land where they have lived for centuries is legally not theirs. Even where they are eligible for compensation, it is common for the officials to calculate compensation amount for land on the lower side, denying them the real value of their properties.

It is no surprise that the tribal people see the current development policies quite differently from the way the government visualises them. For the Government of Orissa, these alone can ensure development for all. On the other hand, the tribal people see them, with their insatiable appetite for lands, forests and other resources, as a direct threat to their survival. In the past, projects involving displacement often left them impoverished, in a condition worse than they were in ever before. Neither does the current increased inflow of private investment give them any hope of a better deal.

Note

1. 'Norway expels Vedanta. SC judgment awaited', *The Times of India* (New Delhi edition), 16 November 2007.

References

Barik, Satyasundar. 2005. 'Legal landmine: Government support to Vedanta's alumina project in Orissa creates more uproar; company pays token fine'. *Down to Earth*, 14(8): 7–14.

———. 2004. 'The iron ore rush: Companies can't wait to mine Orissa's rich deposits: Government goes with the flow'. *Down to Earth*, 13(10): 15.

Barney, I., A. B. Ota, B. Pandey and R. Puranik. 2001. *In focus: Engaging stakeholders: Lessons from three eastern India business case studies.* Swansea: Centre for Development Studies, Resource Centre for the Social Dimensions of Business Practice.

Bose, Ruksan. 2006. 'Mine or yours? Dense forests and tribals caught in a forester-miner fight'. *Down to Earth*, 14(16): 7–8.

Cernea, Michael M. 1995. 'Understanding and preventing impoverishment from displacement: Reflections on the state of knowledge'. Keynote address presented at the 'International Conference on Development-induced Displacement and Impoverishment', 3–7 January, University of Oxford.

———. 1996. 'Understanding and preventing impoverishment from displacement: Reflections on the state of knowledge', in Christopher McDowell (ed.), *Understanding impoverishment: The consequences of development-induced displacement*, pp. 13–32. Providence/Oxford: Berghahn Books.

———. 2000. 'Risks, safeguards, and reconstruction: A model for population displacement and resettlement', in Michael M. Cernea and Christopher McDowell (eds), *Risks and reconstruction: Experiences of resettlers and refugees*, pp. 11–55. Washington DC: The World Bank.

Council for Social Development. 1999. 'Report on the visit of a team of the Council for Social Development to Rayagada and Bhubaneswar, 11–18 January 1999'. New Delhi: Council for Social Development.

Centre for Science and Environment. 2008. 'State of India's environment: Fifth report (Part one: National overview)'. New Delhi: Centre for Science and Environment.

Das, Achyut. 2006. 'Government-NGO collaboration in resettlement', in Hari Mohan Mathur (ed.), *Managing resettlement in India: Approaches, issues, experiences*, pp. 220–41. New Delhi: Oxford University Press.

Das, Prafulla. 2006. 'Spreading resistance: Widespread resistance by tribal people to projects causing displacement forces Orissa government to plan a comprehensive relief and rehabilitation policy'. *Frontline*, 23(2): 35–36.

Down to Earth. 2005. 'Orissa's on overdrive: Has the state overcommitted itself? Why has delivery become so fragile?', *Down to Earth*, 13(22): 27–29.

———. 2006. 'Not bowed down: Clash between tribals and the police at Orissa Steel Complex', *Down to Earth*, 14(17): 12.

Das, Smriti and N. C. Narayanan. 2009. 'Alloyed projects, metalled resistance: A case of bauxite mining in Orissa', in N. C. Narayanan (ed.), *State, natural resource conflicts and challenges to governance: Where do we go from here?*, pp. 221–46. New Delhi: Academic Foundation.

Evans, Geoff, James Goodman and Nina Lansbury. 2002. 'Introduction-globalisation: Threats and opportunities', in Geoff Evans, James Goodman and Nina Lansbury (eds), *Moving mountains: Communities confront mining and globalisation*, pp. xi–xxiii. London and New York: Zed Books.

Government of India. 1984. 'Report of the Working Group on Development of Scheduled Tribes during Seventh Five Year Plan (1985–90)'. New Delhi: Ministry of Home Affairs.

———. 1994. 'National Policy for rehabilitation of persons displaced as a consequence of acquisition of land (Draft)'. New Delhi: Ministry of Rural Development.

Government of Orissa. 2006. 'Orissa Resettlement and Rehabilitation Policy 2006'. Bhubaneswar: Department of Revenue.

Human, Joe and Manoj Pattanaik. 2000. *Community forest management: A casebook from India.* Oxford: Oxfam.

Jena, Manipada. 2006. 'Orissa Draft Resettlement and Rehabilitation Policy, 2006'. *Economic and Political Weekly,* XLI(5): 384–87.

Johnson, Jo. 2006. 'Orissa killings reveal a dark side to India's stellar growth'. *The Financial Times,* 12 January.

Kujur, Joseph Marianus. 'Resettlement debate: Continuing the historical injustice'. *Social Change,* 36(1): 175–90.

Likosky, Michael B. (ed.). 2005. *Privatising development: Transnational law, infrastructure and human rights.* Leiden and Boston: Martinus Nijhoff Publishers.

Mahapatra, L. K. 1998. 'Good intentions or policies are not enough: Reducing impoverishment risks for the tribal oustees', in Hari Mohan Mathur and David Marsden (eds), *Development projects and impoverishment risks: Resettling project-affected people in India,* pp. 217–36 New Delhi: Oxford University Press.

———. 1999a. *Resettlement, impoverishment and reconstruction in India: Development for the deprived.* New Delhi: Vikas Publishing House.

———. 1999b. 'Testing the risks and reconstruction model on India's resettlement experiences', in Michael M. Cernea (ed.), *The economics of involuntary resettlement: questions and challenges.* Washington, DC: World Bank Publications.

———. 2005. *Tribal rights and entitlements in Land, forest and other resources.* Paper prepared for the UNDP Resettlement Policy Project.

Mathur, Hari Mohan and David Marsden. 1998. *Development projects and impoverishment risks: Resettling project-affected people in India.* Delhi: Oxford University Press.

Mathur, Hari Mohan. 1999. 'The impoverishing potential of development projects: Resettlement requires risk analysis'. *D+C Development and Cooperation,* 6: 24–26.

———. 2007. 'Involuntary resettlement policy of Orissa, India: A new deal for the displaced in a globalizing world'. Paper presented at the 'Workshop on Involuntary Population Displacement and the Evolving Policy Response', at the '12th International Metropolis Conference on Migration, Economic Growth, and Social Cohesion', 8–12 October, Melbourne.

———. 2009. 'Tribal land issues in India: Communal management, rights and displacement', in Jayantha Perera (ed.), *Land and cultural survival: The communal land rights of indigenous peoples in Asia*, pp. 163–92. Manila: Asian Development Bank.

Meher, Rajkishor. 2009. 'Globalization, displacement and the livelihood issues of tribal and agriculture dependent poor people: The case of mineral-based industries in India. *Journal of Developing Societies*, 25(4): 457–80.

Menon, Meena. 2005. 'The battle for bauxite in Orissa'. *The Hindu*, 20 April.

Munda, Ram Dayal. 2005. 'Globalization and the challenges of tribal development'. The 2005 Durgbai Deshmukh Memorial Lecture. New Delhi: Council for Social Development and India International Centre.

Panda, Ranjan. 2006. 'Undermined: Orissa villagers say relocate us, we want to leave right away'. *Down to Earth*, 14(20): 32–33.

Padel, Felix and Samarendra Das. 2006. 'Double death: Aluminium's links with genocide'. *Social Scientist*, 34(3–4): 55–81.

———. 2007. '*Agya*, what do you mean by development', in Rakesh Kalshian (ed.), *Caterpillar and the Mahua flower: Tremors in India's mining fields*, pp. 26–46. New Delhi: Panos.

———. 2008. 'Cultural genocide: The real impact of development-induced displacement', in Hari Mohan Mathur (ed.), *India social development report 2008: Development and displacement*, pp. 103–15. New Delhi: Oxford University Press and Council for Social Development.

———. 2010. *Out of this earth: East India adivasis and the aluminum cartel.* New Delhi: Orient Black Swan.

Pandey, Balaji, A. K. Patro, C. V. Rao, K. K. Padhi and S. Mallick. 1998. *Depriving the underprivileged for development.* Bhubaneswar: Institute for Socio-Economic Development.

Perera, Jayantha (ed.). 2009. *Land and cultural survival: The communal land rights of indigenous peoples in Asia.* Manila: Asian Development Bank.

Randeria, Shalini. 2003. 'Cunning states and unaccountable international institutions: Legal plurality, social movements and rights of local communities to common property resources'. *Archives of European Sociology.* KLIV: 27–60.

Sachitanand, N. N. 2005. 'Dark clouds over Orissa projects'. *The Indian Express*, 25 April, Bhubaneswar.

Sarangi, Debarajan. 2004. 'Mining "development" and MNC'. *Economic and Political Weekly*, 39(17): 1648–50.

Sarangi, Debarajan, Rabishankar Pradhan and Saroj Mohanty. 2005. 'State repression in Kashipur'. *Economic and Political Weekly*, XL(13): 1312–14.

Sengupta, Somini. 2006. 'Fatal clash at mill site shows perils of India's rise'. *New York Times*, 13 January.

SETU. 1999. 'Development, equity, and justice: Adivasi communities in India in the era of liberalization and globalization'. Report on a roundtable, 6–9 April 1998, New Delhi. New Delhi: Minority Rights Group.

Shankaran, Deepa. 2009. 'Like a white flag? The gendered dimensions of the Orissa state policy on resettlement and rehabilitation', in Lyla Mehta (ed.), *Displaced by development: Confronting marginalization and gender injustice*, pp. 225–45. New Delhi: Sage.

Sinha, P. 2009. 'Government eases FDI norms: Move to open up all sectors including retail, insurance', *The Times of India*, 12 February.

Shiva, Vandana and Afsar H. Jafri. 1998. 'Stronger than steel: An Indian people's movement against indiscriminate economic development'. *The Ecologist,* 28(6): 349–53.

Srinivas, A. 2005a. 'This land is ours: Why people are fighting mining projects in Orissa'. *The Times of India,* 4 August, New Delhi.

———. 2005b. 'POSCO reveals weak-kneed state'. *The Times of India,* 12 October, New Delhi.

United Nations Environment Programme (UNEP). 2003. *Environmental refugees.* Nairobi: UNEP.

United Nations Industrial Development Organization (UNIDO). 2001. 'Industrial Policy Resolution 2001 of the State of Orissa (Volume 1: Proceedings of the Policy Review Workshop, Economic Analysis and Policy Recommendations; Volume 2: Industrial Growth and Socioeconomic Progress in Orissa)'. Vienna: UNIDO.

Viswanath, Anurag and Rebecca Catching. 2008. 'Orissa steel project tests India's mettle'. *Far Eastern Economic Review,* 171(9): 30–34.

World Bank. 2005. *Orissa: Investment climate assessment 2005: Towards a high performing state.* New Delhi: The World Bank Finance and Private Sector Development Unit, South Asia Region.

Part V

An alternative view

15

The limitations of current approaches to resettlement

Jayantha Perera

This chapter argues that current involuntary resettlement models are of limited value in understanding economic, social and cultural impacts of physical displacement caused by state-sponsored development interventions. The models focus more on how to deal with such impacts than with how to avoid them. As a result, they pay little attention to the processes that generate loss of livelihood and shelter, food insecurity, and social disarticulation. Instead, they emphasise that such displacement, although painful and traumatic, could be converted into 'development opportunities' for the displaced with proper planning and investment. This chapter argues that this rationale of a 'development opportunity' stems from modernisation and development theories, and is of limited value. It also argues that by focusing on post-displacement phases of development interventions, and by labelling them as 'development opportunities', the involuntary resettlement models circumvent the addressing of human rights issues that are related to loss of shelter, income and livelihood sources, and social disarticulation. This chapter makes a plea to discard the current involuntary resettlement models, and to develop another that focuses on human rights-based approaches to development, displacement and resettlement.

The two dominant involuntary resettlement models, namely, the Four-stage Framework and the Impoverishment Risk and Reconstruction Model, are first reviewed to distil the commonalities between the two. Based on this review, the chapter will discuss each model's claim that development-induced displacement would create development opportunities for the displaced people. This is followed by a critique of the models by demonstrating how they share the limitations and false premises of modernisation and development theories. The chapter will then outline key developments in the human rights discourse over the past decades, and how this discourse could provide a solid base for a robust involuntary resettlement model, which focuses on how to protect displaced peoples' human rights.

Resettlement and rehabilitation models

Four-stage framework

Two theoretical models dominate the involuntary resettlement literature: one is Thayer Scudder's Four-stage Framework, and the other is Michael Cernea's Impoverishment Risks and Reconstruction Model. The first was introduced in the early 1980s, while the other in the 1990s. Both focus on physical resettlement of large groups of people. Scudder claims that the Four-stage Framework (FSF) provides 'a successful process of involuntary resettlement with dam construction, with success simply defined as development that is environmentally, economically, institutionally and culturally sustainable into the second generation' (2005: 32). According to him, the framework is 'predictive' and 'behavioral'. It predicts how people who are forced to relocate *en masse* would benefit from such relocation, provided sufficient opportunities and resources are available at relocation sites. Such opportunities and resources would create the correct mindset among them to become risk-taking entrepreneurs by the time the second generation takes over relocation sites. The framework is also prescriptive — it tells how to manage each stage of resettlement so that resettlers and project authorities could share project benefits.

The FSF presents resettlement processes with four distinct temporal stages or phases. The first phase is 'planning and recruitment', which engages all displaced people in project planning and decision making. The prescriptive part of the model says that this is the time to inculcate among them the idea that they will eventually become the project beneficiaries, not mere project-affected persons (PAPs). This phase could start several years before actual physical relocation.

The second phase is 'adjustment and coping', and it starts soon after the physical removal of PAPs from their communities and their relocation at resettlement sites. During this phase, income levels drop, and, as a result, they tend to become 'risk-averse'. Moreover, multi-dimensional stress at the household level peaks; so does household expenditure. They try to build up their own 'closed social systems' to cope with withdrawal anxieties and psychological and socio-cultural shock of their new environment. Cash compensation and other resettlement assistance are hardly sufficient to restore their income and livelihood, or to kick-start economic recovery or to re-establish their broken social networks. In a 'closed' community, therefore, resettlers would not take risks of starting new economic enterprises which would open their closed social system. This phase could last three to 10 years or more.

The third phase is 'community formation and economic development', which is the most critical phase of the four, because, during this phase, resettlers either come out of their closed socioeconomic system to look for opportunities to improve their livelihood, or resign to their fate and continue to lag in poverty without integrating into wider socio-cultural and economic-political systems. Three triggers are required to initiate this giant leap. Radical behavioural changes among resettlers are one. Another is the availability of 'sustainable' development opportunities into which settler initiative can be channelled. Third is the presence of an 'appropriate infrastructure and access to markets' (Scudder 2005: 37). If these triggers are present, resettlers would start to feel 'at home' in their new environment. Moreover, their dependency on project authorities will gradually wither away, as they diversify their income and livelihood sources. With some leisure, fresh identity and improved food security, they would form community organisations to express their identity by building schools, clinics, community centres and religious centres at their resettlement sites. In short, resettlers would by now have rediscovered themselves, and started a new era of their life with self confidence, self identity, and better income and livelihood in an active community.

The final phase of 'handing over and incorporation' marks the successful end of the resettlement process. This phase could last over five to 15 years. The handing-over process will start at several levels. Project authorities hand over project assets to resettlers' organisations, such as water-user associations or to line ministries, or to the private sector. By this time, living standard of the second generation resettlers would be similar to or better than that of their host communities. Resettlers gradually take interest in participating in national and regional political culture, and compete with others for their share in regional and national resources and power systems. If they successfully complete this complicated and risky journey, they would cease to be resettlers.

Impoverishment risks and reconstruction model

The Impoverishment Risks and Reconstruction Model (IRRM), too, follows a linear path, from displacement to relocation and eventually to rehabilitation. It attempts to measure the degree of 'multiple vulnerabilities' that displaced people encounter, and to find ways of offsetting such 'risks'. In other words, it elaborates risks associated with displacement, explains the behavioural responses of displaced people to such risks, and guides the reconstruction of their livelihood and life chances. The IRRM is multi-dimensional and multi-staged. It is multi-dimensional because it includes displaced people, planners and strategists and host populations; it is multi-staged because it covers four stages of recovery and development.

Project authorities, development planners, and displaced people try to understand risks of displacement, impoverishment, and marginalisation during the first stage of the model. This is followed by the second stage, when displaced people react to such risks, especially to the risk of impoverishment. During the third stage, project authorities, financiers and strategists develop resettlement plans to minimise the risks of impoverishment, and to guide displaced people on how to overcome them. Such plans are implemented during the fourth stage in order to restore and improve income and livelihoods of displaced people, making them better off compared to what they were prior to the development intervention that caused their physical displacement (Cernea 1997).

The IRRM emphasises the role of bureaucracy in the key processes of relocation and rehabilitation. Thus, the model is essentially a resettlement planner's tool. The model takes for granted that the displacement of large numbers of people is inevitable in the process of development. It emphasises that development interventions would bring opportunities for PAPs to improve their life chances, and also to share benefits. In other words, the model assumes that a carefully planned and well-executed resettlement program delivers development opportunities for all displaced people of a development intervention, enabling them to improve their income and livelihood, and life chances.

The key concept of the IRRM is 'impoverishment', and the model deals extensively with impoverishment risks inherent in involuntary resettlement. The model is premised on the ground that 'impoverishment is not a fatality and that it should not be tolerated with passive resignation. Displacement is a socially caused disruption, not a natural disaster, and can be counterbalanced. Redressing the inequities caused by displacement and enabling affected people to share in the benefits of growth is not only possible but is also necessary, on both economic and moral grounds' (Cernea 1997: 1570).

The model espouses an egalitarian development policy. Each displaced person, regardless of his economic, social and political status, will have opportunities to improve his life chances. In short, by losing, he could gain more.

The model lists eight risks associated with development-induced displacement: landlessness, unemployment, homelessness, marginalisation, increased morbidity and mortality, food insecurity, loss of access to common property, and social disarticulation. These risks are general sub-processes or trends, and their 'convergent and cumulative effect is the rapid onset of impoverishment' (Cernea 1997: 1572). The emphasis of the model from this point onwards rapidly shifts to post-displacement, that is, the resettlement phase. Although the model identifies a variety of sources of impoverishment associated with physical displacement, it fails to recognise the fact that similar risks exist during the resettlement phase as well. Instead, the model takes the resettlement phase as the period when displaced people could overcome or avoid impoverishment risks associated with physical displacement, by exploiting development opportunities created by the development intervention.

The IRRM suggests that reconstructing and improving the livelihoods of those displaced require 'risk-reversal' through explicit policies and strategies that are backed up by adequate financing. In addition, 'convergence between actions and resources of both the 'agent' that triggers displacement and the population that is displaced is required' (Cernea 1997: 1580). This convergence is to take place as early as possible in the project cycle, and all actors have to contribute to the recovery and improvement of life chances of the displaced. However, the 'agents' who trigger displacement and the

PAPs who suffer, occupy polarised positions. This inequality directly limits displaced peoples' opportunities for benefit-sharing, and the accountability of the 'agent' in implementing 'risk-reversal' strategies described in the model.

The model emphasises that impoverishment risks will undoubtedly become real, but fortunately they can be avoided if anticipated, and purposively counteracted with good planning and by allocating adequate resources to implement the plans. This is the key contradiction in the model — a component of the model destroys its other components. Then, the question is, why do we build models? As Dwivedi (2002: 217) points out, the IRRM has become more a 'self-destroying prophecy' than a development model.

However, despite the internal contradictions, the strength of IRRM lies in four aspects. First, it emphasises the importance of comprehensive resettlement planning after identifying and quantifying the risks associated with displacement. Second, it stresses the importance of identifying and implementing economically viable options for restoring the productive capacity of displaced populations through employment-based strategies. It provides a tool to sensitise planners to different forms of losses confronting a displaced population. It helps them anticipate these losses, and to devise appropriate policies and strategies to prevent, or at least minimise, them. Third, it emphasises the importance of resettlement policies that would help improve the living standards of displaced people. By reversing risks, the model provides development policies that go beyond displacement; the model encapsulates a wider development discourse. Fourth, it extends risk analysis to affected communities as well. It moves away from the conventional risk analysis that concentrated on the investors' risks in the development project and the project's economic rate of return. It recognises that displaced people also share major risks arising from development interventions that displace them.

Comparison between the two models

If the details and the policy prescriptions are removed, the FSF and IRRM show significant similarities. One major similarity between the two is their linear approach to displacement, resettlement and rehabilitation. The stages or phases are well demarcated in both models.

Another common feature is their emphasis on the inevitability of physical displacement. Displacement is considered as unavoidable, and, therefore, is an inevitable characteristic of development. The key message of the two models is that it is not necessary to worry too much about displacement, but that one must find ways and means to minimise physical, economic, social and psychological impacts of physical displacement, by creating opportunities and avenues for those displaced to participate in development interventions, so that they could benefit from them. Both models stress that development interventions trigger growth and benefit not only the displaced persons and communities, but also national or regional populations. For this, vigorous planning is vital, and it is the responsibility of project authorities to formulate resettlement plans and implement them in consultation with PAPs. Thus, both models are essentially planning tools. They claim that through better policies and laws, and planning tools such as 'reconstruction' plans, resettlement experiences could be transformed into development opportunities.

Figure 15.1: Four-stage Framework and impoverishment Risks & Reconstruction Model: Experience of Displaced Persons

Four-stage Framework	*Risk & Reconstruction Model*
Phases	*Phases*
Anxiety, stress, hopelessness	Understanding impoverishment risks
Losses (impoverishment)	Losses (impoverishment)
Gains (development)	Vigorous planning/participation
Consolidation & handover	Reconstruction (reversal of risks/losses)

One important difference, however, between the two models is PAPs' perceptions of their fate. The FSF pays attention to how displaced people feel about their displacement and resettlement. Initial fear of change helps resettlers, according to the FSF, to reconstitute their lives after a major insult to their physiological, psychological and socio-cultural well being. The IRRM, on the other hand, is not concerned with how displaced people feel about the trauma caused by involuntary displacement and resettlement; instead, it expects PAPs to be patient until the project authorities convert the physiological, psychological and socio-cultural trauma generated by development interventions into development opportunities.

Both models fall into what Dwivedi (2002) called the 'reformist-managerial' approach to development. It takes mainstream development as given, and displacement as an unfortunate phase that some people have to go through to achieve 'development' benefits. Both models emphasise that it is worth going through some temporary difficulties to harvest immense project benefits. Thus, displacement, together with resettlement, is a social equalising process that, in the end, makes the world a better place to live for all.

> The tendency is to normalize displacement as a consequence of development that has happened in the past and will happen in the future. The concern of this [approach] is to minimize the adverse outcomes of displacement. As a result resettlement becomes the main problem area of focus ... Since resettlement is the main focus, its inadequacies and failures become main areas of concern. The search is for effective ways of designing and handling resettlement for which appropriate legal, managerial and policy frameworks are sought (Dwivedi 2002: 7120).

Both models use 'resettlement' instead of 'displacement' as their key concept. The word 'displacement' carries certain historical realities, such as forced eviction or practices of acquisition without compensation. But the two models avoid 'displacement' not because of its association with historical realities, but to avoid addressing of human rights such as the right to shelter, decent living and property, which are intrinsically associated with physical displacement. In other words, the two models cater more to the development interventions than to ensuring human rights of displaced people. In fact, a state finds it more comfortable to resolve resettlement problems than avoiding the displacement of large groups of people. As the two models insinuate, 'resettlement' connotes the completion of a process which has bad and adverse roots, that is displacement. 'Resettlement' does not carry the connotation of forced eviction; instead, it informs us that a group of people are being assisted to improve their socioeconomic conditions. The physical location of the operation is, thus, radically shifted from their original lost land to allocated resettlement sites. This shift from displacement to resettlement in both policy and physical senses, in fact, has served a useful purpose of legitimising and labelling of (mainly) state functions associated with development as resettlement and relocation activities, which are far removed from the violation of human rights that are caused by physical displacement of people.

Development opportunity: Is gain possible only with loss?

Gain is possible only with loss: Four-stage Framework

The FSF assumes that land acquisition is inevitable in development interventions, which results in loss of property, livelihood and social networks. Such losses generate a transitional period which is chaotic, and is prone to creating impoverishment. It could continue for many years, sometimes for several generations, corresponding to the first two phases of the framework, namely planning and recruitment, and coping and adjustment. For displaced people, such adjustments often mean poor living standards, multi-dimensional stress, the need to learn new employment skills, spending all earnings on household expenses, and inadequate household labour. Thus, they are involuntary testing times for them in which they have to make critical behavioural changes. The FSF emphasises that if such difficulties and stress are handled carefully, with sufficient resources, planning and stakeholder participation, the transitional period will be reduced to a few years, and soon the project would usher in a golden era for them, which would not only provide them with better life chances but, more importantly, make them risk-taking entrepreneurs and shareholders of development programmes.

As resettlement literature amply demonstrates (Scudder 2005), such gains cannot be guaranteed, as there are several formidable obstacles to overcome before getting an opportunity to share project benefits. One obstacle is displaced persons' unwillingness to take risks that could jeopardise their fragile socioeconomic systems and limited political networks. Another is their desire to stay as 'closed' communities. They tend to consider their host population and those who are engaged in project activities ('others') as hostile strangers, and are reluctant to develop social, cultural, economic and political networks with them. On the other hand, they may think that 'others' consider them as inferior, strange and untrustworthy people, and are unwilling to associate with them (Abeyratne 1982; Perera 1985a, 1985b and 1993; Munsayac 2006). Either way, resettled households tend to live in closed communities, and prefer continuity over change.

Another obstacle to overcome is the limited resources available to generate and sustain development opportunities at resettlement sites. By the time physical constructions are completed, project completion reports are written, accounts are audited, and project officials are withdrawn from the project area, there are hardly any leftover project resources to improve resettlers' livelihood. Rehabilitation works are sporadic and usually are not supported with sufficient funds. Generally, once a project is completed, regardless of whether its resettlement program is completed or not, resettlers will soon be forgotten by project authorities, as in the case of the Batang Ai Resettlement Scheme in Sarawak (Perera 2009). As the FSF predicts, at the most, project benefits would be enjoyed by second or third generations of the original resettlers who went through the trauma of displacement and impoverishment. But there is no assurance that even the second or third generations will benefit from the project, as the obstacles sometimes become insurmountable (Abeyratne 1982; Perera 2003).

Gaining from their losses becomes difficult when resettlers have to compete with their host communities, who would try to usurp limited goods that are available at resettlement sites. Moreover, host communities sometimes try to limit resettlers' access to common resources such as pastures and jungle products. For example, at the Batang Ai Resettlement Scheme, when resettled Ibans communities tried to collect wild ferns from nearby jungles, their host community issued injunc-tions against such land use (Perera 2003).

Although resettlement plans suggest ambitious and appropriate actions on behalf of resettlers, such actions are hardly implemented. The litmus test for the success of such plans is how fast and how well resettlers regain pre-project income and social standards, and then move beyond. The overall picture is that resettlers definitely become poorer and remain poor for a long period of time, despite project activities aimed at helping them. Scudder pointed out that out of 44 dam projects which displaced and resettled people, only three improved their living standards, and only five projects restored them. This is, as Scudder says, an 'unacceptable and unsatisfactory project impact' (2005: 86).

Risk the losses, and gain more: The IRRM

The IRRM takes a straightforward approach to deal with how to gain from loss. It suggests controlling adverse impacts of physical displacement (which causes resettlement and reconstruction) through a strategy.

> The general socioeconomic risks intrinsic to displacement can be controlled by an integrated problem-resolution strategy, but not by piecemeal palliatives; and by allocating adequate financial resources. The adverse effects cannot be tamed simply through cash compensation for lost assets. Only concerted multifaceted cooperation and action by all the social actors involved can pursue development, rather than just risk mitigation. Resettlement is *apt to generate opportunities* to improve lives, not only disrupts them (Cernea 1997: 1580, emphasis added).

The IRRM emphasises that the key task in the resettlement process is to reverse the risks that are identified; in other words, to transform them into development opportunities. The model does not, however, indicate when the risk-reversal process should start, as impoverishment risks of a development intervention could become apparent during the pre-project phase or planning phase, or even during project implementation phase. The starting point of the reversal is vital, as the volume of financial and human resources required for the reversion will be determined by the point of entry in the process. If the process is divided into phases, namely displacement and resettlement, the model seems to emphasise the importance of reversal of risks after physical displacement, and, in fact, as part of the resettlement process. As a result, it is not clear whether the reversal of risks is a component of the 'integrated problem-solution strategy' or not.

In the IRRM, the classification of personal and community losses serves a major diagnostic function towards mapping their form and contours. But losses are depicted as static or blueprint descriptions of a major upheaval a resettler would undergo. In other words, the losses or the risk of losses in the IRRM are not process-based. This allows the model to avoid the difficult task of explaining the anticipated and unanticipated consequences of displacement, including human rights violations, and the humiliation and indignation accruing to those who are to be displaced. As the resettlement literature aptly demonstrates, potential risks are, in fact, not risks, but actual losses that any displaced person or a community would undergo. Unless this cardinal truth is acknowledged, it is difficult to grasp how rapidly and with what certainty displaced people get impoverished in the processes of displacement and resettlement. 'Even if one were to look at the consequences only in terms of losses, an explicit list shows that displaced people potentially lose assets, resources, livelihoods, institutions, networks, traditions, values, identities, rights, entitlements, securities, services and knowledge' (Dwivedi 2002: 718). Some losses can be computed, others cannot be; assets and livelihood losses can be valued, but identities and networks cannot be. On the other hand, what entitlements could be provided to those displaced when they are resettled to compensate the losses, such as loss of community, networks, and human rights violations? What they actually should get in such a situation must not be limited to project-specific 'entitlements' in cash or kind; instead, they should have a *right* to development, a *right* to food security, a *right* to housing, a *right* to live in dignity, and a *right* to earn a decent living. If these rights are recognised, instead of labelling them as risks, and actions are taken to honour these rights and to help displaced people to realise their rights fully, there is some probability that displaced people could overcome impoverishment and social disarticulation.

The encapsulation of losses in a broader context of risks, as suggested by the model, would blur the actual losses a displaced person suffers. If a farmer loses his piece of land to a project, it cannot adequately be replaced by providing a piece of land at a resettlement site. For a farmer in an agrarian community, land means many things in different contexts. It is his means of livelihood, social network source, the determiner of social status, and the licence to exploit the adjacent common property to graze his cattle and to collect firewood and other jungle products. The possession of a piece of land elsewhere will not bring all these back to him. Often its value, even as a livelihood source, is doubtful. Moreover, the farmer may prefer to take the opportunity of becoming a petty businessman in an urban area. But often, he cannot do so because of the lack of capital. In such a situation, providing land for land is certainly not a 'development opportunity' for him.

Old wine in new bottles: Modernisation theory and involuntary resettlement

The rationale of the FSF and IRRM stems from modernisation and development theories which tie up development with change. In fact, it is possible to consider both the FSF and IRRM, too, as modernisation models for a special social group called 'development-induced displaced persons'. In the 1950s and 1960s, modernisation theory was dominant in the development discourse. Modernisation is a process that increases economic and political capabilities of a society through bureaucratisation. Modernisation is widely attractive because it 'enables a society' to move from being poor to being rich (Inglehart 1997: 5). It espouses development as transforming traditional, simple, Third World societies into modern, complex, westernised societies. It prescribes that a wholesale change must take place in under-developed societies in order to break vicious circles of poverty, ignorance, and low productivity. In other words, modernisation requires a society to leave its traditions behind if it wants to become modernised.

Modernisation is premised on development planning, as a key strategy to achieve desired change. The whole development scenario is 'the search for a rationally coordinated system of policy measures that can bring about development' (Myrdal 1968: 58). In this sense, modernisation is a systemic process, in the sense that economic development, cultural change and political change go together in coherent even to some extent, predictable patterns. This is a controversial claim, as it implies that some paths of socioeconomic change are more likely than others — and, consequently, that certain changes are foreseeable (Inglehart 1997).

In many ways, modernisation theory represents an extension of the basic conceptual apparatus of growth theory. Although economic factors continue to occupy a central place in modernisation theory, its scope extends to include the analysis of social and institutional change in an inter-disciplinary manner. This approach, in fact, enriches modernisation theory, as it complements the core focus on economic transformation. Given the social context of Cold War competition in the South within which modernisation theory unfolded, there has also been a tendency towards optimism. This optimism has erased some rather pessimistic and somewhat uncomfortable elements of growth theory. Thus, modernisation theory favours a more positive view of change. It has made capitalist development available to all who would have it. Rather than being difficult to attain, growth and development were made easier to achieve and sustain with bureaucratic ethos and interventions (Mills 2000).

Modernisation theory presents a mixture of development factors, such as technological change, capital accumulation, changing values and attitudes, and migration, which could be analysed from a variety of disciplinary perspectives. Interestingly, these factors could be read and understood as main ingredients of the FSF and IRRM. Some of the key components of modernisation theory, which closely resemble the key components of the two involuntary resettlement models, are discussed in the following paragraphs.

Society, and its values, institutions, social groups and regions, can be divided as 'traditional' and 'modern'. The two spheres are antithetical and, for the most part, exist separately. They are 'duel societies' and could exist for a short while side by side in a country, but the modernisation process eventually dissolves the traditional sphere, giving way to modernised sphere. This key process of modernisation is found in the first two stages of the FSF, where resettlers move from closed social systems to an open social system, with the ability to take more risks and participate in wider social, economic and political arenas. In the IRRM, the concept of 'self-destroying prophesy', and its predictive capacity to warn early, trigger action and inform the adoption of targeted counter-risk measures, tally well with this key dichotomy — tradition and modern — of the modernisation theory.

The direction of change that the modernisation process induces is broadly similar to the third and fourth phases of the FSF, and the reconstruction and reversal of the risks phases of the IRRM. Although the rate of change may vary, and temporary social dislocations may occur among social groups, modernisation is inevitable and assumed to be beneficial to all. Likewise, in the context of involuntary resettlement, although development intervention would displace people from their homes, communities, social networks and economic activities, they as resettlers, will find the intervention as a 'development opportunity' that would improve their living standards and link them with other regions and economic systems, enabling them to move upwards in social, economic and political scales. The direction is linear from 'tradition' to 'modern', from poverty to improved living standards, and from a narrow, particularistic, closed social system to a wider, open social system with many development opportunities.

The modernisation theory postulates that the internal diffusion of key factors of development, such as change in values and attitudes, technical innovations, and investment capital, is the key driver of the modernisation process in the West. In contemporary Third World societies, the diffusion of such factors is normally initiated from outside, through economic resources, transfer of technology and communication. In the FSF and IRRM, innovation, planning and investment funds also come from outside — from bilateral or multilateral donor agencies, regional development funds or rural development programmes sponsored by the state. Such innovation, planning and investment, while bringing development, would certainly displace large number of people, especially in rural and remote areas. But, it is a small price to pay for modernisation, which would improve the life chances of the majority of the population (including those displaced) and usher in egalitarian ethos and democratic institutions into hitherto feudal or highly hierarchical societies, where status, rather than achievement, directed the life chances of an individual or a household.

According to the FSF and IRRM, the ingredients of modernity, such as equality and guaranteed source of income, could more easily be found at resettlement locations than in traditional village communities or in remote areas where indigenous peoples often live. At resettlement locations, each displaced household will get a plot of land of the same size. In agrarian societies, every attempt is made to provide agricultural land of equal size and of good quality to each household (Perera 1993). This post-displacement socialism will place all resettlers in a good stead to start their lives from scratch, and to develop fast with equal development opportunities (Perera 1993 and 2003). 'When opportunities are available, it is interesting that resettlers around the world tend to follow the same development strategies' (Scudder 2005: 39).

A vital component of the modernisation process is radical change in traditional and cultural values and attitudes. At resettlement sites, according to the FSF, the separation from or reduction of past cultural inventory of each household makes innovative activities easier than if resettlement had not occurred, simply because post-displacement behaviour is less culturally constrained (Scudder 2005). On the other hand, the IRRM explains that only through 'convergence' between the actions of project authorities and resettlers, the reversing of the impoverishment risks and the reconstruction of livelihoods could be initiated (Cernea 1997: 1580). In addition, the IRRM urges that the state should pursue a development policy which accommodates such convergence, and supports it by allocating needed resources, including adequate budget, skills and core values, so that sustainable development opportunities become available. In both the FSF and IRRM, the vital role of the state in accelerating the modernisation process through resettlement is clear.

Although the key triggers of development originate from outside, the modernisation process essentially depends on factors internal to each society. Important to the overall process, according to modernisation theory, is the removal of various social and cultural barriers to modernisation. Many barriers are linked to the continuing existence of a traditional sector. Deficiencies resulting from backward internal structures are the fundamental causes of underdevelopment. If structural changes can be introduced, growth and modernisation will follow. This statement is a good summary of the FSF and IRRM — promised equal life chances, light cultural inventory, assistance from outside, and participation in regional and national political systems. These would encourage resettlers to break away from their traditional social, economic and cultural barriers. Such a breakaway would enable them to enjoy sustainable development opportunities, as modern, egalitarian and risk-taking citizens.

Although the state introduces and accelerates the modernisation process in resettlement locations, the speed of diffusion of modern ethos, institutions and practices, within a society, is critically dependent upon the modernising elite of that society. These 'change agents' act as innovators and diffusers. Therefore, development policies should target them, especially during initial phases of modernisation, to facilitate rapid structural transformation. Scudder (2005) explains in the FSF the importance of attitudinal changes, so that resettlers could move from risk aversion to risk taking. This process needs to be identified and facilitated at each resettlement location. A clear sign of such a process is the formation of community organisations by resettlers. Community-building exercises such as the formation of water-user associations, farmer unions and rural councils, are some examples of this process. Such organisations need leaders who are accepted by others as capable of delivering and taking responsibility for community well being. The second generation resettlers with better education and exposure to the outside world often provide such leadership. They are well informed, and ready to take risks and to try out innovations. They are the people who gradually take higher economic risks, diversify their livelihood and make investments. This catalyst function of such community leaders is a key aspect of the second and third phases of the FSF, and also in the 'reversing the risks' phase of the IRRM.

The need for a new paradigm of involuntary resettlement

The modernisation paradigm that dominated the development discourse in the 1970s and 1980s provided a theoretical foundation for the involuntary resettlement policy of World Bank. The involuntary resettlement policy borrowed some key principles from the modernisation paradigm. Among them was the principle that '...large-scale, capital intensive development projects accelerate the pace toward a brighter and better future. If people were uprooted along the way, that was deemed a necessary evil or even an actual good, since it made them more susceptible to change' (Robinson 2003: 10). However, in the 1990s, a new development paradigm highlighted both benefits and costs (or ill effects) of such large-scale development programmes, which physically displaced millions of people every year, without their consent or without paying careful attention to their human rights. The new development paradigm, which emphasises human rights, arose from several movements or processes. First is the rapid development of international legal instruments to safeguard the 'rights' of the people, particularly those who are affected by development programmes. Second is the sheer magnitude of physical displacement and impoverishment created by development projects worldwide in the late 1980s and 1990s. Special applied research institutes such as the Refugee Studies Centre at the Oxford University in the UK, and the North-Eastern Social Research Centre in Guwahati in India, were established to record and analyse displacement and impoverishment of project-affected persons. They heightened awareness among policy and law makers about development-induced displacement of people and their impoverishment. The third is the disproportionate number of marginalised and vulnerable people, such as indigenous peoples, who became the victims of mega infrastructure development projects, such as hydropower, water supply, transport, bridges, dams and railways. Their plight has been widely recorded and made public by various national and international advocacy groups. Such groups have also brought local agitations into the international arena of human rights.

Development discourse and human rights

One of the baffling questions in involuntary resettlement literature is: why have international development agencies largely ignored the steadily growing human rights discourse (which is embedded in various international law instruments) in their involuntary resettlement policies? The main reason is the widespread and continued belief that change is beneficial for developing countries and technological and communication changes would make them 'modern'. This perception has seeped into the involuntary safeguard policies formulated by the agencies even in the 21st century. As infrastructure projects become a stimulus for economic and regional growth, many developing countries borrow money from international donors to build highways, hydropower projects, harbours and airports, which inevitably displace a large number of people. It is much easier for the borrower and the donor to label the impacts of such development interventions as 'development opportunities', than to accept that such activities have direct impacts on displaced persons' human rights, and to take appropriate actions to avoid such impacts or at least to minimise them.

The second reason is the marginal position safeguard policies, such as involuntary resettlement and indigenous peoples policies have held until recent years in overall development policy at international and regional development agencies. At such institutions, a few isolated but determined social scientists, who were concerned about the welfare of displaced people, failed to make a major dent in development thinking. They did not dare to emphasise the importance of human rights aspects of development interventions. Michael Cernea, the first sociologist at the World Bank, for example, could not have taken the involuntary resettlement policy to its current status over a period of 30 years, if he had attempted to highlight 'resettlement entitlements' as 'human rights.' Cernea (1994), in one of his papers — 'Bridging the research divide: Studying refugees and development oustees' — in fact, discussed the importance of paying attention to human rights of 'oustees' and refugees who lost their land and other property. But instead of highlighting the importance of avoiding human rights violations in displacement-induced development, he took the view that ill effects of displacement should be considered as 'risks', and such risks could be avoided through proper project management, which includes consultation, formulation of entitlement matrices and their application, and vigorous monitoring and evaluation of the progress of implementation of resettlement programs. A classic example of sidestepping from paying attention to human rights was the refusal by the management of the World Bank in 1998 to endorse the recommendation of its Operations Evaluation Department to replace 'restoration' of income and livelihood with 'improvement' of income and livelihood of resettlers. The department had convincing arguments, based on the findings of a global study on involuntary resettlement, to recommend the improvement of resettlers' income, instead of restoration of their income:

> In most instances, the upheaval attending relocation should be managed as a development opportunity and funded accordingly. Restoration is an appropriate short-term objective, but improvement of the productivity, living standards, and lifestyles of the displacees is as valid a long-term objective of the projects as are the improvements planned for the primary beneficiaries (World Bank 1998: 73).

The World Bank management pointed out that the benchmark for income levels to achieve are already in operation — 'income restoration' is a criterion to assess the adequacy of resettlement, and 'income improvement' is to be emphasised in case of poor and vulnerable people affected by a project:

> Current Policy provides, as a requirement, that income restoration be the minimum benchmark against which the adequacy of resettlement is assessed. Improvement in the incomes of affected persons is an objective of the policy; it is especially important when the affected people are poor and/or vulnerable. Staff will assess resettlement plans based on a range of feasible options designed to ensure that resettlement arrangements are consistent with the skills and preferences of affected persons (World Bank 1998: 73).

The third reason for sidetracking human rights in the development discourse was the poor rate of ratification of international legal instruments, such as declarations and covenants by the developed and developing countries. Even where they are ratified, their inclusion in domestic laws and application take many years or even decades. Often, states in developing countries are reluctant to recognise basic human rights, such as right to development, right to self-determination, right to participation, right to life and livelihood, and rights of vulnerable communities of their populations. This is mainly because of their fear that such human rights would undermine state sovereignty and the privileges of its favoured ethnic groups. However, during recent decades, in several democratic countries, the judiciary has displayed a vibrant 'judicial activism' in the form of intervention in development project formulation and implementation, in order to safeguard human rights of the affected people. Such activism has encouraged public interest litigation to challenge development projects on human rights grounds. It also has widened the legal standing of NGOs and other community-based organisations, enabling them to articulate and contest the state's actions which could harm the general public, especially vulnerable groups such as slum dwellers (Ahuja 1997).

The concept of 'human rights' often tends to put off development agencies and donors. One reason for this is the poor understanding of human rights, and the misconceptions that surround them. In fact, as Weissbrodt and de La Vaga (2007) articulated, human rights highlight the core values of mankind. Human rights are inherent; they do not have to be bought, earned or inherited. They belong to individuals simply because they are human. Human rights are universal; they are the same for all people, regardless of race, sex, religion, political or other opinions, national or social origins. They are inalienable; they cannot be taken away. They exist even when they are not upheld. Finally, human rights are indivisible; all human beings are entitled to freedom, security and decent standards of living. Thus, human rights set standards for human beings to live with dignity, and provide a common language for action. They help identify and formulate responses to problems.

Over the past 60 years, the United Nations (UN) authoritatively defined human rights listed in the Universal Declaration of Human Rights (1948), and in dozens of subsequent treaties, declarations and other instruments. Among the most important human rights treaties drafted by the United Nations (UN) are the International Covenant on Economic, Social and Cultural Rights and the International Covenant on Civil and Political Rights. Those two human rights covenants have been ratified by 155 and 160 nations, respectively. The covenants, together with the Universal Declaration on Human Rights, comprise the International Bill of Human Rights. In addition, in 1994, the United Nations Sub-commission introduced several draft procedural principles on human rights and environment, which have direct impact on development interventions such as dams, mining and road infrastructure projects in Third World countries. Among the principles, the following are of key value. The right to:

- information concerning the environment;
- receive and disseminate ideas and information;
- participate in planning and decision-making processes;
- freedom of association for the purpose of protecting the environment or the rights of persons affected by environmental harm; and
- effective remedies and redress for environmental harm in administrative and judicial proceedings.

These procedural human rights demonstrate the rapid movement of international law towards development rights of affected people in development interventions. The rights to information and participation, together with the right to effective remedies and redress for environmental harm, are now well established in domestic laws in many developing countries. In several countries, the judiciary, in particular, has taken these procedural human rights as directly applicable to judicial review of administrative decisions pertaining to development.

In international law, involuntary resettlement is not considered as a separate sphere of concern. As a result, involuntary resettlement-related human rights are found in the environment and indigenous peoples rights. The Draft Declaration of the Principles on Human Rights and the Environment 1994, highlighted the close relationship between environment and human rights. It recognised and emphasised the importance of established human rights, such as the right to life, livelihood, health and culture. These human rights display the inseparable link between sustainable development and environmental justice. In international law, three key sets of rights are now well established regarding the relationship between sustainable development and environmental justice: first, 'the right to life, including the right to a healthy environment'; second, 'the traditional and customary property rights of indigenous and other local communities'; and third, 'participatory and procedural rights', such as the right to be informed and right to know.

International human rights law, a branch of international law, takes individuals, their association with communities, and their relationship to environment, as key areas of investigation. In this regard, several bundles of human rights could be identified. One is 'civil and political rights; the second is 'economic and social rights'; and the third is 'solidarity' rights. The earliest manifestation of such rights in an international legal instrument was the two UN covenants of 1966 on 'civil and political rights', and 'economic, social and cultural rights'. 'Civil and political rights' are usually characterised as individual rights entailing freedom from arbitrary governmental interference, or as guaranteeing participatory rights in civil society. They are more readily recognised and protected than other categories of human rights. 'Economic and social rights' encourage governments to pursue policies which create life conditions enabling individuals, or in some cases groups, to develop equally, to their full potential. They require progressive realisation in accordance with available resources. 'Solidarity rights', which include peace, development, and a good environment, generally apply to groups or communities, rather than to individuals, and may require states and international agencies to cooperate with each other and assist those who do not have sufficient resources to achieve the targets.

These three sets of rights serve three useful functions in improving human rights. First, drawing on existing civil and political rights, they can be used to give individuals, groups and NGOs access to information, judicial remedies, and political processes. Thus, this function is one of empowerment, facilitating participatory and informed decision making, and compelling governments to meet minimum standards of protection of life and property. Second, to treat a decent, healthy and viable environment as an economic or social right, comparable to those already protected in the international covenants on civil, political, social and cultural rights (of 1966). The main justification for this function is that it would bestow 'environmental quality' a comparable status to other economic and social rights. The third function is treating 'environmental quality' as a 'solidarity right', which would mainly entail governments and international organisations cooperating to provide the necessary resources, skills and technology to achieve environmental objectives.

The UN Conference on the Human Environment, held in Stockholm in 1972, declared that 'man has the fundamental right to freedom, equality and adequate conditions of life in an environment of a quality that permits a life of dignity and well-being'. Twenty years later, at Rio in 1992, the UN Conference on Environment and Development (the Earth Summit) asserted that 'human beings are at the centre of concerns for sustainable development. They are entitled to a healthy and productive life in harmony with nature'. The failure of the Rio Declaration to emphasise human rights demonstrates continuing uncertainty and debate about the relationship between human rights and international environmental law. Despite this uncertainty, there is a steady growth in the recognition of environmental rights as human rights, which includes both individual and community rights. The fundamental right to a healthy and productive life in harmony with nature has been elaborated to include right to livelihood, right to property, and right to environmental information and decision making. Most of these rights are now considered as environmental rights of individuals and communities, and are also considered paramount in environmental protection. As a result, they are increasingly being incorporated into constitutions and national legal systems either explicitly or by judicial interpretation of other constitutional guarantees.

Since the 1980s, many nations and human rights advocates have devoted their increased attention to strategies for achieving economic, social and cultural rights of indigenous peoples. The UN Declaration on the Rights of Indigenous Peoples (2007) is a good example of international recognition of human rights of hitherto marginalised indigenous peoples. Similarly, at the country level, various legislations have been enacted to recognise their rights. The enactment of the Scheduled Tribes and Other Traditional Forest Dwellers (Recognition of Forest Rights) Act 2006 in India, for example, shows the preparedness of the state to recognise human rights of specific categories of people within its territory.

Involuntary resettlement and human rights

In this context, it is possible to identify several core human rights, which are well established in international law and could be applied directly to development-induced displacement of a large number of people. The rationale and need for reviewing human rights in this chapter arise from the proven inadequacy of so-called 'entitlements' of affected people in resettlement plans prepared by national governments following involuntary resettlement policies. The key issues that are still not resolved fully in these policies are displaced peoples' rights to receive compensation at replacement cost of the property acquired or damaged by a development intervention, assistance to restore and improve their income and livelihood, and to maintain or to re-establish their social networks. In involuntary resettlement literature, such rights are labelled as 'entitlements' or as 'development opportunities'. As discussed earlier, authorities who implement resettlement plans to ensure that such entitlements are provided to the displaced person adequately and promptly, often do not have adequate resources, institutional capacity and a strategy to realise them. What is more disturbing is that, often, a development intervention which is locally funded does not consider the payment of replacement cost of acquired property and improvement of income and livelihood as mandatory. The only compensation that a displaced person or a household would get in such a project is 'statutory' compensation as per domestic land laws or land acquisition laws and regulations. Such minimalist compensation for property is not even sufficient to restore their livelihood and income. Such laws and regulations, in fact, do not even mention the need for the restoration and improvement of livelihood and income of displaced persons. The net result is that most of the displaced people fail (at the least) to restore their pre-intervention income and livelihood, and linger on in poverty (Scudder 2005; Perera 2003; Fernandes 2007). Thus, the remedy of providing 'development opportunities' through 'entitlements' enshrined in international and national involuntary resettlement policies is woefully inadequate to ensure basic human rights of displaced persons.

Ownership of and access to land as a human right

This chapter argues that it is prudent to apply a human rights-based approach to development processes to safeguard human rights of displaced people, so that they could escape from further impoverishment and also benefit from development interventions that have deprived them of their human rights.

There is no specific right to land (except in case of indigenous peoples) which has been recognised by international law. However, there remains the possibility that land rights can be derived from treaty rights, and, in particular, from the right to life, private life, property and access to justice, as recognised by the Universal Declaration of Human Rights, the 1950 European Convention on Human Rights, the UN Covenant on Civil and Political Rights 1966 and the American Convention on Human Rights 1996. Article 17 of the Universal Declaration of Human Rights states: 'Everyone has the right to own property alone as well as in association with others" and "no one shall be arbitrarily deprived of his property'. These key human rights were not codified in the Covenant on Economic, Social and Cultural Rights or in the Covenant on Civil and Political Rights. However, the two covenants state that property cannot be a basis for discrimination. Both covenants also declared within the principle of 'self determination' that 'all peoples may, for their own ends, freely dispose of their natural wealth and resources…, based upon the principle of mutual benefit, and international law. In no case may a people be deprived of its own means of subsistence' (Article 2[1]). While neither of the two covenants specifically protects the right to property, there are several other human rights treaties that protect against discrimination in regard to the right to property. For example, the Convention on the Elimination of All Forms of Racial Discrimination forbids racial discrimination with regard to 'the right to own property alone as well as in association with others' (Article 5[v]) and 'the right to inherit' (Article 5[vi]).

In 2002, the Commission on Human Rights passed a resolution entitled 'Women's equal ownership, access to and control over land and the equal rights to own property and adequate housing' to highlight the importance of the recognition of property and land rights of women. This resolution addresses a vital inadequacy in conventional involuntary resettlement programmes, namely the right of women to be compensated for loss of property and their right to receive resettlement assistance. Quite often, a displaced family is the unit of compensation and resettlement assistance. As a result, the head of the family or household, who is usually a male (husband, father, eldest son), gets the entire compensation package in his name. There are numerous occasions of husbands wasting cash compensation on gambling, or starting a new life with another women abandoning his wife and children by moving to a faraway place. Women who owned property jointly with their husbands, or owned property as part of their dowries, suddenly lose control over such assets with physical displacement. Women's property ownership is rarely recognised at resettlement sites when allocating land and housing facilities.

Right to life and healthy living

Both the right to life and the right to respect private life and property entail more than a simple prohibition on government interference; governments additionally have a positive duty to take appropriate action to secure these rights. This is the key element of the decision of the European Court of Human Rights in the cases of *Guerra v Italy* (1998) and *Lopez Ostra v Spain* (1994).

The right to life has been a fertile source of environmental jurisprudence in several national jurisdictions, especially in India. Indian courts have also used the right to life (Section 21) and the environmental provisions (Section 48A) of the Indian Constitution as the justification for judicial review of executive decisions regarding involuntary land acquisition which lead to impoverishment of people and the degradation of environment. Indian courts have also shown what can be done through litigation to advance not merely procedural rights, but also basic human rights. In India, the courts have not only closed down industries causing harm to health and safety, but have held that 'the right to life includes the right to live with human dignity and all that goes along with it', including the right to live in a 'healthy environment with minimal disturbance of ecological balance'. Thus, the courts have drawn an explicit link between environmental quality and human life. This point of view was also expressed by the Supreme Court of Sri Lanka, especially in the case of *Bulankulama v Minister of Industrial Development* (Eppawala case) (Supreme Court of Sri Lanka, Application No 884/99 FR). One way of reading these court decisions is to consider them as a guarantee of effective remedies (Principle 10 of the Rio Declaration of 1992).

The wide recognition of right to life and healthy living establishes displaced peoples' right to development, housing and livelihood, which, in most cases, is inextricably linked with the right to property, especially to land, as in case of indigenous peoples' rights to communal management of ancestral land (Perera 2009). This right rests on two pillars: the notion of access to subsistence and shelter, and the right to livelihood. It is the state's obligation to ensure the protection of an environment that allows safe living. Safe conditions of living ensure land for livelihood and housing. This is the message of the Special Rapporteur on 'Adequate housing as a component of the right to an adequate standard of living':

> Without the adequate legal recognition of individual as well as collective land rights, the right to adequate housing, in many instances, cannot be effectively realized. The right to land, however, is not just linked to the right to adequate housing but is integrally related to human rights to food, livelihood, work, self-determination, and security of person and home and the sustenance of common property resources. The guarantee of the right to land is thus critical for the majority of the world's population who depend on land and land-based resources for their lives and livelihoods. In the urban context legal recognition of land rights is often critical to protecting the right to adequate housing, including access to essential services and livelihoods, especially for the urban poor (Kothari 2007: 10).

Housing

Article 25 of the Universal Declaration of Human Rights states: 'Everyone has the right to a standard of living adequate for the health and well-being of himself and of his family, including... housing'. The Committee on Economic, Social and Cultural Rights, in 1991, further defined the right to adequate housing in its General Comment 4. The Committee noted that the right to adequate housing is of 'central importance for the enjoyment of all economic, social and cultural rights'. Housing as a right has two components: it is a part of an adequate standard of living, and there can be no discrimination in how it is provided. The General Comment listed seven ways in which housing may be considered to be adequate: legal security of tenure; availability of services, materials, facilities and infrastructure; affordability; habitability; accessibility; location; and cultural adequacy.

Kothari (2007) has convincingly argued that it is necessary to strengthen the legal framework of international law to promote and implement the human right to land, as the framework has direct bearing on implementing the right to adequate housing. He has pointed out that 'land as an entitlement is often an essential element necessary to understand the degree of violation and the extent of realization of the right to adequate housing' (2007: 10). He further pointed out, based on his extensive field visits to many parts of the world, that inadequate housing is directly related to land and land rights. In involuntary resettlement, a household or a community first loses its land, and then housing and other structures that are directly related to its livelihood and social status. Therefore, as Kothari points out, the right to land is a 'cross-cutting issue'.

Forced eviction

The Committee on Economic, Social and Cultural Rights in 1997 adopted General Comment 7, confirming that forced eviction violates the Covenant on Economic, Social and Cultural Rights. In 1991, the Committee was able to convince the Government of Dominican Republic to desist from a plan that would have forced the eviction of 70,000 slum dwellers in a Santo Domingo community. The government had begun to remove thousands of slum dwellers, without providing them with alternative housing facilities, in order to build a national monument. Based on the information provided by Geneva-based NGO Center for Housing Rights and Evictions, the Committee declared that the forced evictions violated Article 11 of the Covenant, and persuaded the government to stop the forced evictions. As a result of the efforts of the NGOs and the Committee, the community in Santo Domingo has received more secure tenure and better social services. This is particularly relevant to the involuntary resettlement policies in many countries, which provide scant protection to squatters and informal dwellers, particularly in urban areas. Their rights to housing and decent livelihood are still to be incorporated into national laws and involuntary resettlement policies of international donor agencies.

Sustainable development

The right to sustainable development can be viewed as the sum of all civil, cultural, economic, political and social rights, with particular focus on the right to a healthy environment. The United Nations' Stockholm Declaration (1972) and Rio De Janeiro Declaration (1992) recognise that the state has the right to exploit its own resources pursuant, however, to its own environmental policies. Rational planning in this regard constitutes an essential tool for recognising any conflict between the needs of development, and the need to protect and improve the environment. Human beings are at the centre of concerns for sustainable development. They are entitled to a healthy and productive life in harmony with nature. In order to achieve sustainable development, environmental protection shall be an integral part of the development process, and cannot be considered in isolation from it.

'Development opportunities' into human rights

In 1997, the Sub-Commission on the Promotion and Protection of Human Rights of the UN Commission on Human Rights affirmed the right of persons to be protected from forcible displacement, and to remain in peace in their homes, on their own lands and in their own countries. The sub-Commission convened a panel of experts in Geneva on the practice of forced evictions. They came out with a report — 'The practice of forced evictions: Comprehensive human rights guidelines on development-based displacement'. They reaffirmed that development is a comprehensive economic, social, cultural and political progress, which aims at the constant improvement of the well being of the entire population and of all individuals, on the basis of their active, free and meaningful participation in development, and in the fair distribution of benefits resulting from them. The guidelines are not exhaustive, but provide a benchmark to develop human rights further to deal with forced eviction, displacement and involuntary resettlement.

The implementation of General Assembly Resolution 60/251 of 15 March 2006, entitled 'Human Rights Council', further strengthened the 1997 guidelines and elaborated the implementation process. They recognise that widespread forced evictions can occur in a variety of contexts, including, but not limited to, conflicts over land rights; development and infrastructure projects, such as the construction of dams or other large-scale energy projects; land acquisition measures associated with urban renewal; housing renovation; and clearing of land for agricultural purposes or macro-urban projects (Robinson 2003; Kothari 2007). The guidelines outline specific preventative obligations related to forced evictions, including development-induced displacement. Some key guidelines are:

- State provides security of tenure and maximum protection against the practice of forced evictions for all persons under their jurisdiction. Special consideration is given to the rights of indigenous peoples, children and women, particularly female-headed households and other vulnerable groups.

- State ensures that no persons, groups or communities are rendered homeless, or are exposed to the violation of any other human rights as a consequence of forced eviction.
- State formulates legislation and policies to protect individuals, groups and communities from forced eviction, paying due regard to their best interests. States are encouraged to adopt constitutional provisions in this regard.
- State fully explores alternatives to any act involving forced eviction, with the full participation of all affected persons, including women, children and indigenous peoples. If a consensus is difficult to achieve, the entity proposing the forced eviction will obtain the assistance of an independent body, such as a court of law, tribunal or ombudsman, to arbitrate the issue and to resolve it.
- State refrains, to the maximum possible extent, from compulsorily acquiring housing or land, unless such acts are legitimate and necessary.

If evictions of persons are required, the guidelines spell out the rights of those affected, including the right to a fair hearing before a competent, impartial and independent court or tribunal, the right to legal counsel and to effective legal remedies, and the right to compensation 'for any losses of land or personal, real or other property or goods. Compensation should include land and access to common property and should not be restricted to cash payments'. Finally, the guidelines assert the 'right to suitable resettlement which includes the right to alternative land or housing which is safe, secure, accessible, affordable and habitable'. Further criteria for resettlement include:

1. Resettlement occurs in a just and equitable manner, and in full accordance with international law and particularly international human rights law.
2. All persons, groups and communities have the right to suitable resettlement, which includes the right to alternative land or housing which is safe, secure, accessible, affordable and habitable.
3. In determining the compatibility of resettlement with guidelines, states should ensure that in the context of physical resettlement the following criteria are adhered to:

(a) No resettlement shall take place until such time that a full resettlement policy consistent with the present guidelines and internationally recognised human rights is in place.
(b) Resettlement must ensure equal rights to women, children and indigenous populations and other vulnerable groups, including the right to property ownership and access to resources. Resettlement policies should include programmes designed for women with respect to education, health, family welfare, and employment opportunities.
(c) The actor proposing and/or carrying out the resettlement shall be required by law to pay any costs associated therewith, including all resettlement costs.
(d) No affected person, groups or communities shall suffer as far as human rights are concerned, nor shall their right to the continuous improvement of living conditions be subject to infringement. This applies equally to host communities at resettlement sites, and affected persons, groups and communities subjected to forced eviction.
(e) The affected persons, groups and communities must provide their full and informed consent as regards the relocation site. The state shall provide all necessary amenities and services and economic opportunities.
(f) Sufficient information shall be provided to affected persons, groups and communities concerning all state projects as well as the planning and implementation processes relating to the resettlement concerned, including information concerning the purpose to which the acquired dwelling or site is to be put, and the persons, groups or communities who will benefit from the site. Particular attention must be given to ensure that indigenous peoples, ethnic minorities, the landless, women and children are represented and included in this process.
(g) The entire resettlement process should be carried out in full consultation with and participation of the affected persons, groups and communities. States should take into account in particular all alternative plans proposed by the affected persons, groups and communities.
(h) If after a full and fair public hearing, it is found that there is a need to proceed with the resettlement, then the affected persons, groups and communities shall be given at least ninety (90) days' notice prior to the date of the resettlement.

These human rights-based guidelines can be adopted by each country as its 'human rights charter' or as a component of the human rights charter, if such a charter already exists. A national-level human rights charter would drastically reduce the need for negotiation to incorporate 'entitlements' of affected persons into project-specific resettlement plans, or for involuntary safeguard policy safeguards formulated by international and regional development agencies from time to time. Moreover, if a human rights charter is adopted by a country, there is high probability that its government would apply the charter to all development projects, irrespective of the source of funds. A charter would also enhance citizens' awareness of their rights and encourage them to demand and obtain appropriate compensation and mitigation measures whenever their rights are at risk or violated.

A comprehensive human rights-based approach

The lingering influence of modernisation and development theories of the 1960s and 1970s can still be seen in policies of and literature on development-induced displacement and resettlement. This influence is particularly evident in dominant theoretical models of resettlement, namely the Four-stage Framework and the Impoverishment Risk and Reconstruction Model. In combination, they have provided a base for developing involuntary resettlement policy frameworks of several international donor agencies and for national involuntary resettlement policies and laws. The popularity of these models among developing countries and major donor agencies derives from their preference for a managerial approach to development, and for treating impoverishment or at least the risks of impoverishment, social disarticulation, and food insecurity arising from physical displacement, as an inevitable precursor of development. But victims of development-induced displacement have a different perspective and viewpoint of such changes. As Sen (1995) pointed out, the people threatened with displacement by the Narmada dam project are not so much against the dam or regional development; they are against the impoverishment arising from inadequate and delayed compensation, or lack of rehabilitation programs to restore their sources of income and livelihood. Their opposition is, thus, derived not from some pure 'traditional' subsistence ethos or a desire to continue to live in a traditional social system, but from the pragmatics of desperate poverty and oppression.

The theoretical models of involuntary resettlement expect that the state, project agency, and affected people to work out a long-term resettlement program so that all will eventually become beneficiaries of the development intervention. This 'aspirational' component of the models has not often been realised, as outcomes of thousands of development interventions all over the world amply demonstrate. There are very few development interventions that have at least restored the pre-intervention income and livelihood standards of the displaced people (Scudder 2005).

As physical displacement of millions of people is reported every year, and considering their hopelessness regarding getting 'entitlements' in time, it is necessary to switch the focus of resettlement and reconstruction models from 'resettlement and rehabilitation' to 'physical and economic displacement', and 'strategies of avoiding or minimising resettlement' to 'strategies of avoiding or minimising displacement.' Such a shift of focus would highlight the plight of displaced persons and the critical need for addressing their rights.

Any form of displacement is a social evil. The best way to address its causes, and to provide remedies, is to follow a comprehensive human right-based approach to handle them. In such an approach to involuntary displacement, 'losses' of persons to a development intervention would become 'triggers' of violation of their human rights. This alone should encourage governments and development agencies to avoid or minimise development-induced displacement, and to remedy the losses adequately and promptly.

Several critical actions are required to move from 'entitlements' to human rights-based development assistance. First, it is necessary to revisit the doctrine of sovereignty of state. This is the stumbling block in introducing human rights approach to development-induced displacement. State sovereignty is to be recast as a concept of responsibility — an instrument for ensuring the protection and welfare of those under a state's jurisdiction. Second, a state's power to acquire private and common property for a public purpose or use (the principle of eminent domain) needs to be balanced against human rights pertaining to life, adequate housing and property. In this sense, the concept of development also needs to be recast to mean protection and welfare of citizens. Third, each state should incorporate the basic human rights, including rights pertaining to displacement and resettlement, into domestic laws. This would avoid the presence of different entitlement packages in a country to deal with development-induced displacement, and eliminate the need to negotiate entitlement packages of each development intervention with donors.

References

Abeyratne, Shyamala. 1982. *Second-generation settlers and their impact on land and water resources in the Gal Oya Irrigation Scheme, Sri Lanka.* Ithaca, New York: Centre for International Studies, Cornell University.

Ahuja, Sangeeta. 1997. *People, law and justice — Casebook on public interest litigation, Vol II.* New Delhi: Orient Longman.

Brohman, John. 1996. *Popular development: Rethinking the theory and practice of development.* UK: Blackwell Publishing.

Cernea, Michael M. 1994. *Bridging the research divide: Studying refugees and development oustees.* Washington DC: Environment Department, The World Bank.

———. 1997. 'The risk and reconstruction model for resettling displaced populations'. *World Development*, 25(10): 1569–87.

Cernea, Michael M. and Hari Mohan Mathur (eds). 2008. *Can compensation prevent impoverishment? Reforming resettlement through investments and benefit-sharing.* New Delhi: Oxford University Press.

Dwivedi, Ranjit. 2002. 'Models and methods in development-induced displacement'. Review article. *Development and Change,* 33(4): 709–32.

Fernandes, Walter. 2007. 'Singur and the displacement scenario'. *Economic and Political Weekly*, 42(3): 203–06.

Government of India. 2006. 'The Scheduled Tribes and Other Traditional Forest Dwellers (Recognition of Forest Rights) Act, 2006'. The Gazette of India (Extraordinary) Part II – Section I. Ministry of Law and Justice, 2 January 2007.

Inglehard, Ronald. 1997. *Modernization and post modernization: Cultural, economic and political change in 43 societies.* Princeton, NJ: Princeton University Press.

International Labour Organization (ILO). 1989. 'Convention concerning Indigenous and Tribal Peoples in Independent Countries (ILO No. 169)'. *72 ILO Official Bulletin 59.* Geneva: ILO.

Jaswal, A. (ed.). 1990. *The role of Supreme Court with regard to the Right to Life and Personal Liberty.* New Delhi: Ashish Publishing House.

Kothari, Miloon. 2007. 'Report of the Special Rapporteur on Adequate Housing as a component of the Right to an Adequate Standard of Living'. UN Implementation of General Assembly Resolution 60/251 of 15 March 2006, entitled 'Human Rights Council', A/HRC/4/18, 4th Session, New York, 5 February 2007.

Mills, C. Wright. 2000. *The sociological imagination.* Fortieth anniversary edition. New York: Oxford University Press.

Munsayac, Jocelyn Erlinda S. 2006. 'Of squatters: Labels and reactions'. MA Sociology thesis (unpublished), University of the Philippines.

Myrdal, Gunnar. 1968. *Asian drama: An inquiry into the poverty of nations.* New York: Pantheon Books.

Perera, Jayantha. 1985a. *New dimensions of social stratification in rural Sri Lanka.* Colombo: Lakehouse Publishers.

———. 1985b. *Conflict and settlement: A portrait of a Sri Lankan village.* Tokyo: University of Tokyo.

———. 1992. 'Trends in agrarian change: Past and present in Wewagama, a village in the Mahaweli Development Project Area, Anuradhapura district', in James Brow and Joe Weeramunda (eds), *Agrarian change in Sri Lanka*, pp. 95–129. New Delhi: Sage.

———. 2003. 'From shifting cultivation to settled cash crop plantations: Displacement and impoverishment of the Ibans in Sarawak, Malaysia', in Dawn Chatty and Marcus Colchester (eds), *Conservation & mobile indigenous peoples*, pp. 87–110. Oxford: Berghahn Books.

———. (ed.). 2009. *Land and cultural survival: Land rights of indigenous peoples in Asia.* Manila: Asian Development Bank.

Robinson, Courtland C. 2003. *Risks and rights: The causes, consequences, and challenges of development-induced displacement.* Washington DC: The Brookings Institution (SAIS Project on Internal Displacement).

Sen, Gita. 1995. 'National development and local environmental action — The case of the river Narmada', in V. Bhaskar and Andrew Glyn (eds) *The North, the south and the environment: ecological constraints and the global economy*. Tokyo: United Nations University Press.

Scott, James C. 1998. *Seeing like a state: How certain schemes to improve the human conditions have failed.* New Haven: Yale University Press.

Scudder Thayer. 2005. *The future of large dams: Dealing with social, environmental, institutional and political costs.* London: Earthscan.

United Nations. 1973. 'Report of the United Nations Conference on the Human Environment'. New York: United Nations.

———. 1992. 'Report of the United Nations Conference on Environment and Development'. New York: United Nations.

———. 1994. 'The Draft Declaration of the Principles on Human Rights and the Environment, International Group of Experts', 16 May, Geneva.

———. 1997. 'Press Release HR/4332'. New York: United Nations.

———. 2000. 'Working Paper on the Relationship and Distinction between the Rights of Persons Belonging to Minorities and Those of Indigenous Peoples', UN Doc/E/CN.4/Sub.2/2000/10. New York: United Nations.

———. 2001. 'Working Paper on the Relationship & Distinction between the Rights of Persons Belonging to Minorities & Those of Indigenous Peoples', UN Doc/E/CAN/Sub.2/20001l0. New York: United Nations.

Weissbrodt, David and Cornie de La Vaga. 2007. *International human rights law: An introduction.* Pennsylvania studies in human rights series. Philadelphia: University of Pennsylvania Press.

About the editor

Hari Mohan Mathur, PhD, is Visiting Professor, Council for Social Development, New Delhi. He has held senior positions in the government and was Chief Secretary to the Government of Rajasthan. He has also served as Vice Chancellor of the University of Rajasthan. He has been United Nations Advisor to the Government of Uganda, and was Development Administration Specialist at the UN Asian and Pacific Development Centre (UNAPDC) in Kuala Lumpur, Malaysia. In addition, he has been staff consultant to several other UN bodies and international organisations, including ADB, FAO, UNDP, UNDTCD, UNESCAP, UNSECO and the World Bank. Dr Mathur has authored and edited several books on anthropology, development and resettlement issues, which include *Administering Development in the Third World* (1986), *Managing Resettlement in India* (2006), *Can Compensation Prevent Impoverishment? Reforming Resettlement with Investments and Benefit-Sharing* (co-edited with Michael M. Cernea, 2008), and *India Social Development Report 2008: Development and Displacement* (2008).

Contributors

Gordon Appleby is a development consultant working with the World Bank, the Millennium Challenge Corporation and various other private-sector clients. In recent decades he has been focussing on the issues thrown up by land acquisition and involuntary resettlement in a range of sectors — dams, roads, irrigated perimeters, and urban upgrading. He was awarded a doctorate in anthropology in 1976 by Stanford University for his work on the regional socio-economic history of wool trade in southern Peru from late colonial to modern times. He also teaches courses in environment and development and rural development at the American University, Washington DC.

Manshi Asher is a researcher and activist working on issues of livelihood and environment rights. More recently she has been tracking, studying and documenting the problems related to Special Economic Zones, a struggle in which she is also involved in direct action and media advocacy. She is currently based in Himachal Pradesh and is associated with campaigns working on sustainable livelihoods, ecological security and environmental justice.

Yamini Atmavilas is Associate Professor and Area Chairperson, Gender Studies, Centre for Human Development, Hyderabad. Her research interests are gender, work, migration, globalisation and economic restructuring and social development in India. She is also involved in capacity building in the areas of gender sensitisation; gender in the workplace; gendering development planning, monitoring and evaluation; social impact analysis; and gender and development.

Tulsi Charan Bisht is at the Department of Sociology and Anthropology, La Trobe University, Melbourne. He has master's degree in sociology from the University of Delhi and an MPhil from Jawaharlal Nehru University, New Delhi. His current research project is an ethnographic study of people displaced by the Tehri dam in the Himalayan state of Uttarakhand, India. His focus is on the way people rebuild their everyday lives following displacement. In India, he has worked with both government and not-for-profit NGOs, including over a year-and-a-half spent with the UN Mission in Haiti as an international observer of human rights and civil policing.

Michael M. Cernea is Research Professor of Anthropology and International Affairs, George Washington University, Washington DC. As the World Bank's Senior Advisor for Social Policy, he was the main author of the resettlement policy adopted by the Bank (1980) and by the aid agencies of all OECD countries (1991). In the last two decades and more, he has contributed to defining many other development and social/cultural policies, strategies and programmes of the World Bank. He has authored and edited many studies on development, including *The Economics of Involuntary Resettlement* (1999), *Risks and Reconstruction: Experiences of Resettlers and Refugees* (2000, edited with Christoph McDowell) and *Can Compensation Prevent Impoverishment: Reforming Resettlement through Investments and Benefit-Sharing* (edited with Hari Mohan Mathur, 2008).

Medha Chandra is a trained architect–urban designer who now works in the field of environmental justice. She obtained her degree in architecture and urban design from the School of Planning and Architecture, New Delhi. Recipient of a Commonwealth Scholarship from the Governments of India and UK, she completed her doctoral studies from University College London. Her doctoral research was on the 74the Amendment to the Indian Constitution, which proposed the decentralisation of powers to urban municipalities, for which she carried out extensive field work in Kolkata. Currently based in San Francisco, she is the coordinator of Pesticide Action Network (PAN) International's Working Group on Pesticides and Corporations, and a team focused on international and domestic pesticide campaigns.

Samarendra Das is an Oriya writer and film-maker. His film *Wira Pdika* (in Kui, a language spoken by the endangered Dongria Kondh tribe of Orissa), *Matrio Poko, Company Loko* (lit. 'Earth Worm, Company Man', 2005) captures the voice of Orissa's tribespeople on the subject of mining. His recent book, co-authored with Felix Padel, is titled *Out of this Earth: East India Adivasis and the Aluminum Cartel* (2010).

Vasudha Dhagamwar is a legal researcher and activist who has been working on issues relating to development-induced displacement for the last 30 years, having first visited Sardar Sarovar in 1980. Trained at Oxford and the University of London, she is a former Director of the Multiple Action Research Group (MARG), based in Delhi, and has also served as a member of the Legal Experts' Group of the National Commission for Women. She has also been involved in industrial and urban displacement, most notably in Korba, Chattisgarh. Author of several books and articles, he published works include *Law, Power and Justice: Protection of Personal Rights under the Indian Penal Code* (1992), *Industrial Development and Displacement: The people of Korba* (co-edited with Subrata De and Nikhil Verma, 2003), and *Role and Image of Law In India: The Tribal Experience* (2006).

Walter Fernandes is Director of North Eastern Social Research Centre, Guwahati. He is a former Director of Indian Social Institute, New Delhi and Editor, Social Action. He has done extensive research on tribal, livelihood and gender issues and has more than 30 books and 100 professional articles to his credit. His main area of specialisation in recent years has been displacement. He has done comprehensive studies of development-induced displacement in the period 1951–95 in several states of India and is now continuing his research in seven states of North Eastern India. He has been a member of several Committees of the Government of India.

Supriya Garikipati did her PhD from the Department of Economics and Politics at the University of Cambridge in 2001. She then worked as a Research Associate at the Department of Applied Economics at Cambridge, before joining the University of Liverpool in 2003. Her research interests are primarily examining the interactions between public policy and household behaviour, with a focus on poverty.

Abhijit Guha is Reader, Department of Anthropology, Vidyasagar University, Medinipur, West Bengal. He was ICSSR Doctoral Fellow in 1984–85 at the Centre for Studies in Social Sciences, Calcutta. His doctoral research was on land acquisition and the displacement of peasants in West Bengal under the Left Front government. He has been teaching at Vidyasagar University for over two decades, and has also taught at the West Bengal National University of Juridical Sciences and was a visiting fellow at the Department of Sociology, Delhi School of Economics. He has published about 80 articles, comments and book reviews, and his most recent book is titled *Land, Law and the Left: The Saga of Disempowerment of the Peasantry in the Era of Globalisation* (2007).

Ramaswamy R. Iyer is Honorary Research Professor at the Centre for Policy Research, New Delhi. A former Secretary, Ministry of Water Resources in the Government of India, Iyer was a member of important review committees of the Sardar Sarovar and Tehri Projects (1993–97). He has been a consultant on different occasions to the World Bank, World Commission on Dams, UNDP, International, Water Management Institute and the European Commission, among others. He has written extensively on water-related issues, and his recent books include *Water: Perspectives, Issues, Concerns* (2003) and *Towards Water Wisdom: Limits, Justice, Harmony,* and *Water Laws in India* (2007).

Felix Padel, a freelance anthropologist, has known Orissa and the Konds for 30 years. He did his BA and PhD at Oxford and his MPhil at the Delhi School of Economics. He divides his time between Orissa and Wales. He is the author of *Sacrificing People: Invasions of a Tribal Landscape* (2009), which is an updated version of a classic case study of colonialism. *Out of this Earth: East India Adivasis and the Aluminum Cartel* (2010) is his most recent book, co-authored with Samarendra Das.

Jayantha Perera, is a Development Anthropologist and a fellow of the Royal Anthropological Institute, London. He is the Principal Safeguards Specialist at the South Asia Department of the Asian Development Bank, Manila, where he plays a key role in shaping policies regarding the environment, involuntary resettlement and indigenous peoples safeguards in South Asia. Dr Perera has taught at several universities including Oxford. He has served as consultant to the World Bank, Asian Development Bank, Japan Bank for International Cooperation, FAO, ILO, IDRC, Swiss Development

Corporation, UNU and several international NGOS. Author of several articles and books, his most recent contribution is an edited volume titled *Land and Cultural Survival: The Land Rights of Indigenous Peoples in Asia.*

M. P. Roy graduated from the Indian Institute of Technology, Kharagpur after studying mining engineering. He is a former Chief General Manager (R&R), World Bank Division, Coal India Limited, Calcutta. His interest in social issues led him to recently obtain MA (Sociology) from the Annamalai University, Tamil Nadu. Presently, he is teaching socio-economic management of environment at the Institute of Social Welfare and Business Management (IISWBM) in Kolkata.

Index

www.ingramcontent.com/pod-product-compliance
Lightning Source LLC
LaVergne TN
LVHW011104300926
849160LV00008B/275

* 9 7 8 1 1 3 8 6 6 2 7 0 4 *